CONSTITUTION OF THE
UNITED

D0889388

CONSTITUTION OF THE
STATE OF CALIFORNIA, 1879

As Last Amended November 4, 2014

and

Related Documents

2015–16

CALIFORNIA STATE LEGISLATURE

LT. GOVERNOR GAVIN NEWSOM
President of the Senate

HON. KEVIN DE LEÓN
President pro Tempore of the Senate

SENATOR BOB HUFF
Minority Floor Leader

DANIEL ALVAREZ
Secretary of the Senate

HON. TONI G. ATKINS
Speaker of the Assembly

HON. KEVIN MULLIN
Speaker pro Tempore

HON. KRISTIN OLSEN
Minority Floor Leader

E. DOTSON WILSON
Chief Clerk of the Assembly

THE STATE FLAG

The Bear Flag was designated California's State Flag by legislative enactment in 1911. It is patterned after the historic flag flown at Sonoma on June 14, 1846, by a group of American settlers in revolt against Mexican rule in California. This short-lived revolution ended on July 9, 1846. The general design and details of the Bear Flag are set forth in Section 420 of the Government Code.

FOREWORD

The California Legislature is privileged to present this compilation of historic documents. Taken together, these compacts, treaties, and charters embody the ongoing evolution of our core principles of representative democracy.

It is important to note that our state Constitution is a living document. It has been amended over 500 times since its adoption in 1879. Some recent amendments have included a change to California's Term Limits law through the passage of Proposition 28 (2012), the Rainy Day Budget Stabilization Act enacted by Proposition 2 (2014), and with the adoption of Proposition 25 (2010), the vote threshold to pass the state budget is now a majority vote.

One hundred and sixty-five years since its inception, the Golden State continues to be a leader throughout the nation and the world. Innovative public policy is often crafted, analyzed, and debated by the Legislature with the collective input of the electorate and its unparalleled commitment to excellence. This sense of progress and purpose can also be found in the documents featured in this publication, as our nation and state continue to strive for a more perfect union.

The framers of our Constitution envisioned a democracy that protected fundamental "freedoms" and "rights." Over time, these freedoms and rights have evolved to embrace a more diverse and inclusive society. Our state Constitution provides such a framework. It is in that spirit of freedom the California Legislature presents these important documents, which shape our collective philosophy and the vision for a government of the people.

DANIEL ALVAREZ
Secretary of the Senate

E. DOTSON WILSON
Chief Clerk of the Assembly

March 2015

i

The design for the Great Seal of the State of California was adopted at the Constitutional Convention in 1849. Thirty-one stars are displayed, one for each state which comprised the Union following the admission of California September 9, 1850. Beneath these stars appears the motto, *Eureka* (in Greek, "I have found it!"). The peaks of the Sierra Nevada stand for the grandeur of nature. Shipping on San Francisco Bay typifies commerce. A miner laboring with pick, rocker, and pan represents industry. Agricultural wealth is seen in a sheaf of wheat and clusters of grapes. Keeping watch over this tableau is the armored figure of Minerva who, in classical Roman mythology, was the goddess of wisdom. Like the political birth of California, she was born full grown from the brain of Jupiter, father of the gods and guardian of law and order. At her feet stands a grizzly bear, independent and formidable, symbolizing the State of California.

THE SEAL OF THE SENATE

The Senate Seal is circular in shape, and the border bears the phrase "Seal of the Senate of the State of California." The center features a quill pen placed diagonally across an open scroll. On the top of the scroll is inscribed "LEGIS" (law) and the Roman numerals MDCCCL, designating 1850, the year California was admitted to the Union. Surrounding the pen and scroll is a cluster of California live oak leaves and acorns. The Senate adopted the seal in 1967.

Senator Kevin de León
President pro Tempore

Senator William W. Monning
Majority Floor Leader

Senator Bob Huff
Minority Floor Leader

THE SENATE RULES COMMITTEE

From left to right: Senator Anthony Cannella, Jean Fuller (Vice Chair),
Kevin de León (Chair), Holly Mitchell, Connie Leyva

Published March 2015   v

THE ASSEMBLY SEAL

The Seal of the Assembly of the State of California was proposed by the Honorable Leo J. Ryan, Assemblyman from the 27th District in San Mateo County, and adopted by the full Assembly in 1967. The official state colors, blue and gold, were used as a background. The "Golden Poppy," the State flower, and the California Grizzly Bear, which are traditional emblems of California, also appear on the Assembly Seal. The gavel in the upper left-hand corner and the Corinthian column in the lower right-hand corner are symbolic of the legislative power of the state. The palm tree and the mountains are representative of the southern and northern parts of our state, respectively. The motto of the California State Assembly is emblazoned on the Seal, "LEGISLATORUM EST JUSTAS LEGES CONDERE" and indicates "It is the duty of the Legislature to make just laws."

Toni G. Atkins
Speaker of the Assembly

Kristin Olsen
Minority Floor Leader

ASSEMBLY RULES COMMITTEE—2015

From left to right: Assembly Members P. Lopez; J. Wood; F. Rodriguez; B. Dodd;
K. Cooley; N. Campos; A. Burke; Chief Clerk E.D. Wilson; Secretary N. Willis;
Chair R. Gordon; Chief Administrative Officer D. Gravert; Sergeant at Arms R. Pane;
Vice Chair L. Chang; M. Waldron; C. Mayes; B. Jones; and J. Obernolte

CONTENTS

Magna Carta
1215

Mayflower Compact
1620

Declarations of Rights
1765 and 1774

The Declaration of Independence
1776

Articles of Confederation
1778

Magna Carta—1215

THE GREAT CHARTER OF ENGLISH LIBERTY, GRANTED BY KING JOHN AT RUNNYMEDE, JUNE 15, A. D. 1215

(From "Select Historical Documents of the Middle Ages," as translated from "Stubb's Charters" by Ernest F. Henderson.)

John, by the grace of God king of England, lord of Ireland, duke of Normandy and Aquitaine, count of Anjou: to the archbishops, bishops, abbots, earls, barons, justices, foresters, sheriffs, prevosts, serving men, and to all his bailiffs and faithful subjects, greeting. Know that we, by the will of God and for the safety of our soul, and of the souls of all our predecessors and our heirs, to the honour of God and for the exalting of the holy church and the bettering of our realm: by the counsel of our venerable fathers Stephen archbishop of Canterbury, primate of all England and cardinal of the holy Roman church; of Henry archbishop of Dublin; of the bishops William of London, Peter of Winchester, Jocelin of Bath and Glastonbury, Hugo of Lincoln, Walter of Worcester, William of Coventry and Benedict of Rochester; of master Pandulf, subdeacon and of the household of the lord pope; of brother Aymeric, master of the knights of the Temple in England; and of the noble men, William Marshall earl of Pembroke, William earl of Salisbury, William earl of Warren, William earl of Arundel, Alan de Galway constable of Scotland, Warin son of Gerold, Peter son of Herbert, Hubert de Burgh seneschal of Poictiers, Hugo de Neville, Matthew son of Herbert, Thomas Basset, Alan Basset, Philip d'Aubigni, Robert de Roppelay, John Marshall, John son of Hugo, and others of our faithful subjects:

1. First of all have granted to God, and, for us and for our heirs forever, have confirmed, by this our present charter, that the English church shall be free and shall have its rights intact and its liberties uninfringed upon. And thus we will that it be observed. As is apparent from the fact that we, spontaneously and of our own free will, before discord broke out between ourselves and our barons, did grant and by our charter confirm—and did cause the lord pope Innocent III, to confirm—freedom of elections, which is considered most important and most necessary to the church of England. Which charter both we ourselves shall observe, and we will that it be observed with good faith by our heirs forever. We have also granted to all free men of our realm, on the part of ourselves and our heirs forever, all the subjoined liberties, to have and to hold, to them and to their heirs, from us and from our heirs:

2. If any one of our earls or barons, or of others holding from us in chief through military service, shall die; and if, at the time of his death, his heir be of full age and owe a relief: he shall have his inheritance by paying the old relief;—the heir, namely, or the heirs of an earl, by paying one hundred pounds for the whole barony of an earl; the heir or heirs of a baron, by paying one hundred pounds for the whole barony; the heir or heirs of a knight, by paying one hundred shillings at most for a whole knight's fee; and he who shall owe less shall give less, according to the ancient custom of fees.

3. But if the heir of any of the above persons shall be under age and in wardship,—when he comes of age he shall have his inheritance without relief and without fine.

4. The administrator of the land of such heir who shall be under age shall take none but reasonable issues from the land of the heir, and reasonable customs and services; and this without destruction and waste of men or goods. And if we shall have committed the custody of any such land to the sheriff or to any other man who ought to be responsible to us for the issues of it, and he cause destruction or waste to what is in his charge: we will fine him, and the land shall be handed over to two lawful and discreet men of that fee who shall answer to us, or to him to whom we shall have referred them, regarding those issues. And if we shall have given or sold to any one the custody of any such land, and he shall have caused destruction or waste to it,—he shall lose that custody, and it shall be given to two lawful and discreet men of that fee, who likewise shall answer to us, as has been explained.

5. The administrator, moreover, so long as he may have the custody of the land, shall keep in order, from the issues of that land, the houses, parks, warrens, lakes, mills, and other things pertaining to it. And he shall restore to the heir when he comes to full age, his whole land stocked with ploughs and wainnages, according as the time of the wainnage requires and the issues of the land will reasonably permit.

6. Heirs may marry without disparagement; so, nevertheless, that, before the marriage is contracted, it shall be announced to the relations by blood of the heir himself.

7. A widow, after the death of her husband, shall straightway, and without difficulty, have her marriage portion and her inheritance, nor shall she give any thing in return for her dowry, her marriage portion, or the inheritance which belonged to her, and which she and her husband held on the day of the death of that husband. And she may remain in the house of her husband, after his death, for forty days; within which her dowry shall be paid over to her.

8. No widow shall be forced to marry when she prefers to live without a husband; so, however, that she gives security not to marry without our consent, if she hold from us, or the consent of the lord from whom she holds, if she hold from another.

9. Neither we nor our bailiffs shall seize any revenue for any debt, so long as the chattels of the debtor suffice to pay the debt; nor shall the sponsors of that debtor be distrained so long as that chief debtor has enough to pay the debt. But if the chief debtor fail in paying the debt, not having the wherewithal to pay it, the sponsors shall answer for the debt. And, if they shall wish, they may have the lands and revenues of the debtor until satisfaction shall have been given them for the debt previously paid for him; unless the chief debtor shall show that he is quit in that respect towards those same sponsors.

10. If any one shall have taken any sum, great or small, as a loan from the money-lenders, and shall die before that debt is paid,—that debt shall not bear interest so long as the heir, from whomever he may hold, shall be under age. And if the debt fall into our hands, we shall take nothing save the chattel contained in the deed.

11. And if any one dies owing a debt to the money-lenders, his wife shall have her dowry, and shall restore nothing of that debt. But if there shall remain children of that dead man, and they shall be under age, the necessaries shall be provided for them according to the nature of the dead man's holding; and, from the residue, the debt shall be paid, saving the service due to the lords. In like manner shall be done concerning debts that are due to others besides money-lenders.

12. No scutage or aid shall be imposed in our realm unless by the common counsel of our realm; except for redeeming our body, and knighting our eldest son, and marrying once our eldest daughter. And for these purposes there shall only be given a reasonable aid. In like manner shall be done concerning the aids of the city of London.

13. And the city of London shall have all its old liberties and free customs as well by land as by water. Moreover we will and grant that all other cities and burroughs, and towns and ports, shall have all their liberties and free customs.

14. And, in order to have the common counsel of the realm in the matter of assessing an aid otherwise than in the aforesaid cases, or of assessing a scutage—we shall cause, under seal through our letters, the archbishops, bishops, abbots, earls, and greater barons to be summoned for a fixed day—for a term, namely, at least forty days distant,—and for a fixed place. And, moreover, we shall cause to be summoned in general, through our sheriffs and bailiffs, all those who hold of us in chief. And in all those letters of summons we shall express the cause of the summons. And when a summons has thus been made, the business shall be proceeded with on the day appointed according to the counsel of those who shall be present, even though not all shall come who were summoned.

15. We will not allow any one henceforth to take an aid from his freemen save for the redemption of his body, and the knighting of his eldest

son, and the marrying, once, of his eldest daughter; and, for these purposes, there shall only be given a reasonable aid.

16. No one shall be forced to do more service for a knight's fee, or for another free holding, than is due from it.

17. Common pleas shall not follow our court but shall be held in a certain fixed place.

18. Assizes of novel disseisin, of mort d'ancestor, and of darrein presentment shall not be held save in their own counties, and in this way: We, or our chief justice, if we shall be absent from the kingdom, shall send two justices through each county four times a year; they, with four knights from each county, chosen by the county, shall hold the aforesaid assizes in the county, and on the day and at the place of the county court.

19. And if on the day of the county court the aforesaid assizes can not be held, a sufficient number of knights and free tenants, from those who were present at the county court on that day, shall remain, so that through them the judgments may be suitably given, according as the matter may have been great or small.

20. A freeman shall only be amerced for a small offence according to the measure of that offence. And for a great offence he shall be amerced according to the magnitude of the offence, saving his contenement; and a merchant, in the same way, saving his merchandize. And a villein, in the same way, if he fall under our mercy, shall be amerced saving his wainnage. And none of the aforesaid fines shall be imposed save upon oath of upright men from the neighbourhood.

21. Earls and barons shall not be amerced save through their peers, and only according to the measure of the offence.

22. No clerk shall be amerced for his lay tenement except according to the manner of the other persons aforesaid; and not according to the amount of his ecclesiastical benefice.

23. Neither a town nor a man shall be forced to make bridges over the rivers, with the exception of those who, from of old and of right ought to do it.

24. No sheriff, constable, coroners, or other bailiffs of ours shall hold the pleas of our crown.

25. All counties, hundreds, wapentakes, and trithings—our demesne manors being excepted—shall continue according to the old farms, without any increase at all.

26. If any one holding from us a lay fee shall die, and our sheriff or bailiff can show our letters patent containing our summons for the debt which the dead man owed to us,—our sheriff or bailiff may be allowed to attach and enroll the chattels of the dead man to the value of that debt, through view of lawful men; in such way, however, that nothing shall be removed thence until the debt is paid which was plainly owed to us. And the residue shall be left to the executors that they may carry out the will of the dead

man. And if nothing is owed to us by him, all the chattels shall go to the use prescribed by the deceased, saving their reasonable portions to his wife and children.

27. If any freeman shall have died intestate his chattels shall be distributed through the hands of his near relatives and friends, by view of the church; saving to any one the debts which the dead man owed him.

28. No constable or other bailiff of ours shall take the corn or other chattels of any one except he straightway give money for them, or can be allowed a respite in that regard by the will of the seller.

29. No constable shall force any knight to pay money for castleward if he be willing to perform that ward in person, or—he for a reasonable cause not being able to perform it himself—through another proper man. And if we shall have led or sent him on a military expedition, he shall be quit of ward according to the amount of time during which, through us, he shall have been in military service.

30. No sheriff nor bailiff of ours, nor any one else, shall take the horses or carts of any freeman for transport, unless by the will of that freeman.

31. Neither we nor our bailiffs shall take another's wood for castles or for other private uses, unless by the will of him to whom the wood belongs.

32. We shall not hold the lands of those convicted of felony longer than a year and a day; and then the lands shall be restored to the lords of the fiefs.

33. Henceforth all the weirs in the Thames and Medway, and throughout all England, save on the sea-coast, shall be done away with entirely.

34. Henceforth the writ which is called *Praecipe* shall not be served on any one for any holding so as to cause a free man to lose his court.

35. There shall be one measure of wine throughout our whole realm, and one measure of ale and one measure of corn—namely, the London quart;—and one width of dyed and russet and hauberk cloths—namely, two ells below the selvage. And with weights, moreover, it shall be as with measures.

36. Henceforth nothing shall be given or taken for a writ of inquest in a matter concerning life or limb; but it shall be conceded gratis, and shall not be denied.

37. If any one hold of us in fee-farm, or in socage, or in burkage, and hold land of another by military service, we shall not, by reason of that fee-farm, or socage, or burkage, have the wardship of his heir or of his land which is held in fee from another. Nor shall we have the wardship of that fee-farm, or socage, or burkage unless that fee-farm owe military service. We shall not, by reason of some petit-serjeanty which some one holds of us through the service of giving us knives or arrows or the like, have the wardship of his heir or of the land which he holds of another by military service.

38. No bailiff, on his own simple assertion, shall henceforth put any one to his law, without producing faithful witnesses in evidence.

39. No freeman shall be taken, or imprisoned, or disseized, or outlawed, or exiled, or in any way harmed—nor will we go upon or send upon him— save by the lawful judgment of his peers or by the law of the land.

40. To none will we sell, to none deny or delay, right or justice.

41. All merchants may safely and securely go out of England, and come into England, and delay and pass through England, as well by land as by water, for the purpose of buying and selling, free from all evil taxes, subject to the ancient and right customs—save in time of war, and if they are of the land at war against us. And if such be found in our land at the beginning of the war, they shall be held, without harm to their bodies and goods, until it shall be known to us or our chief justice how the merchants of our land are to be treated who shall, at that time, be found in the land at war against us. And if ours shall be safe there, the others shall be safe in our land.

42. Henceforth any person, saving fealty to us, may go out of our realm and return to it, safely and securely, by land and by water, except perhaps for a brief period in time of war, for the common good of the realm. But prisoners and outlaws are excepted according to the law of the realm; also people of a land at war against us, and the merchants, with regard to whom shall be done as we have said.

43. If any one hold from any escheat—as from the honour of Wallingford, Nottingham, Boloin, Lancaster, or the other escheats which are in our hands and are baronies—and shall die, his heir shall not give another relief, nor shall he perform for us other service than he would perform for a baron if that barony were in the hand of a baron; and we shall hold it in the same way in which the baron has held it.

44. Persons dwelling without the forest shall not henceforth come before the forest justices, through common summonses, unless they are impleaded or are the sponsors of some person or persons attached for matters concerning the forest.

45. We will not make men justices, constables, sheriffs, or bailiffs, unless they are such as know the law of the realm, and are minded to observe it rightly.

46. All barons who have founded abbeys for which they have charters of the kings of England, or ancient right of tenure, shall have, as they ought to have, their custody when vacant.

47. All forests constituted as such in our time shall straightway be annulled; and the same shall be done for river banks made into places of defense by us in our time.

48. All evil customs concerning forests and warrens, and concerning foresters and warreners, sheriffs and their servants, river banks and their guardians, shall straightway be inquired into in each county, through

twelve sworn knights from that county, and shall be eradicated by them, entirely, so that they shall never be renewed, within forty days after the inquest has been made; in such manner that we shall first know about them, or our justice if we be not in England.

49. We shall straightway return all hostages and charters which were delivered to us by Englishmen as a surety for peace or faithful service.

50. We shall entirely remove from their bailwicks the relatives of Gerard de Athyes, so that they shall henceforth have no bailwick in England: Engelard de Cygnes, Andrew Peter and Gyon de Chanceles, Gyon de Cygnes, Geoffrey de Martin and his brothers, Philip Mark and his brothers, and Geoffrey his nephew, and the whole following of them.

51. And straightway after peace is restored we shall remove from the realm all the foreign soldiers, crossbowmen, servants, hirelings, who may have come with horses and arms to the harm of the realm.

52. If any one shall have been disseized by us, or removed, without a legal sentence of his peers, from his lands, castles, liberties or lawful right, we shall straightway restore them to him. And if a dispute shall arise concerning this matter it shall be settled according to the judgment of the twenty-five barons who are mentioned below as sureties for the peace. But with regard to all those things of which any one was, by king Henry our father or king Richard our brother, disseized or dispossessed without legal judgment of his peers, which we have in our hand or which others hold, and for which we ought to give a guarantee: We shall have respite until the common term for crusaders. Except with regard to those concerning which a plea was moved, or an inquest made by our order, before we took the cross. But when we return from our pilgrimage, or if, by chance, we desist from our pilgrimage, we shall straightway then show full justice regarding them.

53. We shall have the same respite, moreover, and in the same manner, in the matter of showing justice with regard to forests to be annulled and forests to remain, which Henry our father or Richard our brother constituted; and in the matter of wardships of lands which belong to the fee of another—wardships of which kind we have hitherto enjoyed by reason of the fee which some one held from us in military service;—and in the matter of abbeys founded in the fee of another than ourselves—in which the lord of the fee may say that he has jurisdiction. And when we return, or if we desist from our pilgrimage, we shall straightway exhibit full justice to those complaining with regard to these matters.

54. No one shall be taken or imprisoned on account of the appeal of a woman concerning the death of another than her husband.

55. All fines imposed by us unjustly and contrary to the law of the land, and all amerciaments made unjustly and contrary to the law of the land, shall be altogether remitted, or it shall be done with regard to them according to the judgment of the twenty five barons mentioned below as

sureties for the peace, or according to the judgment of the majority of them together with the aforesaid Stephen archibishop of Canterbury, if he can be present, and with others whom he may wish to associate with himself for this purpose. And if he can not be present, the affair shall nevertheless proceed without him; in such way that, if one or more of the said twenty five barons shall be concerned in a similar complaint, they shall be removed as to this particular decision, and, in their place, for this purpose alone, others shall be substituted who shall be chosen and sworn by the remainder of those twenty five.

56. If we have disseized or dispossessed Welshmen of their lands or liberties or other things without legal judgment of their peers, in England or in Wales,—they shall straightway be restored to them. And if a dispute shall arise concerning this, then action shall be taken upon it in the March through judgment of their peers—concerning English holdings according to the law of England, concerning Welsh holdings according to the law of Wales, concerning holdings in the March according to the law of the March. The Welsh shall do likewise with regard to us and our subjects.

57. But with regard to all those things of which any one of the Welsh was, by king Henry our father or king Richard our brother, disseized or dispossessed without legal judgment of his peers, which we have in our hand or which others hold, and for which we ought to give a guarantee: we shall have respite until the common term for crusaders. Except with regard to those concerning which a plea was moved, or an inquest made by our order, before we took the cross. But when we return from our pilgrimage, or if, by chance, we desist from our pilgrimage, we shall straightway then show full justice regarding them, according to the laws of Wales and the aforesaid districts.

58. We shall straightway return the son of Llewelin and all the Welsh hostages, and the charters delivered to us as surety for the peace.

59. We shall act towards Alexander king of the Scots regarding the restoration of his sisters, and his hostages, and his liberties and his lawful right, as we shall act towards our other barons of England; unless it ought to be otherwise according to the charters which we hold from William, his father, the former king of the Scots. And this shall be done through judgment of his peers in our court.

60. Moreover all the subjects of our realm, clergy as well as laity, shall, as far as pertains to them, observe, with regard to their vassals, all these aforesaid customs and liberties which we have decreed shall, as far as pertains to us, be observed in our realm with regard to our own.

61. Inasmuch as, for the sake of God, and for the bettering of our realm, and for the more ready healing of the discord which has arisen between us and our barons, we have made all these aforesaid concessions,—wishing them to enjoy for ever entire and firm stability, we make and grant to them the following security: that the barons, namely, may elect at their pleasure

twenty five barons from the realm, who ought, with all their strength, to observe, maintain and cause to be observed, the peace and privileges which we have granted to them and confirmed by this our present charter. In such wise, namely, that if we, or our justice, or our bailiffs, or any one of our servants shall have transgressed against any one in any respect, or shall have broken some one of the articles of peace or security, and our transgression shall have been shown to four barons of the aforesaid twenty five: those four barons shall come to us, or, if we are abroad, to our justice, showing to us our error; and they shall ask us to cause that error to be amended without delay. And if we do not amend that error, or, we being abroad, if our justice do not amend it within a term of forty days from the time when it was shown to us or, we being abroad, to our justice: the aforesaid four barons shall refer the matter to the remainder of the twenty five barons, and those twenty five barons, with the whole land in common, shall distrain and oppress us in every way in their power,—namely, by taking our castles, lands and possessions, and in every other way that they can, until amends shall have been made according to their judgment. Saving the persons of ourselves, our queen and our children. And when amends shall have been made they shall be in accord with us as they had been previously. And whoever of the land wishes to do so, shall swear that in carrying out all the aforesaid measures he will obey the mandates of the aforesaid twenty five barons, and that, with them, he will oppress us to the extent of his power. And, to any one who wishes to do so, we publicly and freely give permission to swear; and we will never prevent any one from swearing. Moreover, all those in the land who shall be unwilling, themselves and of their own accord, to swear to the twenty five barons as to distraining and oppressing us with them: such ones we shall make to swear by our mandate, as has been said. And if any one of the twenty five barons shall die, or leave the country, or in any other way be prevented from carrying out the aforesaid measures,—the remainder of the aforesaid twenty five barons shall choose another in his place, according to their judgment, who shall be sworn in the same way as the others. Moreover, in all things entrusted to those twenty five barons to be carried out, if those twenty five shall be present and chance to disagree among themselves with regard to some matter, or if some of them, having been summoned, shall be unwilling or unable to be present: that which the majority of those present shall decide or decree shall be considered binding and valid, just as if all the twenty five had consented to it. And the aforesaid twenty five shall swear that they will faithfully observe all the foregoing, and will cause them to be observed to the extent of their power. And we shall obtain nothing from any one, either through ourselves or through another, by which any of those concessions and liberties may be revoked or diminished. And if any such thing shall have been obtained, it shall be vain and invalid, and we shall never make use of it either through ourselves or through another.

62. And we have fully remitted to all, and pardoned, all the ill-will, anger and rancour which have arisen between us and our subjects, clergy and laity, from the time of the struggle. Moreover we have fully remitted to all, clergy and laity, and—as far as pertains to us—have pardoned fully all the transgressions committed, on the occasion of that same struggle, from Easter of the sixteenth year of our reign until the re-establishment of peace. In witness of which, moreover, we have caused to be drawn up for them letters patent of lord Stephen, archbishop of Canterbury, lord Henry, archbishop of Dublin, and the aforesaid bishops and master Pandulf, regarding that surety and the aforesaid concessions.

63. Wherefore we will and firmly decree that the English church shall be free, and that the subjects of our realm shall have and hold all the aforesaid liberties, rights and concessions, duly and in peace, freely and quietly, fully and entirely, for themselves and their heirs, from us and our heirs, in all matters and in all places, forever, as has been said. Moreover it has been sworn, on our part as well as on the part of the barons, that all these above mentioned provisions shall be observed with good faith and without evil intent. The witnesses being the above mentioned and many others. Given through our hand, in the plain called Runnimede between Windsor and Stanes, on the fifteenth day of June, in the seventeenth year of our reign.

The Mayflower Compact—1620

IN THE NAME OF GOD, AMEN.

We whose names are underwritten, the loyal subjects of our dread Sovereign Lord King James, by the Grace of God of Great Britain, France, and Ireland King, Defender of the Faith, etc.

Having undertaken, for the Glory of God and advancement of the Christian Faith and Honour of our King and Country, a Voyage to plant the First Colony in the Northern Parts of Virginia, do by these presents solemnly and mutually in the presence of God and one of another, Covenant and Combine ourselves together into a Civil Body Politic, for our better ordering and preservation and furtherance of the ends aforesaid; and by virtue hereof to enact, constitute and frame such just and equal Laws, Ordinances, Acts, Constitutions and Offices, from time to time, as shall be thought most meet and convenient for the general good of the Colony, unto which we promise all due submission and obedience. In witness whereof we have hereunder subscribed our names at Cape Cod, the 11th of November, in the year of the reign of our Sovereign Lord King James, of England, France and Ireland the eighteenth, and of Scotland the fifty-fourth. Anno Domini 1620.

JOHN CARVER	EDWARD TILLEY	DEGORY PRIEST
WILLIAM BRADFORD	JOHN TILLEY	THOMAS WILLIAMS
EDWARD WINSLOW	FRANCIS COOKE	GILBERT WINSLOW
WILLIAM BREWSTER	THOMAS ROGERS	EDMUND MARGESON
ISSAC ALLERTON	THOMAS TINKER	PETER BROWNE
MYLES STANDISH	JOHN RIGDALE	RICHARD BRITTERIDGE
JOHN ALDEN	EDWARD FULLER	GEORGE SOULE
SAMUEL FULLER	JOHN TURNER	RICHARD CLARKE
CHRISTOPHER MARTIN	FRANCIS EATON	RICHARD GARDINER
WILLIAM MULLINS	JAMES CHILTON	JOHN ALLERTON
WILLIAM WHITE	JOHN CRACKSTON	THOMAS ENGLISH
RICHARD WARREN	JOHN BILLINGTON	EDWARD DOTEY
JOHN HOWLAND	MOSES FLETCHER	EDWARD LEISTER
STEPHEN HOPKINS	JOHN GOODMAN	

Declaration of Rights *

In Congress, at New York, October 19, 1765

The Congress…upon mature deliberation, agreed to the following declarations of the rights and grievances of the colonists in America…

The members of this Congress, sincerely devoted, with the warmest sentiments of affection and duty to His Majesty's person and government; inviolably attached to the present happy establishment of the Protestant succession, and with minds deeply impressed by a sense of the present and impending misfortunes of the British colonies on this continent; having considered as maturely as time would permit, the circumstances of the said colonies, esteem it our indispensable duty to make the following declarations, of our humble opinion, respecting the most essential rights and liberties of the colonists, and of the grievances under which they labor, by reason of several late acts of Parliament.

1st. That His Majesty's subjects in these colonies owe the same allegiance to the Crown of Great Britain, that is owing from his subjects born within the realm, and all due subordination to that august body, the Parliament of Great Britain.

2d. That His Majesty's liege subjects in these colonies are entitled to all the inherent rights and privileges of his natural born subjects within the kingdom of Great Britain.

3d. That it is inseparably essential to the freedom of a people, and the undoubted rights of Englishmen, that no taxes should be imposed on them, but with their own consent, given personally, or by their representatives.

4th. That the people of these colonies are not, and from their local circumstances, cannot be represented in the House of Commons in Great Britain.

5th. That the only representatives of the people of these colonies, are persons chosen therein, by themselves; and that no taxes ever have been, or can be constitutionally imposed on them, but by their respective legislatures.

6th. That all supplies to the Crown, being free gifts of the people, it is unreasonable and inconsistent with the principles and spirit of the British constitution, for the people of Great Britain to grant to His Majesty the property of the colonists.

7th. That trial by jury is the inherent and invaluable right of every British subject in these colonies.

---

* Journal of the Stamp Act Congress, New York, 1765, as printed in the *Republication of the Principles and Acts of the Revolution in America* by Hezekiah Niles (1876).

8th. That the late act of Parliament, entitled, "An act for granting and applying certain stamp duties, and other duties in the British colonies and plantations in America, etc.," by imposing taxes on the inhabitants of these colonies, and the said act, and several other acts, by extending the jurisdiction of the courts of admiralty beyond its ancient limits, have a manifest tendency to subvert the rights and liberties of the colonists.

9th. That the duties imposed by several late acts of Parliament, from their peculiar circumstances of these colonies, will be extremely burthensome and grievous, and from the scarcity of specie, the payment of them absolutely impracticable.

10th. That as the profits of the trade of these colonies ultimately center in Great Britain, to pay for the manufacturers which they are obliged to take from thence, they eventually contribute very largely to all supplies granted there to the Crown.

11th. That the restrictions imposed by several late acts of Parliament, on the trade of these colonies, will render them unable to purchase the manufactures of Great Britain.

12th. That the increase, prosperity and happiness of these colonies, depend on the full and free enjoyment of their rights and liberties, and an intercourse, with Great Britain, mutually affectionate and advantageous.

13th. That it is the right of the British subjects in these colonies, to petition the King or either house of Parliament.

Lastly, that it is the indispensable duty of these colonies to the best of sovereigns, to the mother country, and to themselves, to endeavor by a loyal and dutiful address to His Majesty, and humble application to both houses of Parliament, to procure the repeal of the act for granting and applying certain stamp duties, of all clauses of any other acts of Parliament, whereby the jurisdiction of the admiralty is extended as aforesaid, and of the other late acts for the restriction of the American commerce.

Declaration of Rights *

In Congress, at Philadelphia, October 14, 1774

Whereas, since the close of the last war, the British Parliament, claiming a power of right to bind the people of America, by statute, in all cases whatsoever, hath in some acts expressly imposed taxes on them, and in others, under various pretenses, but in fact for the purpose of raising a revenue, hath imposed rates and duties payable in these colonies established a board of commissioners, with unconstitutional powers, and extended the jurisdiction of courts of admiralty, not only for collecting the said duties, but for the trial of causes merely arising within the body of a county.

And whereas, in consequence of other statutes, judges, who before held only estates at will in their offices, have been made dependent on the Crown alone for their salaries, and standing armies kept in times of peace:

And whereas, it has lately been resolved in Parliament, that by force of a statute, made in the thirty-fifth year of the reign of King Henry the Eighth, colonists may be transported to England, and tried there upon accusations for treasons and misprisions, or concealments of treasons committed in the colonies, and by a late statute, such trials have been directed in cases therein mentioned.

And whereas, in the last session of Parliament, three statutes were made; one, entitled "An act to discontinue, in such manner and for such time as are therein mentioned, the landing and discharging, lading, or shipping of goods, wares and merchandise, at the town, and within the harbor of Boston, in the province of Massachusetts Bay, in North America"; another, entitled "An act for the better regulating the government of the province of the Massachusetts Bay in New England;" and another, entitled "An act for the impartial administration of justice, in the cases of persons questioned for any act done by them in the execution of the law, or for the suppression of riots and tumults, in the province of the Massachusetts Bay, in New England." And another statute was then made, "for making more effectual provision for the government of the province of Quebec, etc." All which statutes are impolitic, unjust and cruel, as well as unconstitutional, and most dangerous and destructive of American rights.

And whereas, assemblies have been frequently dissolved, contrary to the rights of the people, when they attempted to deliberate on grievances; and their dutiful, humble, loyal, and reasonable petitions to the Crown for redress, have been repeatedly treated with contempt by His Majesty's ministers of state:

---

* *Journals of the Continental Congress 1774–1789.* Edited from the original records in the Library of Congress by Worthington Chauncey Ford, Chief, Division of Manuscripts. Washington: Government Printing Office, 1904.

The good people of the several colonies of New Hampshire, Massachusetts Bay, Rhode Island and Providence Plantations, Connecticut, New York, New Jersey, Pennsylvania, New Castle, Kent and Sussex on Delaware, Maryland, Virginia, North Carolina, and South Carolina, justly alarmed at these arbitrary proceedings of Parliament and administration, have severally elected, constituted, and appointed deputies to meet and sit in general congress, in the city of Philadelphia, in order to obtain such establishment, as that their religion, laws, and liberties may not be subverted:

Whereupon the deputies so appointed being now assembled, in a full and free representation of these colonies, taking into their most serious consideration, the best means of attaining the ends aforesaid, do, in the first place, as Englishmen, their ancestors in like cases have usually done, for asserting and vindicating their rights and liberties, declare,

That the inhabitants of the English colonies in North America, by the immutable laws of nature, the principles of the English Constitution, and the several charters or compacts, have the following rights:

Resolved, N. C. D. 1. That they are entitled to life, liberty, and property, and they have never ceded to any sovereign power whatever, a right to dispose of either without their consent.

Resolved, N. C. D. 2. That our ancestors, who first settled these colonies, were at the time of their emigration from the mother country, entitled to all the rights, liberties, and immunities of free and natural born subjects, within the realm of England.

Resolved, N. C. D. 3. That by such emigration they by no means forfeited, surrendered, or lost any of those rights, but that they were, and their descendants now are, entitled to the exercise and enjoyment of all such of them, as their local and other circumstances enable them to exercise and enjoy.

Resolved, 4. That the foundation of English liberty, and of all free government, is a right in the people to participate in their legislative council: and as the English colonists are not represented, and from their local and other circumstances, can not properly be represented in the British Parliament, they are entitled to a free and exclusive power of legislation in their several provincial legislatures, where their right of representation can alone be preserved, in all cases of taxation and internal polity, subject only to the negative of their sovereign, in such manner as has been heretofore used and accustomed. But, from the necessity of the case, and a regard to the mutual interest of both countries, we cheerfully consent to the operation of such acts of the British Parliament, as are bona fide, restrained to the regulation of our external commerce, for the purpose of securing the commercial advantages of the whole empire to the mother country, and the commercial benefits of its respective members; excluding every idea of taxation, internal or external, for raising a revenue on the subjects in America, without their consent.

Resolved, N. C. D. 5. That the respective colonies are entitled to the common law of England, and more especially to the great and inestimable privilege of being tried by their peers of the vicinage, according to the course of that law.

Resolved, N. C. D. 6. That they are entitled to the benefit of such of the English statutes as existed at the time of their colonization; and which they have, by experience, respectively found to be applicable to their several local and other circumstances.

Resolved, N. C. D.7. That these, His Majesty's colonies, are likewise entitled to all the immunities and privileges granted and confirmed to them by royal charters, or secured by their several codes of provincial laws.

Resolved, N. C. D. 8. That they have a right peaceably to assemble, consider of their grievances, and petition the King; and that all prosecutions, prohibitory proclamations, and commitments for the same, are illegal.

Resolved, N. C. D. 9. That the keeping a standing army in these colonies, in times of peace, without the consent of the legislature of that colony, in which such army is kept, is against law.

Resolved, N. C. D. 10. It is indispensably necessary to good government, and rendered essential by the English constitution, that the constituent branches of the legislature be independent of each other; that, therefore, the exercise of legislative power in several colonies, by a council appointed, during pleasure by the Crown, is unconstitutional, dangerous, and destructive to the freedom of American legislation.

All and each of which the aforesaid deputies, in behalf of themselves and their constituents, do claim, demand, and insist on, as their indubitable rights and liberties; which can not be legally taken from them, altered or abridged by any power whatever, without their own consent, by their representatives in their several provincial legislatures.

In the course of our inquiry, we find many infringements and violations of the foregoing rights, which, from an ardent desire, that harmony and mutual intercourse of affection and interest may be restored, we pass over for the present, and proceed to state such acts and measures as have been adopted since the last war, which demonstrate a system formed to enslave America.

Resolved, N. C. D. That the following acts of Parliament are infringements and violations of the rights of the colonists; and that the repeal of them is essentially necessary in order to restore harmony between Great Britain and the American colonies, viz.;

The several acts of 4 Geo. 3. ch. 15, and ch. 34.—5 Geo. 3. ch.25.—6 Geo. 3. ch.52.—7 Geo. 3. ch.41, and ch. 46.—8 Geo. 3. ch.22, which impose duties for the purpose of raising a revenue in America, extend the powers of the admiralty courts beyond their ancient limits, deprive the American subject of trial by jury, authorize the judges' certificate to indemnify the prosecutor from damages, that he might otherwise be liable to, requiring oppressive security from a claimant of ships and goods seized, before he shall be allowed to defend his property, and are subversive of American rights.

Also the 12 Geo. 3. ch. 24, entitled "An act for the better securing His Majesty's dock yards, magazines, ships, ammunition, and stores," which declares a new offense in America, and deprives the American subject of a constitutional trial by jury of the vicinage, by authorizing the trial of any person, charged with the committing any offense described in the said act, out of the realm, to be indicted and tried for the same in any shire or county within the realm.

Also the three acts passed in the last session of Parliament, for stopping the port and blocking up the harbor of Boston, for altering the charter and government of the Massachusetts Bay, and that which is entitled "An act for the better administration of justice," etc.

Also the act passed in the same session for establishing the Roman Catholic religion in the province of Quebec, abolishing the equitable system of English laws, and erecting a tyranny there, to the great danger, from so total a dissimilarity of religion, law, and government of the neighboring British colonies, by the assistance of whose blood and treasure the said country was conquered from France.

Also the act passed in the same session for the better providing suitable quarters for officers and soldiers in His Majesty's service in North America.

Also, that the keeping a standing army in several of these colonies, in time of peace, without the consent of the legislature of that colony in which such army is kept, is against law.

To these grievous acts and measures, Americans can not submit, but in hopes that their fellow subjects in Great Britain will, on a revision of them, restore us to that state in which both countries found happiness and prosperity, we have for the present only resolved to pursue the following peaceable measures:

1st. To enter into a non-importation, non-consumption, and non-exportation agreement or association.

2. To prepare an address to the people of Great Britain, and a memorial to the inhabitants of British America, and

3. To prepare a loyal address to His Majesty; agreeable to resolutions already entered into.

The Declaration of Independence *

(Adopted in Congress July 4, 1776)

The Unanimous Declaration of the Thirteen United States of America

When, in the course of human events, it becomes necessary for one people to dissolve the political bands which have connected them with another, and to assume among the powers of the earth, the separate and equal station to which the laws of nature and of nature's God entitle them, a decent respect to the opinions of mankind requires that they should declare the causes which impel them to the separation.

We hold these truths to be self-evident, that all men are created equal, that they are endowed by their Creator with certain unalienable rights, that among these are life, liberty and the pursuit of happiness. That to secure these rights, governments are instituted among men, deriving their just powers from the consent of the governed, that whenever any form of government becomes destructive of these ends, it is the right of the people to alter or to abolish it, and to institute new government, laying its foundation on such principles and organizing its powers in such form, as to them shall seem most likely to effect their safety and happiness. Prudence, indeed, will dictate that governments long established should not be changed for light and transient causes; and accordingly all experience hath shown that mankind are more disposed to suffer, while evils are sufferable, than to right themselves by abolishing the forms to which they are accustomed. But when a long train of abuses and usurpations, pursuing invariably the same object evinces a design to reduce them under absolute despotism, it is their right, it is their duty, to throw off such government, and to provide new guards for their future security. —Such has been the patient sufferance of these colonies; and such is now the necessity which constrains them to alter their former systems of government. The history of the present King of Great Britain is a history of repeated injuries and usurpations, all having in direct object the establishment of an absolute tyranny over these states. To prove this, let facts be submitted to a candid world.

He has refused his assent to laws, the most wholesome and necessary for the public good.

He has forbidden his governors to pass laws of immediate and pressing importance, unless suspended in their operation till his assent should be obtained; and when so suspended, he has utterly neglected to attend to them.

---

* The Federal and State Constitutions, Colonial Charters, and Other Organic Law of the United States. Compiled under an order of the United States Senate by Ben Perley Poore, Clerk of Printing Records. Washington: Government Printing Office, 1877.

He has refused to pass other laws for the accommodation of large districts of people, unless those people would relinquish the right of representation in the legislature, a right inestimable to them and formidable to tyrants only.

He has called together legislative bodies at places unusual, uncomfortable, and distant from the depository of their public records, for the sole purpose of fatiguing them into compliance with his measures.

He has dissolved representative houses repeatedly, for opposing with manly firmness his invasions on the rights of the people.

He has refused for a long time, after such dissolutions, to cause others to be elected; whereby the legislative powers, incapable of annihilation, have returned to the people at large for their exercise; the state remaining in the meantime exposed to all the dangers of invasion from without, and convulsions within.

He has endeavored to prevent the population of these states; for that purpose obstructing the laws for naturalization of foreigners; refusing to pass others to encourage their migration hither, and raising the conditions of new appropriations of lands.

He has obstructed the administration of justice, by refusing his assent to laws for establishing judiciary powers.

He has made judges dependent on his will alone, for the tenure of their offices, and the amount and payment of their salaries.

He has erected a multitude of new offices, and sent hither swarms of officers to harass our people, and eat out their substance.

He has kept among us, in times of peace, standing armies without the consent of our legislature.

He has affected to render the military independent of and superior to the civil power.

He has combined with others to subject us to a jurisdiction foreign to our constitution, and unacknowledged by our laws; giving his assent to their acts of pretended legislation:

For quartering large bodies of armed troops among us:

For protecting them, by a mock trial, from punishment for any murders which they should commit on the inhabitants of these states:

For cutting off our trade with all parts of the world:

For imposing taxes on us without our consent:

For depriving us in many cases, of the benefits of trial by jury:

For transporting us beyond seas to be tried for pretended offenses:

For abolishing the free system of English laws in a neighboring province, establishing therein an arbitrary government, and enlarging its boundaries so as to render it at once an example and fit instrument for introducing the same absolute rule into these colonies:

For taking away our charters, abolishing our most valuable laws, and altering fundamentally the forms of our governments:

For suspending our own legislatures, and declaring themselves invested with power to legislate for us in all cases whatsoever.

He has abdicated government here, by declaring us out of his protection and waging war against us.

He has plundered our seas, ravaged our coasts, burned our towns, and destroyed the lives of our people.

He is at this time transporting large armies of foreign mercenaries to complete the works of death, desolation and tyranny, already begun with circumstances of cruelty and perfidy scarcely paralleled in the most barbarous ages, and totally unworthy the head of a civilized nation.

He has constrained our fellow citizens taken captive on the high seas to bear arms against their country, to become the executioners of their friends and brethren, or to fall themselves by their hands.

He has excited domestic insurrections amongst us, and has endeavored to bring on the inhabitants of our frontiers, the merciless Indian savages, whose known rule of warfare, is an undistinguished destruction of all ages, sexes and conditions.

In every stage of these oppressions we have petitioned for redress in the most humble terms: our repeated petitions have been answered only by repeated injury. A prince, whose character is thus marked by every act which may define a tyrant, is unfit to be the ruler of a free people.

Nor have we been wanting in attention to our British brethren. We have warned them from time to time of attempts by their legislature to extend an unwarrantable jurisdiction over us. We have reminded them of the circumstances of our emigration and settlement here. We have appealed to their native justice and magnanimity, and we have conjured them by the ties of our common kindred to disavow these usurpations, which, would inevitably interrupt our connections and correspondence. They too have been deaf to the voice of justice and of consanguinity. We must, therefore, acquiesce in the necessity, which denounces our separation, and hold them, as we hold the rest of mankind, enemies in war, in peace friends.

We, therefore, the representatives of the United States of America, in General Congress, assembled, appealing to the Supreme Judge of the world for the rectitude of our intentions, do, in the name, and by the authority of the good people of these colonies, solemnly publish and declare, that these united colonies are, and of right ought to be free and independent states; that they are absolved from all allegiance to the British Crown, and that all political connection between them and the state of Great Britain, is and ought to be totally dissolved; and that as free and independent states, they have full power to levy war, conclude peace, contract alliances, establish commerce, and to do all other acts and things which independent states may of right do. And for the support of this declaration, with a firm reliance on the protection of Divine Providence, we mutually pledge to each other our lives, our fortunes and our sacred honor.

JOHN HANCOCK

New Hampshire
JOSIAH BARTLETT
WM. WHIPPLE
MATTHEW THORTON

Massachusetts Bay
SAML. ADAMS
JOHN ADAMS
ROBT. TREAT PAINE
ELBRIDGE GERRY

Rhode Island
STEP. HOPKINS
WILLIAM ELLERY

Connecticut
ROGER SHERMAN
SAM'EL HUNTINGTON
WM. WILLIAMS
OLIVER WOLCOTT

New York
WM. FLOYD
PHIL LIVINGSTON
FRANS. LEWIS
LEWIS MORRIS

New Jersey
RICHD. STOCKTON
JNO. WITHERSPOON
FRAS. HOPKINSON
JOHN HART
ABRA. CLARK

Pennsylvania
ROBT. MORRIS
BENJAMIN RUSH
BENJA. FRANKLIN
JOHN MORTONS
GEO CLYMER

JAS. SMITH
GEO. TAYLOR
JAMES WILSON GEO. ROSS

Delaware
CAESAR RODNEY
GEO. READ
THO. M'KEAN

Maryland
SAMUEL CHASE
WM. PACA
THOS. STONE
CHARLES CARROLL of Carrollton

Virginia
GEORGE WYTHE
RICHARD HENRY LEE
TH. JEFFERSON
BENJA. HARRISON
THOS. NELSON, JR.
FRANCIS LIGHTFOOT LEE
CARTER BRAXTON

North Carolina
WM. HOOPER
JOSEPH HEWES
JOHN PENN

South Carolina
EDWARD RUTLEDGE
THOS. HEYWARD, JUNR.
THOMAS LYNCH, JUNR.
ARTHUR MIDDLETON

Georgia
BUTTON GWINNETT
LYMAN HALL
GEO. WALTON

Articles of Confederation—1778 *

To all to whom these presents shall come, we the undersigned delegates of the states affixed to our names, send greeting:
WHEREAS the delegates of the United States of America in Congress assembled, did, on the fifteenth day of November in the year of our Lord seventeen seventy-seven, and in the second year of the Independence of America, agree to Certain Articles of Confederation and perpetual union between the states of New Hampshire, Massachusetts Bay, Rhode Island, and Providence Plantations, Connecticut, New York, New Jersey, Pennsylvania, Delaware, Maryland, Virginia, North Carolina, South Carolina and Georgia in the words following viz.:

Articles of Confederation and Perpetual Union Between the States of New Hampshire, Massachusetts Bay, Rhode Island and Providence Plantations, Connecticut, New York, New Jersey, Pennsylvania, Delaware, Maryland, Virginia, North Carolina, South Carolina and Georgia

ARTICLE I. The style of this Confederacy shall be "The United States of America."

ARTICLE II. Each state retains its sovereignty, freedom and independence, and every power, jurisdiction and right which is not by this Confederation expressly delegated to the United States in Congress assembled.

ARTICLE III. The said states hereby severally enter into a firm league of friendship with each other for their common defense, the security of their liberties, and their mutual and general welfare, binding themselves to assist each other against all force offered to, or attacks made upon them, or any of them, on account of religion, sovereignty, trade, or any other pretense whatever.

ARTICLE IV. The better to secure and perpetuate mutual friendship and intercourse among the people of the different States in this Union, the free inhabitants of each of these states, paupers, vagabonds and fugitives from justice excepted, shall be entitled to all privileges and immunities of free citizens in the several states; and the people of each state shall have free ingress and regress to and from any other state, and shall enjoy therein all the privileges of trade and commerce, subject to the same duties, impositions and restrictions as the inhabitants thereof respectively; provided, that such restrictions shall not extend so far as to prevent the removal of property imported into any state, to any other state of which the owner is an inhabitant; provided also, that no imposition, duties or restriction shall be laid by any state on the property of the United States, or either of them.

---

* *The Federal and State Constitutions, Colonial Charters and Other Organic Laws of the United States.* Compiled under an order of the United States Senate by Ben. Perley Poore, Clerk of Printing Records. Washington: Government Printing Offices, 1877.

If any person guilty of or charged with treason, felony, or other high misdemeanor in any state, shall flee from justice, and be found in any of the United States, he shall upon demand of the governor or executive power of the state from which he fled, be delivered up and removed to the state having jurisdiction of his offense.

Full faith and credit shall be given in each of these states to the records, acts and judicial proceedings of the courts and magistrates of every other state.

ARTICLE V. For the more convenient management of the general interests of the United States, delegates shall be annually appointed in such manner as the legislature of each state shall direct, to meet in Congress on the first Monday in November, in every year, with a power reserved to each state, to recall its delegates, or any of them, at any time within the year, and to send others in their stead, for the remainder of the year.

No state shall be represented in Congress by less than two, nor by more than seven members; and no person shall be capable of being a delegate for more than three years in any term of six years; nor shall any person, being a delegate, be capable of holding any office under the United States, for which he, or another for his benefit receives any salary, fees or emolument of any kind.

Each state shall maintain its own delegates in a meeting of the states, and while they act as members of the committee of the states.

In determining questions in the United States, in Congress assembled, each state shall have one vote.

Freedom of speech and debate in Congress shall not be impeached or questioned in any court, or place out of Congress, and the members of Congress shall be protected in their persons from arrests and imprisonments, during the time of their going to and from, and attendance on Congress, except for treason, felony, or breach of the peace.

ARTICLE VI. No state without the consent of the United States in Congress assembled, shall send any embassy to, or receive any embassy from, or enter into any conference, agreement, alliance or treaty with any king, prince or state; nor shall any person holding any office of profit or trust under the United States, or any of them, accept of any present, emolument, office or title of any kind whatever from any king, prince or foreign state; nor shall the United States in Congress assembled, or any of them, grant any title of nobility.

No two or more states shall enter into any treaty, confederation or alliance whatever between them, without the consent of the United States in Congress assembled, specifying accurately the purposes for which the same is to be entered into, and how long it shall continue.

No state shall lay any imposts or duties, which may interfere with any stipulations in treaties, entered into by the United States in Congress assembled, with any king, prince or state, in pursuance of any treaties already proposed by Congress, to the courts of France and Spain.

No vessels of war shall be kept up in time of peace by any state, except such number only as shall be deemed necessary by the United States in Congress assembled, for the defense of such state, or its trade; nor shall any body of forces be kept up by any state, in time of peace, except such number only, as in the judgment of the United States, in Congress assembled, shall be deemed requisite to garrison the forts necessary for the defense of such state; but every state shall always keep up a well regulated and disciplined militia, sufficiently armed and accoutered, and shall provide and constantly have ready for use, in public stores, a due number of field pieces and tents, and a proper quantity of arms, ammunition and camp equipage.

No state shall engage in any war without the consent of the United States in Congress assembled, unless such state be actually invaded by enemies, or shall have received certain advice of a resolution being formed by some nation of Indians to invade such state, and the danger is so imminent as not to admit of a delay, till the United States in Congress assembled can be consulted: nor shall any state grant commissions to any ships or vessels of war, nor letters of marque or reprisal, except it be after a declaration of war, by the United States in Congress assembled, and then only against the kingdom or state and the subjects thereof, against which war has been so declared, and under such regulations as shall be established by the United States in Congress assembled, unless such state be infested by pirates, in which case vessels of war may be fitted out for that occasion, and kept so long as the danger shall continue, or until the United States in Congress assembled shall determine otherwise.

ARTICLE VII. When land forces are raised by any state for the common defense, all officers of or under the rank of colonel, shall be appointed by the Legislature of each state respectively by whom such forces shall be raised, or in such manner as such state shall direct, and all vacancies shall be filled up by the state which first made the appointment.

ARTICLE VIII. All charges of war, and all other expenses that shall be incurred for the common defense or general welfare, and allowed by the United States in Congress assembled, shall be defrayed out of a common treasury, which shall be supplied by the several states, in proportion to the value of all land within each state, granted to or surveyed for any person, as such land and the buildings and improvements thereon shall be estimated according to such mode as the United States in Congress assembled, shall from time to time direct and appoint.

The taxes for paying that proportion shall be laid and levied by the authority and direction of the legislatures of the several states within the time agreed upon by the United States in Congress assembled.

ARTICLE IX.   The United States in Congress assembled, shall have the sole and exclusive right and power of determining on peace and war except in the cases mentioned in the sixth article—of sending and receiving ambassadors—entering into treaties and alliances; provided that no treaty of commerce shall be made whereby the legislative power of the respective states shall be restrained from imposing such imposts and duties on foreigners, as their own people are subjected to, or from prohibiting the exportation or importation of any species of goods or commodities whatsoever—of establishing rules for deciding in all cases, what captures on land or water shall be legal, and in what manner prizes taken by land or naval forces in the service of the United States shall be divided or appropriated—of granting letters of marque and reprisal in times of peace—appointing courts for the trial of piracies and felonies committed on the high seas and establishing courts for receiving and determining finally appeals in all cases of captures, provided that no member of Congress shall be appointed a judge of any of the said courts.

The United States in Congress assembled shall also be the last resort on appeal in all disputes and differences now subsisting or that hereafter may arise between two or more states concerning boundary, jurisdiction or any other cause whatever; which authority shall always be exercised in the manner following. Whenever the legislative or executive authority or lawful agent of any state in controversy with another shall present a petition to Congress, stating the matter in question and praying for a hearing, notice thereof shall be given by order of Congress to the legislative or executive authority of the other state in controversy, and a day assigned for the appearance of the parties by their lawful agents, who shall then be directed to appoint by joint consent commissioners or judges to constitute a court for hearing and determining the matter in question: but if they can not agree, Congress shall name three persons out of each of the United States, and from the list of such persons each party shall alternately strike out one, the petitioners beginning, until the number shall be reduced to thirteen; and from that number not less than seven, nor more than nine names, as Congress shall direct, shall in the presence of Congress be drawn out by lot, and the persons whose names shall be so drawn or any five of them, shall be commissioners or judges, to hear and finally determine the controversy, so always as a major part of the judges who shall hear the cause shall agree in the determination: and if either party shall neglect to attend at the day appointed, without showing reasons, which Congress shall judge sufficient, or being present shall refuse to strike, the Congress shall proceed to nominate three persons out of each state, and the Secretary of Congress shall strike in behalf of such party absent or refusing; and the judgment and sentence of the court to be appointed, in the manner before prescribed, shall be final and conclusive; and if any of the parties shall refuse to submit to the authority of such court, or to appear or defend their claim or cause, the court shall, nevertheless proceed to pronounce sentence, or judgment, which shall in like manner be final and decisive, the judgment or sentence and other proceedings being in either case transmitted to Congress, and lodged among the acts of Congress for the security of the parties concerned: provided that every commissioner, before he sits in judgment, shall take an oath to be administered by one of the judges of the supreme or superior court of the state where the cause shall be tried, "well and truly to hear and determine the matter in question, according to the best of his judgment, without favor, affection, or hope of reward": provided also that no state shall be deprived of territory for the benefit of the United States.

All controversies concerning the private right of soil claimed under different grants of two or more states, whose jurisdiction as they may respect such lands, and the states which passed such grants are adjusted, the said grants or either of them being at the same time claimed to have originated antecedent to such settlement of jurisdiction, shall on the petition of either party to the Congress of the United States, be finally determined as near as may be in the same manner as is before prescribed for deciding disputes respecting territorial jurisdiction between different states.

The United States in Congress assembled shall also have the sole and exclusive right and power of regulating the alloy and value of coin struck by their own authority, or by that of the respective states—fixing the standard of weights and measures throughout the United States—regulating the trade, and managing all affairs with the Indians, not members of any of the states, provided that the legislative right of any state within its own limits be not infringed or violated—establishing and regulating post offices from one state to another, throughout all the United States, and exacting such postage on the papers passing through the same as may be requisite to defray the expenses of the said office—appointing all officers of the land forces, in the service of the United States, excepting regimental officers—appointing all the officers of the naval forces, and commissioning all officers whatever in the service of the United States—making rules for the government and regulation of the said land and naval forces, and directing their operations.

The United States in Congress assembled shall have authority to appoint a committee, to sit in the recess of Congress, to be denominated "a Committee of the States," and to consist of one delegate from each state; and to appoint such other committees and civil officers as may be necessary for managing the general affairs of the United States under their direction—to appoint one of their number to preside, provided that no person be allowed to serve in the office of president more than one year in any term of three years; to ascertain the necessary sums of money to be raised for the service of the United States, and to appropriate and apply the same for defraying the public expenses—to borrow money, or emit bills on the credit of the United States, transmitting every half year to the respective states an account of the sums of money so borrowed or emitted—to build and equip a navy—to agree upon the number of land forces, and to make requisitions from each state for its quota, in proportion to the number of white inhabitants in such state; which requisition shall be binding, and thereupon the legislature of each state shall appoint the regimental officers, raise the men and clothe, arm and equip them in a soldierlike manner, at the expense of the United States; and the officers and men so clothed, armed and equipped shall march to the place appointed, and within the time agreed on by the United States in Congress assembled: but if the United States in Congress assembled shall, on consideration of circumstances judge proper that any state should not raise men, or should raise a smaller number than its quota, and that any other state should raise a greater number of men than the quota thereof, such extra number shall be raised, officered, clothed, armed and equipped in the same manner as the quota of such state, unless the legislature of such state shall judge that such extra number can not be safely spared out of the same, in which case they shall raise, officer, clothe, arm and equip as many of such extra number as they judge can be safely spared. And the officers and men so clothed, armed and equipped, shall march to the place appointed, and within the time agreed on by the United States in Congress assembled.

The United States in Congress assembled shall never engage in a war, nor grant letters of marque and reprisal in time of peace, nor enter into any treaties or alliances, nor coin money, nor regulate the value thereof, nor ascertain the sums and expenses necessary for the defense and welfare of the United States, or any of them, nor emit bills, nor borrow money on the credit of the United States, nor appropriate money, nor agree upon the number of vessels of war, to be built or purchased, or the number of land or sea forces to be raised, nor appoint a commander-in-chief of the army or navy, unless nine states assent to the same: nor shall a question on any other point, except for adjourning from day to day be determined, unless by the votes of a majority of the United States in Congress assembled.

The Congress of the United States shall have power to adjourn to any time within the year, and to any place within the United States, so that no period of adjournment be for a longer duration than the space of six months; and shall publish the journal of their proceedings monthly, except such parts thereof relating to treaties, alliances or military operations, as in their judgment require secrecy; and the yeas and nays of the delegates of each state on any question shall be entered on the journal, when it is desired by any delegate; and the delegates of a state, or any of them, at his or their request, shall be furnished with a transcript of the said journal, except such parts as are above excepted, to lay before the legislatures of the several states.

ARTICLE X. The Committee of the States, or any nine of them shall be authorized to execute, in the recess of Congress, such of the powers of Congress as the United States in Congress assembled, by the consent of nine states, shall from time to time think expedient to vest them with; provided that no power be delegated to the said committee, for the exercise of which, by the Articles of Confederation, the voice of nine states in the Congress of the United States assembled is requisite.

ARTICLE XI. Canada acceding to this Confederation, and joining in the measures of the United States, shall be admitted into, and entitled to all the advantages of this Union: but no other colony shall be admitted into the same, unless such admission be agreed to by nine states.

ARTICLE XII. All bills of credit emitted, moneys borrowed and debts contracted by, or under the authority of Congress, before the assembling of the United States, in pursuance of the present Confederation, shall be deemed and considered as a charge against the United States, for payment and satisfaction whereof the said United States, and the public faith are hereby solemnly pledged.

ARTICLE XIII. Every state shall abide by the determinations of the United States in Congress assembled, on all questions which by this Confederation are submitted to them. And the Articles of this Confederation shall be inviolably observed by every state, and the Union shall be perpetual; nor shall any alteration at any time hereafter be made in any of them, unless such alteration be agreed to in a Congress of the United States, and be afterwards confirmed by the legislatures of every state.

AND WHEREAS it hath pleased the Great Governor of the world to incline the hearts of the legislatures we respectively represent in Congress, to approve of, and to authorize us to ratify the said Articles of Confederation and perpetual Union. Know ye that we the undersigned delegates, by virtue of the power and authority to us given for that purpose, do by these presents, in the name and in behalf of our respective constituents, fully and entirely ratify and confirm each and every of the said Articles of Confederation and perpetual Union, and all and singular the matters and things therein contained: and we do further solemnly plight and engage the faith of our respective constituents, that they shall abide by the determinations of the United States in Congress assembled, on all questions, which by the said Confederation are submitted to them. And that the articles thereof shall be inviolably observed by the states we respectively represent, and that the Union shall be perpetual.

IN WITNESS WHEREOF we have hereunto set our hands in Congress Done at Philadelphia in the State of Pennsylvania the ninth day of July in the year of our Lord one thousand seven hundred and seventy-eight, and in the third year of the independence of America.

JOSIAH BARTLETT	JOHN WENTWORTH, JUNR. August 8th, 1778 }	On the part and behalf of the State of New Hampshire.
JOHN HANCOCK SAMUEL ADAMS ELBRIDGE GERRY	FRANCIS DANA JAMES LOVELL SAMUEL HOLTON }	On the part and behalf of the State of Massachusetts Bay.
WILLIAM ELLERY HENRY MARCHANT	JOHN COLLINS }	On the part and behalf of the State of Rhode island and Providence Plantations.
ROGER SHERMAN SAMUEL HUNTINGTON OLIVER WOOLCOTT	TITUS HOSMER ANDREW ADAMS }	On the part and behalf of the State of Connecticut.
JAS. DUANE FRA. LEWIS	WM. DUER GOUV. MORRIS }	On the part and behalf of the State of New York.
JNO. WITHERSPOON	NATHL. SCUDDER }	On the part and behalf of the State of New Jersey Novr. 26, 1778.
ROBT. MORRIS DANIEL ROBERDEAU JONA. BAYARD SMITH	WILLIAM CLINGAN JOSEPH REED 22d July, 1778 }	On the part and behalf of the State of Pennsylvania.
THO. M'KEAN Feby. 12, 1779	JOHN DICKINSON May 5th, 1779 NICHOLAS VAN DYKE }	On the part and behalf of the State of Delaware.
JOHN HANSON March 1, 1781	DANIEL CARROLL Mar. 1, 1781 }	On the part and behalf of the State of Maryland.
RICHARD HENRY LEE JOHN BANISTER THOMAS ADAMS	JNO. HARVIE FRANCIS LIGHTFOOT LEE }	On the part and behalf of the State of Virginia.
JOHN PENN July 21st, 1778	CORNS. HARNETT JNO. WILLIAMS }	On the part and behalf of the State of North Carolina.
HENRY LAURENS WILLIAM HENRY DRAYTON JNO. MATHEWS	RICHD. HUTSON THOS. HEYWARD JUNR. }	On the part and behalf of the State of South Carolina.
JNO. WALTON 24th July, 1778	EDWD. TELFAIR EDWD. LANGWORTHY }	On the part and behalf of the State of Georgia.

The Articles of Confederation were ratified by the States as follows:

South Carolina .... Feb. 5, 1778	Massachusetts .... Mar. 10, 1778
New York .... Feb. 6, 1778	North Carolina .... April 5, 1778
Rhode Island .... Feb. 9, 1778	New Jersey .... Nov. 19, 1778
Connecticut .... Feb. 12, 1778	Virginia .... Dec. 15, 1778
Georgia .... Feb. 26, 1778	Delaware .... Feb. 1, 1779
New Hampshire .... Mar. 4, 1778	Maryland .... Jan. 30, 1781
Pennsylvania .... Mar. 5, 1778	

The ratification by all the States was formally announced to the public March 1, 1781.

Constitution of the
United States
1787

Constitution of the United States

(In Convention, September 17, 1787)

PREAMBLE

We the people of the United States, in order to form a more perfect union, establish justice, insure domestic tranquillity, provide for the common defense, promote the general welfare, and secure the blessings of liberty to ourselves and our posterity, do ordain and establish this Constitution for the United States of America.

ARTICLE I. LEGISLATIVE DEPARTMENT*

Section 1. Congress*

*Powers Are Vested in Senate and House**

1.* All legislative powers herein granted shall be vested in a Congress of the United States, which shall consist of a Senate and House of Representatives.

Section 2. House of Representatives

Election of Representatives

1. The House of Representatives shall be composed of members chosen every second year by the people of the several states, and the electors in each state shall have the qualifications requisite for electors of the most numerous branch of the state legislature.

Qualifications of Representatives

2. No person shall be a Representative who shall not have attained to the age of twenty-five years, and been seven years a citizen of the United States, and who shall not, when elected, be an inhabitant of that state in which he shall be chosen.

---

* Headings and paragraph numbers have been inserted to assist the reader, and are not to be construed as a part of the Constitution. The original Constitution contains only article and section numbers. The modern style of capitalization has been used in the printing of this edition; and obsolete spelling of such words as "chuse" and "controul" has been changed to conform to the modern spelling prescribed by Webster's Dictionary. We have followed the text of the *UNITED STATES CONSTITUTION, 1787* Bicentennial Edition 1987, prepared by the Commission on the Bicentennial of the United States Constitution.

Apportionment of Representatives

3. Representatives and direct taxes shall be apportioned among the several states which may be included within this union, according to their respective numbers, which shall be determined by adding to the whole number of free persons, including those bound to service for a term of years, and excluding Indians not taxed, three-fifths of all other persons. The actual enumeration shall be made within three years after the first meeting of the Congress of the United States, and within every subsequent term of ten years, in such manner as they shall by law direct. The number of Representatives shall not exceed one for every thirty thousand, but each state shall have at least one Representative; and until such enumeration shall be made, the State of New Hampshire shall be entitled to choose three, Massachusetts eight, Rhode Island and Providence plantations one, Connecticut five, New York six, New Jersey four, Pennsylvania eight, Delaware one, Maryland six, Virginia ten, North Carolina five, South Carolina five, and Georgia three.

This clause has been superseded, so far as it relates to representation, by Section 2 of the Fourteenth Amendment to the Constitution.

Vacancies

4. When vacancies happen in the representation from any state, the executive authority thereof shall issue writs of election to fill such vacancies.

Officers of the House—Impeachment

5. The House of Representatives shall choose their Speaker and other officers; and shall have the sole power of impeachment.

Section 3.   The Senate

Number of Senators

1. The Senate of the United States shall be composed of two Senators from each state, chosen by the legislature thereof, for six years; and each Senator shall have one vote.

Superseded by Amendment XVII.

Classification of Senators
2. Immediately after they shall be assembled in consequence of the first election, they shall be divided as equally as may be into three classes. The seats of the Senators of the first class shall be vacated at the expiration of the second year, of the second class at the expiration of the fourth year, and of the third class at the expiration of the sixth year, so that one-third may be chosen every second year; and if vacancies happen by resignation, or otherwise, during the recess of the legislature of any state, the executive thereof may make temporary appointments until the next meeting of the legislature, which shall then fill such vacancies.

Modified by Amendment XVII.

Qualification of Senators
3. No person shall be a Senator who shall not have attained to the age of thirty years, and been nine years a citizen of the United States, and who shall not, when elected, be an inhabitant of that state for which he shall be chosen.

President of Senate
4. The Vice President of the United States shall be President of the Senate, but shall have no vote, unless they be equally divided.

Officers of Senate
5. The Senate shall choose their other officers, and also a President pro Tempore, in the absence of the Vice President, or when he shall exercise the office of President of the United States.

Trial of Impeachment
6. The Senate shall have the sole power to try all impeachments. When sitting for that purpose, they shall be on oath or affirmation. When the President of the United States is tried, the Chief Justice shall preside: and no person shall be convicted without the concurrence of two-thirds of the members present.

Judgment on Conviction of Impeachment
7. Judgment in cases of impeachment shall not extend further than to removal from office, and disqualification to hold and enjoy any office of honor, trust or profit under the United States: but the party convicted shall nevertheless be liable and subject to indictment, trial, judgment and punishment, according to law.

Section 4. Election of Senators and Representatives— Meetings of Congress

Election of Members of Congress

1. The times, places and manner of holding elections for Senators and Representatives, shall be prescribed in each state by the legislature thereof; but the Congress may at any time by law make or alter such regulations, except as to the places of choosing Senators.

See Amendment XX.

Congress to Meet Annually

2. The Congress shall assemble at least once in every year, and such meeting shall be on the first Monday in December, unless they shall by law appoint a different day.

Changed to January 3d by Amendment XX.

Section 5. Powers and Duties of Each House of Congress

Sole Judge of Qualifications of Members

1. Each house shall be the judge of the elections, returns and qualifications of its own members, and a majority of each shall constitute a quorum to do business; but a smaller number may adjourn from day to day, and may be authorized to compel the attendance of absent members, in such manner, and under such penalties as each house may provide.

Rules of Proceedings—Punishment of Members

2. Each house may determine the rules of its proceedings, punish its members for disorderly behavior, and, with the concurrence of two-thirds, expel a member.

Journals

3. Each house shall keep a journal of its proceedings, and from time to time publish the same, excepting such parts as may in their judgment require secrecy; and the yeas and nays of the members of either house on any question shall, at the desire of one-fifth of those present, be entered on the journal.

Adjournment

4. Neither house, during the session of Congress, shall, without the consent of the other, adjourn for more than three days, nor to any other place than that in which the two houses shall be sitting.

Section 6.   Compensation, Privileges and Disabilities, of Senators and Representatives

Compensation—Privileges

1. The Senators and Representatives shall receive a compensation for their services, to be ascertained by law, and paid out of the Treasury of the United States. They shall in all cases, except treason, felony and breach of the peace, be privileged from arrest during their attendance at the session of their respective houses, and in going to and returning from the same; and for any speech or debate in either house, they shall not be questioned in any other place.

See also Amendment XXVII.

Disability to Hold Other Offices

2. No Senator or Representative shall, during the time for which he was elected, be appointed to any civil office under the authority of the United States, which shall have been created, or the emoluments whereof shall have been increased during such time; and no person holding any office under the United States, shall be a member of either house during his continuance in office.

See also Section 3 of the Fourteenth Amendment.

Section 7.   Mode of Passing Laws

SPECIAL PROVISIONS AS TO REVENUE LAWS

1. All bills for raising revenue shall originate in the House of Representatives; but the Senate may propose or concur with amendments as on other bills.

Laws, How Enacted

2. Every bill which shall have passed the House of Representatives and the Senate, shall, before it become a law, be presented to the President of the United States; if he approve he shall sign it, but if not he shall return it, with his objections to that house in which it shall have originated, who shall enter the objections at large on their journal, and proceed to reconsider it. If after such reconsideration two-thirds of that house shall agree to pass the bill, it shall be sent, together with the objections, to the other house, by which it shall likewise be reconsidered, and if approved by two-thirds of that house, it shall become a law. But in all such cases the votes of both houses shall be determined by yeas and nays, and the names of the persons voting for and against the bill shall be entered on the journal of each house respectively. If any bill shall not be returned by the President within ten days (Sundays excepted) after it shall have been presented to

him, the same shall be a law, in like manner as if he had signed it, unless the Congress by their adjournment prevent its return, in which case it shall not be a law.

Resolutions, Etc.

3. Every order, resolution, or vote to which the concurrence of the Senate and House of Representatives may be necessary (except on a question of adjournment) shall be presented to the President of the United States; and before the same shall take effect, shall be approved by him, or, being disapproved by him, shall be repassed by two-thirds of the Senate and House of Representatives, according to the rules and limitations prescribed in the case of a bill.

Section 8. Powers Granted to Congress

Taxation

1. The Congress shall have power to lay and collect taxes, duties, imposts and excises, to pay the debts and provide for the common defense and general welfare of the United States; but all duties, imposts and excises shall be uniform throughout the United States;

Loans

2. To borrow money on the credit of the United States;

Commerce

3. To regulate commerce with foreign nations, and among the several states, and with the Indian tribes;

Naturalization and Bankruptcies

4. To establish an uniform rule of naturalization, and uniform laws on the subject of bankruptcies throughout the United States;

Coin

5. To coin money, regulate the value thereof, and of foreign coin, and fix the standard of weights and measures;

Counterfeiting

6. To provide for the punishment of counterfeiting the securities and current coin of the United States;

Post Office

7. To establish post offices and post roads;

Patents and Copyrights
8. To promote the progress of science and useful arts, by securing for limited times to authors and inventors the exclusive right to their respective writings and discoveries;

Courts
9. To constitute tribunals inferior to the Supreme Court;

Piracies
10. To define and punish piracies and felonies committed on the high seas, and offenses against the law of nations;

War
11. To declare war, grant letters of marque and reprisal, and make rules concerning captures on land and water;

Army
12. To raise and support armies, but no appropriation of money to that use shall be for a longer term than two years;

Navy
13. To provide and maintain a navy;

Military and Naval Rules
14. To make rules for the government and regulation of the land and naval forces;

Militia, Calling Forth
15. To provide for calling forth the militia to execute the laws of the union, suppress insurrections and repel invasions;

Militia, Organizing and Arming
16. To provide for organizing, arming, and disciplining the militia, and for governing such part of them as may be employed in the service of the United States, reserving to the states respectively, the appointment of the officers, and the authority of training the militia according to the discipline prescribed by Congress;

Federal District and Other Places
17. To exercise exclusive legislation in all cases whatsoever, over such district (not exceeding ten miles square) as may, by cession of particular states, and the acceptance of Congress, become the seat of the government of the United States, and to exercise like authority over all places pur-

chased by the consent of the legislature of the state in which the same shall be, for the erection of forts, magazines, arsenals, dockyards and other needful buildings;—And

Make Laws to Carry Out Foregoing Powers
18. To make all laws which shall be necessary and proper for carrying into execution the foregoing powers, and all other powers vested by this Constitution in the government of the United States, or in any department or officer thereof.

For other powers, see Article II, Section 1; Article III, Sections 2 and 3; Article IV, Sections 1–3; Article V; and Amendments XIII–XVI and XIX–XXI.

Section 9. Limitations on Powers Granted to the United States

Slave Trade
1. The migration or importation of such persons as any of the states now existing shall think proper to admit, shall not be prohibited by the Congress prior to the year one thousand eight hundred and eight, but a tax or duty may be imposed on such importation, not exceeding ten dollars for each person.

Habeas Corpus
2. The privilege of the writ of habeas corpus shall not be suspended, unless when in cases of rebellion or invasion the public safety may require it.

Ex Post Facto Law
3. No bill of attainder or ex post facto law shall be passed.

Direct Taxes
4. No capitation, or other direct, tax shall be laid, unless in proportion to the census or enumeration hereinbefore directed to be taken.

Duties on Exports
5. No tax or duty shall be laid on articles exported from any state.

No Commercial Discrimination to Be Made Between States
6. No preference shall be given by any regulation of commerce or revenue to the ports of one state over those of another: nor shall vessels bound to, or from, one state, be obliged to enter, clear, or pay duties in another.

Money, How Drawn From Treasury
7. No money shall be drawn from the Treasury, but in consequence of appropriations made by law; and a regular statement and account of the receipts and expenditures of all public money shall be published from time to time.

Titles of Nobility
8. No title of nobility shall be granted by the United States; and no person holding any office of profit or trust under them, shall, without the consent of the Congress, accept of any present, emolument, office, or title, of any kind whatever, from any King, Prince, or foreign state.

For other limitations see Amendments I–X.

Section 10.   Powers Prohibited to the States

Powers Prohibited, Absolutely
1. No state shall enter into any treaty, alliance, or confederation; grant letters of marque and reprisal; coin money; emit bills of credit; make any thing but gold and silver coin a tender in payment of debts; pass any bill of attainder, ex post facto law, or law impairing the obligation of contracts, or grant any title of nobility.

Powers Concerning Duties on Imports or Exports
2. No state shall, without the consent of the Congress, lay any imposts or duties on imports or exports, except what may be absolutely necessary for executing its inspection laws: and the net produce of all duties and imposts, laid by any state on imports or exports, shall be for the use of the Treasury of the United States; and all such laws shall be subject to the revision and control of the Congress.

Powers Permitted With Consent of Congress
3. No state shall, without the consent of Congress, lay any duty of tonnage, keep troops, or ships of war in time of peace, enter into any agreement or compact with another state, or with a foreign power, or engage in war, unless actually invaded, or in such imminent danger as will not admit of delay.

ARTICLE II.   EXECUTIVE DEPARTMENT

Section 1.   The President

Executive Power Vested in President—Term of Office
1. The executive power shall be vested in a President of the United States of America. He shall hold his office during the term of four years, and, together with the Vice President, chosen for the same term, be elected, as follows:

Appointment and Number of Presidential Electors
2. Each state shall appoint, in such manner as the legislature thereof may direct, a number of electors, equal to the whole number of Senators and

Representatives to which the state may be entitled in the Congress: but no Senator or Representative, or person holding an office of trust or profit under the United States, shall be appointed an elector.

Mode of Electing President and Vice President

3. The electors shall meet in their respective states and vote by ballot for two persons, of whom one at least shall not be an inhabitant of the same state with themselves. And they shall make a list of all the persons voted for, and of the number of votes for each; which list they shall sign and certify, and transmit sealed to the seat of the government of the United States, directed to the President of the Senate. The President of the Senate shall, in the presence of the Senate and House of Representatives, open all the certificates, and the votes shall then be counted. The person having the greatest number of votes shall be the President, if such number be a majority of the whole number of electors appointed; and if there be more than one who have such majority, and have an equal number of votes, then the House of Representatives shall immediately choose by ballot one of them for President; and if no person have a majority, then from the five highest on the list the said house shall in like manner choose the President. But in choosing the President, the vote shall be taken by states, the representation from each state having one vote; a quorum for this purpose shall consist of a member or members from two-thirds of the states, and a majority of all the states shall be necessary to a choice. In every case, after the choice of the President, the person having the greatest number of votes of the electors shall be the Vice President. But if there should remain two or more who have equal votes, the Senate shall choose from them by ballot the Vice President.

This paragraph has been superseded by the Twelfth Amendment to the Constitution.

See Amendment XX.

Time of Choosing Electors and Casting Electoral Vote

4. The Congress may determine the time of choosing the electors, and the day on which they shall give their votes; which day shall be the same throughout the United States.

Qualifications of President

5. No person except a natural born citizen, or a citizen of the United States, at the time of the adoption of this Constitution, shall be eligible to the office of President; neither shall any person be eligible to that office who shall not have attained to the age of thirty-five years, and been fourteen years a resident within the United States.

See also Fourteenth Amendment.

Presidential Succession

6. In case of the removal of the President from office, or of his death, resignation, or inability to discharge the powers and duties of the said office, the same shall devolve on the Vice President, and the Congress may by law provide for the case of removal, death, resignation or inability, both of the President and Vice President, declaring what officer shall then act as President, and such officer shall act accordingly, until the disability be removed, or a President shall be elected.

NOTE—*United States Code Annotated, Title 3, Sec. 19,* provides as follows:

§ 19. (a) (1) If, by reason of death, resignation, removal from office, inability, or failure to qualify, there is neither a President nor Vice President to discharge the powers and duties of the office of President, then the Speaker of the House of Representatives shall, upon his resignation as Speaker and as Representative in Congress, act as President.

(2) The same rule shall apply in the case of the death, resignation, removal from office, or inability of an individual acting as President under this subsection.

(b) If, at the time when under subsection (a) of this section a Speaker is to begin the discharge of the powers and duties of the office of President, there is no Speaker, or the Speaker fails to qualify as Acting President, then the President pro Tempore of the Senate shall, upon his resignation as President pro Tempore and as Senator, act as President.

(c) An individual acting as President under subsection (a) or subsection (b) of this section shall continue to act until the expiration of the then current Presidential term, except that—

(1) if his discharge of the powers and duties of the office is founded in whole or in part on the failure of both the President-elect and the Vice-President-elect to qualify, then he shall act only until a President or Vice President qualifies; and

(2) if his discharge of the powers and duties of the office is founded in whole or in part on the inability of the President or Vice President, then he shall act only until the removal of the disability of one of such individuals.

(d) (1) If, by reason of death, resignation, removal from office, inability, or failure to qualify, there is no President pro Tempore to act as President under subsection (b) of this section, then the officer of the United States who is highest on the following list, and who is not under disability to discharge the powers and duties of the office of President shall act as President: Secretary of State, Secretary of the Treasury, Secretary of Defense, Attorney General, Postmaster General, Secretary of the Interior, Secretary of Agriculture, Secretary of Commerce, Secretary of Labor, Secretary of Health, Education, and Welfare, Secretary of Housing and Urban Development.

(2) An individual acting as President under this subsection shall continue so to do until the expiration of the then current Presidential term, but not after a qualified and prior-entitled individual is able to act, except that the removal of the disability of an individual higher on the list contained in paragraph (1) of this subsection or the ability to qualify on the part of an individual higher on such list shall not terminate his service.

(3) The taking of the oath of office by an individual specified in the list in paragraph (1) of this subsection shall be held to constitute his resignation from the office by virtue of the holding of which he qualifies to act as President.

(e) Subsections (a), (b), and (d) of this section shall apply only to such officers as are eligible to the office of President under the Constitution. Subsection (d) of this section shall apply only to officers appointed, by and with the advice and consent of the Senate, prior to the time of the death, resignation, removal from office, inability, or failure to qualify, of the President pro Tempore, and only to officers not under impeachment by the House of Representatives at the time the powers and duties of the office of President devolve upon them.

(f) During the period that any individual acts as President under this section, his compensation shall be at the rate then provided by law in the case of the President.

Salary of President

7. The President shall, at stated times, receive for his services a compensation, which shall neither be increased nor diminished during the period for which he shall have been elected, and he shall not receive within that period any other emolument from the United States, or any of them.

Oath of Office of President

8. Before he enter on the execution of his office, he shall take the following oath or affirmation;—"I do solemnly swear (or affirm) that I will faithfully execute the office of President of the United States, and will to the best of my ability, preserve, protect and defend the Constitution of the United States."

Section 2.   Powers of the President

Commander-in-Chief

1. The President shall be commander in chief of the Army and Navy of the United States, and of the militia of the several states, when called into the actual service of the United States; he may require the opinion, in writing, of the principal officer in each of the executive departments, upon any subject relating to the duties of their respective offices, and he shall have power to grant reprieves and pardons for offenses against the United States, except in cases of impeachment.

Treaties and Appointments
2. He shall have power, by and with the advice and consent of the Senate, to make treaties, provided two-thirds of the Senators present concur; and he shall nominate, and by and with the advice and consent of the Senate, shall appoint ambassadors, other public ministers and consuls, judges of the Supreme Court, and all other officers of the United States, whose appointments are not herein otherwise provided for, and which shall be established by law: but the Congress may by law vest the appointment of such inferior officers, as they think proper, in the President alone, in the courts of law, or in the heads of departments.

Filling Vacancies
3. The President shall have power to fill up all vacancies that may happen during the recess of the Senate, by granting commissions which shall expire at the end of their next session.

Section 3.   Duties of the President

Message to Congress—Adjourn and Call Special Session
He shall from time to time give to the Congress information of the state of the union, and recommend to their consideration such measures as he shall judge necessary and expedient; he may, on extraordinary occasions, convene both houses, or either of them, and in case of disagreement between them, with respect to the time of adjournment, he may adjourn them to such time as he shall think proper; he shall receive ambassadors and other public ministers; he shall take care that the laws be faithfully executed, and shall commission all the officers of the United States.

See also Article I, Section 5.

Section 4.   Removal of Executive and Civil Officers

Impeachment of President and Other Officers
The President, Vice President and all civil officers of the United States, shall be removed from office on impeachment for, and conviction of, treason, bribery, or other high crimes and misdemeanors.

See also Article I, Sections 2 and 3.

ARTICLE III. JUDICIAL DEPARTMENT

Section 1. Judicial Powers Vested in Federal Courts

Courts—Terms of Office and Salary of Judges

The judicial power of the United States shall be vested in one supreme court, and in such inferior courts as the Congress may from time to time ordain and establish. The judges, both of the Supreme and inferior courts, shall hold their offices during good behavior, and shall, at stated times, receive for their services, a compensation, which shall not be diminished during their continuance in office.

Section 2. Jurisdiction of United States Courts

Cases That May Come Before United States Courts

1. The judicial power shall extend to all cases, in law and equity, arising under this Constitution, the laws of the United States, and treaties made, or which shall be made, under their authority; to all cases affecting ambassadors, other public ministers and consuls; to all cases of admiralty and maritime jurisdiction; to controversies to which the United States shall be a party; to controversies between two or more states, between a state and citizens of another state, between citizens of different states, between citizens of the same state claiming lands under grants of different states, and between a state, or the citizens thereof, and foreign states, citizens or subjects.

See also Eleventh Amendment.

Jurisdiction of Supreme and Appellate Courts

2. In all cases affecting ambassadors, other public ministers and consuls, and those in which a state shall be party, the Supreme Court shall have original jurisdiction. In all the other cases before mentioned, the Supreme Court shall have appellate jurisdiction, both as to law and fact, with such exceptions, and under such regulations as the Congress shall make.

Trial of Crimes

3. The trial of all crimes, except in cases of impeachment, shall be by jury; and such trial shall be held in the state where the said crimes shall have been committed; but when not committed within any state, the trial shall be at such place or places as the Congress may by law have directed.

See also Fifth, Sixth, Seventh, and Eighth Amendments.

Section 3. Treason

Treason—Definition and Conviction
1. Treason against the United States, shall consist only in levying war against them, or in adhering to their enemies, giving them aid and comfort. No person shall be convicted of treason unless on the testimony of two witnesses to the same overt act, or on confession in open court.

Punishment
2. The Congress shall have power to declare the punishment of treason, but no attainder of treason shall work corruption of blood, or forfeiture except during the life of the person attainted.

ARTICLE IV. THE STATES AND THE FEDERAL GOVERNMENT

Section I. Official Acts of the States

Full Faith and Credit
   Full faith and credit shall be given in each state to the public acts, records, and judicial proceedings of every other state. And the Congress may by general laws prescribe the manner in which such acts, records and proceedings shall be proved, and the effect thereof.

See also Fourteenth Amendment.

Section 2. Citizens of the States

Interstate Privileges of Citizens
1. The citizens of each state shall be entitled to all privileges and immunities of citizens in the several states.

Fugitives From Justice
2. A person charged in any state with treason, felony, or other crime, who shall flee from justice, and be found in another state, shall, on demand of the executive authority of the state from which he fled, be delivered up, to be removed to the state having jurisdiction of the crime.

Fugitives From Service
3. No person held to service or labor in one state, under the laws thereof, escaping into another, shall, in consequence of any law or regulation therein, be discharged from such service or labor, but shall be delivered up on claim of the party to whom such service or labor may be due.

"Person" here includes slave. This was the basis of the Fugitive Slave Laws of 1793 and 1850. It is now superseded by the Thirteenth Amendment, by which slavery is prohibited.

Section 3.   New States

Admission or Division of States

1. New states may be admitted by the Congress into this union; but no new state shall be formed or erected within the jurisdiction of any other state; nor any state be formed by the junction of two or more states, or parts of states, without the consent of the legislatures of the states concerned as well as of the Congress.

Control of the Property and Territory of the Union

2. The Congress shall have power to dispose of and make all needful rules and regulations respecting the territory or other property belonging to the United States; and nothing in this Constitution shall be so construed as to prejudice any claims of the United States, or of any particular state.

Section 4.   Protection of States Guaranteed

Republican Form of Government

The United States shall guarantee to every state in this union a republican form of government, and shall protect each of them against invasion; and on application of the legislature, or of the executive (when the legislature cannot be convened) against domestic violence.

ARTICLE V.   AMENDMENTS

Amendments, How Proposed and Adopted

The Congress, whenever two-thirds of both houses shall deem it necessary, shall propose amendments to this Constitution, or, on the application of the legislatures of two-thirds of the several states, shall call a convention for proposing amendments, which, in either case, shall be valid to all intents and purposes, as part of this Constitution, when ratified by the legislatures of three-fourths of the several states, or by conventions in three-fourths thereof, as the one or the other mode of ratification may be proposed by the Congress; provided that no amendment which may be made prior to the year one thousand eight hundred and eight shall in any manner affect the first and fourth clauses in the ninth section of the first article; and that no state, without its consent, shall be deprived of its equal suffrage in the Senate.

ARTICLE VI. GENERAL PROVISIONS

The Public Debt

1. All debts contracted and engagements entered into, before the adoption of this Constitution, shall be as valid against the United States under this Constitution, as under the Confederation.

See also Fourteenth Amendment, Section 4.

Supreme Law of the Land

2. This Constitution, and the laws of the United States which shall be made in pursuance thereof; and all treaties made, or which shall be made, under the authority of the United States, shall be the supreme law of the land; and the judges in every state shall be bound thereby, any thing in the Constitution or laws of any state to the contrary notwithstanding.

Oath of Office—No Religious Test Required

3. The Senators and Representatives before mentioned, and the members of the several state legislatures, and all executive and judicial officers, both of the United States and of the several states, shall be bound by oath or affirmation, to support this Constitution; but no religious test shall ever be required as a qualification to any office or public trust under the United States.

ARTICLE VII. RATIFICATION OF THE CONSTITUTION *

Ratification of Nine States Required

The ratification of the conventions of nine states, shall be sufficient for the establishment of this Constitution between the states so ratifying the same.

DONE in convention by the unanimous consent of the states present the seventeenth day of September in the year of our Lord one thousand seven hundred and eighty-seven and of the Independence of the United States of America the twelfth. In witness whereof we have hereunto subscribed our names.†

---

*The Constitution was ratified by the States in the following order:
  1. Delaware—December 7, 1787.
  2. Pennsylvania—December 12, 1787.
  3. New Jersey—December 19, 1787.
  4. Georgia—January 2, 1788.
  5. Connecticut—January 9, 1788.
  6. Massachusetts—February 6, 1788.
  7. Maryland—April 28, 1788.
  8. South Carolina—May 23, 1788.
  9. New Hampshire—June 21, 1788.
 10. Virginia—June 25, 1788.
 11. New York—July 26, 1788.
 12. North Carolina—November 21, 1789.
 13. Rhode Island—May 29, 1790.

† *The Records of the Federal Convention,* as edited by Farrand, is the source for all of Warren's figures cited here. Farrand's work is highly respected, and has been referred to as "the basic document for the study of the Convention." (P. Bator et al, eds., *The Federal Courts and the Federal System,* 2nd ed., 1973, at p. 2.)
  There were 74 delegates chosen to the convention: 19 did not attend; 16 declined or failed to sign: 39 signed.

G[o] WASHINGTON—Presid[t]
and deputy from Virginia

New Hampshire
{ JOHN LANGDON
NICHOLAS GILMAN

Massachusetts
{ NATHANIEL GORHAM
RUFUS KING

Connecticut
{ W[M] SAM[L] JOHNSON
ROGER SHERMAN

New York : : :   ALEXANDER HAMILTON

New Jersey
{ WIL: LIVINGSTON
DAVID BREARLEY.
W[M] PATERSON.
JONA: DAYTON

Pennsylvania
{ B FRANKLIN
THOMAS MIFFLIN
ROB[T] MORRIS
GEO. CLYMER
THO[S] FITZSIMONS
JARED INGERSOLL
JAMES WILSON
GOUV MORRIS

Delaware
{ GEO: READ
GUNNING BEDFORD jun
JOHN DICKINSON
RICHARD BASSETT
JACO: BROOM

Maryland
{ JAMES M[C]HENRY
DAN OF S[T] THO[S] JENIFER
DAN[L] CARROLL

Virginia
{ JOHN BLAIR—
JAMES MADISON JR.

North Carolina
{ W[M] BLOUNT
RICH[D] DOBBS SPAIGHT.
HU WILLIAMSON

South Carolina
{ J. RUTLEDGE
CHARLES COTESWORTH PINCKNEY
CHARLES PINCKNEY
PIERCE BUTLER

Georgia
{ WILLIAM FEW
ABR BALDWIN

The word, "the," being interlined between the seventh and eighth lines of the first page, the word "thirty" being partly written on an erasure in the fifteenth line of the first page, the words "is tried" being interlined between the thirty-second and thirty-third lines of the first page and the word "the" being interlined between the forty-third and forty-fourth lines of the second page.

Attest WILLIAM JACKSON Secretary

Amendments

AMENDMENT I

Restrictions on Powers of Congress

[SECTION 1 *.]　Congress shall make no law respecting an establishment of religion, or prohibiting the free exercise thereof; or abridging the freedom of speech, or of the press; or the right of the people peaceably to assemble, and to petition the government for a redress of grievances.

Proposed September 25, 1789; ratified December 15, 1791.

AMENDMENT II

Right to Bear Arms

[SECTION 1.]　A well regulated militia, being necessary to the security of a free state, the right of the people to keep and bear arms, shall not be infringed.

Proposed September 25, 1789; ratified December 15, 1791.

AMENDMENT III

Billeting of Soldiers

[SECTION 1.]　No soldier shall, in time of peace be quartered in any house, without the consent of the owner, nor in time of war, but in a manner to be prescribed by law.

Proposed September 25, 1789; ratified December 15, 1791.

AMENDMENT IV

Seizures, Searches and Warrants

[SECTION 1.]　The right of the people to be secure in their persons, houses, papers and effects, against unreasonable searches and seizures, shall not be violated, and no warrants shall issue, but upon probable cause, supported by oath or affirmation, and particularly describing the place to be searched, and the persons or things to be seized.

Proposed September 25, 1789; ratified December 15, 1791.

---

* Words in brackets added.

AMENDMENT V

Criminal Proceedings and Condemnation of Property

[SECTION 1.] No person shall be held to answer for a capital, or otherwise infamous crime, unless on a presentment or indictment of a grand jury, except in cases arising in the land or naval forces, or in the militia, when in actual service in time of war or public danger; nor shall any person be subject for the same offense to be twice put in jeopardy of life or limb; nor shall be compelled in any criminal case to be a witness against himself, nor be deprived of life, liberty, or property, without due process of law; nor shall private property be taken for public use without just compensation.

Proposed September 25, 1789; ratified December 15, 1791.

AMENDMENT VI

Mode of Trial in Criminal Proceedings

[SECTION 1.] In all criminal prosecutions, the accused shall enjoy the right to a speedy and public trial, by an impartial jury of the state and district wherein the crime shall have been committed, which district shall have been previously ascertained by law, and to be informed of the nature and cause of the accusation; to be confronted with the witnesses against him; to have compulsory process for obtaining witnesses in his favor, and to have the assistance of counsel for his defense.

Proposed September 25, 1789; ratified December 15, 1791.

AMENDMENT VII

Trial by Jury

[SECTION 1.] In suits at common law, where the value in controversy shall exceed twenty dollars, the right of trial by jury shall be preserved, and no fact tried by a jury shall be otherwise reexamined in any court of the United States, than according to the rules of the common law.

Proposed September 25, 1789; ratified December 15, 1791.

AMENDMENT VIII

Bails—Fines—Punishments

[SECTION 1.] Excessive bail shall not be required, nor excessive fines imposed, nor cruel and unusual punishments inflicted.

Proposed September 25, 1789; ratified December 15, 1791.

AMENDMENT IX

Certain Rights Not Denied to the People

[SECTION 1.] The enumeration in the Constitution of certain rights shall not be construed to deny or disparage others retained by the people.

Proposed September 25, 1789; ratified December 15, 1791.

AMENDMENT X

State Rights

[SECTION 1.] The powers not delegated to the United States by the Constitution, nor prohibited by it to the states, are reserved to the states respectively, or to the people.

Proposed September 25, 1789; ratified December 15, 1791.

AMENDMENT XI

Judicial Powers

[SECTION 1.] The judicial power of the United States shall not be construed to extend to any suit in law or equity, commenced or prosecuted against one of the United States by citizens of another state, or by citizens or subjects of any foreign state.

Proposed March 4, 1794; ratified February 7, 1795; declared ratified January 8, 1798.

AMENDMENT XII

Election of President and Vice President

[SECTION 1.] The electors shall meet in their respective states and vote by ballot for President and Vice President, one of whom, at least, shall not be an inhabitant of the same state with themselves; they shall name in their ballots the person voted for as President, and in distinct ballots, the person voted for as Vice President, and they shall make distinct lists of all persons voted for as President, and of all persons voted for as Vice President, and of the number of votes for each, which lists they shall sign and certify, and transmit sealed to the seat of the government of the United States, directed to the President of the Senate;—The President of the Senate shall, in the presence of the Senate and House of Representatives, open all the certificates and the votes shall then be counted;—The person having the greatest number of votes for President, shall be the President, if such number be a majority of the whole number of electors appointed; and if no person have such majority, then from the persons having the highest numbers not exceeding three on the list of those voted for as President, the House of Representatives shall choose immediately, by ballot, the President. But in choosing the President, the votes shall be taken by states, the representation from each state having one vote; a quorum for this purpose shall consist of a member or members from two-thirds of the states, and a majority of all the states shall be necessary to a choice. And if the House of Representatives shall not choose a President whenever the right of choice shall devolve upon them, before the fourth day of March next following, then the Vice President shall act as President, as in the case of the death or other constitutional disability of the President.

The person having the greatest number of votes as Vice President, shall be the Vice President, if such number be a majority of the whole number of electors appointed, and if no person have a majority, then from the two highest numbers on the list, the Senate shall choose the Vice President; a quorum for the purpose shall consist of two-thirds of the whole number of Senators, and a majority of the whole number shall be necessary to a choice. But no person constitutionally ineligible to the office of President shall be eligible to that of Vice President of the United States.

Passed both Houses December 9, 1803; proposed (signed) December 12, 1803; declared ratified September 25, 1804.

AMENDMENT XIII

Slavery

SECTION 1.   Neither slavery nor involuntary servitude, except as a punishment for crime whereof the party shall have been duly convicted, shall exist within the United States, or any place subject to their jurisdiction.

SECTION 2.   Congress shall have power to enforce this article by appropriate legislation.

Proposed January 31, 1865; ratified December 6, 1865; certified December 18, 1865.

AMENDMENT XIV

Citizenship, Representation, and Payment of Public Debt

Citizenship

SECTION 1.   All persons born or naturalized in the United States and subject to the jurisdiction thereof, are citizens of the United States and of the state wherein they reside. No state shall make or enforce any law which shall abridge the privileges or immunities of citizens of the United

States; nor shall any state deprive any person of life, liberty, or property, without due process of law; nor deny to any person within its jurisdiction the equal protection of the laws.

Apportionment of Representatives

SECTION 2. Representatives shall be apportioned among the several states according to their respective numbers, counting the whole number of persons in each state, excluding Indians not taxed. But when the right to vote at any election for the choice of electors for President and Vice President of the United States, Representatives in Congress, the executive and judicial officers of a state, or the members of the legislature thereof, is denied to any of the male inhabitants of such state, being twenty-one years of age, and citizens of the United States, or in any way abridged, except for participation in rebellion or other crime, the basis of representation therein shall be reduced in the proportion which the number of such male citizens shall bear to the whole number of male citizens twenty-one years of age in such state.

Disqualification for Public Office

SECTION 3. No person shall be a Senator or Representative in Congress, or elector of President and Vice President, or hold any office, civil or military, under the United States, or under any state, who, having previously taken an oath, as a member of Congress, or as an officer of the United States, or as a member of any state legislature, or as an executive or judicial officer of any state, to support the Constitution of the United States, shall have engaged in insurrection or rebellion against the same, or given aid or comfort to the enemies thereof. But Congress may by a vote of two-thirds of each house, remove such disability.

Public Debt, Guarantee of

SECTION 4. The validity of the public debt of the United States, authorized by law, including debts incurred for payment of pensions and bounties for services in suppressing insurrection or rebellion, shall not be questioned. But neither the United States nor any state shall assume or pay any debt or obligation incurred in aid of insurrection or rebellion against the United States, or any claim for the loss or emancipation of any slave; but all such debts, obligations and claims shall be held illegal and void.

Power of Congress

SECTION 5. The Congress shall have power to enforce, by appropriate legislation, the provisions of this article.

Proposed June 13, 1866; ratified July 9, 1868; certified July 28, 1868.

AMENDMENT XV

Elective Franchise

Right of Citizens to Vote
SECTION 1. The right of citizens of the United States to vote shall not be denied or abridged by the United States or by any state on account of race, color, or previous condition of servitude.

Power of Congress
SECTION 2. The Congress shall have power to enforce this article by appropriate legislation.

Proposed February 26, 1869; ratified February 3, 1870; certified March 30, 1870.

AMENDMENT XVI

Income Tax—Congress Given Power to Lay and Collect

The Congress shall have power to lay and collect taxes on incomes, from whatever source derived, without apportionment among the several states, and without regard to any census or enumeration.

Proposed July 2, 1909; ratified February 3, 1913; certified February 25, 1913.

AMENDMENT XVII

Popular Election of Senators

[SECTION 1.] The Senate of the United States shall be composed of two Senators from each state, elected by the people thereof, for six years; and each Senator shall have one vote. The electors in each state shall have the qualifications requisite for electors of the most numerous branch of the state legislatures.

[SECTION 2.] When vacancies happen in the representation of any state in the Senate, the executive authority of such state shall issue writs of election to fill such vacancies: *Provided,* That the legislature of any state may empower the executive thereof to make temporary appointments until the people fill the vacancies by election as the legislature may direct.

[SECTION 3.] This amendment shall not be so construed as to affect the election or term of any Senator chosen before it becomes valid as part of the Constitution.

Proposed May 13, 1912; ratified April 8, 1913; certified May 31, 1913.

NOTE.—The Seventeenth Amendment was proposed as a direct amendment of Article I, Section 3, of the Constitution.

AMENDMENT XVIII

Prohibition—States Given Concurrent Power to Enforce

SECTION 1. After one year from the ratification of this article the manufacture, sale, or transportation of intoxicating liquors within, the importation thereof into, or the exportation thereof from the United States and all territory subject to the jurisdiction thereof for beverage purposes is hereby prohibited.

SECTION 2. The Congress and the several states shall have concurrent power to enforce this article by appropriate legislation.

SECTION 3. This article shall be inoperative unless it shall have been ratified as an amendment to the Constitution by the legislatures of the several states, as provided in the Constitution, within seven years from the date of the submission hereof to the states by the Congress.

Proposed December 18, 1917; ratified January 16, 1919; certified January 29, 1919. Effective January 29, 1920. For repeal see Amendment XXI.

AMENDMENT XIX

Equal Suffrage

[SECTION 1.] The right of citizens of the United States to vote shall not be denied or abridged by the United States or by any state on account of sex.

[SECTION 2.] Congress shall have power to enforce this article by appropriate legislation.

Proposed June 4, 1919; ratified August 18, 1920; certified August 26, 1920.

AMENDMENT XX

Commencement of Congressional and Presidential Terms

End of Terms

SECTION 1. The terms of the President and Vice President shall end at noon on the 20th day of January, and the terms of Senators and Representatives at noon on the 3d day of January, of the years in which such terms would have ended if this article had not been ratified; and the terms of their successors shall then begin.

Assembling of Congress

SECTION 2. The Congress shall assemble at least once in every year, and such meeting shall begin at noon on the 3d day of January, unless they shall by law appoint a different day.

Congress Provides for Acting President
SECTION 3. If, at the time fixed for the beginning of the term of the President, the President-elect shall have died, the Vice President-elect shall become President. If a President shall not have been chosen before the time fixed for the beginning of his term, or if the President-elect shall have failed to qualify, then the Vice President-elect shall act as President until a President shall have qualified; and the Congress may by law provide for the case wherein neither a President-elect nor a Vice President-elect shall have qualified, declaring who shall then act as President, or the manner in which one who is to act shall be selected, and such person shall act accordingly until a President or Vice President shall have qualified.

Congress Has Power Over Unusual Elections
SECTION 4. The Congress may by law provide for the case of the death of any of the persons from whom the House of Representatives may choose a President whenever the right of choice shall have devolved upon them, and for the case of the death of any of the persons from whom the Senate may choose a Vice President whenever the right of choice shall have devolved upon them.

Date in Effect
SECTION 5. Sections 1 and 2 shall take effect on the 15th day of October following the ratification of this article.

Conditions of Ratification
SECTION 6. This article shall be inoperative unless it shall have been ratified as an amendment to the Constitution by the legislatures of three-fourths of the several states within seven years from the date of its submission.

Proposed March 2, 1932; ratified January 23, 1933; certified February 6, 1933.

AMENDMENT XXI

Repeal of Prohibition

Repeal of 18th Amendment
SECTION 1. The eighteenth article of amendment to the Constitution of the United States is hereby repealed.

Control of Interstate Liquor Transportation
SECTION 2. The transportation or importation into any state, territory, or possession of the United States for delivery or use therein of intoxicating liquors, in violation of the laws thereof, is hereby prohibited.

Condition of Ratification

SECTION 3. This article shall be inoperative unless it shall have been ratified as an amendment to the Constitution by conventions in the several states, as provided in the Constitution, within seven years from the date of the submission hereof to the states by the Congress.

Proposed February 20, 1933; ratified December 5, 1933; certified December 5, 1933.

Ratified by the California State Convention on July 24, 1933.

AMENDMENT XXII

Terms of Office of the President

Limitation on Number of Terms

SECTION 1. No person shall be elected to the office of the President more than twice, and no person who has held the office of President, or acted as President, for more than two years of a term to which some other person was elected President shall be elected to the office of the President more than once.

But this article shall not apply to any person holding the office of President when this article was proposed by the Congress, and shall not prevent any person who may be holding the office of President, or acting as President, during the term within which this article becomes operative from holding the office of President or acting as President during the remainder of such term.

Condition of Ratification

SECTION 2. This article shall be inoperative unless it shall have been ratified as an amendment to the Constitution by the legislatures of three-fourths of the several states within seven years from the date of its submission to the states by the Congress.

Proposed March 24, 1947; ratified February 27, 1951; certified March 1, 1951 [16 Fed. Reg. 2019 (1951)].

AMENDMENT XXIII

District of Columbia

SECTION 1. The district constituting the seat of government of the United States shall appoint in such manner as the Congress may direct:

A number of electors of President and Vice President equal to the whole number of Senators and Representatives in Congress to which the district would be entitled if it were a state, but in no event more than the least populous state; they shall be in addition to those appointed by the states, but they shall be considered, for the purposes of the election of President and Vice President, to be electors appointed by a state; and they shall meet in the district and perform such duties as provided by the twelfth article of amendment.

SECTION 2. The Congress shall have power to enforce this article by appropriate legislation.

Proposed June 16, 1960; ratified March 29, 1961; certified April 3, 1961.

AMENDMENT XXIV

Qualifications of Electors; Poll Tax

SECTION 1. The right of citizens of the United States to vote in any primary or other election for President or Vice President, for electors for President or Vice President, or for Senator or Representative in Congress, shall not be denied or abridged by the United States or any state by reason of failure to pay any poll tax or other tax.

SECTION 2. The Congress shall have power to enforce this article by appropriate legislation.

Proposed September 14, 1962; ratified January 23, 1964; certified February 4, 1964.

AMENDMENT XXV

Succession to Presidency and Vice Presidency; Disability of President

SECTION 1. In case of the removal of the President from office or of his death or resignation, the Vice President shall become President.

SECTION 2. Whenever there is a vacancy in the office of the Vice President, the President shall nominate a Vice President who shall take office upon confirmation by a majority vote of both houses of Congress.

SECTION 3. Whenever the President transmit to the President pro Tempore of the Senate and the Speaker of the House of Representatives his written declaration that he is unable to discharge the powers and duties of his office, and until he transmits to them a written declaration to the contrary, such powers and duties shall be discharged by the Vice President as Acting President.

SECTION 4. Whenever the Vice President and a majority of either the principal officers of the executive departments or of such other body as Congress may by law provide, transmit to the President pro Tempore of the Senate and the Speaker of the House of Representatives their written declaration that the President is unable to discharge the powers and duties of his office, the Vice President shall immediately assume the powers and duties of the office as Acting President.

Thereafter, when the President transmits to the President pro Tempore of the Senate and the Speaker of the House of Representatives his written declaration that no inability exists, he shall resume the powers and duties of his office unless the Vice President and a majority of either the principal officers of the executive department or of such other body as Congress may by law provide, transmit within four days to the President pro Tempore of the Senate and the Speaker of the House of Representatives their written declaration that the President is unable to discharge the powers and duties of his office. Thereupon Congress shall decide the issue, assembling within forty-eight hours for that purpose if not in session. If the Congress, within twenty-one days after receipt of the latter written declaration, or, if Congress is not in session, within twenty-one days after Congress is required to assemble, determines by two-thirds vote of both houses that the President is unable to discharge the powers and duties of his office, the Vice President shall continue to discharge the same as Acting President; otherwise, the President shall resume the powers and duties of his office.

Proposed July 6, 1965; certified February 23, 1967.

AMENDMENT XXVI

Voting Age — Eighteen

SECTION 1.   The right of citizens of the United States, who are eighteen years of age or older, to vote shall not be denied or abridged by the United States or by any state on account of age.

SECTION 2.   The Congress shall have power to enforce this article by appropriate legislation.

Proposed March 23, 1971; ratified July 1, 1971; certified July 7, 1971.

AMENDMENT XXVII

Compensation of Members of Congress

No law, varying the compensation for the services of the Senators and Representatives, shall take effect, until an election of Representatives shall have intervened.

Proposed September 25, 1789; ratified May 7, 1992; certified May 18, 1992 [57 Fed. Reg. 21187 (1992)].

Ratified by the California State Legislature July 1, 1992.

Index to the Constitution of
the United States

Index to Constitution of the United States

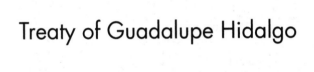

Treaty of Guadalupe Hidalgo

TREATY OF GUADALUPE HIDALGO[*]

TREATY OF PEACE, FRIENDSHIP, LIMITS, AND SETTLEMENT WITH THE REPUBLIC OF MEXICO[£]

In the name of Almighty God:

The United States of America and the United Mexican States, animated by a sincere desire to put an end to the calamities of the war which unhappily exists between the two republics, and to establish upon a solid basis relations of peace and friendship, which shall confer reciprocal benefits upon the citizens of both, and assure the concord, harmony, and mutual confidence wherein the two people should live, as good neighbors, have for that purpose appointed their respective plenipotentiaries—that is to say, the President of the United States has appointed Nicholas P. Trist, a citizen of the United States, and the President of the Mexican republic has appointed Don Luis Gonzaga Cuevas, Don Bernardo Couto, and Don Miguel Atristain, citizens of the said republic, who, after a reciprocal communication of their respective full powers, have, under the protection of Almighty God, the author of peace, arranged, agreed upon, and signed the following

Treaty of Peace, Friendship, Limits, and Settlement between the United States of America and the Mexican Republic.

ARTICLE I.

There shall be firm and universal peace between the United States of America and the Mexican republic, and between their respective countries, territories, cities, towns, and people, without exception of places or persons.

ARTICLE II.

Immediately upon the signature of this treaty, a convention shall be entered into between a commissioner or commissioners appointed by the General-in-chief of the forces of the United States, and such as may be appointed by the Mexican government, to the end that a provisional suspension of hostilities shall take place, and that, in the places occupied by the said forces, constitutional order may be reëstablished, as regards the political, administrative, and judicial branches, so far as this shall be permitted by the circumstances of military occupation.

---

[*] Concluded at Guadalupe Hidalgo, February 2, 1848; The United States Senate, with amendments, advised and consented to the ratification March 10, 1848; With all signatories agreeing, the President ratified the Treaty, March 16, 1848; Ratifications exchanged at Queretaro, May 30, 1848; Proclaimed, July 4, 1848.

[£] The text here printed is taken from Volume 3, West's Annotated California Codes, 1996, pg. 387.

ARTICLE III.

Immediately upon the ratification of the present treaty by the government of the United States, orders shall be transmitted to the commanders of their land and naval forces, requiring the latter (provided this treaty shall then have been ratified by the government of the Mexican republic, and the ratifications exchanged) immediately to desist from blockading any Mexican ports; and requiring the former (under the same condition) to commence, at the earliest moment practicable, withdrawing all troops of the United States then in the interior of the Mexican republic, to points that shall be selected by common agreement, at a distance from the seaports not exceeding thirty leagues; and such evacuation of the interior of the republic shall be completed with the least possible delay; the Mexican government hereby binding itself to afford every facility in its power for rendering the same convenient to the troops, on their march and in their new positions, and for promoting a good understanding between them and the inhabitants. In like manner orders shall be despatched to the persons in charge of the custom-houses at all ports occupied by the forces of the United States, requiring them (under the same condition) immediately to deliver possession of the same to the persons authorized by the Mexican government to receive it, together with all bonds and evidences of debt for duties on importations and on exportations, not yet fallen due. Moreover, a faithful and exact account shall be made out, showing the entire amount of all duties on imports and on exports, collected at such custom-houses, or elsewhere in Mexico, by authority of the United States, from and after the day of the ratification of this treaty by the government of the Mexican republic; and also an account of the cost of collection; and such entire amount, deducting only the cost of collection, shall be delivered to the Mexican government, at the city of Mexico, within three months after the exchange of ratifications.

The evacuation of the capital of the Mexican republic by the troops of the United States, in virtue of the above stipulation, shall be completed in one month after the orders there stipulated for shall have been received by the commander of said troops, or sooner if possible.

ARTICLE IV.

Immediately after the exchange of ratifications of the present treaty, all castles, forts, territories, places, and possessions, which have been taken or occupied by the forces of the United States during the present war, within the limits of the Mexican republic, as about to be established by the following article, shall be definitively restored to the said republic, together with all the artillery, arms, apparatus of war, munitions, and other public property, which were in the said castles and forts when captured, and which shall remain there at the time when this treaty shall be duly ratified by the government of the Mexican republic. To this end, immediately upon the signature of this treaty, orders shall be despatched to the American officers commanding such castles and forts, securing against the removal or destruction of any such artillery, arms, apparatus of war, munitions, or other public property. The city of Mexico, within the inner line of intrenchments surrounding the said city, is comprehended in the above stipulations, as regards the restoration of artillery, apparatus of war, & c.

The final evacuation of the territory of the Mexican republic, by the forces of the United States, shall be completed in three months from the said exchange of ratifications, or sooner if possible: the Mexican government hereby engaging, as in the foregoing article, to use all means in its power for facilitating such evacuation, and rendering it convenient to the troops, and for promoting a good understanding between them and the inhabitants.

If, however, the ratification of this treaty by both parties should not take place in time to allow the embarcation of the troops of the United States to be completed before the commencement of the sickly season, at the Mexican ports on the Gulf of Mexico, in such case a friendly arrangement shall be entered into between the General-in-chief of the said troops and the Mexican government, whereby healthy and otherwise suitable places, at a distance from the ports not exceeding thirty leagues, shall be designated for the residence of such troops as may not yet have embarked, until the return of the healthy season. And the space of time here referred to as comprehending the sickly season, shall be understood to extend from the first day of May to the first day of November.

All prisoners of war taken on either side, on land or on sea, shall be restored as soon as practicable after the exchange of ratifications of this treaty. It is also agreed that if any Mexicans should now be held as captives by any savage tribe within the limits of the United States, as about to be established by the following article, the government of the said United States will exact the release of such captives, and cause them to be restored to their country.

ARTICLE V.

The boundary line between the two republics shall commence in the Gulf of Mexico, three leagues from land, opposite the mouth of the Rio Grande, otherwise called Rio Bravo del Norte, or opposite the mouth of its deepest branch, if it should have more than one branch emptying directly into the sea; from thence up the middle of that river, following the deepest channel, where it has more than one, to the point where it strikes the southern boundary of New Mexico; thence, westwardly, along the whole southern boundary of New Mexico (which runs north of the town called *Paso*) to its western termination; thence, northward, along the western line of

New Mexico, until it intersects the first branch of the River Gila; (or if it should not intersect any branch of that river, then to the point on the said line nearest to such branch, and thence in a direct line to the same;) thence down the middle of the said branch and of the said river, until it empties into the Rio Colorado; thence across the Rio Colorado, following the division line between Upper and Lower California, to the Pacific Ocean.

The southern and western limits of New Mexico, mentioned in this article, are those laid down in the map entitled *"Map of the United Mexican States, as organized and defined by various acts of the Congress of said republic, and constructed according to the best authorities. Revised edition. Published at New York, in 1847, by J. Disturnell."* Of which map a copy is added to this treaty, bearing the signatures and seals of the undersigned plenipotentiaries. And, in order to preclude all difficulty in tracing upon the ground the limit separating Upper from Lower California, it is agreed that the said limit shall consist of a straight line drawn from the middle of the Rio Gila, where it unites with the Colorado, to a point on the coast of the Pacific Ocean distant one marine league due south of the southernmost point of the port of San Diego, according to the plan of said port made in the year 1782 by Don Juan Pantoja, second sailing-master of the Spanish fleet, and published at Madrid in the year 1802, in the Atlas to the voyage of the schooners *Sutil* and *Mexicana*, of which plan a copy is hereunto added, signed and sealed by the respective plenipotentiaries.

In order to designate the boundary line with due precision, upon authoritative maps, and to establish upon the ground landmarks which shall show the limits of both republics, as described in the present article, the two governments shall each appoint a commissioner and a surveyor, who, before the expiration of one year from the date of the exchange of ratifications of this treaty, shall meet at the port of San Diego, and proceed to run and mark the said boundary in its whole course to the mouth of the Rio Bravo del Norte. They shall keep journals and make out plans of their operations; and the result agreed upon by them shall be deemed a part of this treaty, and shall have the same force as if it were inserted therein. The two governments will amicably agree regarding what may be necessary to these persons, and also as to their respective escorts, should such be necessary.

The boundary line established by this article shall be religiously respected by each of the two republics, and no change shall ever be made therein, except by the express and free consent of both nations, lawfully given by the general government of each, in conformity with its own constitution.

ARTICLE VI.

The vessels and citizens of the United States shall, in all time, have a free and uninterrupted passage by the Gulf of California, and by the River Colorado below its confluence with the Gila, to and from their possessions situated north of the boundary line defined in the preceding article; it being understood that this passage is to be by navigating the Gulf of California and the River Colorado, and not by land, without the express consent of the Mexican government.

If, by the examinations which may be made, it should be ascertained to be practicable and advantageous to construct a road, canal, or railway, which should in whole or in part run upon the River Gila, or upon its right or its left bank, within the space of one marine league from either margin of the river, the governments of both republics will form an agreement regarding its construction, in order that it may serve equally for the use and advantage of both countries.

ARTICLE VII.

The River Gila, and the part of the Rio Bravo del Norte lying below the southern boundary of New Mexico, being, agreeably to the fifth article, divided in the middle between the two republics, the navigation of the Gila and of the Bravo below said boundary shall be free and common to the vessels and citizens of both countries; and neither shall, without the consent of the other, construct any work that may impede or interrupt, in whole or in part, the exercise of this right; not even for the purpose of favoring new methods of navigation. Nor shall any tax or contribution, under any denomination or title, be levied upon vessels, or persons navigating the same, or upon merchandise or effects transported thereon, except in the case of landing upon one of their shores. If, for the purpose of making the said rivers navigable, or for maintaining them in such state, it should be necessary or advantageous to establish any tax or contribution, this shall not be done without the consent of both governments.

The stipulations contained in the present article shall not impair the territorial rights of either republic within its established limits.

ARTICLE VIII.

Mexicans now established in territories previously belonging to Mexico, and which remain for the future within the limits of the United States, as defined by the present treaty, shall be free to continue where they now reside, or to remove at any time to the Mexican republic, retaining the property which they possess in the said territories, or disposing thereof, and removing the proceeds wherever they please, without their being subjected, on this account, to any contribution, tax, or charge whatever.

Those who shall prefer to remain in the said territories, may either retain the title and rights of Mexican citizens, or acquire those of citizens of the United States. But they shall be under the obligation to make their election within one year from the date of the exchange of ratifications of this treaty; and those who shall remain in the said territories after the expiration of that year, without having declared their intention to retain the character of Mexicans, shall be considered to have elected to become citizens of the United States.

In the said territories, property of every kind, now belonging to Mexicans not established there, shall be inviolably respected. The present owners, the heirs of these, and all Mexicans who may hereafter acquire said property by contract, shall enjoy with respect to it guaranties equally ample as if the same belonged to citizens of the United States.

ARTICLE IX.

Mexicans who, in the territories aforesaid, shall not preserve the character of citizens of the Mexican republic, conformably with what is stipulated in the preceding article, shall be incorporated into the Union of the United States, and be admitted at the proper time (to be judged of by the Congress of the United States) to the enjoyment of all the rights of citizens of the United States, according to the principles of the constitution; and in the mean time shall be maintained and protected in the free enjoyment of their liberty and property, and secured in the free exercise of their religion without restriction.

ARTICLE X.
[Stricken out.]

ARTICLE XI.

Considering that a great part of the territories which, by the present treaty, are to be comprehended for the future within the limits of the United States, is now occupied by savage tribes, who will hereafter be under the exclusive control of the government of the United States, and whose incursions within the territory of Mexico would be prejudicial in the extreme, it is solemnly agreed that all such incursions shall be forcibly restrained by the government of the United States whensoever this may be necessary; and that when they cannot be prevented, they shall be punished by the said government, and satisfaction for the same shall be exacted—all in the same way, and with equal diligence and energy, as if the same incursions were mediated or committed within its own territory, against its own citizens.

It shall not be lawful, under any pretext whatever, for any inhabitant of the United States to purchase or acquire any Mexican, or any foreigner residing in Mexico, who may have been captured by Indians inhabiting the territory of either of the two republics, nor to purchase or acquire horses, mules, cattle, or property of any kind, stolen within Mexican territory by such Indians.

And in the event of any person or persons, captured within Mexican territory by Indians, being carried into the territory of the United States, the government of the latter engages and binds itself, in the most solemn manner, so soon as it shall know of such captives being within its territory, and shall be able so to do, through the faithful exercise of its influence and power, to rescue them and return them to their country, or deliver them to the agent or representative of the Mexican government. The Mexican authorities will, as far as practicable, give to the government of the United States notice of such captures; and its agent shall pay the expenses incurred in the maintenance and transmission of the rescued captives; who, in the mean time, shall be treated with the utmost hospitality by the American authorities at the place where they may be. But if the government of the United States, before receiving such notice from Mexico, should obtain intelligence, through any other channel, of the existence of Mexican captives within its territory, it will proceed forthwith to effect their release and delivery to the Mexican agent, as above stipulated.

For the purpose of giving to these stipulations the fullest possible efficacy, thereby affording the security and redress demanded by their true spirit and intent, the government of the United States will now and hereafter pass, without unnecessary delay, and always vigilantly enforce, such laws as the nature of the subject may require. And finally, the sacredness of this obligation shall never be lost sight of by the said government when providing for the removal of the Indians from any portion of the said territories, or for its being settled by citizens of the United States; but on the contrary, special care shall then be taken not to place its Indian occupants under the necessity of seeking new homes, by committing those invasions which the United States have solemnly obliged themselves to restrain.

ARTICLE XII.

In consideration of the extension acquired by the boundaries of the United States, as defined in the fifth article of the present treaty, the government of the United States engages to pay to that of the Mexican republic the sum of fifteen millions of dollars.

Immediately after this treaty shall have been duly ratified by the government of the Mexican republic, the sum of three millions of dollars shall be paid to the said government by that of the United States, at the city of Mexico, in the gold or silver coin of Mexico. The remaining twelve millions of dollars shall be paid at the same place, and in the same coin, in annual instalments of three millions of dollars each, together with interest on the same at the rate of six per centum per annum. This interest shall begin to run upon the whole sum of twelve millions from the day of the ratification of the present treaty by the Mexican government, and the first of the instalments shall be paid at the expiration of one year from the same day. Together with each annual instalment, as it falls due, the whole interest accruing on such instalment from the beginning shall also be paid.

ARTICLE XIII.

The United States engage, moreover, to assume and pay to the claimants all the amounts now due them, and those hereafter to become due, by reason of the claims already liquidated and decided against the Mexican republic, under the conventions between the two republics severally concluded on the eleventh day of April, eighteen hundred and thirty-nine, and on the thirtieth day of January, eighteen hundred and forty-three; so that the Mexican republic shall be absolutely exempt, for the future, from all expense whatever on account of the said claims.

ARTICLE XIV.

The United States do furthermore discharge the Mexican republic from all claims of citizens of the United States, not heretofore decided against the Mexican government, which may have arisen previously to the date of the signature of this treaty; which discharge shall be final and perpetual, whether the said claims be rejected or be allowed by the board of commissioners provided for in the following article, and whatever shall be the total amount of those allowed.

ARTICLE XV.

The United States, exonerating Mexico from all demands on account of the claims of their citizens mentioned in the preceding article, and considering them entirely and forever cancelled, whatever their amount may be, undertake to make satisfaction for the same, to an amount not exceeding three and one quarter millions of dollars. To ascertain the validity and amount of those claims, a board of commissioners shall be established by the government of the United States, whose awards shall be final and conclusive: provided, that in deciding upon the validity of each claim, the board shall be guided and governed by the principles and rules of decision prescribed by the first and fifth articles of the unratified convention, concluded at the city of Mexico on the twentieth day of November, one thousand eight hundred and forty-three; * and in no case shall an award be made in favor of any claim not embraced by these principles and rules.

If, in the opinion of the said board of commissioners, or of the claimants, any books, records, or documents in the possession or power of the government of the Mexican republic, shall be deemed necessary to the just decision of any claim, the commissioners, or the claimants through them, shall, within such period as Congress may designate, make an application in writing for the same, addressed to the Mexican Minister for Foreign Affairs, to be transmitted by the Secretary of State of the United States; and the Mexican government engages, at the earliest possible moment after the receipt of such demand, to cause any of the books, records, or documents, so specified, which shall be in their possession or power, (or authenticated copies or extracts of the same,) to be transmitted to the said Secretary of State, who shall immediately deliver them over to the said board of commissioners: *Provided*, That no such application shall be made by, or at the instance of, any claimant, until the facts which it is expected to prove by such books, records, or documents, shall have been stated under oath or affirmation.

* *First and Fifth Articles of the unratified Convention between the United States and the Mexican Republic of the 20th November, 1843.*

ARTICLE I.

All claims of citizens of the Mexican republic against the government of the United States, which shall be presented in the manner and time hereinafter expressed, and all claims of citizens of the United States against the government of the Mexican republic, which, for whatever cause, were not submitted to, nor considered, nor finally decided by, the commission, nor by the arbiter appointed by the convention of 1839, and which shall be presented in the manner and time hereinafter specified, shall be referred to four commissioners, who shall form a board, and shall be appointed in the following manner, that is to say: Two commissioners shall be appointed by the President of the Mexican republic, and the other two by the President of the United States, with the approbation and consent of the Senate. The said commissioners, thus appointed, shall, in the presence of each other, take an oath to examine and decide impartially the claims submitted to them, and which may lawfully be considered, according to the proofs which shall be presented, the principles of right and justice, the law of nations, and the treaties between the two republics.

ARTICLE V.

All claims of citizens of the United States against the government of the Mexican republic, which were considered by the commissioners, and referred to the umpire appointed under the convention of the eleventh April, 1839, and which were not decided by him, shall be referred to, and decided by, the umpire to be appointed, as provided by this convention, on the points submitted to the umpire under the late convention, and his decision shall be final and conclusive. It is also agreed, that if the respective commissioners shall deem it expedient, they may submit to the said arbiter new arguments upon the said claims.

ARTICLE XVI.

Each of the contracting parties reserves to itself the entire right to fortify whatever point within its territory it may judge proper so to fortify, for its security.

ARTICLE XVII.

The treaty of amity, commerce, and navigation, concluded at the city of Mexico on the fifth day of April, A.D. 1831, between the United States of America and the United Mexican States, except the additional article, and except so far as the stipulations of the said treaty may be incompatible with any stipulation contained in the present treaty, is hereby revived for the period of eight years from the day of the exchange of ratifications of this treaty, with the same force and virtue as if incorporated therein; it being understood that each of the contracting parties reserves to itself the right, at any time after the said period of eight years shall have expired, to terminate the same by giving one year's notice of such intention to the other party.

Article XVIII.

All supplies whatever for troops of the United States in Mexico, arriving at ports in the occupation of such troops previous to the final evacuation thereof, although subsequently to the restoration of the custom-houses at such ports, shall be entirely exempt from duties and charges of any kind; the government of the United States hereby engaging and pledging its faith to establish, and vigilantly to enforce, all possible guards for securing the revenue of Mexico, by preventing the importation, under cover of this stipulation, of any articles other than such, both in kind and in quantity, as shall really be wanted for the use and consumption of the forces of the United States during the time they may remain in Mexico. To this end, it shall be the duty of all officers and agents of the United States to denounce to the Mexican authorities at the respective ports any attempts at a fraudulent abuse of this stipulation which they may know of or may have reason to suspect, and to give to such authorities all the aid in their power with regard thereto; and every such attempt, when duly proved and established by sentence of a competent tribunal, shall be punished by the confiscation of the property so attempted to be fraudulently introduced.

Article XIX.

With respect to all merchandise, effects, and property whatsoever, imported into ports of Mexico whilst in the occupation of the forces of the United States, whether by citizens of either republic, or by citizens or subjects of any neutral nation, the following rules shall be observed:—

1.   All such merchandise, effects, and property, if imported previously to the restoration of the custom-houses to the Mexican authorities, as stipulated for in the third article of this treaty, shall be exempt from confiscation, although the importation of the same be prohibited by the Mexican tariff.

2.   The same perfect exemption shall be enjoyed by all such merchandise, effects, and property, imported subsequently to the restoration of the custom-houses, and previously to the sixty days fixed in the following article for the coming into force of the Mexican tariff at such ports respectively; the said merchandise, effects, and property being, however, at the time of their importation, subject to the payment of duties, as provided for in the said following article.

3.   All merchandise, effects, and property described in the two rules foregoing shall, during their continuance at the place of importation, and upon their leaving such place for the interior, be exempt from all duty, tax, or impost of every kind, under whatsoever title or denomination. Nor shall they be there subjected to any charge whatsoever upon the sale thereof.

4.   All merchandise, effects, and property, described in the first and second rules, which shall have been removed to any place in the interior whilst such place was in the occupation of the forces of the United States, shall, during their continuance therein, be exempt from all tax upon the sale or consumption thereof, and from every kind of impost or contribution, under whatsoever title or denomination.

5.   But if any merchandise, effects, or property, described in the first and second rules, shall be removed to any place not occupied at the time by the forces of the United States, they shall, upon their introduction into such place, or upon their sale or consumption there, be subject to the same duties which, under the Mexican laws, they would be required to pay in such cases if they had been imported in time of peace, through the maritime custom-houses, and had there paid the duties conformably with the Mexican tariff.

6.   The owners of all merchandise, effects, or property described in the first and second rules, and existing in any port of Mexico, shall have the right to reship the same, exempt from all tax, impost, or contribution whatever.

With respect to the metals, or other property, exported from any Mexican port whilst in the occupation of the forces of the United States, and previously to the restoration of the custom-house at such port, no person shall be required by the Mexican authorities, whether general or state, to pay any tax, duty, or contribution upon any such exportation, or in any manner to account for the same to the said authorities.

Article XX.

Through consideration for the interests of commerce generally, it is agreed, that if less than sixty days should elapse between the date of the signature of this treaty and the restoration of the custom-houses, conformably with the stipulation in the third article, in such case all merchandise, effects, and property whatsoever, arriving at the Mexican ports after the restoration of the said custom-houses, and previously to the expiration of sixty days after the day of the signature of this treaty, shall be admitted to entry; and no other duties shall be levied thereon than the duties established by the tariff found in force at such custom-houses at the time of the restoration of the same. And to all such merchandise, effects, and property, the rules established by the preceding article shall apply.

ARTICLE XXI.

If unhappily any disagreement should hereafter arise between the governments of the two republics, whether with respect to the interpretation of any stipulation in this treaty, or with respect to any other particular concerning the political or commercial relations of the two nations, the said governments, in the name of those nations, do promise to each other that they will endeavor, in the most sincere and earnest manner, to settle the differences so arising, and to preserve the state of peace and friendship in which the two countries are now placing themselves; using, for this end, mutual representations and pacific negotiations. And if, by these means, they should not be enabled to come to an agreement, a resort shall not, on this account, be had to reprisals, aggression, or hostility of any kind, by the one republic against the other, until the government of that which deems itself aggrieved shall have maturely considered, in the spirit of peace and good neighborship, whether it would not be better that such difference should be settled by the arbitration of commissioners appointed on each side, or by that of a friendly nation. And should such course be proposed by either party, it shall be acceded to by the other, unless deemed by it altogether incompatible with the nature of the difference, or the circumstances of the case.

ARTICLE XXII.

If (which is not to be expected, and which God forbid!) war should unhappily break out between the two republics, they do now, with a view to such calamity, solemnly pledge themselves to each other and to the world, to observe the following rules; absolutely where the nature of the subject permits, and as closely as possible in all cases where such absolute observance shall be impossible:—

1. The merchants of either republic then residing in the other shall be allowed to remain twelve months, (for those dwelling in the interior,) and six months (for those dwelling at the seaports,) to collect their debts and settle their affairs; during which periods, they shall enjoy the same protection, and be on the same footing, in all respects, as the citizens or subjects of the most friendly nations; and, at the expiration thereof, or at any time before, they shall have full liberty to depart, carrying off all their effects without molestation or hinderance, conforming therein to the same laws which the citizens or subjects of the most friendly nations are required to conform to. Upon the entrance of the armies of either nation into the territories of the other, women and children, ecclesiastics, scholars of every faculty, cultivators of the earth, merchants, artisans, manufacturers, and fishermen, unarmed and inhabiting unfortified towns, villages, or places, and in general all persons whose occupations are for the common subsistence and benefit of mankind, shall be allowed to continue their respective

employments unmolested in their persons. Nor shall their houses or goods be burnt or otherwise destroyed, nor their cattle taken, nor their fields wasted, by the armed force into whose power, by the events of war, they may happen to fall; but if the necessity arise to take any thing from them for the use of such armed force, the same shall be paid for at an equitable price. All churches, hospitals, schools, colleges, libraries, and other establishments for charitable and beneficent purposes, shall be respected, and all persons connected with the same protected in the discharge of their duties, and the pursuit of their vocations.

2. In order that the fate of prisoners of war may be alleviated, all such practices as those of sending them into distant inclement or unwholesome districts, or crowding them into close and noxious places, shall be studiously avoided. They shall not be confined in dungeons, prison-ships, or prisons; nor be put in irons, or bound, or otherwise restrained in the use of their limbs. The officers shall enjoy liberty on their paroles, within convenient districts, and have comfortable quarters; and the common soldier shall be disposed in cantonments, open and extensive enough for air and exercise, and lodged in barracks as roomy and good as are provided by the party in whose power they are for its own troops. But if any officer shall break his parole by leaving the district so assigned him, or any other prisoner shall escape from the limits of his cantonment, after they shall have been designated to him, such individual, officer, or other prisoner, shall forfeit so much of the benefit of this article as provides for his liberty on parole or in cantonment. And if any officer so breaking his parole, or any common soldier so escaping from the limits assigned him, shall afterwards be found in arms, previously to his being regularly exchanged, the person so offending shall be dealt with according to the established laws of war. The officers shall be daily furnished by the party in whose power they are, with as many rations, and of the same articles, as are allowed, either in kind or by commutation, to officers of equal rank in its own army; and all others shall be daily furnished with such ration as is allowed to a common soldier in its own service: the value of all which supplies shall, at the close of the war, or at periods to be agreed upon between the respective commanders, be paid by the other party, on a mutual adjustment of accounts for the subsistence of prisoners; and such accounts shall not be mingled with or set off against any others, nor the balance due on them be withheld, as a compensation or reprisal for any cause whatever, real or pretended. Each party shall be allowed to keep a commissary of prisoners, appointed by itself, with every cantonment of prisoners, in possession of the other; which commissary shall see the prisoners as often as he pleases; shall be allowed to receive, exempt from all duties or taxes, and to distribute, whatever comforts may be sent to them by their friends; and shall be free to transmit his reports in open letters to the party by whom he is employed.

And it is declared that neither the pretence that war dissolves all treaties, nor any other whatever, shall be considered as annulling or suspending the solemn covenant contained in this article. On the contrary, the state of war is precisely that for which it is provided; and during which, its stipulations are to be as sacredly observed as the most acknowledged obligations under the law of nature or nations.

ARTICLE XXIII.

This treaty shall be ratified by the President of the United States of America, by and with the advice and consent of the Senate thereof; by the President of the Mexican republic, with the previous approbation of its General Congress; and the ratifications shall be exchanged in the city of Washington, or at the seat of government of Mexico, in four months from the date of the signature hereof, or sooner if practicable.

In faith whereof, we, the respective plenipotentiaries, have signed this treaty of peace, friendship, limits, and settlement; and have hereunto affixed our seals respectively. Done in quintuplicate, at the city of Guadalupe Hidalgo, on the second day of February, in the year of our Lord one thousand eight hundred and forty-eight.

N.P. Trist, [L.S.]
Luis G. Cuevas, [L.S.]
Bernardo Couto, [L.S.]
Migl. Atristain, [L.S.]

Act for the Admission of California Into the Union
1850

Act for the Admission of California Into the Union *

Whereas, the people of California have presented a constitution and asked admission into the Union, which constitution was submitted to Congress by the President of the United States, by message dated February thirteenth, eighteen hundred and fifty, and which, on due examination, is found to be republican in its form of government:

Be it enacted by the Senate and House of Representatives of the United States of America in Congress assembled, That the State of California shall be one, and is hereby declared to be one, of the United States of America, and admitted into the Union on an equal footing with the original States in all respects whatever.

SEC. 2. *And be it further enacted,* That until the representatives in Congress shall be apportioned according to an actual enumeration of the inhabitants of the United States, the State of California shall be entitled to two representatives in Congress.

SEC. 3. *And be it further enacted,* That the said State of California is admitted into the Union upon the express condition that the people of said State, through their legislature or otherwise, shall never interfere with the primary disposal of the public lands within its limits, and shall pass no law and do no act whereby the title of the United States to, and right to dispose of, the same shall be impaired or questioned; and that they shall never lay any tax or assessment of any description whatsoever upon the public domain of the United States, and in no case shall non-resident proprietors, who are citizens of the United States, be taxed higher than residents; and that all the navigable waters within the said State shall be common highways, and forever free, as well to the inhabitants of said State as to the citizens of the United States, without any tax, impost, or duty therefor. *Provided,* That nothing herein contained shall be construed as recognizing or rejecting the propositions tendered by the people of California as articles of compact in the ordinance adopted by the convention which formed the constitution of that State.

Approved, September 9, 1850. †

---

*The text here printed is taken from Volume 9, Statutes at Large, page 452.
†The following provision appears in an act approved September 28, 1850, Volume 9, Statutes at Large, page 521:
"That all the laws of the United States which are not locally inapplicable shall have the same force and effect within the said State of California as elsewhere within the United States."

Constitutional History
of California

Constitutional History of California

By PAUL MASON

GOVERNMENT DURING THE SPANISH PERIOD
Spanish Plan of Government

Earliest Government of California

Beginning with the first Spanish settlement in California in 1769 the government was divided between the Padres who exercised an ecclesiastical control of the missions, and commandantes who exercised military control over the soldiers and presidios and generally over crimes.

With the establishment of pueblos a short time later, a civil government was established which consisted merely of a Governor, but for a long period of time it was of no practical importance.

The independence of Mexico was secured from Spain in 1821.

In 1837 a new constitution was drawn up by which the government of the provinces was substantially altered and the missions were confiscated.

Government of California in 1846 [1]

At the time of the occupation of California by the Americans the province was governed by the laws of March 20 and May 23, 1837, which provided for a government divided into executive, legislative and judicial departments. The division was not as carefully followed as in our state and national governments, but was more closely followed than in our county governments. The government was also decidedly more centralized than our own.

The Executive Department

The Executive Department of the Government consisted of a Governor appointed by the Government of Mexico, prefects appointed by the Governor and approved by the Federal Government of Mexico, and subprefects appointed by the prefects and approved by the Governor. Both prefects and subprefects were responsible to the Governor for the administration of the government in their local districts.

The position of prefect, or subprefect, is more comparable to our sheriffs than to any other of our officers.

The Governor, through the prefects, subprefects and town councils (ayuntamientos), where they existed, was responsible for the public order of the department, the disposal of the armed force assigned to him for police purposes, and was authorized when necessary to require the service of troops from the commandante. It was his duty to publish and execute the

---

[1] Browne Debates, Translation of Mexican Laws, XXIV, XLIV; 1 Cal. 559, 587.

laws of the department and of the general government, to remit to the government all acts of the Departmental Legislature, to watch over the revenues and the public health of the department, to take care that there was no want of elementary schools, to see that the school teachers possessed good moral character and the necessary qualifications, and to send vagabonds and idle persons to work shops or agricultural establishments.

The Governor also had power to issue search warrants, to appoint officers for a term not to exceed three years, to suspend the town councils with the consent of the Legislature, to decide disputes concerning local elections, to preside over the Departmental Legislature and to vote in case of a tie, and to preside over public meetings.

The law provided for a secretary whose duties correspond closely with the duties of the secretaries of state in our own states, and who was also to act as a private secretary to the Governor.

The Legislative Department

The Departmental Legislature consisted of seven members who were elected every four years. The duties of the Legislature were to pass laws relating to taxes, public education, industry, trade and municipal administrations; to establish schools in all of the towns of the department; and to collect and assign funds to the schools; to order the establishment and repair of the roads; to make regulations for the improvement of public education, and the improvement of agricultural industries and commerce; to audit municipal financial reports, and to advise with the Governor when he should require it. The Legislature was prohibited from imposing illegal or unauthorized contributions; from raising armies except when ordered by the general government and from exercising authority other than that granted by the laws of Mexico.

The Judicial Department

The Judicial Department as provided by the laws of March 20 and May 23, 1837, called for Supreme (Superior) Court, courts of second instance, courts of first instance, and courts of alcaldes and justices of the peace. The Supreme Court (Tribunal Superior) was to consist of four Justices (Minestros) and an Attorney General (Fiscal). The courts of second instance (segunda instancia) were constituted by the Judges of the Supreme Court sitting separately. The Supreme Court and courts of second instance were courts of appellate jurisdiction.[2] The courts of first instance (primeria instancia) were the district courts of original jurisdiction. The judges of courts of first instance were appointed by the Governor upon the

---

[2] 1 California Reports, 575.

recommendation of the Supreme Court. The alcaldes were municipal officers who exercised judicial functions, and the courts of the justices of the peace (jueces depaz) were local courts having jurisdiction of cases involving the less important matters.

By a decree of March 2, 1843, alcaldes and justices of the peace of California were empowered to perform the functions of judges of first instance in those districts in which there were no judges of courts of first instance.[3]

The Departmental Legislature and the Governor were especially enjoined to provide for the appointment of a sufficient number of justices of the peace so that there should be one in "every ward and populous ranchería distant from a town." The justices of the peace were to be appointed by the prefects upon the recommendation of the subprefects.

The justices of the peace were granted the same authority that had been previously exercised by the alcaldes which they were to replace everywhere in California except in the capital city.[4] The town councils in which the alcalde was the chief officer continued to exist, however, in most of the towns, until the organization of the state government by the Americans.

The judicial system provided for the provinces of Mexico corresponds very closely with the present judicial system of California; the tribunal and courts of segunda instancia correspond with our Supreme and appellate courts; the courts of primeria instancia, with our superior courts; the alcaldes courts, with our municipal courts and the justices' courts with our own justices' courts. The judicial system adopted by the first constitution was the system already established in California under the laws of Mexico.

Judicial Procedure

The judicial procedure was, except in two particulars, very similar to our own. In civil disputes before the case could go to the regular courts a hearing was required before a justice of the peace or alcalde for the purpose of attempting to effect a reconciliation. A special type of proceeding was also provided for civil cases in which the amount involved did not exceed $100 and for criminal cases respecting trifling injuries. In these cases formal procedure was dispensed with and all pleadings were oral. The procedure in these cases was very similar to that in our small claims courts. It appears that small cases were rarely tried by the aid of attorneys, but instead each party brought a friend to assist him.

Local Administration of Justice

The alcaldes and justices of the peace were responsible for the good order and public tranquility of the place of their residence and were required

---

[3] Mena vs. LeRoy, 1 California Reports, 220.
[4] 1 California Reports, 575.

to watch over the execution of the police regulations and laws and for the purpose of maintaining order they were authorized to ask for assistance from the military commandante. They were required to bring any person arrested by them before a judge within three days, and to reprimand the idle, vagabonds, persons of bad character or conduct, and those of no known occupation. They were authorized on their own authority to levy and collect fines to the amount of $25 (which were paid into the municipal treasury) and to impose sentences of not to exceed four days at hard labor or eight days confinement in prison.

Municipal Government

The capital of the department and certain other towns were authorized to establish town councils (ayuntamientos) and the town councils were to consist of not more than six magistrates (alcaldes), 12 councilmen (regidores) and two clerks (síndicas). Monterey, the capital of the province, was the only city in California which was by the laws of 1837 entitled to a town council.[5]

The alcalde was the principal municipal officer and performed the duties ordinarily performed in our own cities by the mayor, and in the absence of justices of the peace or judges of first instance, he performed the duties of these offices.

The duties of the town councils were to take care of the streets, public places, and public squares, to provide burial grounds, to watch over the quality of food and drugs, to provide supplies of water, to take charge of prisons and hospitals, and in case of epidemics to organize and establish health committees. They were to keep records of births, marriages, etc., and to endeavor as far as possible to have the streets straight, paved and lighted; to provide for the construction and repair of bridges and to license amusements. The town councils were given power to make and enforce local police regulations and were required to pay careful attention to the establishment of schools.

General Riley's Summary of the Government

General Riley in his proclamation of June 3, 1849, calling the constitutional convention, described the government of California, as he believed it should be organized under the Mexican law, as follows:

"It consists first of a Governor, appointed by the Supreme Government; in default of such appointment the office is temporarily vested in the commanding officer of the Department. The powers and duties of the Governor are of a limited character, and fully defined and pointed out by the laws. Second, a secretary, whose duties and powers are also properly defined. Third, a territorial or Departmental Legislature, with

---

5 1 California Reports, 574.

limited powers to pass laws of a local character. Fourth, a Superior Court (Tribunal Superior) of the Territory, consisting of four judges and a Fiscal. Fifth, a Prefect and Sub-Prefect for each district, who are charged with the preservation of public order and the execution of the laws; their duties correspond in a great measure with those of District Marshals and Sheriffs. Sixth, a Judge of First Instance for each district. This office is by a custom not inconsistent with the laws, vested in the First Alcalde of the District. Seventh, Alcaldes who have concurrent jurisdiction among themselves in the same district are subordinate to the higher judicial tribunals. Eighth, Local Justices of the Peace. Ninth, Ayuntamientos or Town Councils. The powers and functions of all these officers are fully defined in the laws of this country, and are almost identical with those of the corresponding officers in the Atlantic and Western States."

The Actual Government

The Alcalde System

The actual government, however, appears to have been very different from that provided by the laws of 1837. In a department where revolution and disorder were the rule, and law and order the exception, the Mexican judiciary consisted primarily of alcaldes and justices of the peace, and the Governor in person was the appellate court.

"When a neighborhood needed the services of a magistrate, an alcalde was chosen on the spot, and he either acted for a single occasion, or continued to act for a longer or shorter period according to the pleasure of those who put him into his precarious office." [6]

The executive and legislative departments of the government appear to have functioned in a manner very similar to that prescribed by the law, although revolutions frequently caused changes of the personnel, and there were almost constant disputes between the governor, representing the civil authority, and the commandante, representing the military authority.

When the Americans took control of the province of California, many of them were unfamiliar with the Mexican system. And particularly after the immigration following the discovery of gold, the proportion who had any knowledge of the Spanish system was very small.

In the north the settlements were in a region where the Mexican government or law were never established and where there was no governmental organization whatever.

---

[6] R. A. Wilson, Judge of First Instance, Sacramento, 1 California Reports, 574.

The Americans, after the occupation of California in 1846, revived the alcalde system. Wherever a group of Americans collected, they proceeded to elect an American alcalde [7] who served as an adjuster of disputes and an administrator of the few local regulations. In cases involving the more serious criminal offenses, difficulties arose. When a regularly appointed judge was not available the miners frequently tried the cases by a jury without a judge. These "miner's courts" had the advantage of quickly and finally disposing of the cases. The administration of justice in the more remote mining districts appears to have been about as primitive and in many respects very similar to the administration of justice by the petty chiefs and "hundred courts" among the early Saxons.

The Law Which Was Administered

It was very seriously doubted at that time by the majority of the settlers, and even denied in the constitutional convention [8] that any of the former Mexican laws were actually in effect in the territory, although it was affirmed that "the laws of California, not inconsistent with the laws, Constitution and treaties of the United States, are still in force, and must continue to be until changed by competent authority." [9]

The American alcaldes were usually completely ignorant of local Spanish customs and had no knowledge whatever of the civil or Spanish law, so that the law which was actually applied, insofar as it followed any system of law, was the common law.

And this, in spite of the fact that it was clear that there was no authorization for applying the common law, until it had been adopted by the legislature. [10]

Government Under the United States

At the same time that delegates were elected to the constitutional convention, officers to fill the administration and judicial offices as they were created by the Mexican law were voted upon. The prefects and judges of First Instance were executive appointments but General Riley called for an advisory vote and appointed those persons securing the largest vote. [11]

The legislature was never organized but the prefects, subprefects and judicial officers held office until January 1, 1850.

---

[7] Wilson, 1 California Reports, 577 (Appendix).

[8] Browne, Debates, 274–277.

[9] Riley, Proclamation Calling Convention, Browne, Debates, 3.

[10] April 13, 1850.

[11] Riley, Proclamation Calling the Convention, Browne, Debates, p. 4; Justice Bennett, Preface 1 California Reports, p. VII. The election returns are in the archives of the office of the Secretary of State.

Judicial Opinions

When the American government was established the courts accepted jurisdiction of appeals from the alcaldes as well as from the courts which were instituted by General Riley.[12]

The Supreme Court decided that the whole body of Mexican law had been applicable to California, insofar as it did not conflict with the Constitution or the laws of the United States, until it was officially replaced by the Constitution of the State and the laws enacted by the legislatures.

The courts also gave the authority of law to customs which appeared to have been established in California, even when in direct conflict with the Mexican or Spanish law.[13]

American Immigration and Occupation

Early American Immigration

For several years previous to the war with Mexico, Americans had been moving into California as they had previously moved into Texas.

The number of Americans in California before about 1846 is not definitely known, but John Bidwell, an immigrant of 1841, said that in 1844 the Americans could not have mustered more than one hundred men, although most of the immigrants were able-bodied men.[14] It is estimated that the population of California, exclusive of Indians, in 1846 was 10,000, about 2,000 of whom were foreigners and that most of these were Americans.[15]

New American immigration was primarily to the northern part of California. Yerba Buena, which later became San Francisco, was primarily an American settlement, though most of the Americans settled on large ranchos north and east of San Francisco Bay in the Napa, Sonoma and Sacramento Valleys.

This immigration, however, did not affect to an important degree the Spanish-Californian settlements of the south. Los Angeles was the largest city and San Diego, Santa Barbara, San Luis Obispo and San Buena Ventura were settlements of some importance. Farther north, Monterey, the capital, was the chief seaport and had as yet been almost unaffected by the American immigration. San Jose and Sonoma were the only important truly Spanish settlements farther north. Sutter's Fort, which could scarcely be called Spanish, had already become an important establishment.

---

[12] Preface to Cal. Reports by Justice Bennett, p. VII.

[13] Von Schmidt vs. Huntington, 1 California Reports, 64; Farrand vs. Jones, 1 California Reports, 488.

[14] Bidwell, Overland Monthly XVI, 563.

[15] Hunt, The Genesis of California's First Constitution, John Hopkins Studies, Vol. 13, 30.

The Policy of the United States

The policy of the United States from the beginning of Polk's administration seemed to have been fixed on the annexation of California.[16] Larkin, the American Consul at Monterey, under instructions from Washington, was undertaking to establish a sentiment in California favorable to annexation.[17] The slave states particularly appeared to desire more slave territory. All the relations of California with the government of the United States were influenced and largely controlled by the slavery question in Congress.

Occupation of California

With the outbreak of the war with Mexico the United States Government directed the seizure of California by the American naval forces and dispatched General Kearny overland with troops.[18]

Commodore Sloat seized Monterey on July 7, 1846, and followed with the occupation of the other seaports and then the settlements of the interior, the occupation being complete by August 17, 1846.[19]

A group of American settlers at the instigation of Fremont, who was then on an exploring expedition in the west, had seized Sonoma and captured General Vallejo on June 14, 1846.

The Mexican government in California was not able to render any effective opposition to the occupation. The province was generally without military supplies and the population appeared almost entirely indifferent. They regarded Mexico almost as a foreign nation, and many of their leaders favored annexation to some foreign nation. There was a rather strong group, including Pio Pico, the governor, who favored annexation to England; but many more were favorable to annexation to the United States. General Vallejo appears to have been the leader of those favoring annexation to the United States.[20]

The Mexican officials failed to cooperate in resisting occupation. At the time the occupation began, the governor, Pico, and the commandante, Castro, were attempting to raise armies for military operations against each other.[21] There was no actual military opposition to the occupation.

Relation of California to the United States

The seizure of California as a military measure warranted only the occupation of the province during the period of the war but the expectation that California was to be annexed was clearly shown by Sloat in his first

---

[16] Schouler, History IV, 446; 31st Congress, 1st Session, Dec. 17.

[17] Bancroft, XXII, 54.

[18] Bancroft, XXII, 195.

[19] Bancroft, XXII, 230, 283.

[20] Bancroft, XXII, 67, 75.

[21] Bancroft, XXII, 30, 53.

proclamation issued at Monterey, July 7, 1846, in which, after charging Mexico with the responsibility of the war, he said:
"I declare to the inhabitants of California that, although I come in arms with a powerful force, I do not come among them as an enemy to California; on the contrary, I come as their friend, as henceforward California will be a portion of the United States, and its peaceful inhabitants will enjoy the same rights and privileges as the citizens of any other portion of that territory, with all the rights and privileges they now enjoy, together with the privilege of choosing their own magistrates and other officers for the administration of justice among themselves; and the same protection will be extended to them as to any other state in the Union . . . With full confidence in the honor and integrity of the inhabitants of the country, I invite the judges, alcaldes, and other civil officers to retain their offices, and to execute their functions as heretofore, that the public tranquility may not be disturbed; at least until the government of the territory can be more definitely arranged. All persons holding titles to real estate, or in quiet possession of lands under a color of right, shall have those titles and rights guaranteed to them." [22]
Sloat was soon replaced by Stockton, who had a far less conciliatory attitude toward the native Californians but who did make promises of a civil government. In his first proclamation, July 29, 1846, he said:
" . . . and all persons who may have belonged to the government of Mexico, but who from this day acknowledge the authority of the existing laws, are to be treated in the same manner as other citizens of the United States, provided they are obedient to the law and to the orders they shall receive from me or by my authority. The commander-in-chief does not desire to possess himself of one foot of California for any other reason than as the only means to save from destruction the lives and property of the foreign residents, and citizens of the territory who have invoked his protection. As soon, therefore, as the officers of the civil law return to their proper duties, under a regularly organized government, and give security for life, liberty, and property, alike to all, the forces under my command will be withdrawn, and the people left to manage their own affairs in their own way." [23]

Revolt of the Californians

Sloat had assumed a very friendly attitude toward the Californians and had promised a stable government. Stockton, on the other hand, though he had renewed promises of a civil government, was of a very different temperament and assumed the attitude of an intimidating conqueror, and en-

---

[22] Bancroft, XXII, 235.
[23] Bancroft, XXII, 256.

forced strict military law. The organization of a civil government by Stockton was delayed by a revolt in the southern part of the province, centering in Los Angeles; though it does appear that he had planned a civil government with Fremont as governor.[24]

Civil Governors, But No Government

Before the revolt had been suppressed General Kearny had arrived overland from the "States" with instructions to organize a civil government. In a proclamation issued by General Kearny he promised the people that they would "soon be called upon to exercise their rights as free men, in electing their own representatives to make such laws as may be deemed best for the interest and welfare."[25]

Kearny was unable to organize a civil government according to his plan, before he was succeeded by Colonel Mason."[26]

Absence of Law and Government

By May, 1846, it appears that although the laws of Mexico were, according to international usages still in effect, the people had begun to feel that there were no laws actually in force but "the divine laws and the law of nature." And the editor of the *California Star*[27] was unable to discover any general written laws whatever.

Already the settlers had become very clamorous for a civil government and began to feel that they had been seriously wronged, if not wilfully deceived, with promises of a self-government.

Mason undoubtedly had full power to establish a temporary civil government, and apparently began studying the conditions and collecting and translating the Mexican laws which he believed to be in force.

"Mason's Code" appears to have been completed and possibly printed. Bancroft says that "Mason formerly promulgated a code printed in English and Spanish."[28] It appears certain, however, that the code of law was never actually promulgated, and probably not printed, though the *Californian* states distinctly that a code was printed.[29]

Delay in Government

The expectation of peace with Mexico and a scheme for a civil government from Washington apparently caused a delay and possibly a relinquishment of Colonel Mason's plans for a civil government. It was expected that Congress, which was then in session, would certainly provide

---

[24] Bancroft, XXII, 413, 432, 468.

[25] *Californian,* March 13, 1847.

[26] May 31, 1847.

[27] March 27, 1847.

[28] Bancroft, XXII, 263.

[29] August 14, 1848.

some sort of government for California, irrespective of whether peace was declared. And Mason, rather than proceeding with his idea of a civil government, assumed a policy of "watchful waiting." Congress adjourned without providing any form of government.

No Action by Congress

The next session of Congress opened in December. President Polk, in his annual message, recommended that a "stable, responsible and free government be provided for California and New Mexico." [30] Congress, however, failed to take any action. Meanwhile gold had been discovered and when the news became disseminated a large immigration began.

Local Government Broken Down

To this time apparently there was little injury done through the absence of a civil government. In the south, the government continued with slight change. In the north, the majority of the American settlers and other foreigners had lived under the Mexican system and were somewhat familiar, at least, with the general system of government. They proceeded to elect alcaldes from among themselves and maintained at least a fair degree of order. [31] With the new immigration conditions were changed. Many of the immigrants were of a lawless nature and as a whole they were reckless and adventuresome.

Most of the immigrants had come for gold with no idea of remaining permanently. The new immigration completely destroyed what appearance of government had remained in the north and the lawabiding persons became still more insistent upon some type of government. The people of San Francisco met the situation by organizing a new local government. [32]

Effect of Peace

Even before immigrants began to arrive in large numbers, news was received of peace with Mexico. Legally, this terminated military rule. Tidings of peace were received by the people as opening the brightest possible prospect. Instead, however, of giving the people a civil government, the effect of peace was merely to take away the authority of the military government and leave the military organization with no further authority to act for the people than that of the presumed consent of the inhabitants.

Only two courses were open—to wait for Congress to provide a civil government or for the people to take the power into their own hands and

---

[30] 30th Congress, 2d Session, H. Ex., Doc. 1, 17.

[31] 1 California Reports, 577.

[32] Annals of San Francisco; 1 California Reports, 583.

organize a territorial or state government for themselves as the people of San Francisco had previously organized a municipal government.

In the *Star and Californian* of November, 1848, it was reported that Colonel Mason had, after a conference with Commodore Jones, decided that if Congress failed to provide for a government, he would immediately recommend "the appointment of delegates by the people to frame laws and to make their necessary arrangements for a provincial government for California." [33] By this time the population generally appears to have despaired of any action by Congress.

People Take Action

On December 11, 1848, the citizens of San Jose met "for the purpose of taking into consideration the propriety of establishing a provincial territorial government for the better protection of life and property" until Congress should provide a government for California. They adopted resolutions recommending that a general convention meet in San Jose. [34] Similar meetings were held in Sacramento, San Francisco and Sonoma. [35] There appears to have been a general popular feeling supporting the movement for the organization of an effective government.

In the spring of 1849, General Riley became *de facto* Governor, succeeding General Smith, who had been Governor for a short time following Colonel Mason. General Riley continued the policy of awaiting action of Congress.

From the time the treaty of peace was signed with Mexico, California had been practically without government, except that provided by the local alcaldes, and yet Congress adjourned for the third time without having made any provision for a government for California.

After gold had been discovered, even the few soldiers who remained under the control of the military governor and the sailors on the ships deserted, and conditions became so bad that there were scarcely men enough to guard the few military supplies. [36]

The population had increased from 10,000 in the summer of 1846 to 26,000 by the end of 1848, and to 50,000 by August of the next year. [37] The new settlements usually elected alcaldes and when drastic action became necessary "miner's courts" convened and took such summary action as the conditions appeared to require. [38]

---

[33] *Star and Californian*, December 16, 1848.

[34] *Star and Californian*, December 23, 1848.

[35] *Alta Californian*, January 25, February 22, March 22, 1849.

[36] Bancroft XXIV, 445–460.

[37] *Californian*, August 22, 1846; Overland Monthly XVI, 287.

[38] 1 California Reports, 577.

General Riley Calls the Constitutional Convention

General Riley proved to be more energetic than his predecessors and upon receipt of news that Congress had adjourned without provision for a government in California, he immediately asserted his authority by issuing a call for a constitutional convention. The people through local meetings in the various communities had already recommended the calling of a convention, and were inclined to dispute the authority of General Riley.[39] The difficulty was adjusted by the local organizations changing the date of their proposed convention to the date fixed by General Riley in his proclamation. The convention was called to meet at Monterey on September 1, 1849.

THE FIRST CONSTITUTION
The Constitutional Convention

On September 1, 1849, 10 delegates to the constitutional convention met at Colton Hall in Monterey. They elected a temporary chairman and secretary and adjourned until Monday, September 3. On Monday there were 28 members present.

The first matter taken up was the eligibility of members and the distribution of the representation. In the proclamation calling the convention General Riley had directed that "the district of San Diego will elect two delegates, of Los Angeles four, of Santa Barbara two, of San Luis Obispo two, of Monterey five, of San Jose five, of San Francisco five, of Sonoma four, of Sacramento four, of San Joaquin four. Should any district think itself entitled to a greater number of delegates than the above named, they may elect supernumeraries, who, on the organization of the convention, will be admitted or not at the pleasure of that body."[40]

In order to make a proper adjustment for the increasing population in some of the districts and possibly to adjust an unequal apportionment, the convention provided that the districts should be entitled to the following representation:

"San Diego, two; Los Angeles, seven; Santa Barbara, three; San Luis Obispo, two; Monterey, five; San Jose, seven; San Francisco, nine; Sonoma, six; Sacramento, fifteen; and San Joaquin, fifteen."[41]

---

[39] Hunt, Genesis of California's First Constitution, 29.
[40] Browne, Debates, 4.
[41] Browne, Debates, 4.

The Delegates

The persons who actually took part in the convention were the following: [42]

Name	Age	Where born	District in California	Length of residence	Profession
J. D. Hoppe	35	Maryland	San Jose	3 years	Merchant
Joseph Aram	39	New York	San Jose	3 years	Farmer
Elam Brown	52	New York	San Jose	3 years	Farmer
Jacob R. Snyder	34	Pennsylvania	Sacramento	4 years	Surveyor
Winfield S. Sherwood	32	New York	Sacramento	4 months	Lawyer
H. W. Halleck	32	New York	Monterey	3 years	U. S. Engineer
L. W. Hastings	30	Ohio	Sacramento	6 years	Lawyer
J. A. Sutter	47	Switzerland	Sacramento	10 years	Farmer
John McDougal	32	Ohio	Sacramento	7 months	Merchant
E. O. Crosby	34	New York	Sacramento	7 months	Lawyer
M. M. McCarver	42	Kentucky	Sacramento	1 year	Farmer
Julian Hanks	39	Connecticut	San Jose	10 years	Farmer
Kimball H. Dimmick	34	New York	San Jose	3 years	Lawyer
Thomas O. Larkin	47	Massachusetts	Monterey	16 years	Trader
Lewis Dent	26	Massachusetts	Monterey	3 years	Lawyer
Rodman M. Price	30	New York	San Francisco	4 years	U. S. Navy
Ch. T. Botts	40	Virginia	Monterey	16 months	Attorney at Law
M. G. Vallejo	42	California	Sonoma	All my life	Military
Manl. Dominguez	46	California	Los Angeles	All my life	Banker
Antonio M. Pico	40	California	San Jose	All my life	Agriculturist
Jacinto Rodrigues	36	California	Santa Barbara	All my life	Agriculturist
Henry A. Tefft	26	New York	San Luis Obispo	4 months	Lawyer
Pedro Sansevaine	31	France	San Jose	11 years	Negotiant
Hugo Reid	38	Scotland	Los Angeles	16 years	Farmer
Stephen C. Foster	28	Maine	Los Angeles	3 years	Agriculturist
J. McH. Hollingsworth	25	Maryland	San Joaquin	3 years	Lieut. Volunteers
Joseph Hobson	39	Maryland	San Francisco	5 months	Merchant
Pacificus Ord	34	Maryland	Monterey	8 months	Lawyer
O. M. Wosencraft	34	Ohio	San Joaquin	4 months	Physician
J. P. Walker	52	Virginia	Sonoma	13 months	Farmer
W. E. Shannon	27	Ireland	Sacramento	3 years	Lawyer
Abel Stearns	51	Massachusetts	Los Angeles	20 years	Merchant
Thos. L. Vermeule	35	New Jersey	San Joaquin	3 years	Lawyer
Benj. S. Lippincott	34	New York	San Joaquin	3½ years	Trader
Myron Norton	27	New York	San Francisco	1 year	Lawyer
W. M. Steuart	29	Maryland	San Francisco	1 year	Attorney at Law
B. F. Moore	29	Florida	San Joaquin	1 year	Elegant leisure
A. J. Ellis	33	New York	San Francisco	2½ years	Merchant
Edw. Gilbert	27	New York	San Francisco	2½ years	Printer
J. M. Jones	25	Kentucky	San Joaquin	4 months	Attorney at Law
W. M. Gwin	44	Tennessee	San Francisco	4 months	Farmer
Jose Anto. Carrillo	53	California	Los Angeles	All my life	Labrador (Sp.) Farmer
Francis J. Lippitt	37	Rhode Island	San Francisco	2 years 7 months	Lawyer
Henry Hill	33	Virginia	San Diego	1 year 5 months	U. S. Army
Miguel de Pedroena	41	Spain	San Diego	12 years	Merchant
R. Semple	42	Kentucky	Sonoma	5 years	Printer
P. de la Guerra	36	California	Santa Barbara		
J. M. Covarrubias	40	California	San Luis Obispo and Santa Barbara		

---

[42] Browne, Debates, 478.

It will be noticed that the original number of delegates called by General Riley was 37; that the representation as apportioned by the convention was 73, but that only 48 members attended the convention. The northern districts in particular did not send the number of delegates allotted to them. Most of the members were young men, more than thirty of them were less than 40 years of age, nine were less than 30 years of age, and the oldest was 53. The occupations were varied. There were 14 lawyers, 11 farmers and 7 merchants. It is probable that a large number of the members were, temporarily at least, miners. Fifteen of the members may be considered as from the southern states and there were 23 members from the northern states. The northern members had also on the average been in California for a greater number of years. There were seven native Californians, and five foreign-born members, one from France, one from Scotland, one from Switzerland, one from Ireland and one from Spain.

Organization of the Convention

The convention was organized on September 4th. Robert Semple, delegate from Sonoma, was elected president and William G. Marcy was elected secretary. W. E. P. Hartnell was elected translator for the Spanish-speaking members and various other lesser officers were elected. J. Ross Browne was elected reporter.

There are several of the members who deserve particular mention. [43] The president, Dr. Semple, who had been a resident of California for five years, proved to be a tactful and capable presiding officer, although technically, many of his decisions on procedure were not correct. He had been the founder of Benicia and had taken an active part in the revolt of the American settlers in 1846. H. W. Halleck was acting as Secretary of State under General Riley, in addition to being a member of the convention and appears to have served both offices very well. He later received some note as a general during the Civil War. William M. Gwin, a southerner, who had last resided in Louisiana, was one of the leading members of the convention. He had been a member of Congress, had recently sat in the constitutional convention in Iowa and had come to California but four months before in order to become a Senator from the new State. Thomas O. Larkin had been the United States Consul to California and had taken an active part in the occupation. Edward Gilbert, publisher of the *Alta Californian*, was a leading member from San Francisco. Foster, Crosby, Dimmick and Hastings were leading northern men. Botts, a Virginian, was one of the most capable southern members and a lawyer of ability. James M. Jones was also another capable lawyer and supporter of the south. The more prominent Spanish members were Carrillo, De la Guerra and Vallejo who appears to have been strongly pro-American in spite of humiliating treat-

---

[43] The descriptions of the members are taken from Bancroft XXII, 285, 287.

ment received during the revolt in 1846. Of the foreign-born delegates Captain Sutter stands out very prominently.

State vs. Territorial Government

Before the convention proceeded with the drawing up of the Constitution, Halleck secured a direct vote on the question of whether a state or territorial government was to be organized. The only opposition to a State Government came from the southern part of the State. The vote favoring a state government was 28 to 8. [44]

Procedure in the Convention

When the convention proceeded to the formation of the new Constitution, McCarver moved that the committee take the Constitution of Iowa as a basis for the proposed Constitution. Mr. Gwin explained that he had selected the Constitution of Iowa to be used as a basis for the new Constitution "because it was one of the latest and shortest" and that he had secured several copies for the use of the convention. [45] The method of procedure adopted was that proposed by Mr. Gilbert, of appointing a committee of two members from each district who should propose the new Constitution article by article. The first article, the "Bill of Rights," was reported on September 7th and the committee reported additional articles as each article was disposed of.

Important Problems of the Convention

The Bill of Rights as submitted by the committee made no reference to the question of slavery, but on motion of Mr. Shannon a section prohibiting slavery was adopted without opposition.

The first question upon which there was much debate was as to the matter of excluding free Negroes. It was finally decided to leave that question to the Legislature.

Another matter of controversy arose as to the right of a judge in charging juries to "state the testimony and declare the law." Yet finally the convention adopted the report of the committee giving the judges that power. Violent opposition was shown to corporations and particularly to banking corporations. Reference was frequently made to the panic of 1837, which was still fresh in the minds of many of the members. It was finally provided that "corporations may be formed under general laws, but shall not be created by special act," and "that no corporate body shall be created, renewed or extended with the privileges of making, issuing or putting in circulation any bill, check, ticket, certificate, promissory note, or other paper, or the paper of any bank to circulate as money." [46]

---

[44] Browne, Debates, 23.
[45] Browne, Debates, 24.
[46] Browne, Debates, 119.

In providing for a school system it was expected that the Government of the United States would allot considerable land to be used for school purposes and so no other provisions were made for financing the schools, but it was provided that "the Legislature shall encourage by all suitable means the promotion of intellectual, scientific, moral and agricultural improvements" and schools were required to be maintained for at least three months each year. [47]

Questions of taxation were generally left to the Legislature, except that it was provided that assessors shall be elected by the local districts. This was a concession to the southern part of the State where most of the taxable property was located. The Legislature was authorized to secure a loan of not to exceed $300,000.

A section was adopted which provided that married women might have separate property. This was adopting a principle of the civil law in preference to the common law and continuing in effect the law as it had previously existed in California. [48]

The Boundary Question

The problem of the convention over which there was the most controversy was the fixing of the eastern boundary. [49] One group wished the eastern boundary to be the Sierra Nevada Mountains, while another wished to include the entire region ceded to the United States by Mexico, and which would include Utah and Nevada. After much heated discussion the present boundary was decided upon as a compromise, though it is scarcely east of the mountains. The arguments against the larger state were that the State would be so large that it could not be fairly represented in the Legislature nor the laws efficiently or effectively administered; that the large size would probably cause the State to be divided later, in which case it might lose some of its most valuable territory; that Congress would hesitate and might delay or deny the admission of the entire territory as one state. But the argument which appeared to finally settle the dispute was that there was in Utah a population of about 30,000, who had no representation in the convention, and the convention had no right to include them in the proposed State without their consent.

The Government Provided

The government provided for California by the convention was very similar to the present State Government. There were to be a Governor, Lieutenant Governor, Secretary of State and certain other elective executive and administrative officers. The Legislative Department was to consist of two houses to be called the Senate and the Assembly. The Governor was given the usual veto power. The Judicial Department, while very simi-

---

[47] Constitution of 1849, Art. IX.

[48] Art. XI, Sec. 13.

[49] Browne, Debates, 154, 123–124, 167–169, 418–461.

lar to that of the other states, was a continuation of the Mexican courts established by the law of 1837 with the one modification, that the Justices of the Supreme Court did not sit separately as judges of the district courts as the corresponding judges had done under the Mexican system. The Committee on the Constitution recommended that the Mexican system of courts be continued but the proposed article was amended to provide that Judges of the Supreme Court should not sit separately as judges of the courts of second instance, which were to be called district courts.

Sources of the Constitution

The Constitution of 1849 is rather a compilation of parts of the constitutions of the other states than an original document.

The members of the convention were well suited by experience for the work of compilation. Thirty-eight of the delegates had been citizens of 21 different states, and the 14 lawyers had been citizens of 11 of the states.

The constitutions of all of the states appear to have been used by the convention. On four different occasions the constitutions were referred to collectively and on one occasion Halleck stated that the committee on the Constitution was working "with the constitutions of every state in the Union before it." [50]

Twenty of the state constitutions and the Federal Constitution were mentioned in the debates, some of them several times. [51]

It is not always possible to determine the exact influence the various constitutions had on the Constitution of California, but most of the sections can be traced back to the constitutions of particular states.

In arrangement, the Constitution follows generally the Constitution of Iowa. Sixty-six of the 137 sections of the original Constitution of California appear to have been taken from the Constitution of Iowa, and 19 from the Constitution of New York. It is clear also that sections from the Constitutions of the States of Louisiana, Wisconsin, Michigan, Texas and Mississippi, and of the United States, were adopted. The sources of the other sections of the constitution are not clear. Some sections appear to be modifications of sections from other constitutions and some sections appear to be original. [52]

The First Constitution

The Constitution was divided into 13 parts consisting of 12 articles and a schedule.

---

[50] Browne, Debates, 25, 27, 36, 40, 221.

[51] Browne, Debates, 37, 56, 69, 70, 77, 110, 132, 165, 235, 248, 250, 292, 371, 380, 384.

[52] For further information on the sources of the Constitution see Goodwin, *The Establishment of State Government in California*, 230–243.

Article I—The Bill of Rights

The first article was a declaration of rights, which provided that all men were free and independent, [53] that political power was inherent in the people, [54] guaranteed trial by jury [55] and freedom of religion, [56] that the writ of habeas corpus should not be suspended, [57] that excessive bail should not be required, [58] guaranteed free speech, [59] the right of free assembly, [60] provided that laws of a general nature should have a uniform operation. [61] It provided that the military power should be subordinate to civil power, [62] and that soldiers should not be quartered in private houses in time of peace. [63] It required that representation should be apportioned according to population. [64] No person should be imprisoned for debt, [65] and no bill of indenture, ex post facto law or law impairing operation of contract should be passed. [66] Foreigners who were residents of the State were granted the same right with respect to possession, enjoyment and inheritance of property as citizens. [67] Slavery was prohibited. [68] Unreasonable searches were forbidden. [69] Treason against the State was defined. [70] It was provided that the enumeration of rights should not be construed to deny others retained by the people. [71]

Article II—Suffrage

The right of suffrage was granted to "every white male citizen of the United States and every white male citizen of Mexico who shall have elected to become a citizen of the United States under the terms of the Treaty of Peace exchanged at Querétaro on the thirtieth day of May, 1848, of the age of 21 years, who shall have been a resident of the United States for six months preceding the election and the county or district for 30 days in which he claims to vote," and the Legislature was authorized by a two-thirds vote to admit Indians or descendants of Indians to the right of suffrage. [72] Electors were privileged from arrest, except for treason, felony, breach of peace, during attendance at elections, [73] and were not to be re-

---

[53] Sec. 1.
[54] Sec. 2.
[55] Sec. 3.
[56] Sec. 4.
[57] Sec. 5.
[58] Secs. 6, 7.
[59] Sec. 9.
[60] Sec. 10.
[61] Sec. 11.
[62] Sec. 12.
[63] Sec. 13.
[64] Sec. 14.
[65] Sec. 15.
[66] Sec. 16.
[67] Sec. 17.
[68] Sec. 18.
[69] Sec. 19.
[70] Sec. 20.
[71] Sec. 21.
[72] Sec. 1.
[73] Sec. 2.

quired to perform military duty on election day except in time of war or public danger. [74] Residence for the purpose of voting was not gained or lost by the presence in or absence from the district while employed by the United States or in commerce, on the high seas, or as students. [75] Idiots, insane persons, and persons convicted of crime were not eligible to vote. [76] All elections were to be by ballot. [77]

Article III—Distribution of Powers

Article III contained the provision concerning separation of powers and was as follows:

"The powers of the government of the State of California shall be divided into three separate departments: the legislative, the executive, and judicial; and no person charged with the exercise of powers properly belonging to one of these departments shall exercise any functions pertaining to either of the others, except in the cases hereinafter expressly directed or permitted."

Article IV—Legislative Department

The legislative power of the State was vested in the Senate and Assembly. [78] Sessions of the Legislature [79] and elections of Assemblymen were to be annually. [80] Senators were to be elected biennially [81] and were to be divided into two classes as nearly equal as practicable, one-half of whom were to be chosen each year. [82] Members were required to be qualified electors of the district from which elected. [83] Each house was to choose its own officers and to be judge of the election of its members, [84] to determine its own rules, [85] and to keep a journal of its proceedings. [86] A majority was to constitute a quorum. [87] Members were privileged from arrest and civil process except for treason, felony or breach of the peace, from 15 days before the commencement until 15 days after the termination of each session. [88] The Governor was to issue writs of election to fill vacancies. [89] The sessions were to be public except when in the opinion of the house secrecy

---

[74] Sec. 3.
[75] Sec. 4.
[76] Sec. 5.
[77] Sec. 6.
[78] Sec. 1.
[79] Sec. 2.
[80] Sec. 3.
[81] Sec. 5.
[82] Secs. 6, 7.
[83] Sec. 4.
[84] Sec. 8.
[85] Sec. 10.
[86] Sec. 11.
[87] Sec. 9.
[88] Sec. 12.
[89] Sec. 13.

was required. [90] Neither house was to adjourn for more than three days without the consent of the other. [91] Bills might originate in either house and be amended in the other. [92]

After a bill had been passed by both houses it was to be submitted to the Governor for his approval; if he disapproved of it he should return it with his objections and the bill should be reconsidered and in case it received a two-thirds vote of the members of each house, it should become a law despite the Governor's objection. In case the bill should not be returned within 10 days, Sunday excepted, it should become a law unless the Legislature by adjournment prevented the return.

No Member of the Legislature was to be eligible to an office which was created or the salary of which was increased during the time of his service, [93] nor might he hold any lucrative office under the United States. [94] The Assembly was given the power of impeachment and impeachments were to be tried by the Senate. [95] The officers subject to impeachment were the Governor, the state administrative officers and justices of the Supreme and district courts. [96] Every person convicted of embezzlement was declared to be ineligible to any office of the State. [97] Money might be drawn from the Treasury only in consequence of appropriations made by law. [98]

Every law was required to have but one subject which should be stated in the title and when any section was amended it was required to be reenacted and published at length. [99]

The Legislature was denied the right to grant divorces [100] or authorize lotteries. [101]

A census was required to be taken in 1852, in 1855 and every 10 years thereafter. [102] The Legislature was to divide the State into legislative districts [103] but no county should be divided in the making of such districts. [104]

"Corporations may be formed under the general laws but shall not be created by special act except for municipal purposes." [105] Each stockholder of a corporation was made personally liable for his proportion of

---

[90] Sec. 14.
[91] Sec. 15.
[92] Sec. 16.
[93] Secs. 20, 24.
[94] Sec. 21.
[95] Sec. 18.
[96] Sec. 19.
[97] Sec. 22.
[98] Sec. 23.
[99] Sec. 25.
[100] Sec. 26.
[101] Sec. 26.
[102] Sec. 28.
[103] Sec. 29.
[104] Sec. 30.
[105] Sec. 31.

its liabilities, [106] and the corporators were to be liable for fees from corporations [107] and joint stock companies. [108]
The Legislature was required to provide for the organization of cities. [109] In elections by the legislatures the members were required to vote viva voce and the votes were to be entered in the journal." [110]

Article V—Executive Department

The supreme executive power of the State was vested in the Governor, [111] who was to be elected in the same manner as Members of the Assembly, and to hold office for two years. [112] To be eligible to the office of Governor, a person was required to be a citizen of the United States, a resident of the State for two years and to be 25 years of age. [113]

The election returns for the office of Governor were required to be submitted to the Legislature and to be opened and published in the presence of both houses. [114]

The Governor was made commander in chief of the militia. [115] He was directed to transact all executive business [116] and to see that the laws were faithfully executed. [117] Whenever a vacancy in a state office occurred where no provision for a succesor had been made the Governor was authorized to fill the vacancy until the next election. [118]

The Governor was empowered to call special sessions of the Legislature, [119] and directed to present his message on the condition of the State at each session [120] and in case of a disagreement as to the time of adjournment, he might adjourn the Legislature. [121]

No person while holding an office of the United States was eligible to act as Governor. [122]

The Governor was authorized to grant reprieves and pardons, a record of which he was required to transmit to the next session of the Legislature. [123]

---

[106] Sec. 36.
[107] Sec. 32.
[108] Sec. 33.
[109] Sec. 37.
[110] Sec. 38.
[111] Sec. 1.
[112] Sec. 2.
[113] Sec. 3.
[114] Sec. 4.
[115] Sec. 5.
[116] Sec. 6.
[117] Sec. 7.
[118] Sec. 8.
[119] Sec. 9.
[120] Sec. 10.
[121] Sec. 11.
[122] Sec. 12.
[123] Sec. 13.

The Great Seal of the State was to be kept by the Governor [124] and all grants and commissions made in the name of the State were to be sealed by such seal. [125]

The Lieutenant Governor was to be elected in the same manner as the Governor. He was to be President of the Senate and have a vote in case of a tie. [126]

In case of a vacancy in the office of Governor, the Lieutenant Governor should act as Governor. [127] During any vacancy in the office of Governor and Lieutenant Governor the President pro Tempore of the Senate should act as Governor. [128]

A Comptroller, a Treasurer, an Attorney General and a Surveyor General were to be elected in the same manner and for the same term as the Governor. [129]

The Secretary of State was to be appointed by the Governor with the advice and consent of the Senate. [130] The other executive state officers to act during the first term were to be chosen by the joint vote of the two houses of the Legislature. [131]

The executive officers were to receive a regular compensation but were to receive no fees for the performance of their duties. [132]

Article VI—Judicial Department

The judicial power of the State was vested in a Supreme Court, in district courts, county courts and justices' courts. [133]

The Supreme Court was to consist of a Chief Justice and two associate Justices, [134] who were to be elected by the people for six-year terms. [135] The Supreme Court was given appellate jurisdiction in all cases in which the matter in dispute exceeded $200 in value, in all cases involving the legality of taxes and in questions of law in criminal cases amounting to felonies. [136]

The Legislature was directed to divide the State into judicial districts in which were to be organized district courts. The judges of the district courts were to be elected by the people for terms of six years. [137] The district courts were given original jurisdiction in civil cases where the amount in

---

[124] Sec. 14.
[125] Sec. 15.
[126] Sec. 16.
[127] Sec. 17.
[128] Sec. 16.
[129] Sec. 18.
[130] Sec. 19.
[131] Sec. 20.
[132] Sec. 21.
[133] Sec. 1.
[134] Sec. 2.
[135] Sec. 16.
[136] Sec. 6.
[137] Sec. 5.

dispute exceeded $200, and unlimited jurisdiction in criminal cases and questions of fact raised in probate cases. [138]

The Legislature was to provide for the election by the people of district attorneys, sheriffs, and the other necessary officers. [139]

There was to be a county court in each county. The judge was to be elected for a term of four years. These courts were to have jurisdiction of probate cases, of appeals from justices' courts [140] and such other cases as the Legislature might prescribe. [141]

The Legislature was directed to determine the number of justices of the peace to be elected in the different counties and cities and fix their powers, duties and responsibilities. [142]

No judicial officers except justices of the peace were to receive fees. [143]

The Legislature was authorized to establish courts of arbitration, whose decisions were to be binding only when the parties had voluntarily submitted their dispute. [144]

The judges of the Supreme and district courts were to receive salaries which were not to be increased during their terms of office [145] and they were made ineligible to any other office during such terms. [146]

Judges were forbidden to "charge juries with respect to matter of fact, but may state the testimony and declare the law." [147]

All process was to be in the name of the "People of the State of California." [148]

The Legislature was directed to provide for a speedy publication of the statutes and judicial decisions. [149]

Article VII—The Militia

The Legislature was directed to provide for a militia [150] which might be called out by the Governor. [151] The officers were to be selected in a manner provided by the Legislature and commissioned by the Governor. [152]

Article VIII—State Debts

The Legislature was authorized to incur indebtedness of not to exceed $300,000 without special authorization, and was also authorized to incur,

---

[138] Sec. 6.
[139] Sec. 7.
[140] Sec. 8.
[141] Sec. 9.
[142] Sec. 14.
[143] Sec. 11.
[144] Sec. 13.
[145] Sec. 15.
[146] Sec. 16.
[147] Sec. 17.
[148] Sec. 18.
[149] Sec. 12.
[150] Sec. 1.
[151] Sec. 3.
[152] Sec. 2.

with the approval of the voters at a general election, further debt "for some single object or work, to be distinctly specified."

Article IX—Education

A Superintendent of Public Instruction was to be elected to serve for a term of three years. [153] A system of common schools was to be maintained [154] and any money derived from land granted by the United States for the use of the common schools was to be held as a trust fund for that purpose. [155] Similar provision was made for a state university.

Article X—Mode of Amending and Revising the Constitution

Amendments to the Constitution were to be proposed at two successive sessions of the Legislature by a majority vote of all the members elected to each house, subject to approval by "a majority of the electors qualified to vote for Members of the Legislature." [156] A convention to revise the Constitution might be proposed by two-thirds of the members of both houses. [157]

Article XI—Miscellaneous Provisions

San Jose was to be the "permanent seat of government until removed by law." [158] Any citizen who should fight a duel was disfranchised. [159] State officers were to take a prescribed oath. [160] The Legislature was to provide a system of county and town governments [161] and for the election of county boards of supervisors. [162] Officers whose selection was not provided for were to be elected or appointed as the Legislature might direct. [163] Terms of office were not to exceed four years. [164] The fiscal year was to begin on July 1st. [165] Each political subdivision was to support its own officers. [166] The state credit was not to be loaned. [167] Suits against the State were to be regulated by law. [168] Marriages were not invalidated by failure to comply with requirements of any religious sect. [169] Taxes were to be uniform throughout the State, and assessors and tax collectors were to be elected by the district in which the property to be taxed was situated. [170] Owner-

---

[153] Sec. 1.
[154] Sec. 2.
[155] Sec. 3.
[156] Sec. 1.
[157] Sec. 2.
[158] Sec. 1.
[159] Sec. 2.
[160] Sec. 3.
[161] Sec. 4.
[162] Sec. 5.
[163] Sec. 6.
[164] Sec. 7.
[165] Sec. 8.
[166] Sec. 9.
[167] Sec. 10.
[168] Sec. 11.
[169] Sec. 12.
[170] Sec. 13.

ship of separate property was provided for married women, [171] and homesteads were to be protected from forced sale. [172] Perpetuities were not allowed except for eleemosynary purposes. [173] Conviction for crime was to disqualify for office. [174] Absence from the State on the business of the State or of the United States was not to affect the question of residence. [175] A plurality of votes was to elect. [176] All laws, decrees, etc., which required publication were to be published in both English and Spanish. [177]

Article XII—Boundary
The boundary was fixed as it now exists.

Schedule
A schedule followed the other provisions of the Constitution and provided for the vote upon it and for its taking effect.

Adoption of the Constitution
The constitutional convention adjourned on October 13, 1849, and the date for the vote on the adoption of the Constitution and the election of prospective Governor and Lieutenant Governor and Members of the Legislature was November 13. Copies of the proposed Constitution were printed and distributed as quickly as possible. Candidates were nominated by mass meetings and usually ran without party designation.

The vote on the Constitution was 12,872 for and 811 against. [178] The small vote was probably due to the election day being very stormy. Most of the votes against the Constitution were cast in the Sacramento and San Joaquin districts.

Organization of the State Government
The first Legislature met at San Jose on December 15, 1849. When the election returns were canvassed Peter H. Burnett was found to be elected Governor, and John McDougal, Lieutenant Governor. John C. Fremont and William M. Gwin were elected Senators. State administrative officers and justices of the Supreme Court were also elected. [179]

The Legislature authorized a loan of $200,000 [180] and provided a system of taxation. [181]

---

[171] Sec. 14.
[172] Sec. 15.
[173] Sec. 16.
[174] Secs. 17 and 18.
[175] Sec. 19.
[176] Sec. 20.
[177] Sec. 21.
[178] The official returns are in the archives of the Secretary of State at Sacramento.
[179] Bancroft XXIII, 311–314.
[180] Journals of the California Legislature, 1850, pp. 630, 640, 650.
[181] Statutes of 1850, p. 54.

The common law was adopted as the law of the State. [182] Governor Burnett had recommended that the English merchant law and the definitions of crimes and the Civil Code and Code of Procedure of Louisiana be adopted.

The Legislature passed acts fixing the jurisdiction of the courts and rather comprehensive acts governing criminal and civil procedure. [183]

The State was divided into 25 counties, [184] and provision was made for the incorporation of cities. [185]

The State was organized and began to function exactly as though it were a part of the Union.

Admission of California Into the Union

The Legislature elected Senators to the United States Senate and sent them with representatives to Washington to urge the admission of California into the Union as a state. These senators were John C. Fremont and William M. Gwin. The delegation worked strenuously to secure the admission of the State to the Union at an early date. There was still further delay and California was not finally admitted to the Union until September 9, 1850.

Amendments to the First Constitution

The only important amendments to the first Constitution were adopted in 1862, although minor amendments were adopted in 1857 and 1871. They provided that the term of the Governor be increased from two to four years, that the Secretary of State be elected, and completely revised and re-enacted Article VI, relating to the Judicial Department. The effect of the amendments was to provide for recorder's courts and court commissioners, and in general to revise and amplify the provisions of the Constitution relating to the courts.

Defects of the First Constitution

The first Constitution was not entirely satisfactory, as no constitution or law can ever be. The principal faults charged to the new Constitution were faults of omission. [186] It was said that the old Constitution was "dumb" on the subject of finance, that all of the regulations concerning taxation "did not occupy four lines." The Legislature might impose any tax which it might desire and as a result much capital had been driven from the State. The expenditure of money was entirely unchecked. The Legislature was unlimited as to the salaries it might allow to its members or other state officers. No check was established against extravagant fees which might be allowed for any official service. There was nothing to prevent the Legisla-

---

[182] Journals of the California Legislature, 1850, pp. 323, 1123, 1204.

[183] Statutes 1850, p. 275.

[184] Journals of the California Legislature, 1850, pp. 156, 849; Statutes 1850, p. 58.

[185] Journals of the California Legislature, 1850, pp. 190, 229, 944, 1026; Statutes 1850, p. 87.

[186] Summarized in Bancroft XXIV, 370, 371.

ture from disposing of the entire property of the State. No provision was made for separate senatorial and assembly districts and the members elected at large from the more populous counties controlled the Legislature. The number of members of the Assembly was limited to 40 and yet there were counties which had no representation in that house. Another defect frequently objected to was the unlimited pardoning power of the Governor. The real dissatisfaction which resulted in calling the second constitutional convention appears to have arisen from the financial depression of the time. In San Francisco, desire for radical changes in the Constitution had been particularly evident. A native of that city named Denis Kearney had gathered about himself a group of radicals and organized a "workingman's" party which demanded some substantial changes.

The Second Constitution

The Convention Called

The Legislature had proposed the calling of a second constitutional convention in 1859, 1860 and 1873, but each time the proposal had been voted down at the election. A convention was again proposed in 1877. This time it was approved at the election and provision was made for the immediate meeting of the convention. As early as April, 1878, attempts were made to organize a single nonpartisan organization. The 152 delegates who were elected to the convention in September were divided into three groups: There were 85 nonpartisan delegates, 50 "Kearneyites or Workingman's Party delegates" and 17 elected on the regular party tickets, nine of whom were Republicans and eight Democrats. The large number of foreign-born delegates caused considerable comment at the time. There were 35 foreign-born delegates in the convention, most of whom were Irish and 19 of whom were from San Francisco. [187]

The Convention

No members of the convention were particularly conspicuous. Joseph F. Hoge of San Francisco was elected president and appeared to be a capable presiding officer. Edwin F. Smith was elected secretary of the convention. The work of the convention was divided between 23 committees, each of which reported on a particular part of the proposed constitution. The work of the convention consisted primarily in making the new Constitution more specific and detailed. The opponents of the new Constitution described it as a code of law rather than a constitution.

The Bill of Rights

Probably the most conspicuous new clauses were those added to the Bill of Rights which provided that "no property qualification shall ever be re-

---

[187] Bancroft, XXIV, 373, 407.

quired for any person to vote or hold office" and that "the provisions of this Constitution are mandatory and prohibitory unless by express words they are declared to be otherwise." [188]

The Legislative Department

The powers of the Legislature [189] were considerably restricted. Appropriations of money for the use of institutions not under the exclusive control of the State were forbidden, except for orphanages or homes for the indigent. [190]

Special legislation was forbidden in a large number of cases, including the regulation of the duties of judicial officers, punishment of crimes and misdemeanors, regulating practice of courts of justice, providing for change of venue in civil and criminal actions, granting divorces, changing the names of persons or places, laying out streets, etc., summoning and impanelling grand and petty juries, regulating county and township business, election of township officers, and assessment or collection of taxes. Special legislation was also forbidden affecting estates, extending the time for the collection of taxes, giving effect to invalid debts, wills or other instruments, refunding money paid into the State Treasury, repudiating debts of any municipal corporation, declaring persons of age, legalizing except against the State any unauthorized act, granting any rights or privileges to corporations, exempting property from taxation, changing county seats, restoring citizenship, regulating interest rate on money, controlling liens, providing for the management of common schools, remitting fines, effecting fees or salaries of any officers, changing the law of descent, authorizing the adopting of children, limiting civil or criminal actions, and "all other cases where a general law can be made applicable." [191]

The Legislature was directed to pass laws to regulate or prohibit the sale of stock of corporations, by any exchange under the control of any association, and all sales of stock on a margin or for future delivery were declared void. [192]

No appropriation or allotment of money might be made from any public source for the aid of any religious school or hospital. [193]

The Legislature was prohibited from lending the credit of the State, [194] and no gifts of public money might be made. [195]

The Legislature was directed to enact laws limiting the charges of telegraph and gas companies and the charges of storage, wharfage, etc. [196]

---

[188] Article I, Secs. 22, 24.
[189] Article IV.
[190] Article IV, Sec. 22.
[191] Article IV, Sec. 25.
[192] Article XII, Sec. 26.
[193] Article IV, Sec. 30; Article IX, Sec. 8.
[194] Article IV, Sec. 33.
[195] Article IV, Sec. 26.
[196] Article IV, Sec. 33.

The Executive Department

There was but slight change made in the Executive Department. The term of office of the Governor had been increased in 1862 from two to four years. The Governor might veto a bill but each house by a two-thirds vote could pass a bill over his veto. The Governor might convene extra sessions of the Legislature, which should have no power to legislate except on the subjects named in the call. [197]

The Governor was directed to report to the Legislature any and all pardons he had granted since the last session, and no person twice convicted of a felony might be pardoned except on the recommendation of a majority of judges of the Supreme Court. [198]

The Judicial Department

The Judicial Department was completely reorganized. [199] The Supreme Court was to consist of a Chief Justice and six Associate Justices who might sit in two departments of three judges each.

The decision of each department was to be final except when a hearing in bank was granted. The Chief Justice was to apportion the business to the departments. The concurrence of four judges was necessary to a judgment in bank. All decisions of the Supreme Court were required to be in writing and the grounds for the decisions stated. Under the first Constitution decisions were not always made in writing. [200]

The Justices of the Supreme Court were to be elected in three separate classes and were to hold office for 12 years. [201]

The county and district courts were to be replaced by superior courts. [202]

Corporations

Considerable attention was given to the "evils" of corporations and "monopolies." Corporations were to be formed only under general laws and each stockholder was to be individually liable for his proportion of all the debts of the corporation. [203]

The directors were liable to the creditors for all money embezzled or misappropriated. [204]

The Legislature could not grant a charter for banking purposes but banks might be formed under general laws. [205]

The State was specifically given a right to take property of individuals or corporations by eminent domain for public use. [206]

---

[197] Article VI, Sec. 9.
[198] Article VII.
[199] Article IV, Sec. 2.
[200] Heuston vs. Williams, 13 Cal. 24.
[201] Article VI, Sec. 3.
[202] Article VI, Sec. 6.
[203] Article XII, Secs. 1, 2.
[204] Article XII, Sec. 3.
[205] Article XII, Sec. 5.
[206] Article XII, Sec. 8.

No corporation might engage in any business other than that authorized in its charter and no corporation might hold real estate not necessary to its business for more than five years. [207] No corporation might issue stock or bonds except for actual payment in money, labor or property, and all fictitious increase of stock or indebtedness was void. [208] Cumulative voting was authorized in corporations. Common carriers were made subject to legislative control. Transportation companies might not grant free passes to persons holding office, and the acceptance of such a pass by any public officer, except a railroad commissioner, caused the forfeiture of the office. [209]

Any common carrier which reduced its rates for the purpose of competition might not increase such rates until authorized. [210]

The State was divided into three districts in each of which a railroad commissioner was to be elected. The duty of the railroad commissioner was to supervise and regulate the rates of transportation. [211]

Taxation

Mortgages, deeds of trust and any instruments by which debts were secured were subject to taxation as interests in such property, and property was declared to include "moneys, credits, bonds, stocks, dues, franchises, and all other matters and things, real and personal and mixed, capable of private ownership." [212]

Special attention was given to making taxes on large amounts of property proportional to those upon smaller divisions.

Chinese

An entire article was devoted to the Chinese which provided that every means should be taken to prohibit their immigration, that they should not be employed by corporations or any public works, and that the Legislature should make necessary regulations for the protection of the state political subdivisions from the burdens arising from their presence. [213]

Education

A new provision required that the state school money be used only for the common schools. [214] Examinations for teachers' certificates were to be conducted by local boards instead of by the state board. Sectarian doctrines were not to be taught in any of the public schools of the State. [215]

---

[207] Article XII, Sec. 9.
[208] Article XII, Sec. 11.
[209] Article XII, Sec. 19.
[210] Article XII, Sec. 20.
[211] Article XII, Sec. 22.
[212] Article XIII, Sec. 1.
[213] Article XIX.
[214] Article IX, Sec. 4.
[215] Article IX, Sec. 7.

Miscellaneous Provisions

Several restrictions were placed upon the organization of counties under general laws. [216] Provisions were made for granting charters to cities. [217] Amendments to the Constitution might be proposed by two-thirds of the members elected to each house of the Legislature. [218]

The Constitution Adopted

The provisions of the Constitution regulating corporations and some of the provisions relating to cities and counties, particularly those relating to the granting of charters, caused considerable opposition to the proposed Constitution.

San Francisco, where the strongest demand for a new Constitution had been evident, rejected the new Constitution by a majority of 1,500 out of 38,000; but the Constitution was adopted by a majority of 10,000 out of a total State vote of 145,000 and went into effect for some purposes on July 4, 1879. [219]

Some of the limitations that were incorporated to appease the radical members were so worded that they failed to accomplish the purposes intended or, as in the case of the provision prohibiting the employment of Chinese by corporations, were found to be in conflict with the Federal Constitution and treaties.

Amendments

The large amount of legislation contained in the Constitution has necessitated frequent change. From 1880 to 1940 inclusive, there were amendments proposed to 733 sections of the Constitution, of which 343 were adopted and 390 rejected. Among the more important amendments adopted were those providing for the initiative and referendum, [220] and recall, [221] the executive budget, [222] the district courts of appeal, [223] municipal courts, [224] absent voting, [225] increasing the powers of the Railroad Commission, [226] establishing the Judicial Council, [227] regulating the sale of liquor, [228] and establishing a state civil service system. [229]

---

[216] Article XI.
[217] Article XI, Sec. 8.
[218] Article XVIII.
[219] Bancroft XXIV, 400; Article XXII, Sec. 12.
[220] Article IV, Sec. 1.
[221] Article XXIII.
[222] Article IV, Sec. 34.
[223] Article VI, Sec. 4.
[224] Article VI, Sec. 11.
[225] Article II, Sec. 1.
[226] Article XII, Secs. 22, 23, 23a.
[227] Article VI, Sec. 1a.
[228] Article XX, Sec. 22.
[229] Article XXIV.

Proposed Constitutional Convention

During recent years there has been considerable discussion of the advisability of calling a constitutional convention. In 1933 the Legislature submitted the question of calling a constitutional convention to the voters. [230] This proposal received a vote of 705,915 for to 668,080 against. When the Legislature undertook to make provision for the convention it was noticed that the proposition approved by the people had provided that the convention must meet within three months of the election calling it. The election having been November 6, 1934, the three months would expire February 6, 1935. The Legislature met on January 7, 1935, and it was impossible for the Legislature to pass the necessary legislation to provide for the convention for the election to be called, the results canvassed and the delegates to meet within 29 days. It was argued by some that the provision concerning time was only directory and that the convention should be called at a later date. Other defects in the proposal were pointed out; the cost of the special elections were considered. The Legislature finally took no action.

Revision of the Constitution

At every session of the Legislature, from 1935 to 1947, there were proposals for a Constitutional convention and for revision of the Constitution. The proposals were given thorough consideration but none of them passed. Finally, in 1947, Assembly Concurrent Resolution No. 89 was proposed for the purpose of setting up a joint committee for making recommendations concerning constitutional revision. This resolution passed and the joint committee consisting of 10 members from each house was appointed. A large and representative advisory committee was selected and a competent staff was secured.

The resolution directed the committee to study the Constitution of California and those of other states and to prepare a draft of a revised Constitution appropriate for use in case revision of the Constitution as a whole was effected and a series of drafts of the several parts of the Constitution appropriate for use in case needed changes were effected by amendment instead of by way of revision.

A study of the problems of revision indicated that a complete revision of the Constitution rather than the submission of individual amendments would be more feasible. An amendment was prepared to Article XVIII of the Constitution authorizing the Legislature to submit a revision of the Constitution to the electors, but this proposal was not submitted.

Very little was accomplished because the advisory committee recommended that the committee restrict itself to the elimination of obsolete provisions in the Constitution rather than a revision in substance and that recommendation was accepted by the committee. A series of seven Con-

---

[230] Assembly Concurrent Resolution No. 17.

stitutional amendments were submitted by the Legislature to the voters for the purpose of eliminating purely obsolete material from the Constitution. After submission it was discovered that one of these proposals might contain defects in drafting. At the special election November 8, 1949, the voters adopted six of these proposals thereby eliminating the more obviously obsolete proposals of the Constitution. These amendments on the whole eliminated approximately 14,500 words from the Constitution.

The California Constitution
Revision Commission

The California Constitution Revision Commission

BY HON. BRUCE W. SUMNER*

History of the Commission

In 1962, the voters of California approved a proposition submitted to them by the Legislature which launched a vast project to modernize and update the state's antiquated Constitution through the creation of the California Constitution Revision Commission.

Until 1962, the only certain way to revise the California Constitution was by a constitutional convention. While Article XVIII, Section 1, provided for amendments to be proposed by the Legislature it was generally felt that judicial construction of the term "amendment" might preclude overall constitutional revision.[1]

Following the 1949 Special Election at which much obsolete language was deleted from the Constitution by amendments, proposals for revision were considered at nearly every session of the Legislature. As legislators and other interested citizens became increasingly concerned about the length and content of the State Constitution, general support for complete revision was evident.

In 1959, the Assembly of the California Legislature adopted a resolution directing the Citizens' Legislative Advisory Commission to study the legislative techniques and procedures which should be used to secure a revision of the State Constitution.[2] A preliminary report of the commission's findings was submitted to the Legislature in April, 1960, in which the commission stated that the State Constitution was in need of fundamental review.[3] The commission's final report recommended that Article XVIII be amended to permit the Legislature to submit to the people a revised constitution, or a revision of any part, and that a commission be established by statute to study the Constitution and make recommendations for a total or partial revision.[4]

Concurrently with the citizen's commission study, the Assembly Interim Committee on Constitutional Amendments undertook an examination of the need for constitutional reform. In its 1960 report to the Legislature, the committee stated that the California Constitution was in need of fundamental revision in both substance and form.[5] The committee also

---

* Judge, Superior Court, Orange County; Chairman, California Constitution Revision Commission; Member, California Legislature 1957–1962.

[1] *McFadden v. Jordan,* 32 Cal. 2d 330, 196 P.2d 787, *cert. denied,* 336 U.S. 918 (1948); *Livermore v. Waite,* 102 Cal. 113, 36 Pac. 424 (1894).

[2] Assembly House Resolution No. 278, Stats. 1959 Regular Session.

[3] Citizens' Legislative Advisory Commission, *Second Progress Report the Citizens of California,* September, 1960.

[4] Citizens' Legislative Advisory Commission, *Final Report to the California Legislature and to the Citizens of California,* March, 1962.

[5] *Report of the Assembly Interim Committee on Constitutional Amendments to the California Legislature,* November, 1960.

recommended that Article XVIII be amended to authorize the Legislature to submit an entire revision to the people.[6]

Acting on these recommendations the Legislature in 1961 adopted Assembly Constitutional Amendment No. 14 by Assemblyman Busterud.[7] The measure proposed an amendment to Article XVIII to authorize the Legislature to act, in effect, as a constitutional convention by allowing it to submit proposals for revision of the Constitution to the voters. The amendment was placed on the November, 1962 ballot as Proposition 7 and was approved by the voters by a margin of more than 2 to 1.[8]

To implement Proposition 7, the Legislature in 1963 adopted resolutions which called for the creation of a Constitutional Revision Commission, under the auspices of the Joint Committee on Legislative Organization, to provide the Legislature and the joint committee "with facts and recommendations relating to the revision of the Constitution of the State of California."[9]

By the terms of the implementing resolutions, the commission was to be composed of not less than 25 nor more than 50 citizen members, appointed by the Joint Committee on Legislative Organization, and six legislative members. In addition, the members of the joint committee were named as ex officio members of the commission. The resolutions provided that "The Commission membership shall be broadly representative of the various political, economic and social groupings within the State."[10]

This initial legislation provided that "The existence of the Commission shall terminate 90 days after the termination of the 1965 Regular Session of the Legislature."[11] During the 1965 Regular Session, the Legislature extended the life of the commission to October 1, 1966, and increased the maximum number of citizen members to 60.[12]

Subsequent legislation has renamed the commission The Constitution Revision Commission and continued its existence for an indefinite period.[13]

Under these resolutions, the commission selects its own chairman, adopts its own rules of procedure and reports its findings to the Legislature. Members of the commission "serve without compensation but each member is allowed actual expenses incurred in the discharge of his duties,

---

[6] *Ibid.*

[7] Assembly Constitutional Amendment No. 14, ch. 222, Stats. 1961 Regular Session.

[8] 2,901,537–1,428,034. Secretary of State, *Statement of the Vote*, General Election, 1962.

[9] Assembly Concurrent Resolution No. 77, ch. 181, Stats. 1963 Regular Session; Assembly Concurrent Resolution No. 7, ch. 7, Stats. 1963 First Extraordinary Session.

[10] Assembly Concurrent Resolution No. 7, ch. 7, Stats. 1963 First Extraordinary Session.

[11] *Ibid.*

[12] Assembly Concurrent Resolution No. 130, ch. 179, Stats. 1965 Regular Session.

[13] Assembly Concurrent Resolution No. 144, ch. 212, Stats. 1965 Regular Session; Senate Concurrent Resolution No. 6, ch. 74, Stats. 1966 First Extraordinary Session; Assembly Concurrent Resolution No. 107, ch. 163, Stats. 1967 Regular Session; Assembly Concurrent Resolution No. 102, ch. 202, Stats. 1968 Regular Session.

including travel expenses." All necessary staff and materials are provided by the Joint Committee on Legislative Organization.[14] When it first met on February 20, 1964, the commission consisted of 43 citizen members. At the first session the commission elected the late James C. Sheppard of Los Angeles and Robert Gordon Sproul of Berkeley, cochairman, Mrs. Robert Zurbach of Pasadena, secretary, and Paul Mason of Sacramento, parliamentarian. On July 31, 1964, Burnham Enersen of San Francisco was elected vice chairman of the commission. With the passing of James C. Sheppard the commission on November 4, 1964, elected Judge Bruce W. Sumner of Laguna Beach, cochairman. On November 18, 1965, Robert Gordon Sproul resigned as cochairman and Judge Sumner was elected chairman.

The revision commission has organized its study of the Constitution on an article by article basis. Usually meeting monthly for two or three day public sessions, the commission chairman determines which articles will be considered and may name a committee of the commission to study an article in depth. Committees report their recommendations to the full commission for consideration. Before an article is considered by a committee, or the commission, a background study is prepared by the commission staff or by a special consultant under staff supervision. The study includes an analysis of the provisions of the article being considered, relevant sections of other articles, relevant constitutional provisions in other state constitutions and other source material. After studying an article in detail the commission adopts its recommendations for revision of both the substance and language of the article.

Revision Phase I

On February 22, 1966, the commission, in an historic session in Sacramento, made its initial report to the Legislature. It contained recommended revisions of Articles III, IV, V, VI, VII, VIII, and XXIV of the Constitution, which deal with the legislative, executive and judicial branches of government and the civil service system. These articles comprised approximately one-third of the Constitution.

Since 1966 was a budget session there was a question whether the Legislature would be permitted, at that time, to consider the recommendations of the commission. The question was resolved when Governor Edmund G. Brown placed constitution revision on special call and the commission's proposals were submitted to the Legislature in the form of Assembly Constitutional Amendment No. 13 by Assemblyman James Mills of San Diego, Chairman of the Joint Committee on Legislative Organization.[15] A companion measure, Assembly Bill No. 147 by Assemblymen Mills and

---

[14] Assembly Concurrent Resolution No. 7, *supra* note 11.

[15] *Governor's Proclamations Nos. 54, 55, 56*, Stats. 1966 First Extraordinary Session, pp. 250, 251; Assembly Constitutional Amendment No. 13, ch. 139, Stats. 1966 First Extraordinary Session.

Elliott, contained the nonfundamental matters which were to be deleted from the Constitution by the revision and converted to statutes. [16]

Strong bipartisan support represented by Assembly Speaker Jesse M. Unruh and Assembly Minority Leader Robert T. Monagan, together with the inherent strength of the commission through its many prominent and politically active members, gave the commission's proposals ready support in the Assembly. However, because the State Senate in 1966 was meeting in an historic last session under court-voided apportionment laws, there was some question whether passage could be obtained through that house. Bipartisan support and active commission endorsement also produced Senate approval of the recommendations which were placed on the November 8, 1966, ballot as Proposition 1-A.

The momentum obtained by the passage of the measure through both houses by the necessary two-thirds vote, along with unanimous commission endorsement, caused the campaign for voter adoption of the revision to proceed virtually without opposition. Both Governor Brown and Ronald Reagan, then candidate for Governor, endorsed Proposition 1-A and appeared on television in support of its passage. The result was approval by the people by a vote of 4,156,416 to 1,499,675, a 73.7 percent "Yes" vote. [17]

The 1966 revision in addition to deleting approximately 16,000 words effected the following basic changes and redrafted the articles involved so that the citizens of California could read and understand them.

Article III—Separation of Powers

The 1966 revision retained, with only changes in wording, the concept that our legislative, executive and judicial branches of government must be separate. The article was rephrased to state its meaning concisely and accurately.

Article IV—Legislative

This article effected a number of important substantive changes relative to the legislative branch.

Under the former Constitution the Legislature met in general session only during odd-numbered years. In even-numbered years the Legislature met in budget session. The 1966 revision eliminated the restricted budget session and provided for annual general sessions.

Regular sessions of the Legislature formerly could not exceed 120 days, excluding Saturdays and Sundays. Experience showed this to be, in effect, a minimum as well as a maximum period. The limitation on the length of the regular session was removed.

Legislative compensation was formerly set at $500 a month, and any adjustment required a constitutional amendment. Subject to a two-thirds vote

---

[16] Assembly Bill No. 147, ch. 161, Stats. 1966 First Extraordinary Session.

[17] Secretary of State, *Statement of Vote,* General Election, 1966.

of each house, the Governor's veto, and the initiative and referendum, the Legislature, under the 1966 revision, was permitted to set its own compensation by statute. Increases of more than 5 percent per year cannot be passed, however, and any compensation adjustment adopted in one session may not take effect until after the next general election. Thus, before an increase in compensation can be realized, the action of the legislators may be reviewed by the people at the polls.

No mention was made of conflict of interest in the former Constitution. Under the 1966 revision the Senate and Assembly were mandated to pass conflict-of-interest statutes. In anticipation of the passage of Proposition 1-A, the 1966 Legislature passed a conflict-of-interest law. Under the law, restrictions were imposed on legislators' expense and retirement benefits, travel expense reimbursement was limited to the fare of common carriers, and control over per diem determinations given to the Board of Control.[18]

California's two basic initiative provisions are the initiative statute and the initiative constitutional amendment. The initiative statute enacts or amends statutes; the initiative constitutional amendment enacts or amends a provision of the Constitution. Each type of initiative is commenced by filing a petition signed by a number of voters equal to 8 percent of the votes cast at the last election for Governor. Each type of initiative must be approved by a majority of the voters.

The 1966 revision reduced the signature requirement for initiative statute petitions from 8 to 5 percent, but retained the 8 percent signature requirement for constitutional amendments. This was done to encourage persons wishing to sponsor initiative petitions to use the initiative statute, thus protecting the Constitution from addition of unnecessary detail.

The former Constitution contained a provision for an indirect initiative. Like that for the initiative statute, the procedure prescribed began with a petition to enact or change a statute. The petition was signed by a number of voters equal to 5 percent of the votes cast at the last election for Governor. The indirect initiative and initiative statute differed, however, in that the former was directed to the Legislature rather than to the people for a vote. If the Legislature approved the proposed statute, it became law. If it did not approve, the proposed statute was submitted to the people for their approval or rejection.

As noted above, the 1966 revision reduced the signatures required for an initiative statute from 8 to 5 percent, the same as required for the indirect initiative. With the same signature requirement, the indirect initiative merely added an additional step to accomplish the result which could be realized under the direct initiative. Moreover, the indirect initiative had been used only four times, and only once successfully. For these reasons

---

[18] Assembly Bill No. 173, ch. 163, Stats. 1966 First Extraordinary Session.

the 1966 revision deleted the indirect initiative as unnecessary. This, however, did not impair the right of the people to propose laws through the initiative procedure.

Article V—Executive

Article V (Executive Powers), Article VII (Pardoning Power), and Article VIII (Militia) were all separate articles in the former Constitution. The 1966 revision combined these articles into revised Article V. This placed all the primary duties of the executive branch in one article.

Reorganization of the executive branch was not specifically mentioned in the former Constitution. The 1966 revision authorized the Legislature to allow the Governor to reorganize the executive branch of government which furnishes the Governor more direct control over his own area of responsibility.

The former Constitution contained a detailed order of succession to the offices of Governor and Lieutenant Governor. The 1966 revision deleted this list and provided that successors to the Governor, after the Lieutenant Governor, were to be designated by statute. The result simplified constitutional language.

The 1966 revision added a new provision authorizing the California Supreme Court to determine when the Governor is unable to carry out his duties and should be removed from office. Authority to raise questions regarding the Governor's ability to perform his duties was vested in a special body to be created by statute. [19]

The former Constitution provided that money could not be spent by the state unless first authorized by the Legislature. This principle of fiscal management is followed in other states and by the federal government. An unused exception in the former Constitution, however, allowed the Governor and the Controller to bypass the Legislature and give money to the Attorney General without legislative appropriation. The 1966 revision deleted this special funding provision and required the Attorney General to receive legislative approval for his funds, as do all other state officers and agencies.

The Attorney General's salary was fixed by the former Constitution at the amount paid to an Associate Justice of the State Supreme Court. The 1966 revision also deleted this provision, so that the Attorney General's salary, like those of all other elected state officers, could be determined by the Legislature.

Article VI—Judicial

Relatively few substantive changes were proposed in the operation of the judicial branch, since California's system is envied by most of the nation.

---

[19] Assembly Bill No. 164, ch. 162, Stats. 1966 First Extraordinary Session.

The former Constitution provided for Supreme Court operation in two separate departments to relieve heavy caseloads. With the creation of District Courts of Appeal in 1904, the department system became obsolete and never was used again. The 1966 revision recognized this fact and deleted this obsolete provision.

The 1966 revision continued the requirement of a superior court in each county, but deleted the requirement of at least one judge in each county and instead permitted the Legislature to provide that one or more superior court judges be selected to serve more than one county. Concurrence of the boards of supervisors of the affected counties was required for adoption of the system. The change provides financial savings to small counties that do not need the full-time services of a superior court judge and which prefer to share a judge with other counties.

Under the former Constitution an appeal from a superior court, in many cases, went directly to the State Supreme Court. The Supreme Court normally transferred these cases for hearing to the intermediate appellate court. The 1966 revision adhered to orderly appellate procedure by requiring appeals to be taken from a superior court to a court of appeals before the case could proceed to the Supreme Court. An exception was made for unique cases in that the Supreme Court can always order a matter transferred to it from a court of appeals. Cases imposing the death sentence were excepted and still are appealable directly from a superior court to the Supreme Court.

Five years admission to practice law in this state was required by the former Constitution for eligibility to a judgeship in any court of record. To encourage placement of experienced men as judges, the 1966 revision increased the admission requirement to 10 years for future judges of the superior and appellate courts.

The former Constitution provided that the names of incumbent judges of the superior court in counties of 700,000 population or more need not appear on the election ballot if no one ran against them or petitioned to have the name appear. This system met with widespread approval and the 1966 revision allowed the Legislature to extend it to any trial court in the state without regard to population.

The election or appointment of superior and municipal court judges to nonjudicial office during their terms was permitted under the former Constitution. Acceptance of the new position, however, constituted a resignation from their judicial office. The 1966 revision recognized that judges should be, as far as possible, removed from politics. Accordingly, it prohibited appointment of any judge to nonjudicial office during his judicial term and it required a judge of a municipal or superior court to take a leave of absence without pay before running for nonjudicial office. The prohibition against appellate judges running for other than judicial office during their terms was retained.

Under the former Constitution a judge was suspended from office without pay after conviction for a crime involving moral turpitude. The 1966 revision provided for suspension when a judge is convicted of any felony, as well as a crime involving moral turpitude. In addition, a provision was added providing that a judge charged with a serious crime is disqualified, without loss of pay, from sitting on the bench until he is cleared of the charge.

Revision Phase II

Even before the voters had accepted Proposition 1-A, work on the second phase of constitutional revision had begun. This phase, which became Proposition I on the November, 1968 General Election ballot, presented to the voters a proposed revision of Articles: IX (Education), X (State Institutions), XI (Local Government), XII (Corporations and Public Utilities), XVII (Land, and Homestead Exemption), XVIII (Amending and Revising the Constitution) and XXIV (State Civil Service).

After two years of deliberations and public meetings held throughout California, the revision commission submitted its second phase recommendations to the Legislature on February 28, 1968.[20] The recommendations were introduced in the Assembly in the form of Assembly Constitutional Amendment No. 30 by Assemblyman Joe Gonsalves, Chairman of the Joint Committee on Legislative Organization.[21]

There followed extensive public hearings in both the Assembly and the Senate. These hearings were announced publicly by the Legislature and were preceded by written notices to interested persons and groups throughout the state.

In July of 1968, Proposition I passed both houses of the Legislature by the required two-thirds vote. Before the measure could be presented to the voters, however, it was necessary that Governor Reagan approve and sign a companion measure, Assembly Bill No. 918, also by Assemblyman Gonsalves, which contained deleted constitutional material recommended for enactment into statutory law.[22] The bill was signed thereby allowing Proposition I to appear on the November ballot and insuring that, on adoption by the people, the provisions transferred from the Constitution to the statutes would become effective immediately.

In spite of strong legislative support and the endorsement of Proposition I by such groups as the California League of Cities, County Supervisors' Association, and the State Chamber of Commerce, Proposition I failed to attain the necessary majority vote for its adoption.[23]

---

[20] *Report of the California Constitution Revision Commission,* v.II, February, 1968.

[21] Assembly Constitutional Amendment No. 30, ch. 184, Stats. 1968 Regular Session.

[22] Assembly Bill No. 918, ch. 767, Stats. 1968 Regular Session.

[23] 2,562,378–3,406,029, Secretary of State, *Statement of the Vote,* General Election, 1968.

A brief description of the changes which would have been effected if the second phase proposal had been approved follows:

Article IX—Education

The revised article would simply state "the Legislature shall provide for and support a free public school system." This is a mandate to the Legislature and a concise declaration of what shall be done as a minimum in the field of education. A similar mandate is contained in the existing Constitution.

The amended version would require that the Legislature grant basic financial aid to school districts and mandate the Legislature to create intermediate and local school districts. The general requirement that the Legislature provide financial aid would be a change from specific dollar amounts in the existing Constitution, which have been exceeded by statutory provisions.

The revised article would also provide that school districts shall have an executive officer appointed by an elected board, and that at the county or intermediate unit level there shall continue to be elected school boards and elected superintendents, unless the Legislature, by enactment of a statute passed by a two-thirds vote of the members of each house, provides for a different method of selection. This would mean no change in the present method of selecting county superintendents of schools in general law counties. Charter counties and cities now have and would continue to have autonomy in this area.

The revision would make no change in the present provisions concerning the State Board of Education. The amendment states that the State Superintendent of Public Instruction would continue to be elected by the people, unless the Legislature, by enactment of a statute passed by a two-thirds vote of all the members elected to each house, provides for a different method of selection. It is well to note that such a statute would be subject to veto by the Governor and the people's right of referendum.

The revision proposal provides that the State Board of Education shall continue to adopt and furnish textbooks at state expense for use in the elementary schools throughout the state.

The proposed article would continue the present constitutional mandate for a minimum annual salary for teachers. As in the case of financial aid to school districts, the specific dollar amount would be deleted, however, a general mandate to the Legislature would be retained.

The sections of existing Article IX dealing with higher education would not have been altered by Proposition I. Recommendations concerning these sections will be submitted to the Legislature in 1970.

The existing sections dealing with the financial aspects of education, other than basic financing, would be transferred to Article XIII (Revenue and Taxation) with no change in their text.

Article X—State Institutions

The first two paragraphs of existing Article X would be deleted from the Constitution as unnecessary statements of power clearly inherent in the Legislature. The third paragraph dealing with the use of convict labor would be transferred without change to Article XX (Miscellaneous) for future consideration by the revision commission and the Legislature.

Article XI—Local Government

This article has been described as one of the two most amended articles in the California Constitution. By itself, it is as long as the entire United States Constitution, and it contains much material which the commission and the Legislature found to be statutory in nature.

The revised article would continue to provide for counties as legal subdivisions of the state and would guarantee an elected governing body. The present Constitution does not mandate that the governing body of counties be elected. Existing provisions governing the formation of cities would not be substantively altered.

The revision proposal would continue to provide for the adoption by cities and counties of governing charters. The extensive procedural provisions covering this process in the existing Constitution would be reenacted as statutes. Existing provisions governing the powers of chartered cities would be retained.

The minimum number of members of the local governing body of charter counties would be increased from three to five, recognizing that no charter county at present has fewer than five members.

Consolidation of cities and counties would be authorized under the revised provisions, as provided by statute, subject to the condition that all cities within the county be included and that the consolidated city and county have a charter.

The police powers of local governments would be preserved without change. In addition there would be no change in the existing constitutional provisions which allow the Legislature to provide that counties may perform municipal functions at the request of cities within them, and if provided by their respective charters, a county may agree with the city within it to assume and discharge specific municipal functions. The existing constitutional provisions concerning public works would also be retained.

A prohibition on local government bodies from granting extra compensation or extra allowance to a public officer, employee, or contractor, after service has been rendered, or to pay a claim without authority of law would be added. There is a similar prohibition in the existing Constitution on the Legislature.

The existing provisions prohibiting delegation by the Legislature of certain powers over local matters and allowing the Legislature to prescribe a procedure for the presentation of claims against the local government and its agents and employees would be retained with minor changes.

Article XII—Corporations and Public Utilities

The first 16 sections of existing Article XII, with two exceptions, would be deleted by the revision proposal since they concern corporation matters which are extensively dealt with by statute. It was unanimously acknowledged that these provisions are inappropriate in the State Constitution and can better be dealt with by statute. Existing Section I, which authorizes the Legislature to amend or repeal laws concerning corporations would be retained and transferred to Article XX (Miscellaneous) and existing Section 13 dealing with the extension of credit by the state and other financial matters would be retained and transferred to Article XIII (Revenue and Taxation) for future consideration by the commission and the Legislature.

The balance of existing Article XII concerns the Public Utilities Commission. The revision would continue the constitutional status of the commission with five or more members and would classify certain activities and entities as public utilities without changing the substance of existing provisions.

The jurisdiction of the Public Utilities Commission would be defined more specifically than the present Constitution and in accordance with existing law and practice.

Under the proposed revision the Legislature would be authorized to provide, on request of a condemnor and condemnee, that the Public Utilities Commission may fix the just compensation for public utility property taken by eminent domain. Present law restricts this option to the condemning authority.

Article XVII—Land, and the Homestead Exemption

The first provision of existing Article XVII, is a statement of policy requiring the Legislature to provide for homestead protection. This policy declaration is not self-executing, is unenforceable, and has been exceeded in scope by current statutes. To provide for homestead protection is clearly within the inherent power of the Legislature.

The second provision of the existing article declares that it is against the public interest for individuals or corporations to hold uncultivated and unimproved tracts of land. In light of the adoption in 1966, of Article XXVIII declaring it to be in the best interest of the state to maintain open space land, this 1879 provision appears contrary to current public policy. The revision proposal would delete these two sections of Article XVII entirely.

A third section in existing Article XVII provides for a system of granting state lands to settlers. This provision would be transferred to the statutes.

Article XVIII—Amending and Revising the Constitution

Revised Article XVIII would continue to provide for legislatively proposed amendments and revisions. It contains a substantive change which will allow the Legislature, after an amendment or revision has passed both houses, to amend or withdraw the measure by the two-thirds vote required to pass it. This will allow necessary changes in proposed amendments before they are submitted to the people where changes are agreed to by two-thirds vote of each house. Initiative constitutional amendments would not be affected by this provision.

The revised article would continue the requirement that the Legislature provide for a constitutional convention when approved by the electors. A provision would be added requiring that constitutional convention delegates must be voters elected from districts of substantially equal population.

There is no existing provision in Article XVIII providing that the people may amend the Constitution by Initiative. However, detailed provisions governing initiative amendments are found in Article IV. Reference to amending the Constitution by initiative would be placed in Article XVIII as well to assure the article mentions all methods for changing the Constitution.

A further provision would be added stating that all amendments to the Constitution would take effect the day after election unless the measure otherwise provides. Under existing law, amendments to the Constitution proposed by the Legislature take effect on election day, and initiative constitutional amendments take effect five days after the date of the official declaration of vote by the Secretary of State. The Legislature and the commission have agreed that the effective date of amendments to the Constitution should be the same whether proposed by the Legislature or by the people directly.

Article XXIV—State Civil Service

This article was the subject of recommended revisions submitted to the Legislature in 1966. Because it was not placed on a special call by the Governor, it was not considered by the Legislature or the people with the rest of the first phase revisions. The Legislature included the recommended revisions of Article XXIV in the 1968 revision proposal.

The revised article would substantially retain the existing provisions concerning the state civil service system. It would continue to provide for a five member State Personnel Board, appointed by the Governor and approved by the Senate for 10 year terms, for selection and promotion of state employees by competitive examination, and for exemptions from civil service. The existing exemptions would be augmented by the employees of the Lieutenant Governor. Additional exempt positions in the office of Legislative Counsel would also be authorized. The revised article would add a provision requiring the State Personnel Board to include within the state civil service system employees of a county, city, district, department or agency where the functions of the local or federal agency have been assumed by the state.

Conclusion

Proposition I dealt with more than fourteen thousand words in the existing Constitution and would have reduced the verbiage in the articles affected to approximately nineteen hundred carefully chosen words. In general, its effect would have been to strengthen local government, lend clarity to existing provisions, and provide flexibility in our state system. The Constitution Revision Commission is continuing its work. The members of the commission are striving to complete their recommendations for Constitutional Revision in time for submission to the Legislature at the 1970 session. The members have donated five years and thousands of hours in making their recommendations to the Legislature. They do so as volunteer citizens who believe that state and local government must have an efficient and concise statement of constitutional power under which to work if these vital governmental entities are to continue to play an important role in our way of life. Whether the people adopt or reject these final recommendations or those previously submitted in Proposition I, an important chapter in the history of California's Constitution has been written.

Constitution of the State of California
1879

CONSTITUTIONAL AMENDMENTS
APPROVED AT STATEWIDE ELECTIONS
JUNE 2014–NOVEMBER 2014

Sub-division	Affected By Election	Prop.	Effect	Year Res. Ch.	Sub-division	Affected By Election	Prop.	Effect	Year Res. Ch.
Art. I					**Art. XVI** (Cont.)				
Sec. 3	6-3-14	42	Am	13:123	Sec. 21	11-4-14	2	Ad	2X 14:1
(b)	6-3-14	42	Am	13:123	(a)	11-4-14	2	Ad	2X 14:1
					(b)	11-4-14	2	Ad	2X 14:1
Art. IV					(c)	11-4-14	2	Ad	2X 14:1
Sec. 12.5	11-4-14	2	Ad	2X 14:1	(d)	11-4-14	2	Ad	2X 14:1
(a)	11-4-14	2	Ad	2X 14:1	(e)	11-4-14	2	Ad	2X 14:1
(b)	11-4-14	2	Ad	2X 14:1	(f)	11-4-14	2	Ad	2X 14:1
					(g)	11-4-14	2	Ad	2X 14:1
Art. XIII B					(h)	11-4-14	2	Ad	2X 14:1
Sec. 6	6-3-14	42	Am	13:123	(i)	11-4-14	2	Ad	2X 14:1
(a)	6-3-14	42	Am	13:123	(j)	11-4-14	2	Ad	2X 14:1
					(k)	11-4-14	2	Ad	2X 14:1
Art. XVI					(l)	11-4-14	2	Ad	2X 14:1
Sec. 20	11-4-14	2	R & Ad	2X 14:1					
(a)	11-4-14	2	R & Ad	2X 14:1	Sec. 22	11-4-14	2	Ad	2X 14:1
(b)	11-4-14	2	R & Ad	2X 14:1	(a)	11-4-14	2	Ad	2X 14:1
(c)	11-4-14	2	R & Ad	2X 14:1	(b)	11-4-14	2	Ad	2X 14:1
(d)	11-4-14	2	R & Ad	2X 14:1					
(e)	11-4-14	2	R & Ad	2X 14:1					
(f)	11-4-14	2	R & Ad	2X 14:1					
(g)	11-4-14	2	Ad	2X 14:1					
(h)	11-4-14	2	Ad	2X 14:1					

Abbreviations

Ad = Added
Am = Amended
Art. = Article
R & Ad = Repealed and Added
Sec. = Section

TABLE OF CONTENTS

CONSTITUTION OF THE STATE OF CALIFORNIA*

AS AMENDED AND IN FORCE NOVEMBER 4, 2014

PREAMBLE

We, the People of the State of California, grateful to Almighty God for our freedom, in order to secure and perpetuate its blessings, do establish this Constitution.

ARTICLE I

DECLARATION OF RIGHTS

SECTION 1. [*Repealed November 5, 1974. See Section 1, below.*]

[Inalienable Rights]

SECTION 1. All people are by nature free and independent and have inalienable rights. Among these are enjoying and defending life and liberty, acquiring, possessing, and protecting property, and pursuing and obtaining safety, happiness, and privacy. [*New section adopted November 5, 1974.*]

[Liberty of Speech and of the Press—Newspersons' Refusal to Disclose Information Sources Not Adjudged in Contempt]

SEC. 2. (a) Every person may freely speak, write and publish his or her sentiments on all subjects, being responsible for the abuse of this right. A law may not restrain or abridge liberty of speech or press.

(b) A publisher, editor, reporter, or other person connected with or employed upon a newspaper, magazine, or other periodical publication, or by a press association or wire service, or any person who has been so connected or employed, shall not be adjudged in contempt by a judicial, legislative, or administrative body, or any other body having the power to issue subpoenas, for refusing to disclose the source of any information procured while so connected or employed for publication in a newspaper, magazine or other periodical publication, or for refusing to disclose any unpublished information obtained or prepared in gathering, receiving or processing of information for communication to the public.

Nor shall a radio or television news reporter or other person connected with or employed by a radio or television station, or any person who has been so connected or employed, be so adjudged in contempt for refusing to disclose the source of any information procured while so connected or employed for news or news commentary purposes on radio or television, or for refusing to disclose any unpublished information obtained or prepared in gathering, receiving or processing of information for communication to the public.

---

* Adopted by the people on May 7, 1879. Certain spelling and capitalization variances reflect State Printer's style in effect at time of adoption of amendments.

As used in this subdivision, "unpublished information" includes information not disseminated to the public by the person from whom disclosure is sought, whether or not related information has been disseminated and includes, but is not limited to, all notes, outtakes, photographs, tapes or other data of whatever sort not itself disseminated to the public through a medium of communication, whether or not published information based upon or related to such material has been disseminated. [*As amended June 3, 1980.*]

[*Right to Assemble and to Petition—Right of Access to Government Information*]

Sec. 3.   (a) The people have the right to instruct their representatives, petition government for redress of grievances, and assemble freely to consult for the common good.

(b) (1) The people have the right of access to information concerning the conduct of the people's business, and, therefore, the meetings of public bodies and the writings of public officials and agencies shall be open to public scrutiny.

(2) A statute, court rule, or other authority, including those in effect on the effective date of this subdivision, shall be broadly construed if it furthers the people's right of access, and narrowly construed if it limits the right of access. A statute, court rule, or other authority adopted after the effective date of this subdivision that limits the right of access shall be adopted with findings demonstrating the interest protected by the limitation and the need for protecting that interest.

(3) Nothing in this subdivision supersedes or modifies the right of privacy guaranteed by Section 1 or affects the construction of any statute, court rule, or other authority to the extent that it protects that right to privacy, including any statutory procedures governing discovery or disclosure of information concerning the official performance or professional qualifications of a peace officer.

(4) Nothing in this subdivision supersedes or modifies any provision of this Constitution, including the guarantees that a person may not be deprived of life, liberty, or property without due process of law, or denied equal protection of the laws, as provided in Section 7.

(5) This subdivision does not repeal or nullify, expressly or by implication, any constitutional or statutory exception to the right of access to public records or meetings of public bodies that is in effect on the effective date of this subdivision, including, but not limited to, any statute protecting the confidentiality of law enforcement and prosecution records.

(6) Nothing in this subdivision repeals, nullifies, supersedes, or modifies protections for the confidentiality of proceedings and records of the Legislature, the Members of the Legislature, and its employees, committees, and caucuses provided by Section 7 of Article IV, state law, or legislative rules adopted in furtherance of those provisions; nor does it affect

the scope of permitted discovery in judicial or administrative proceedings regarding deliberations of the Legislature, the Members of the Legislature, and its employees, committees, and caucuses.

(7) In order to ensure public access to the meetings of public bodies and the writings of public officials and agencies, as specified in paragraph (1), each local agency is hereby required to comply with the California Public Records Act (Chapter 3.5 (commencing with Section 6250) of Division 7 of Title 1 of the Government Code) and the Ralph M. Brown Act (Chapter 9 (commencing with Section 54950) of Part 1 of Division 2 of Title 5 of the Government Code), and with any subsequent statutory enactment amending either act, enacting a successor act, or amending any successor act that contains finding demonstrating that the statutory enactment furthers the purposes of this section. [*As amended June 3, 2014.*]

SEC. 4.   [*Repealed November 5, 1974. See Section 4, below.*]

[*Liberty of Conscience*]

SEC. 4.   Free exercise and enjoyment of religion without discrimination or preference are guaranteed. This liberty of conscience does not excuse acts that are licentious or inconsistent with the peace or safety of the State. The Legislature shall make no law respecting an establishment of religion.

A person is not incompetent to be a witness or juror because of his or her opinions on religious beliefs. [*New section adopted November 5, 1974.*]

SEC. 5.   [*Repealed November 5, 1974. See Section 5, below.*]

[*The Military*]

SEC. 5.   The military is subordinate to civil power. A standing army may not be maintained in peacetime. Soldiers may not be quartered in any house in wartime except as prescribed by law, or in peacetime without the owner's consent. [*New section adopted November 5, 1974.*]

SEC. 6.   [*Repealed November 5, 1974. See Section 6, below.*]

[*Slavery Prohibited*]

SEC. 6.   Slavery is prohibited. Involuntary servitude is prohibited except to punish crime. [*New section adopted November 5, 1974.*]

[*Due Process of Law—Use of Pupil School Assignment or Pupil Transportation*]

SEC. 7.   (a) A person may not be deprived of life, liberty, or property without due process of law or denied equal protection of the laws; provided, that nothing contained herein or elsewhere in this Constitution imposes upon the State of California or any public entity, board, or official any obligations or responsibilities which exceed those imposed by the Equal Protection Clause of the 14th Amendment to the United States Constitution with respect to the use of pupil school assignment or pupil transportation. In enforcing this subdivision or any other provision of this Constitution, no court of this State may impose upon the State of California or any public entity, board, or official any obligation or responsibility with respect to the use of pupil school assignment or pupil transportation, (1) except to remedy a specific violation by such party that would also constitute a violation of the Equal Protection Clause of the 14th Amendment to the United States Constitution, and (2) unless a federal court would be permitted under federal decisional law to impose that obligation or responsibility upon such party to remedy the specific violation of the Equal Protection Clause of the 14th Amendment of the United States Constitution.

Except as may be precluded by the Constitution of the United States, every existing judgment, decree, writ, or other order of a court of this State, whenever rendered, which includes provisions regarding pupil school assignment or pupil transportation, or which requires a plan including any such provisions shall, upon application to a court having jurisdiction by any interested person, be modified to conform to the provisions of this subdivision as amended, as applied to the facts which exist at the time of such modification.

In all actions or proceedings arising under or seeking application of the amendments to this subdivision proposed by the Legislature at its 1979–80 Regular Session, all courts, wherein such actions or proceedings are or may hereafter be pending, shall give such actions or proceedings first precedence over all other civil actions therein.

Nothing herein shall prohibit the governing board of a school district from voluntarily continuing or commencing a school integration plan after the effective date of this subdivision as amended.

In amending this subdivision, the Legislature and people of the State of California find and declare that this amendment is necessary to serve compelling public interests, including those of making the most effective use of the limited financial resources now and prospectively available to support public education, maximizing the educational opportunities and protecting the health and safety of all public school pupils, enhancing the ability of parents to participate in the educational process, preserving harmony and tranquility in this State and its public schools, preventing the waste of scarce fuel resources, and protecting the environment.

[*Privileges and Immunities*]

(b) A citizen or class of citizens may not be granted privileges or immunities not granted on the same terms to all citizens. Privileges or immunities granted by the Legislature may be altered or revoked. [*As amended November 6, 1979.*]

[*Marriage*]

SEC. 7.5. Only marriage between a man and a woman is valid or recognized in California. [*New section adopted November 4, 2008. Initiative measure.*]

[*Sex, Race, Etc., Not a Disqualification for Business*]

SEC. 8. A person may not be disqualified from entering or pursuing a business, profession, vocation, or employment because of sex, race, creed, color, or national or ethnic origin. [*Former Section 18 of Article XX, as renumbered and amended November 5, 1974.*]

SEC. 9. [*Repealed November 5, 1974. See Section 9, below.*]

[*Bill of Attainder—Ex Post Facto Law—Obligation of Contract*]

SEC. 9. A bill of attainder, ex post facto law, or law impairing the obligation of contracts may not be passed. [*New section adopted November 5, 1974.*]

SEC. 10. [*Repealed November 5, 1974. See Section 10, below.*]

[*Detention of Witnesses—No Imprisonment for Debt*]

SEC. 10. Witnesses may not be unreasonably detained. A person may not be imprisoned in a civil action for debt or tort, or in peacetime for a militia fine. [*New section adopted November 5, 1974.*]

SEC. 11. [*Repealed November 5, 1974. See Section 11, below.*]

[*Suspension of Habeas Corpus*]

SEC. 11. Habeas corpus may not be suspended unless required by public safety in cases of rebellion or invasion. [*New section adopted November 5, 1974.*]

[*Bail—Release on Own Recognizance*]

SEC. 12. A person shall be released on bail by sufficient sureties, except for:

(a) Capital crimes when the facts are evident or the presumption great;

(b) Felony offenses involving acts of violence on another person, or felony sexual assault offenses on another person, when the facts are evident or the presumption great and the court finds based upon clear and convincing evidence that there is a substantial likelihood the person's release would result in great bodily harm to others; or

(c) Felony offenses when the facts are evident or the presumption great and the court finds based on clear and convincing evidence that the person has threatened another with great bodily harm and that there is a substantial likelihood that the person would carry out the threat if released.

Excessive bail may not be required. In fixing the amount of bail, the court shall take into consideration the seriousness of the offense charged, the previous criminal record of the defendant, and the probability of his or her appearing at the trial or hearing of the case.

A person may be released on his or her own recognizance in the court's discretion. [*As amended November 8, 1994.*]

Sec. 13. [*Repealed November 5, 1974. See Section 13, below.*]

[*Unreasonable Seizure and Search—Warrant*]

Sec. 13. The right of the people to be secure in their persons, houses, papers, and effects against unreasonable seizures and searches may not be violated; and a warrant may not issue except on probable cause, supported by oath or affirmation, particularly describing the place to be searched and the persons and things to be seized. [*New section adopted November 5, 1974.*]

Sec. 14. [*Repealed November 5, 1974. See Section 14, below.*]

[*Felony Defendant Before Magistrate—Prosecutions*]

Sec. 14. Felonies shall be prosecuted as provided by law, either by indictment or, after examination and commitment by a magistrate, by information.

A person charged with a felony by complaint subscribed under penalty of perjury and on file in a court in the county where the felony is triable shall be taken without unnecessary delay before a magistrate of that court. The magistrate shall immediately give the defendant a copy of the complaint, inform the defendant of the defendant's right to counsel, allow the defendant a reasonable time to send for counsel, and on the defendant's request read the complaint to the defendant. On the defendant's request the magistrate shall require a peace officer to transmit within the county where the court is located a message to counsel named by defendant.

A person unable to understand English who is charged with a crime has a right to an interpreter throughout the proceedings. [*New section adopted November 5, 1974.*]

[*Felony—Prosecution by Indictment*]

Sec. 14.1. If a felony is prosecuted by indictment, there shall be no postindictment preliminary hearing. [*New section adopted June 5, 1990. Initiative measure.*]

Sec. 14½. [*Repealed November 5, 1974.*]

Sec. 15. [*Repealed November 5, 1974. See Section 15, below.*]

[*Criminal Prosecutions—Rights of Defendant—Due Process of Law—Jeopardy— Depositions—Assistance of Counsel*]

Sec. 15. The defendant in a criminal cause has the right to a speedy public trial, to compel attendance of witnesses in the defendant's behalf, to have the assistance of counsel for the defendant's defense, to be personally present with counsel, and to be confronted with the witnesses against the defendant. The Legislature may provide for the deposition of a witness in the presence of the defendant and the defendant's counsel.

Persons may not twice be put in jeopardy for the same offense, be compelled in a criminal cause to be a witness against themselves, or be deprived of life, liberty, or property without due process of law. [*New section adopted November 5, 1974.*]

[*Trial by Jury*]

SEC. 16.   Trial by jury is an inviolate right and shall be secured to all, but in a civil cause three-fourths of the jury may render a verdict. A jury may be waived in a criminal cause by the consent of both parties expressed in open court by the defendant and the defendant's counsel. In a civil cause a jury may be waived by the consent of the parties expressed as prescribed by statute.

[*Number of Jurors in Civil Trials*]

In civil causes the jury shall consist of 12 persons or a lesser number agreed on by the parties in open court. In civil causes other than causes within the appellate jurisdiction of the court of appeal the Legislature may provide that the jury shall consist of eight persons or a lesser number agreed on by the parties in open court.

[*Number of Jurors in Criminal Trials*]

In criminal actions in which a felony is charged, the jury shall consist of 12 persons. In criminal actions in which a misdemeanor is charged, the jury shall consist of 12 persons or a lesser number agreed on by the parties in open court. [*As amended June 2, 1998.*]

SEC. 17.   [*Repealed November 5, 1974. See Section 17, below.*]

[*Unusual Punishment—Excessive Fines*]

SEC. 17.   Cruel or unusual punishment may not be inflicted or excessive fines imposed. [*New section adopted November 5, 1974.*]

SEC. 18.   [*Repealed November 5, 1974. See Section 18, below.*]

[*Treason*]

SEC. 18.   Treason against the State consists only in levying war against it, adhering to its enemies, or giving them aid and comfort. A person may not be convicted of treason except on the evidence of two witnesses to the same overt act or by confession in open court. [*New section adopted November 5, 1974.*]

SEC. 19.   [*Repealed November 5, 1974. See Section 19, below.*]

[*Eminent Domain*]

SEC. 19.   (a) Private property may be taken or damaged for a public use and only when just compensation, ascertained by a jury unless waived, has first been paid to, or into court for, the owner. The Legislature may provide for possession by the condemnor following commencement of eminent domain proceedings upon deposit in court and prompt release to the owner of money determined by the court to be the probable amount of just compensation.

(b) The State and local governments are prohibited from acquiring by eminent domain an owner-occupied residence for the purpose of conveying it to a private person.

(c) Subdivision (b) of this section does not apply when State or local government exercises the power of eminent domain for the purpose of protecting public health and safety; preventing serious, repeated criminal activity; responding to an emergency; or remedying environmental contamination that poses a threat to public health and safety.

(d) Subdivision (b) of this section does not apply when State or local government exercises the power of eminent domain for the purpose of acquiring private property for a public work or improvement.

(e) For the purpose of this section:

1. "Conveyance" means a transfer of real property whether by sale, lease, gift, franchise, or otherwise.

2. "Local government" means any city, including a charter city, county, city and county, school district, special district, authority, regional entity, redevelopment agency, or any other political subdivision within the State.

3. "Owner-occupied residence" means real property that is improved with a single-family residence such as a detached home, condominium, or townhouse and that is the owner or owners' principal place of residence for at least one year prior to the State or local government's initial written offer to purchase the property. Owner-occupied residence also includes a residential dwelling unit attached to or detached from such a single-family residence which provides complete independent living facilities for one or more persons.

4. "Person" means any individual or association, or any business entity, including, but not limited to, a partnership, corporation, or limited liability company.

5. "Public work or improvement" means facilities or infrastructure for the delivery of public services such as education, police, fire protection, parks, recreation, emergency medical, public health, libraries, flood protection, streets or highways, public transit, railroad, airports and seaports; utility, common carrier or other similar projects such as energy-related, communication-related, water-related and wastewater-related facilities or infrastructure; projects identified by a State or local government for recovery from natural disasters; and private uses incidental to, or necessary for, the public work or improvement.

6. "State" means the State of California and any of its agencies or departments. [*As amended June 3, 2008. Initiative measure.*]

Sec. 20. [*Repealed November 5, 1974. See Section 20, below.*]

[*Rights of Noncitizens*]

Sec. 20. Noncitizens have the same property rights as citizens. [*New section adopted November 5, 1974.*]

Sec. 21. [*Repealed November 5, 1974. See Section 21, below.*]

[*Separate Property of Husband and Wife*]

Sec. 21. Property owned before marriage or acquired during marriage by gift, will, or inheritance is separate property. [*Former Section 8 of Article XX, as renumbered November 5, 1974.*]

Sec. 22. [*Repealed November 5, 1974. See Section 22, below.*]

[*No Property Qualification for Electors*]

Sec. 22. The right to vote or hold office may not be conditioned by a property qualification. [*New section adopted November 5, 1974.*]

Sec. 23. [*Repealed November 5, 1974. See Section 23, below.*]

[*Grand Juries*]

Sec. 23. One or more grand juries shall be drawn and summoned at least once a year in each county. [*New section adopted November 5, 1974.*]

[*Constitutional Rights—Rights Reserved*]

Sec. 24. Rights guaranteed by this Constitution are not dependent on those guaranteed by the United States Constitution.

In criminal cases the rights of a defendant to equal protection of the laws, to due process of law, to the assistance of counsel, to be personally present with counsel, to a speedy and public trial, to compel the attendance of witnesses, to confront the witnesses against him or her, to be free from unreasonable searches and seizures, to privacy, to not be compelled to be a witness against himself or herself, to not be placed twice in jeopardy for the same offense, and to not suffer the imposition of cruel or unusual punishment, shall be construed by the courts of this State in a manner consistent with the Constitution of the United States. This Constitution shall not be construed by the courts to afford greater rights to criminal defendants than those afforded by the Constitution of the United States, nor shall it be construed to afford greater rights to minors in juvenile proceedings on criminal causes than those afforded by the Constitution of the United States.

This declaration of rights may not be construed to impair or deny others retained by the people. [*As amended June 5, 1990. Initiative measure.*]

[*Right to Fish*]

SECTION 25. The people shall have the right to fish upon and from the public lands of the State and in the waters thereof, excepting upon lands set aside for fish hatcheries, and no land owned by the State shall ever be sold or transferred without reserving in the people the absolute right to fish thereupon; and no law shall ever be passed making it a crime for the people to enter upon the public lands within this State for the purpose of fishing in any water containing fish that have been planted therein by the State; *provided*, that the Legislature may by statute, provide for the season when and the conditions under which the different species of fish may be taken. [*New section adopted November 8, 1910.*]

SEC. 26. [*Renumbered Section 1 of Article II June 8, 1976. See Section 26, below.*]

[*Constitution Mandatory and Prohibitory*]

SEC. 26. The provisions of this Constitution are mandatory and prohibitory, unless by express words they are declared to be otherwise. [*Former Section 28, as renumbered June 8, 1976.*]

SEC. 26a. [*Repealed November 8, 1949.*]

[*Death Penalty*]

SEC. 27. All statutes of this State in effect on February 17, 1972, requiring, authorizing, imposing, or relating to the death penalty are in full force and effect, subject to legislative amendment or repeal by statute, initiative, or referendum.

The death penalty provided for under those statutes shall not be deemed to be, or to constitute, the infliction of cruel or unusual punishments within the meaning of Article 1, Section 6 nor shall such punishment for such offenses be deemed to contravene any other provision of this constitution. [*New section adopted November 7, 1972. Initiative measure.*]

[*"The Victims' Bill of Rights"*]

SEC. 28. (a) The People of the State of California find and declare all of the following:

(1) Criminal activity has a serious impact on the citizens of California. The rights of victims of crime and their families in criminal prosecutions are a subject of grave statewide concern.

(2) Victims of crime are entitled to have the criminal justice system view criminal acts as serious threats to the safety and welfare of the people of California. The enactment of comprehensive provisions and laws ensuring a bill of rights for victims of crime, including safeguards in the criminal justice system fully protecting those rights and ensuring that crime victims are treated with respect and dignity, is a matter of high public importance. California's victims of crime are largely dependent upon the

proper functioning of government, upon the criminal justice system and upon the expeditious enforcement of the rights of victims of crime described herein, in order to protect the public safety and to secure justice when the public safety has been compromised by criminal activity.

(3) The rights of victims pervade the criminal justice system. These rights include personally held and enforceable rights described in paragraphs (1) through (17) of subdivision (b).

(4) The rights of victims also include broader shared collective rights that are held in common with all of the People of the State of California and that are enforceable through the enactment of laws and through good-faith efforts and actions of California's elected, appointed, and publicly employed officials. These rights encompass the expectation shared with all of the people of California that persons who commit felonious acts causing injury to innocent victims will be appropriately and thoroughly investigated, appropriately detained in custody, brought before the courts of California even if arrested outside the State, tried by the courts in a timely manner, sentenced, and sufficiently punished so that the public safety is protected and encouraged as a goal of highest importance.

(5) Victims of crime have a collectively shared right to expect that persons convicted of committing criminal acts are sufficiently punished in both the manner and the length of the sentences imposed by the courts of the State of California. This right includes the right to expect that the punitive and deterrent effect of custodial sentences imposed by the courts will not be undercut or diminished by the granting of rights and privileges to prisoners that are not required by any provision of the United States Constitution or by the laws of this State to be granted to any person incarcerated in a penal or other custodial facility in this State as a punishment or correction for the commission of a crime.

(6) Victims of crime are entitled to finality in their criminal cases. Lengthy appeals and other post-judgment proceedings that challenge criminal convictions, frequent and difficult parole hearings that threaten to release criminal offenders, and the ongoing threat that the sentences of criminal wrongdoers will be reduced, prolong the suffering of crime victims for many years after the crimes themselves have been perpetrated. This prolonged suffering of crime victims and their families must come to an end.

(7) Finally, the People find and declare that the right to public safety extends to public and private primary, elementary, junior high, and senior high school, and community college, California State University, University of California, and private college and university campuses, where students and staff have the right to be safe and secure in their persons.

(8) To accomplish the goals it is necessary that the laws of California relating to the criminal justice process be amended in order to protect the legitimate rights of victims of crime.

(b) In order to preserve and protect a victim's rights to justice and due process, a victim shall be entitled to the following rights:

(1) To be treated with fairness and respect for his or her privacy and dignity, and to be free from intimidation, harassment, and abuse, throughout the criminal or juvenile justice process.

(2) To be reasonably protected from the defendant and persons acting on behalf of the defendant.

(3) To have the safety of the victim and the victim's family considered in fixing the amount of bail and release conditions for the defendant.

(4) To prevent the disclosure of confidential information or records to the defendant, the defendant's attorney, or any other person acting on behalf of the defendant, which could be used to locate or harass the victim or the victim's family or which disclose confidential communications made in the course of medical or counseling treatment, or which are otherwise privileged or confidential by law.

(5) To refuse an interview, deposition, or discovery request by the defendant, the defendant's attorney, or any other person acting on behalf of the defendant, and to set reasonable conditions on the conduct of any such interview to which the victim consents.

(6) To reasonable notice of and to reasonably confer with the prosecuting agency, upon request, regarding, the arrest of the defendant if known by the prosecutor, the charges filed, the determination whether to extradite the defendant, and, upon request, to be notified of and informed before any pretrial disposition of the case.

(7) To reasonable notice of all public proceedings, including delinquency proceedings, upon request, at which the defendant and the prosecutor are entitled to be present and of all parole or other post-conviction release proceedings, and to be present at all such proceedings.

(8) To be heard, upon request, at any proceeding, including any delinquency proceeding, involving a post-arrest release decision, plea, sentencing, post-conviction release decision, or any proceeding in which a right of the victim is at issue.

(9) To a speedy trial and a prompt and final conclusion of the case and any related post-judgment proceedings.

(10) To provide information to a probation department official conducting a pre-sentence investigation concerning the impact of the offense on the victim and the victim's family and any sentencing recommendations before the sentencing of the defendant.

(11) To receive, upon request, the pre-sentence report when available to the defendant, except for those portions made confidential by law.

(12) To be informed, upon request, of the conviction, sentence, place and time of incarceration, or other disposition of the defendant, the sched-

uled release date of the defendant, and the release of or the escape by the defendant from custody.

(13) To restitution.

(A) It is the unequivocal intention of the People of the State of California that all persons who suffer losses as a result of criminal activity shall have the right to seek and secure restitution from the persons convicted of the crimes causing the losses they suffer.

(B) Restitution shall be ordered from the convicted wrongdoer in every case, regardless of the sentence or disposition imposed, in which a crime victim suffers a loss.

(C) All monetary payments, monies, and property collected from any person who has been ordered to make restitution shall be first applied to pay the amounts ordered as restitution to the victim.

(14) To the prompt return of property when no longer needed as evidence.

(15) To be informed of all parole procedures, to participate in the parole process, to provide information to the parole authority to be considered before the parole of the offender, and to be notified, upon request, of the parole or other release of the offender.

(16) To have the safety of the victim, the victim's family, and the general public considered before any parole or other post-judgment release decision is made.

(17) To be informed of the rights enumerated in paragraphs (1) through (16).

(c) (1) A victim, the retained attorney of a victim, a lawful representative of the victim, or the prosecuting attorney upon request of the victim, may enforce the rights enumerated in subdivision (b) in any trial or appellate court with jurisdiction over the case as a matter of right. The court shall act promptly on such a request.

(2) This section does not create any cause of action for compensation or damages against the State, any political subdivision of the State, any officer, employee, or agent of the State or of any of its political subdivisions, or any officer or employee of the court.

(d) The granting of these rights to victims shall not be construed to deny or disparage other rights possessed by victims. The court in its discretion may extend the right to be heard at sentencing to any person harmed by the defendant. The parole authority shall extend the right to be heard at a parole hearing to any person harmed by the offender.

(e) As used in this section, a "victim" is a person who suffers direct or threatened physical, psychological, or financial harm as a result of the commission or attempted commission of a crime or delinquent act. The term "victim" also includes the person's spouse, parents, children, siblings, or guardian, and includes a lawful representative of a crime victim who is deceased, a minor, or physically or psychologically incapacitated. The term "victim" does not include a person in custody for an offense, the accused, or a person whom the court finds would not act in the best interests of a minor victim.

(f) In addition to the enumerated rights provided in subdivision (b) that are personally enforceable by victims as provided in subdivision (c), victims of crime have additional rights that are shared with all of the People of the State of California. These collectively held rights include, but are not limited to, the following:

(1) Right to Safe Schools. All students and staff of public primary, elementary, junior high, and senior high schools, and community colleges, colleges, and universities have the inalienable right to attend campuses which are safe, secure and peaceful.

(2) Right to Truth-in-Evidence. Except as provided by statute hereafter enacted by a two-thirds vote of the membership in each house of the Legislature, relevant evidence shall not be excluded in any criminal proceeding, including pretrial and post conviction motions and hearings, or in any trial or hearing of a juvenile for a criminal offense, whether heard in juvenile or adult court. Nothing in this section shall affect any existing statutory rule of evidence relating to privilege or hearsay, or Evidence Code Sections 352, 782 or 1103. Nothing in this section shall affect any existing statutory or constitutional right of the press.

(3) Public Safety Bail. A person may be released on bail by sufficient sureties, except for capital crimes when the facts are evident or the presumption great. Excessive bail may not be required. In setting, reducing or denying bail, the judge or magistrate shall take into consideration the protection of the public, the safety of the victim, the seriousness of the offense charged, the previous criminal record of the defendant, and the probability of his or her appearing at the trial or hearing of the case. Public safety and the safety of the victim shall be the primary considerations.

A person may be released on his or her own recognizance in the court's discretion, subject to the same factors considered in setting bail.

Before any person arrested for a serious felony may be released on bail, a hearing may be held before the magistrate or judge, and the prosecuting attorney and the victim shall be given notice and reasonable opportunity to be heard on the matter.

When a judge or magistrate grants or denies bail or release on a person's own recognizance, the reasons for that decision shall be stated in the record and included in the court's minutes.

(4) Use of Prior Convictions. Any prior felony conviction of any person in any criminal proceeding, whether adult or juvenile, shall subsequently be used without limitation for purposes of impeachment or enhancement of sentence in any criminal proceeding. When a prior felony conviction is

an element of any felony offense, it shall be proven to the trier of fact in open court.

(5) Truth in Sentencing. Sentences that are individually imposed upon convicted criminal wrongdoers based upon the facts and circumstances surrounding their cases shall be carried out in compliance with the courts' sentencing orders, and shall not be substantially diminished by early release policies intended to alleviate overcrowding in custodial facilities. The legislative branch shall ensure sufficient funding to adequately house inmates for the full terms of their sentences, except for statutorily authorized credits which reduce those sentences.

(6) Reform of the parole process. The current process for parole hearings is excessive, especially in cases in which the defendant has been convicted of murder. The parole hearing process must be reformed for the benefit of crime victims.

(g) As used in this article, the term "serious felony" is any crime defined in subdivision (c) of Section 1192.7 of the Penal Code, or any successor statute. [*As amended November 4, 2008. Initiative measure.*]

[Criminal Cases—Due Process of Law—Speedy and Public Trial]

Sec. 29.   In a criminal case, the people of the State of California have the right to due process of law and to a speedy and public trial. [*New section adopted June 5, 1990. Initiative measure.*]

[Criminal Cases—Jointure-Hearsay Evidence—Discovery]

Sec. 30.   (a) This Constitution shall not be construed by the courts to prohibit the joining of criminal cases as prescribed by the Legislature or by the people through the initiative process.

(b) In order to protect victims and witnesses in criminal cases, hearsay evidence shall be admissible at preliminary hearings, as prescribed by the Legislature or by the people through the initiative process.

(c) In order to provide for fair and speedy trials, discovery in criminal cases shall be reciprocal in nature, as prescribed by the Legislature or by the people through the initiative process. [*New section adopted June 5, 1990. Initiative measure.*]

[Prohibition Against Discrimination or Preferential Treatment]

Sec. 31.   (a) The State shall not discriminate against, or grant preferential treatment to, any individual or group on the basis of race, sex, color, ethnicity, or national origin in the operation of public employment, public education, or public contracting.

(b) This section shall apply only to action taken after the section's effective date.

(c) Nothing in this section shall be interpreted as prohibiting bona fide qualifications based on sex which are reasonably necessary to the normal operation of public employment, public education, or public contracting.

(d) Nothing in this section shall be interpreted as invalidating any court order or consent decree which is in force as of the effective date of this section.

(e) Nothing in this section shall be interpreted as prohibiting action which must be taken to establish or maintain eligibility for any federal program, where ineligibility would result in a loss of federal funds to the State.

(f) For the purposes of this section, "State" shall include, but not necessarily be limited to, the State itself, any city, county, city and county, public university system, including the University of California, community college district, school district, special district, or any other political subdivision or governmental instrumentality of or within the State.

(g) The remedies available for violations of this section shall be the same, regardless of the injured party's race, sex, color, ethnicity, or national origin, as are otherwise available for violations of then-existing California antidiscrimination law.

(h) This section shall be self-executing. If any part or parts of this section are found to be in conflict with federal law or the United States Constitution, the section shall be implemented to the maximum extent that federal law and the United States Constitution permit. Any provision held invalid shall be severable from the remaining portions of this section. [*New section adopted November 5, 1996. Initiative measure.*]

ARTICLE II.   [*Repealed November 7, 1972. See Article II, below.*]

ARTICLE II *

VOTING, INITIATIVE AND REFERENDUM, AND RECALL

[*Heading as amended June 8, 1976.*]

SEC. 1.   [*Renumbered Section 2 June 8, 1976. See Section 1, below.*]

[*Purpose of Government*]

SECTION 1.   All political power is inherent in the people. Government is instituted for their protection, security, and benefit, and they have the right to alter or reform it when the public good may require. [*Former Section 26 of Article I, as renumbered June 8, 1976.*]

SEC. 1½.   [*Repealed November 7, 1972.*]

SEC. 2.   [*Renumbered Section 3 June 8, 1976. See Section 2, below.*]

---

* New Article II adopted November 7, 1972.

[*Right to Vote*]

SEC. 2.   A United States citizen 18 years of age and resident in this State may vote. [*Former Section 1, as renumbered June 8, 1976.*]

SEC. 2.5.   [*Repealed November 7, 1972. See Section 2.5, below.*]

[*Right to Have Vote Counted*]

SEC. 2.5.   A voter who casts a vote in an election in accordance with the laws of this State shall have that vote counted. [*New Section adopted November 5, 2002.*]

SEC. 2¾.   [*Repealed November 7, 1972.*]

SEC. 3.   [*Renumbered Section 4 June 8, 1976. See Section 3, below.*]

[*Residence—Registration—Free Elections*]

SEC. 3.   The Legislature shall define residence and provide for registration and free elections. [*Former Section 2, as renumbered June 8, 1976.*]

SEC. 4.   [*Renumbered Section 5 June 8, 1976. See Section 4, below.*]

[*Improper Practices That Affect Elections—Mentally Incompetent, Etc.*]

SEC. 4.   The Legislature shall prohibit improper practices that affect elections and shall provide for the disqualification of electors while mentally incompetent or imprisoned or on parole for the conviction of a felony. [*Former Section 3, as renumbered June 8, 1976.*]

SEC. 5.   [*Renumbered Section 6 June 8, 1976. See Section 5, below.*]

[*Voter-Nominated Primary Election—Partisan Elections—Open Presidential Primary—Election Rights of Political Parties*]

SEC. 5.   (a) A voter-nomination primary election shall be conducted to select the candidates for congressional and state elective offices in California. All voters may vote at a voter-nominated primary election for any candidate for congressional and state elective office without regard to the political party preference disclosed by the candidate or the voter, provided that the voter is otherwise qualified to vote for candidates for the office in question. The candidates who are the top two vote-getters at a voter-nominated primary election for a congressional or state elective office shall, regardless of party preference, compete in the ensuing general election.

(b) Except as otherwise provided by Section 6, a candidate for a congressional or state elective office may have his or her political party preference, or lack of political party preference, indicated upon the ballot for the office in the manner provided by statute. A political party or party central committee shall not nominate a candidate for any congressional or state elective office at the voter-nominated primary. This subdivision shall not be interpreted to prohibit a political party or party central committee from endorsing, supporting, or opposing any candidate for a congressional or state elective office. A political party or party central committee shall not have the right to have its preferred candidate participate in the general election for a voter-nominated office other than a candidate who is one of the two highest vote-getters at the primary election, as provided in subdivision (a).

(c) The Legislature shall provide for partisan elections for presidential candidates, and political party and party central committees, including an open presidential primary whereby the candidates on the ballot are those found by the Secretary of State to be recognized candidates throughout the nation or throughout California for the office of President of the United States, and those whose names are placed on the ballot by petition, but excluding any candidate who has withdrawn by filing an affidavit of noncandidacy.

(d) A political party that participated in a primary election for a partisan office pursuant to subdivision (c) has the right to participate in the general election for that office and shall not be denied the ability to place on the general election ballot the candidate who received, at the primary election, the highest vote among that party's candidates. [*As amended June 8, 2010.*]

[*Nonpartisan Offices*]

SEC. 6.   (a) All judicial, school, county, and city offices, including the Superintendent of Public Instruction, shall be nonpartisan.

(b) A political party or party central committee shall not nominate a candidate for nonpartisan office, and the candidate's party preference shall not be included on the ballot for the nonpartisan office. [*As amended June 8, 2010.*]

[*Voting—Secret*]

SEC. 7.   Voting shall be secret. [*Former Section 6, as renumbered June 8, 1976.*]

[*Initiative*]

SEC. 8.   (a) The initiative is the power of the electors to propose statutes and amendments to the Constitution and to adopt or reject them.

(b) An initiative measure may be proposed by presenting to the Secretary of State a petition that sets forth the text of the proposed statute or amendment to the Constitution and is certified to have been signed by electors equal in number to 5 percent in the case of a statute, and 8 percent in the case of an amendment to the Constitution, of the votes for all candidates for Governor at the last gubernatorial election.

(c) The Secretary of State shall then submit the measure at the next general election held at least 131 days after it qualifies or at any special statewide election held prior to that general election. The Governor may call a special statewide election for the measure.

(d) An initiative measure embracing more than one subject may not be submitted to the electors or have any effect.

(e) An initiative measure may not include or exclude any political subdivision of the State from the application or effect of its provisions based upon approval or disapproval of the initiative measure, or based upon the casting of a specified percentage of votes in favor of the measure, by the electors of that political subdivision.

(f) An initiative measure may not contain alternative or cumulative provisions wherein one or more of those provisions would become law depending upon the casting of a specified percentage of votes for or against the measure. [*As amended June 2, 1998.*]

[Referendum]

SEC. 9.   (a) The referendum is the power of the electors to approve or reject statutes or parts of statutes except urgency statutes, statutes calling elections, and statutes providing for tax levies or appropriations for usual current expenses of the State.

(b) A referendum measure may be proposed by presenting to the Secretary of State, within 90 days after the enactment date of the statute, a petition certified to have been signed by electors equal in number to 5 percent of the votes for all candidates for Governor at the last gubernatorial election, asking that the statute or part of it be submitted to the electors. In the case of a statute enacted by a bill passed by the Legislature on or before the date the Legislature adjourns for a joint recess to reconvene in the second calendar year of the biennium of the legislative session, and in the possession of the Governor after that date, the petition may not be presented on or after January 1 next following the enactment date unless a copy of the petition is submitted to the Attorney General pursuant to subdivision (d) of Section 10 of Article II before January 1.

(c) The Secretary of State shall then submit the measure at the next general election held at least 31 days after it qualifies or at a special statewide election held prior to that general election. The Governor may call a special statewide election for the measure. [*As amended June 5, 1990.*]

[Initiative and Referendum — Vote and Effective Date — Conflicts — Legislative Repeal or Amendment — Titling]

SEC. 10.   (a) An initiative statute or referendum approved by a majority of votes thereon takes effect the day after the election unless the measure provides otherwise. If a referendum petition is filed against a part of a statute the remainder shall not be delayed from going into effect.

(b) If provisions of 2 or more measures approved at the same election conflict, those of the measure receiving the highest affirmative vote shall prevail.

(c) The Legislature may amend or repeal referendum statutes. It may amend or repeal an initiative statute by another statute that becomes effective only when approved by the electors unless the initiative statute permits amendment or repeal without their approval.

(d) Prior to circulation of an initiative or referendum petition for signatures, a copy shall be submitted to the Attorney General who shall prepare a title and summary of the measure as provided by law.

(e) The Legislature shall provide the manner in which petitions shall be circulated, presented, and certified, and measures submitted to the electors. [*Former Section 24 of Article IV, as renumbered June 8, 1976.*]

[Initiative and Referendum—Cities or Counties]

SEC. 11.   (a) Initiative and referendum powers may be exercised by the electors of each city or county under procedures that the Legislature shall provide. Except as provided in subdivisions (b) and (c), this section does not affect a city having a charter.

(b) A city or county initiative measure may not include or exclude any part of the city or county from the application or effect of its provisions based upon approval or disapproval of the initiative measure, or based upon the casting of a specified percentage of votes in favor of the measure, by the electors of the city or county or any part thereof.

(c) A city or county initiative measure may not contain alternative or cumulative provisions wherein one or more of those provisions would become law depending upon the casting of a specified percentage of votes for or against the measure. [*As amended June 2, 1998.*]

[Naming Individual or Private Corporation to Office or Duty Prohibited]

SEC. 12.   No amendment to the Constitution, and no statute proposed to the electors by the Legislature or by initiative, that names any individual to hold any office, or names or identifies any private corporation to perform any function or to have any power or duty, may be submitted to the electors or have any effect. [*Former Section 26 of Article IV, as renumbered June 8, 1976.*]

[Recall Defined]

SEC. 13.   Recall is the power of the electors to remove an elective officer. [*New section adopted June 8, 1976.*]

[Recall Petitions]

SEC. 14.   (a) Recall of a state officer is initiated by delivering to the Secretary of State a petition alleging reason for recall. Sufficiency of reason is not reviewable. Proponents have 160 days to file signed petitions.

(b) A petition to recall a statewide officer must be signed by electors equal in number to 12 percent of the last vote for the office, with signatures from each of 5 counties equal in number to 1 percent of the last vote for the office in the county. Signatures to recall Senators, members of the Assembly, members of the Board of Equalization, and judges of courts of appeal and trial courts must equal in number 20 percent of the last vote for the office.

(c) The Secretary of State shall maintain a continuous count of the signatures certified to that office. [*New section adopted June 8, 1976.*]

[*Recall Elections*]

SEC. 15.　(a) An election to determine whether to recall an officer and, if appropriate, to elect a successor shall be called by the Governor and held not less than 60 days nor more than 80 days from the date of certification of sufficient signatures.

(b) A recall election may be conducted within 180 days from the date of certification of sufficient signatures in order that the election may be consolidated with the next regularly scheduled election occurring wholly or partially within the same jurisdiction in which the recall election is held, if the number of voters eligible to vote at that next regularly scheduled election equal at least 50 percent of all the voters eligible to vote at the recall election.

(c) If the majority vote on the question is to recall, the officer is removed and, if there is a candidate, the candidate who receives a plurality is the successor. The officer may not be a candidate, nor shall there be any candidacy for an office filled pursuant to subdivision (d) of Section 16 of Article VI. [*As amended November 8, 1994.*]

[*Legislature to Provide for Petitions, Etc.*]

SEC. 16.　The Legislature shall provide for circulation, filing, and certification of petitions, nomination of candidates, and the recall election. [*New section adopted June 8, 1976.*]

[*Recall of Governor or Secretary of State*]

SEC. 17.　If recall of the Governor or Secretary of State is initiated, the recall duties of that office shall be performed by the Lieutenant Governor or Controller, respectively. [*New section adopted June 8, 1976.*]

[*Reimbursement of Recall Election Expenses*]

SEC. 18.　A state officer who is not recalled shall be reimbursed by the State for the officer's recall election expenses legally and personally incurred. Another recall may not be initiated against the officer until six months after the election. [*New section adopted June 8, 1976.*]

[*Recall of Local Officers*]

SEC. 19.　The Legislature shall provide for recall of local officers. This section does not affect counties and cities whose charters provide for recall. [*New section adopted June 8, 1976.*]

[*Terms of Elective Offices*]

SEC. 20. Terms of elective offices provided for by this Constitution, other than Members of the Legislature, commence on the Monday after January 1 following election. The election shall be held in the last even-numbered year before the term expires. [*New section adopted June 8, 1976.*]

ARTICLE III.   [*Repealed November 7, 1972. See Article III, below.*]

ARTICLE III *

STATE OF CALIFORNIA

[*United States Constitution Supreme Law*]

SECTION 1. The State of California is an inseparable part of the United States of America, and the United States Constitution is the supreme law of the land. [*New section adopted November 7, 1972.*]

[*Boundaries of the State—Sacramento Seat of Government*]

SEC. 2. The boundaries of the State are those stated in the Constitution of 1849 as modified pursuant to statute. Sacramento is the capital of California. [*New section adopted November 7, 1972.*]

[*Separation of Powers*]

SEC. 3. The powers of state government are legislative, executive, and judicial. Persons charged with the exercise of one power may not exercise either of the others except as permitted by this Constitution. [*New section adopted November 7, 1972.*]

[*Administrative Agencies: Declaration Statute Unenforceable or Unconstitutional Prohibited*]

SEC. 3.5. An administrative agency, including an administrative agency created by the Constitution or an initiative statute, has no power:

(a) To declare a statute unenforceable, or refuse to enforce a statute, on the basis of it being unconstitutional unless an appellate court has made a determination that such statute is unconstitutional;

(b) To declare a statute unconstitutional;

(c) To declare a statute unenforceable, or to refuse to enforce a statute on the basis that federal law or federal regulations prohibit the enforcement of such statute unless an appellate court has made a determination that the enforcement of such statute is prohibited by federal law or federal regulations. [*New section adopted June 6, 1978.*]

---

* New Article III adopted November 7, 1972.

[Salaries of Elected State Officers—Salaries of Judges]

SEC. 4. (a) Except as provided in subdivision (b), salaries of elected state officers may not be reduced during their term of office. Laws that set these salaries are appropriations.

(b) Beginning on January 1, 1981, the base salary of a judge of a court of record shall equal the annual salary payable as of July 1, 1980, for that office had the judge been elected in 1978. The Legislature may prescribe increases in those salaries during a term of office, and it may terminate prospective increases in those salaries at any time during a term of office, but it shall not reduce the salary of a judge during a term of office below the highest level paid during that term of office. Laws setting the salaries of judges shall not constitute an obligation of contract pursuant to Section 9 of Article I or any other provision of law. [*As amended November 4, 1980.*]

[Suits Against State]

SEC. 5. Suits may be brought against the State in such manner and in such courts as shall be directed by law. [*New section adopted November 7, 1972.*]

[Official State Language]

SEC. 6. (a) Purpose.

English is the common language of the people of the United States of America and the State of California. This section is intended to preserve, protect and strengthen the English language, and not to supersede any of the rights guaranteed to the people by this Constitution.

(b) English as the Official Language of California.

English is the official language of the State of California.

(c) Enforcement.

The Legislature shall enforce this section by appropriate legislation. The Legislature and officials of the State of California shall take all steps necessary to insure that the role of English as the common language of the State of California is preserved and enhanced. The Legislature shall make no law which diminishes or ignores the role of English as the common language of the State of California.

(d) Personal Right of Action and Jurisdiction of Courts.

Any person who is a resident of or doing business in the State of California shall have standing to sue the State of California to enforce this section, and the Courts of record of the State of California shall have jurisdiction to hear cases brought to enforce this section. The Legislature may provide reasonable and appropriate limitations on the time and manner of suits brought under this section. [*New section adopted November 4, 1986. Initiative measure.*]

[*Retirement Benefits for Elected Constitutional Officers*]

SEC. 7.   (a) The retirement allowance for any person, all of whose credited service in the Legislators' Retirement System was rendered or was deemed to have been rendered as an elective officer of the State whose office is provided for by the California Constitution, other than a judge and other than a Member of the Senate or Assembly, and all or any part of whose retirement allowance is calculated on the basis of the compensation payable to the officer holding the office which the member last held prior to retirement, or for the survivor or beneficiary of such a person, shall not be increased or affected in any manner by changes on or after November 5, 1986, in the compensation payable to the officer holding the office which the member last held prior to retirement.

(b) This section shall apply to any person, survivor, or beneficiary described in subdivision (a) who receives, or is receiving, from the Legislators' Retirement System a retirement allowance on or after November 5, 1986, all or any part of which allowance is calculated on the basis of the compensation payable to the officer holding the office which the member last held prior to retirement.

(c) It is the intent of the people, in adopting this section, to restrict retirement allowances to amounts reasonably to be expected by certain members and retired members of the Legislators' Retirement System and to preserve the basic character of earned retirement benefits while prohibiting windfalls and unforeseen advantages which have no relation to the real theory and objective of a sound retirement system. It is not the intent of this section to deny any member, retired member, survivor, or beneficiary a reasonable retirement allowance. Thus, this section shall not be construed as a repudiation of a debt nor the impairment of a contract for a substantial and reasonable retirement allowance from the Legislators' Retirement System.

(d) The people and the Legislature hereby find and declare that the dramatic increase in the retirement allowances of persons described in subdivision (a) which would otherwise result when the compensation for those offices increases on November 5, 1986, or January 5, 1987, are not benefits which could have reasonably been expected. The people and the Legislature further find and declare that the Legislature did not intend to provide in its scheme of compensation for those offices such windfall benefits. [*New section adopted November 4, 1986.*]

[*California Citizens Compensation Commission*]

SEC. 8.   (a) The California Citizens Compensation Commission is hereby created and shall consist of seven members appointed by the Governor. The commission shall establish the annual salary and the medical, dental, insurance, and other similar benefits of state officers.

(b) The commission shall consist of the following persons:

(1) Three public members, one of whom has expertise in the area of compensation, such as an economist, market researcher, or personnel manager; one of whom is a member of a nonprofit public interest organization; and one of whom is representative of the general population and may include, among others, a retiree, homemaker, or person of median income. No person appointed pursuant to this paragraph may, during the 12 months prior to his or her appointment, have held public office, either elective or appointive, have been a candidate for elective public office, or have been a lobbyist, as defined by the Political Reform Act of 1974.

(2) Two members who have experience in the business community, one of whom is an executive of a corporation incorporated in this State which ranks among the largest private sector employers in the State based on the number of employees employed by the corporation in this State and one of whom is an owner of a small business in this State.

(3) Two members, each of whom is an officer or member of a labor organization.

(c) The Governor shall strive insofar as practicable to provide a balanced representation of the geographic, gender, racial, and ethnic diversity of the State in appointing commission members.

(d) The Governor shall appoint commission members and designate a chairperson for the commission not later than 30 days after the effective date of this section. The terms of two of the initial appointees shall expire on December 31, 1992, two on December 31, 1994, and three on December 31, 1996, as determined by the Governor. Thereafter, the term of each member shall be six years. Within 15 days of any vacancy, the Governor shall appoint a person to serve the unexpired portion of the term.

(e) No current or former officer or employee of this State is eligible for appointment to the commission.

(f) Public notice shall be given of all meetings of the commission, and the meetings shall be open to the public.

(g) On or before December 3, 1990, the commission shall, by a single resolution adopted by a majority of the membership of the commission, establish the annual salary and the medical, dental, insurance, and other similar benefits of state officers. The annual salary and benefits specified in that resolution shall be effective on and after December 3, 1990.

Thereafter, at or before the end of each fiscal year, the commission shall, by a resolution adopted by a majority of the membership of the commission, adjust the medical, dental, insurance, and other similar benefits of state officers. The benefits specified in the resolution shall be effective on and after the first Monday of the next December.

Thereafter, at or before the end of each fiscal year, the commission shall adjust the annual salary of state officers by a resolution adopted by a majority of the membership of the commission. The annual salary specified in the resolution shall be effective on and after the first Monday of the next

December, except that a resolution shall not be adopted or take effect in any year that increases the annual salary of any state officer if, on or before the immediately preceding June 1, the Director of Finance certifies to the commission, based on estimates for the current fiscal year, that there will be a negative balance on June 30 of the current fiscal year in the Special Fund for Economic Uncertainties in an amount equal to, or greater than, 1 percent of estimated General Fund revenues.

(h) In establishing or adjusting the annual salary and the medical, dental, insurance, and other similar benefits, the commission shall consider all of the following:

(1) The amount of time directly or indirectly related to the performance of the duties, functions, and services of a state officer.

(2) The amount of the annual salary and the medical, dental, insurance, and other similar benefits for other elected and appointed officers and officials in this State with comparable responsibilities, the judiciary, and, to the extent practicable, the private sector, recognizing, however, that state officers do not receive, and do not expect to receive, compensation at the same levels as individuals in the private sector with comparable experience and responsibilities.

(3) The responsibility and scope of authority of the entity in which the state officer serves.

(4) Whether the Director of Finance estimates that there will be a negative balance in the Special Fund for Economic Uncertainties in an amount equal to or greater than 1 percent of estimated General Fund revenues in the current fiscal year.

(i) Until a resolution establishing or adjusting the annual salary and the medical, dental, insurance, and other similar benefits for state officers takes effect, each state officer shall continue to receive the same annual salary and the medical, dental, insurance, and other similar benefits received previously.

(j) All commission members shall receive their actual and necessary expenses, including travel expenses, incurred in the performance of their duties. Each member shall be compensated at the same rate as members, other than the chairperson, of the Fair Political Practices Commission, or its successor, for each day engaged in official duties, not to exceed 45 days per year.

(k) It is the intent of the Legislature that the creation of the commission should not generate new state costs for staff and services. The Department of Personnel Administration, the Board of Administration of the Public Employees' Retirement System, or other appropriate agencies, or their successors, shall furnish, from existing resources, staff and services to the commission as needed for the performance of its duties.

(l) "State officer," as used in this section, means the Governor, Lieutenant Governor, Attorney General, Controller, Insurance Commissioner,

Secretary of State, Superintendent of Public Instruction, Treasurer, member of the State Board of Equalization, and Member of the Legislature. [*As amended May 19, 2009.*]

[*Sale of Surplus State Property*]

Sec. 9.   The proceeds from the sale of surplus state property occurring on or after the effective date of this section, and any proceeds from the previous sale of surplus state property that have not been expended or encumbered as of that date, shall be used to pay the principal and interest on bonds issued pursuant to the Economic Recovery Bond Act authorized at the March 2, 2004, statewide primary election. Once the principal and interest on those bonds are fully paid, the proceeds from the sale of surplus state property shall be deposited into the Special Fund for Economic Uncertainties, or any successor fund. For purposes of this section, surplus state property does not include property purchased with revenues described in Article XIX or any other special fund moneys. [*New section adopted November 2, 2004.*]

ARTICLE IV

LEGISLATIVE

[*Heading as amended November 8, 1966.*]

Section 1.   [*Repealed November 8, 1966. See Section 1, below.*]

[*Legislative Power*]

Section 1.   The legislative power of this State is vested in the California Legislature which consists of the Senate and Assembly, but the people reserve to themselves the powers of initiative and referendum. [*New section adopted November 8, 1966.*]

Sec. 1a.   [*Renumbered Section 20 of Article XIII and amended November 8, 1966.*]

Sec. 1b.   [*Repealed November 8, 1966.*]
Sec. 1c.   [*Repealed November 8, 1966.*]
Sec. 1d.   [*Repealed November 8, 1966.*]

[*Legislators—Limitation on Incumbency—Restriction of Retirement Benefits—Limitation of Staff and Support Services—Number of Terms*]

Sec. 1.5.   The people find and declare that the Founding Fathers established a system of representative government based upon free, fair, and competitive elections. The increased concentration of political power in the hands of incumbent representatives has made our electoral system less free, less competitive, and less representative.

The ability of legislators to serve unlimited number of terms, to establish their own retirement system, and to pay for staff and support services at state expense contribute heavily to the extremely high number of incumbents who are reelected. These unfair incumbent advantages discourage qualified candidates from seeking public office and create a class of career politicians, instead of the citizen representatives envisioned by the Founding Fathers. These career politicians become representatives of the bureaucracy, rather than of the people whom they are elected to represent.

To restore a free and democratic system of fair elections, and to encourage qualified candidates to seek public office, the people find and declare that the powers of incumbency must be limited. Retirement benefits must be restricted, state-financed incumbent staff and support services limited, and limitations placed upon the number of terms which may be served. [*New section adopted November 6, 1990. Initiative measure.*]

[*Senate and Assembly—Membership—Elections—Number of Terms and Years of Service—Qualifications—Vacancies*]

SEC. 2.   (a) (1) The Senate has a membership of 40 Senators elected for 4-year terms, 20 to begin every 2 years.

(2) The Assembly has a membership of 80 members elected for 2-year terms.

(3) The terms of a Senator or a Member of the Assembly shall commence on the first Monday in December next following her or his election.

(4) During her or his lifetime a person may serve no more than 12 years in the Senate, the Assembly, or both, in any combination of terms. This subdivision shall apply only to those Members of the Senate or the Assembly who are first elected to the Legislature after the effective date of this subdivision and who have not previously served in the Senate or Assembly. Members of the Senate or Assembly who were elected before the effective date of this subdivision may serve only the number of terms allowed at the time of the last election before the effective date of this subdivision.

(b) Election of members of the Assembly shall be on the first Tuesday after the first Monday in November of even-numbered years unless otherwise prescribed by the Legislature. Senators shall be elected at the same time and places as members of the Assembly.

(c) A person is ineligible to be a member of the Legislature unless the person is an elector and has been a resident of the legislative district for one year, and a citizen of the United States and a resident of California for 3 years, immediately preceding the election, and service of the full term of office to which the person is seeking to be elected would not exceed the maximum years of service permitted by subdivision (a) of this section.

(d) When a vacancy occurs in the Legislature the Governor immediately shall call an election to fill the vacancy. [*As amended June 5, 2012. Initiative measure.*]

[Legislative Sessions—Regular and Special Sessions]

SEC. 3. (a) The Legislature shall convene in regular session at noon on the first Monday in December of each even-numbered year and each house shall immediately organize. Each session of the Legislature shall adjourn sine die by operation of the Constitution at midnight on November 30 of the following even-numbered year.

(b) On extraordinary occasions the Governor by proclamation may cause the Legislature to assemble in special session. When so assembled it has power to legislate only on subjects specified in the proclamation but may provide for expenses and other matters incidental to the session. [*As amended June 8, 1976.*]

[Legislators—Conflict of Interest—Prohibited Compensation—Earned Income]

SEC. 4. (a) To eliminate any appearance of a conflict with the proper discharge of his or her duties and responsibilities, no Member of the Legislature may knowingly receive any salary, wages, commissions, or other similar earned income from a lobbyist or lobbying firm, as defined by the Political Reform Act of 1974, or from a person who, during the previous 12 months, has been under a contract with the Legislature. The Legislature shall enact laws that define earned income. However, earned income does not include any community property interest in the income of a spouse. Any Member who knowingly receives any salary, wages, commissions, or other similar earned income from a lobbyist employer, as defined by the Political Reform Act of 1974, may not, for a period of one year following its receipt, vote upon or make, participate in making, or in any way attempt to use his or her official position to influence an action or decision before the Legislature, other than an action or decision involving a bill described in subdivision (c) of Section 12 of this article, which he or she knows, or has reason to know, would have a direct and significant financial impact on the lobbyist employer and would not impact the public generally or a significant segment of the public in a similar manner. As used in this subdivision, "public generally" includes an industry, trade, or profession.

[Legislators—Travel and Living Expenses]

(b) Travel and living expenses for Members of the Legislature in connection with their official duties shall be prescribed by statute passed by rollcall vote entered in the journal, two-thirds of the membership of each house concurring. A Member may not receive travel and living expenses during the times that the Legislature is in recess for more than three calendar days, unless the Member is traveling to or from, or is in attendance at, any meeting of a committee of which he or she is a member, or a meeting, conference, or other legislative function or responsibility as authorized by the rules of the house of which he or she is a member, which is held at a location at least 20 miles from his or her place of residence.

[Legislators—Retirement]

(c) The Legislature may not provide retirement benefits based on any portion of a monthly salary in excess of five hundred dollars ($500) paid to any Member of the Legislature unless the Member receives the greater amount while serving as a Member in the Legislature. The Legislature may, prior to their retirement, limit the retirement benefits payable to Members of the Legislature who serve during or after the term commencing in 1967.

When computing the retirement allowance of a Member who serves in the Legislature during the term commencing in 1967 or later, allowance may be made for increases in cost of living if so provided by statute, but only with respect to increases in the cost of living occurring after retirement of the Member. However, the Legislature may provide that no Member shall be deprived of a cost of living adjustment based on a monthly salary of five hundred dollars ($500) which has accrued prior to the commencement of the 1967 Regular Session of the Legislature. [*As amended June 5, 1990.*]

[Legislators—Retirement]

Sec. 4.5.   Notwithstanding any other provision of this Constitution or existing law, a person elected to or serving in the Legislature on or after November 1, 1990, shall participate in the Federal Social Security (Retirement, Disability, Health Insurance) Program and the State shall pay only the employer's share of the contribution necessary to such participation. No other pension or retirement benefit shall accrue as a result of service in the Legislature, such service not being intended as a career occupation. This Section shall not be construed to abrogate or diminish any vested pension or retirement benefit which may have accrued under an existing law to a person holding or having held office in the Legislature, but upon adoption of this Act no further entitlement to nor vesting in any existing program shall accrue to any such person, other than Social Security to the extent herein provided. [*New section adopted November 6, 1990. Initiative measure.*]

[Legislators—Qualifications—Expulsion]

Sec. 5.   (a) Each house shall judge the qualifications and elections of its Members and, by rollcall vote entered in the journal, two thirds of the membership concurring, may expel a Member.

[*Legislators—Honoraria*]

(b) No Member of the Legislature may accept any honorarium. The Legislature shall enact laws that implement this subdivision.

[*Legislators—Gifts—Conflict of Interest*]

(c) The Legislature shall enact laws that ban or strictly limit the acceptance of a gift by a Member of the Legislature from any source if the acceptance of the gift might create a conflict of interest.

[*Legislators—Prohibited Compensation or Activity*]

(d) No Member of the Legislature may knowingly accept any compensation for appearing, agreeing to appear, or taking any other action on behalf of another person before any state government board or agency. If a Member knowingly accepts any compensation for appearing, agreeing to appear, or taking any other action on behalf of another person before any local government board or agency, the Member may not, for a period of one year following the acceptance of the compensation, vote upon or make, participate in making, or in any way attempt to use his or her official position to influence an action or decision before the Legislature, other than an action or decision involving a bill described in subdivision (c) of Section 12 of this article, which he or she knows, or has reason to know, would have a direct and significant financial impact on that person and would not impact the public generally or a significant segment of the public in a similar manner. As used in this subdivision, "public generally" includes an industry, trade, or profession. However, a Member may engage in activities involving a board or agency which are strictly on his or her own behalf, appear in the capacity of an attorney before any court or the Workers' Compensation Appeals Board, or act as an advocate without compensation or make an inquiry for information on behalf of a person before a board or agency. This subdivision does not prohibit any action of a partnership or firm of which the Member is a member if the Member does not share directly or indirectly in the fee, less any expenses attributable to that fee, resulting from that action.

[*Legislators—Lobbying*]

(e) The Legislature shall enact laws that prohibit a Member of the Legislature whose term of office commences on or after December 3, 1990, from lobbying, for compensation, as governed by the Political Reform Act of 1974, before the Legislature for 12 months after leaving office.

[*Legislators—Conflict of Interest*]

(f) The Legislature shall enact new laws, and strengthen the enforcement of existing laws, prohibiting Members of the Legislature from engaging in activities or having interests which conflict with the proper discharge of their duties and responsibilities. However, the people reserve to themselves the power to implement this requirement pursuant to Article II. [*As amended June 5, 1990. Subdivision (b) operative December 3, 1990.*]

SEC. 6.   [*Repealed June 3, 1980. See Section 6, below.*]

[*Senatorial and Assembly Districts*]

SEC. 6.   For the purpose of choosing members of the Legislature, the State shall be divided into 40 Senatorial and 80 Assembly districts to be called Senatorial and Assembly Districts. Each Senatorial district shall choose one Senator and each Assembly district shall choose one member of the Assembly. [*New section adopted June 3, 1980.*]

[*House Rules—Officers—Quorum*]

SEC. 7.   (a) Each house shall choose its officers and adopt rules for its proceedings. A majority of the membership constitutes a quorum, but a smaller number may recess from day to day and compel the attendance of absent members.

[*Journals*]

(b) Each house shall keep and publish a journal of its proceedings. The rollcall vote of the members on a question shall be taken and entered in the journal at the request of 3 members present.

[*Public Proceedings—Closed Sessions*]

(c) (1) The proceedings of each house and the committees thereof shall be open and public. However, closed sessions may be held solely for any of the following purposes:

(A) To consider the appointment, employment, evaluation of performance, or dismissal of a public officer or employee, to consider or hear complaints or charges brought against a Member of the Legislature or other public officer or employee, or to establish the classification or compensation of an employee of the Legislature.

(B) To consider matters affecting the safety and security of Members of the Legislature or its employees or the safety and security of any buildings and grounds used by the Legislature.

(C) To confer with, or receive advice from, its legal counsel regarding pending or reasonably anticipated, or whether to initiate, litigation when discussion in open session would not protect the interests of the house or committee regarding the litigation.

(2) A caucus of the Members of the Senate, the Members of the Assembly, or the Members of both houses, which is composed of the members of the same political party, may meet in closed session.

(3) The Legislature shall implement this subdivision by concurrent resolution adopted by rollcall vote entered in the journal, two-thirds of the membership of each house concurring, or by statute, and shall prescribe that, when a closed session is held pursuant to paragraph (1), reasonable

notice of the closed session and the purpose of the closed session shall be provided to the public. If there is a conflict between a concurrent resolution and statute, the last adopted or enacted shall prevail.

[*Recess*]

(d) Neither house without the consent of the other may recess for more than 10 days or to any other place. [*As amended June 5, 1990. Subdivision (c) operative December 3, 1990.*]

[*Legislature—Total Aggregate Expenditures*]

SEC. 7.5. In the fiscal year immediately following the adoption of this Act, the total aggregate expenditures of the Legislature for the compensation of members and employees of, and the operating expenses and equipment for, the Legislature may not exceed an amount equal to nine hundred fifty thousand dollars ($950,000) per member for that fiscal year or 80 percent of the amount of money expended for those purposes in the preceding fiscal year, whichever is less. For each fiscal year thereafter, the total aggregate expenditures may not exceed an amount equal to that expended for those purposes in the preceding fiscal year, adjusted and compounded by an amount equal to the percentage increase in the appropriations limit for the State established pursuant to Article XIII B. [*New section adopted November 6, 1990. Initiative measure.*]

[*Bills and Statutes—30-day Waiting Period*]

SEC. 8.   (a) At regular sessions no bill other than the budget bill may be heard or acted on by committee or either house until the 31st day after the bill is introduced unless the house dispenses with this requirement by rollcall vote entered in the journal, three fourths of the membership concurring.

[*Bills and Statutes—3 Readings*]

(b) The Legislature may make no law except by statute and may enact no statute except by bill. No bill may be passed unless it is read by title on 3 days in each house except that the house may dispense with this requirement by rollcall vote entered in the journal, two thirds of the membership concurring. No bill may be passed until the bill with amendments has been printed and distributed to the members. No bill may be passed unless, by rollcall vote entered in the journal, a majority of the membership of each house concurs.

[*Bills and Statutes—Effective Date*]

(c) (1) Except as provided in paragraphs (2) and (3) of this subdivision, a statute enacted at a regular session shall go into effect on January 1 next following a 90-day period from the date of enactment of the statute and a statute enacted at a special session shall go into effect on the 91st day after adjournment of the special session at which the bill was passed.

(2) A statute, other than a statute establishing or changing boundaries of any legislative, congressional, or other election district, enacted by a bill passed by the Legislature on or before the date the Legislature adjourns for a joint recess to reconvene in the second calendar year of the biennium of the legislative session, and in the possession of the Governor after that date, shall go into effect on January 1 next following the enactment date of the statute unless, before January 1, a copy of a referendum petition affecting the statute is submitted to the Attorney General pursuant to subdivision (d) of Section 10 of Article II, in which event the statute shall go into effect on the 91st day after the enactment date unless the petition has been presented to the Secretary of State pursuant to subdivision (b) of Section 9 of Article II.

(3) Statutes calling elections, statutes providing for tax levies or appropriations for the usual current expenses of the State, and urgency statutes shall go into effect immediately upon their enactment.

[*Bills and Statutes—Urgency Statutes*]

(d) Urgency statutes are those necessary for immediate preservation of the public peace, health, or safety. A statement of facts constituting the necessity shall be set forth in one section of the bill. In each house the section and the bill shall be passed separately, each by rollcall vote entered in the journal, two thirds of the membership concurring. An urgency statute may not create or abolish any office or change the salary, term, or duties of any office, or grant any franchise or special privilege, or create any vested right or interest. [*As amended June 5, 1990.*]

[*Ballot Measures—Application*]

SEC. 8.5.   An act amending an initiative statute, an act providing for the issuance of bonds, or a constitutional amendment proposed by the Legislature and submitted to the voters for approval may not do either of the following:

(a) Include or exclude any political subdivision of the State from the application or effect of its provisions based upon approval or disapproval of the measure, or based upon the casting of a specified percentage of votes in favor of the measure, by the electors of that political subdivision.

(b) Contain alternative or cumulative provisions wherein one or more of those provisions would become law depending upon the casting of a specified percentage of votes for or against the measure. [*New section adopted June 2, 1998.*]

SEC. 9.   [*Repealed November 8, 1966. See Section 9, below.*]

[*Statutes—Title—Section*]

SEC. 9. A statute shall embrace but one subject, which shall be expressed in its title. If a statute embraces a subject not expressed in its title, only the part not expressed is void. A statute may not be amended by reference to its title. A section of a statute may not be amended unless the section is re-enacted as amended. [*New section adopted November 8, 1966.*]

[*Governor's Veto—Bill Introduction in Biennial Session—Fiscal Emergencies*]

SEC. 10. (a) Each bill passed by the Legislature shall be presented to the Governor. It becomes a statute if it is signed by the Governor. The Governor may veto it by returning it with any objections to the house of origin, which shall enter the objections in the journal and proceed to reconsider it. If each house then passes the bill by rollcall vote entered in the journal, two-thirds of the membership concurring, it becomes a statute.

(b) (1) Any bill, other than a bill which would establish or change boundaries of any legislative, congressional, or other election district, passed by the Legislature on or before the date the Legislature adjourns for a joint recess to reconvene in the second calendar year of the biennium of the legislative session, and in the possession of the Governor after that date, that is not returned within 30 days after that date becomes a statute.

(2) Any bill passed by the Legislature before September 1 of the second calendar year of the biennium of the legislative session and in the possession of the Governor on or after September 1 that is not returned on or before September 30 of that year becomes a statute.

(3) Any other bill presented to the Governor that is not returned within 12 days becomes a statute.

(4) If the Legislature by adjournment of a special session prevents the return of a bill with the veto message, the bill becomes a statute unless the Governor vetoes the bill within 12 days after it is presented by depositing it and the veto message in the office of the Secretary of State.

(5) If the 12th day of the period within which the Governor is required to perform an act pursuant to paragraph (3) or (4) of this subdivision is a Saturday, Sunday, or holiday, the period is extended to the next day that is not a Saturday, Sunday, or holiday.

(c) Any bill introduced during the first year of the biennium of the legislative session that has not been passed by the house of origin by January 31 of the second calendar year of the biennium may no longer be acted on by the house. No bill may be passed by either house on or after September 1 of an even-numbered year except statutes calling elections, statutes providing for tax levies or appropriations for the usual current expenses of the State, and urgency statutes, and bills passed after being vetoed by the Governor.

(d) The Legislature may not present any bill to the Governor after November 15 of the second calendar year of the biennium of the legislative session.

(e) The Governor may reduce or eliminate one or more items of appropriation while approving other portions of a bill. The Governor shall append to the bill a statement of the items reduced or eliminated with the reasons for the action. The Governor shall transmit to the house originating the bill a copy of the statement and reasons. Items reduced or eliminated shall be separately reconsidered and may be passed over the Governor's veto in the same manner as bills.

(f) (1) If, following the enactment of the budget bill for the 2004–05 fiscal year or any subsequent fiscal year, the Governor determines that, for that fiscal year, General Fund revenues will decline substantially below the estimate of General Fund revenues upon which the budget bill for that fiscal year, as enacted, was based, or General Fund expenditures will increase substantially above that estimate of General Fund revenues, or both, the Governor may issue a proclamation declaring a fiscal emergency and shall thereupon cause the Legislature to assemble in special session for this purpose. The proclamation shall identify the nature of the fiscal emergency and shall be submitted by the Governor to the Legislature, accompanied by proposed legislation to address the fiscal emergency.

(2) If the Legislature fails to pass and send to the Governor a bill or bills to address the fiscal emergency by the 45th day following the issuance of the proclamation, the Legislature may not act on any other bill, nor may the Legislature adjourn for a joint recess, until that bill or those bills have been passed and sent to the Governor.

(3) A bill addressing the fiscal emergency declared pursuant to this section shall contain a statement to that effect. [*As amended March 2, 2004.*]

[*Committees*]

SEC. 11.   The Legislature or either house may by resolution provide for the selection of committees necessary for the conduct of its business, including committees to ascertain facts and make recommendations to the Legislature on a subject within the scope of legislative control. [*As amended November 7, 1972.*]

[*Governor's Budget—Budget Bill—Other Appropriations*]

SEC. 12.   (a) Within the first 10 days of each calendar year, the Governor shall submit to the Legislature, with an explanatory message, a budget for the ensuing fiscal year containing itemized statements for recommended state expenditures and estimated state revenues. If recommended expenditures exceed estimated revenues, the Governor shall recommend the sources from which the additional revenues should be provided.

(b) The Governor and the Governor-elect may require a state agency, officer or employee to furnish whatever information is deemed necessary to prepare the budget.

(c) (1) The budget shall be accompanied by a budget bill itemizing recommended expenditures.

(2) The budget bill shall be introduced immediately in each house by the persons chairing the committees that consider the budget.

(3) The Legislature shall pass the budget bill by midnight on June 15 of each year.

(4) Until the budget bill has been enacted, the Legislature shall not send to the Governor for consideration any bill appropriating funds for expenditure during the fiscal year for which the budget bill is to be enacted, except emergency bills recommended by the Governor or appropriations for the salaries and expenses of the Legislature.

(d) No bill except the budget bill may contain more than one item of appropriation, and that for one certain, expressed purpose. Appropriations from the General Fund of the State, except appropriations for the public schools and appropriations in the budget bill and in other bills providing for appropriations related to the budget bill, are void unless passed in each house by rollcall vote entered in the journal, two-thirds of the membership concurring.

(e) (1) Notwithstanding any other provision of law or of this Constitution, the budget bill and other bills providing for appropriations related to the budget bill may be passed in each house by rollcall vote entered in the journal, a majority of the membership concurring, to take effect immediately upon being signed by the Governor or upon a date specified in the legislation. Nothing in this subdivision shall affect the vote requirement for appropriations for the public schools contained in subdivision (d) of this section and in subdivision (b) of Section 8 of this article.

(2) For purposes of this section, "other bills providing for appropriations related to the budget bill" shall consist only of bills identified as related to the budget in the budget bill passed by the Legislature.

(f) The Legislature may control the submission, approval, and enforcement of budgets and the filing of claims for all state agencies.

(g) For the 2004–05 fiscal year, or any subsequent fiscal year, the Legislature may not send to the Governor for consideration, nor may the Governor sign into law, a budget bill that would appropriate from the General Fund, for that fiscal year, a total amount that, when combined with all appropriations from the General Fund for that fiscal year made as of the date of the budget bill's passage, and the amount of any General Fund moneys transferred to the Budget Stabilization Account for that fiscal year pursuant to Section 20 of Article XVI, exceeds General Fund revenues for that fiscal year estimated as of the date of the budget bill's passage. That estimate of General Fund revenues shall be set forth in the budget bill passed by the Legislature.

(h) Notwithstanding any other provision of law or of this Constitution, including subdivision (c) of this section, Section 4 of this article, and Sections 4 and 8 of Article III, in any year in which the budget bill is not passed by the Legislature by midnight on June 15, there shall be no appropriation from the current budget or future budget to pay any salary or reimbursement for travel or living expenses for Members of the Legislature during any regular or special session for the period from midnight on June 15 until the day that the budget bill is presented to the Governor. No salary or reimbursement for travel or living expenses forfeited pursuant to this subdivision shall be paid retroactively. [*As amended November 2, 2010. Initiative measure.*]

[*General Fund—Revenues and Expenditures—Estimates*]

SEC. 12.5.   Within 10 days following the submission of a budget pursuant to subdivision (a) of Section 12, following the proposed adjustments to the Governor's Budget required by subdivision (e) of Section 13308 of the Government Code or a successor statute, and following the enactment of the budget bill, or as soon as feasible thereafter, the Director of Finance shall submit to the Legislature both of the following:

(a) Estimates of General Fund revenues for the ensuing fiscal year and for the three fiscal years thereafter.

(b) Estimates of General Fund expenditures for the ensuing fiscal year and for the three fiscal years thereafter. [*New section adopted November 4, 2014.*]

[*Legislators—Ineligible for Certain Offices*]

SEC. 13.   A member of the Legislature may not, during the term for which the member is elected, hold any office or employment under the State other than an elective office. [*As amended November 5, 1974.*]

SEC. 14.   [*Repealed November 8, 1966. See Section 14, below.*]

[*Members—Not Subject to Civil Process*]

SEC. 14.   A member of the Legislature is not subject to civil process during a session of the Legislature or for 5 days before and after a session. [*New section adopted November 8, 1966.*]

[*Influencing Action or Vote of a Member—Felony*]

SEC. 15.   A person who seeks to influence the vote or action of a member of the Legislature in the member's legislative capacity by bribery, promise of reward, intimidation, or other dishonest means, or a member of the Legislature so influenced, is guilty of a felony. [*As amended November 5, 1974.*]

[Uniform Operation of General Laws—Special Statute—Invalid]

SEC. 16.   (a) All laws of a general nature have uniform operation.

(b) A local or special statute is invalid in any case if a general statute can be made applicable. [*As amended November 5, 1974.*]

SEC. 17.   [*Repealed November 8, 1966. See Section 17, below.*]

[Grant of Extra Compensation or Allowance Prohibited]

SEC. 17.   The Legislature has no power to grant, or to authorize a city, county, or other public body to grant, extra compensation or extra allowance to a public officer, public employee, or contractor after service has been rendered or a contract has been entered into and performed in whole or in part, or to authorize the payment of a claim against the State or a city, county, or other public body under an agreement made without authority of law. [*New section adopted November 8, 1966.*]

SEC. 18.   [*Repealed November 8, 1966. See Section 18, below.*]

[Impeachment]

SEC. 18.   (a) The Assembly has the sole power of impeachment. Impeachments shall be tried by the Senate. A person may not be convicted unless, by rollcall vote entered in the journal, two thirds of the membership of the Senate concurs.

(b) State officers elected on a statewide basis, members of the State Board of Equalization, and judges of state courts are subject to impeachment for misconduct in office. Judgment may extend only to removal from office and disqualification to hold any office under the State, but the person convicted or acquitted remains subject to criminal punishment according to law. [*New section adopted November 8, 1966.*]

[Lotteries—Horse Races Regulated—Bingo Games and Raffles for Charitable Purposes—Gaming on Tribal Lands]

SEC. 19.   (a) The Legislature has no power to authorize lotteries and shall prohibit the sale of lottery tickets in the State.

(b) The Legislature may provide for the regulation of horse races and horse race meetings and wagering on the results.

(c) Notwithstanding subdivision (a), the Legislature by statute may authorize cities and counties to provide for bingo games, but only for charitable purposes.

(d) Notwithstanding subdivision (a), there is authorized the establishment of a California State Lottery.

(e) The Legislature has no power to authorize, and shall prohibit, casinos of the type currently operating in Nevada and New Jersey.

(f)* Notwithstanding subdivisions (a) and (e), and any other provision of state law, the Governor is authorized to negotiate and conclude compacts, subject to ratification by the Legislature, for the operation of slot machines and for the conduct of lottery games and banking and percentage card games by federally recognized Indian tribes on Indian lands in California in accordance with federal law. Accordingly, slot machines, lottery games, and banking and percentage card games are hereby permitted to be conducted and operated on tribal lands subject to those compacts.

(f)† Notwithstanding subdivision (a), the Legislature may authorize private, nonprofit, eligible organizations, as defined by the Legislature, to conduct raffles as a funding mechanism to provide support for their own or another private, nonprofit, eligible organization's beneficial and charitable works, provided that (1) at least 90 percent of the gross receipts from the raffle go directly to beneficial or charitable purposes in California, and (2) any person who receives compensation in connection with the operation of a raffle is an employee of the private nonprofit organization that is conducting the raffle. The Legislature, two-thirds of the membership of each house concurring, may amend the percentage of gross receipts required by this subdivision to be dedicated to beneficial or charitable purposes by means of a statute that is signed by the Governor. [*As amended March 7, 2000.*]

SEC. 20. [*Repealed November 8, 1966. See Section 20, below.*]

[Fish and Game—Districts and Commission]

SEC. 20. (a) The Legislature may provide for division of the State into fish and game districts and may protect fish and game in districts or parts of districts.

(b) There is a Fish and Game Commission of 5 members appointed by the Governor and approved by the Senate, a majority of the membership concurring, for 6-year terms and until their successors are appointed and qualified. Appointment to fill a vacancy is for the unexpired portion of the term. The Legislature may delegate to the commission such powers relating to the protection and propagation of fish and game as the Legislature sees fit. A member of the commission may be removed by concurrent resolution adopted by each house, a majority of the membership concurring. [*New section adopted November 8, 1966.*]

[War- or Enemy-Caused Disaster]

SEC. 21. To meet the needs resulting from war-caused or enemy-caused disaster in California, the Legislature may provide for:

---

* Ballot Proposition 1A (SCA 11) March 7, 2000.
† Ballot Proposition 17 (SCA 4) March 7, 2000.

(a) Filling the offices of members of the Legislature should at least one fifth of the membership of either house be killed, missing, or disabled, until they are able to perform their duties or successors are elected.

(b) Filling the office of Governor should the Governor be killed, missing, or disabled, until the Governor or the successor designated in this Constitution is able to perform the duties of the office of Governor or a successor is elected.

(c) Convening the Legislature.

(d) Holding elections to fill offices that are elective under this Constitution and that are either vacant or occupied by persons not elected thereto.

(e) Selecting a temporary seat of state or county government. [*As amended November 5, 1974.*]

[*Accountability—Session Goals and Objectives*]

SEC. 22.   It is the right of the people to hold their legislators accountable. To assist the people in exercising this right, at the convening of each regular session of the Legislature, the President pro Tempore of the Senate, the Speaker of the Assembly, and the minority leader of each house shall report to their house the goals and objectives of that house during that session and, at the close of each regular session, the progress made toward meeting those goals and objectives. [*New section adopted June 5, 1990.*]

SEC. 22a.   [*Repealed November 8, 1966.*]

SEC. 23.   [*Renumbered Section 9 of Article II June 8, 1976.*]

SEC. 23a.   [*Repealed November 8, 1966.*]

SEC. 23b.   [*Repealed November 8, 1966.*]

SEC. 24.   [*Renumbered Section 10 of Article II June 8, 1976.*]

SEC. 25.   [*Renumbered Section 11 of Article II June 8, 1976.*]

SEC. 25a.   [*Repealed November 8, 1966.*]

SEC. 25½.   [*Repealed November 8, 1966.*]

SEC. 25⅝.   [*Renumbered Section 22 of Article XIII and amended November 8, 1966.*]

SEC. 25¾.   [*Renumbered Section 25.7 and amended November 6, 1962.*]

SEC. 25.7.   [*Repealed November 8, 1966.*]

SEC. 26.   [*Renumbered Section 12 of Article II June 8, 1976.*]

SEC. 27.   [*Repealed June 3, 1980.*]

[*State Capitol Maintenance—Appropriations*]

SEC. 28.   (a) Notwithstanding any other provision of this Constitution, no bill shall take effect as an urgency statute if it authorizes or contains an appropriation for either (1) the alteration or modification of the color, detail, design, structure or fixtures of the historically restored areas of the first, second, and third floors and the exterior of the west wing of the State Capitol from that existing upon the completion of the project of restoration or rehabilitation of the building conducted pursuant to Section 9124 of the Government Code as such section read upon the effective date of this section, or (2) the purchase of furniture of different design to replace that restored, replicated, or designed to conform to the historic period of the historically restored areas specified above, including the legislators' chairs and desks in the Senate and Assembly Chambers.

(b) No expenditures shall be made in payment for any of the purposes described in subdivision (a) of this section unless funds are appropriated expressly for such purposes.

(c) This section shall not apply to appropriations or expenditures for ordinary repair and maintenance of the State Capitol building, fixtures and furniture. [*New Section adopted June 3, 1980.*]

SEC. 29. [*Renumbered Section 23 of Article XIII and amended November 8, 1966.*]

SEC. 30. [*Renumbered Section 24 of Article XIII and amended November 8, 1966.*]

SEC. 31. [*Renumbered Section 25 of Article XIII and amended November 8, 1966.*]

SEC. 31a. [*Renumbered Section 26 of Article XIII and amended November 8, 1966.*]

SEC. 31b. [*As adopted by Assembly Constitutional Amendment 14 of 1931, repealed November 6, 1956.*]

SEC. 31b. [*As adopted November 8, 1932, renumbered Section 27 of Article XIII and amended November 8, 1966.*]

SEC. 31c. [*As adopted November 3, 1936, renumbered Section 28 of Article XIII and amended November 8, 1966.*]

SEC. 31c. [*As adopted November 3, 1942, repealed November 6, 1956.*]

SEC. 31d. [*Repealed November 6, 1956.*]

SEC. 32. [*Repealed November 8, 1966.*]

SEC. 33. [*Repealed November 8, 1966.*]

SEC. 34. [*Repealed November 8, 1966.*]

SEC. 34a. [*Repealed November 8, 1966.*]

SEC. 35. [*Repealed November 8, 1966.*]

SEC. 36. [*Repealed November 8, 1966.*]

SEC. 37. [*Repealed November 8, 1966.*]

SEC. 38. [*Repealed November 8, 1966.*]

ARTICLE V. [*Repealed November 8, 1966. See Article V, below.*]

ARTICLE V *

EXECUTIVE

[*Executive Power Vested in Governor*]

SECTION 1.   The supreme executive power of this State is vested in the Governor. The Governor shall see that the law is faithfully executed. [*As amended November 5, 1974.*]

[*Election—Eligibility—Number of Terms*]

SEC. 2.   The Governor shall be elected every fourth year at the same time and places as members of the Assembly and hold office from the Monday after January 1 following the election until a successor qualifies. The Governor shall be an elector who has been a citizen of the United States and a resident of this State for 5 years immediately preceding the Governor's election. The Governor may not hold other public office. No Governor may serve more than 2 terms. [*As amended November 6, 1990. Initiative measure.*]

[*Report to Legislature—Recommendations*]

SEC. 3.   The Governor shall report to the Legislature each calendar year on the condition of the State and may make recommendations. [*As amended November 7, 1972.*]

SEC. 4.   [*Repealed November 8, 1966. See Section 4, below.*]

[*Information From Executive Officers, Etc.*]

SEC. 4.   The Governor may require executive officers and agencies and their employees to furnish information relating to their duties. [*New section adopted November 8, 1966.*]

[*Filling Vacancies—Confirmation by Legislature*]

SEC. 5.   (a) Unless the law otherwise provides, the Governor may fill a vacancy in office by appointment until a successor qualifies.

(b) Whenever there is a vacancy in the office of the Superintendent of Public Instruction, the Lieutenant Governor, Secretary of State, Controller, Treasurer, or Attorney General, or on the State Board of Equalization, the Governor shall nominate a person to fill the vacancy who shall take office upon confirmation by a majority of the membership of the Senate and a majority of the membership of the Assembly and who shall hold office for the balance of the unexpired term. In the event the nominee is neither confirmed nor refused confirmation by both the Senate and the Assembly within 90 days of the submission of the nomination, the nominee shall take office as if he or she had been confirmed by a majority of the Senate and

---

* New Article V adopted November 8, 1966.

Assembly; provided, that if such 90-day period ends during a recess of the Legislature, the period shall be extended until the sixth day following the day on which the Legislature reconvenes. [*As amended November 2, 1976.*]

SEC. 6. [*Repealed November 8, 1966. See Section 6, below.*]

[*Executive Assignment and Agency Reorganization*]

SEC. 6. Authority may be provided by statute for the Governor to assign and reorganize functions among executive officers and agencies and their employees, other than elective officers and agencies administered by elective officers. [*New section adopted November 8, 1966.*]

[*Commander of Militia*]

SEC. 7. The Governor is commander in chief of a militia that shall be provided by statute. The Governor may call it forth to execute the law. [*As amended November 5, 1974.*]

[*Reprieves—Pardons—Commutations*]

SEC. 8. (a) Subject to application procedures provided by statute, the Governor, on conditions the Governor deems proper, may grant a reprieve, pardon, and commutation, after sentence, except in case of impeachment. The Governor shall report to the Legislature each reprieve, pardon, and commutation granted, stating the pertinent facts and the reasons for granting it. The Governor may not grant a pardon or commutation to a person twice convicted of a felony except on recommendation of the Supreme Court, 4 judges concurring.

(b) No decision of the parole authority of this State with respect to the granting, denial, revocation, or suspension of parole of a person sentenced to an indeterminate term upon conviction of murder shall become effective for a period of 30 days, during which the Governor may review the decision subject to procedures provided by statute. The Governor may only affirm, modify, or reverse the decision of the parole authority on the basis of the same factors which the parole authority is required to consider. The Governor shall report to the Legislature each parole decision affirmed, modified, or reversed, stating the pertinent facts and reasons for the action. [*As amended November 8, 1988.*]

[*Lieutenant Governor—Qualifications—Casting Vote*]

SEC. 9. The Lieutenant Governor shall have the same qualifications as the Governor. The Lieutenant Governor is President of the Senate but has only a casting vote. [*As amended November 5, 1974.*]

[*Succession*]

SEC. 10. The Lieutenant Governor shall become Governor when a vacancy occurs in the office of Governor.

The Lieutenant Governor shall act as Governor during the impeachment, absence from the State, or other temporary disability of the Governor or of a Governor-elect who fails to take office.

The Legislature shall provide an order of precedence after the Lieutenant Governor for succession to the office of Governor and for the temporary exercise of the Governor's functions.

The Supreme Court has exclusive jurisdiction to determine all questions arising under this section.

Standing to raise questions of vacancy or temporary disability is vested exclusively in a body provided by statute. [*As amended November 5, 1974.*]

[Other State Officers—Election—Number of Terms]

SEC. 11.   The Lieutenant Governor, Attorney General, Controller, Secretary of State, and Treasurer shall be elected at the same time and places and for the same term as the Governor. No Lieutenant Governor, Attorney General, Controller, Secretary of State, or Treasurer may serve in the same office for more than 2 terms. [*As amended November 6, 1990. Initiative measure.*]

SEC. 12.   [*Repealed June 5, 1990.*]

[Attorney General—Chief Law Officer]

SEC. 13.   Subject to the powers and duties of the Governor, the Attorney General shall be the chief law officer of the State. It shall be the duty of the Attorney General to see that the laws of the State are uniformly and adequately enforced. The Attorney General shall have direct supervision over every district attorney and sheriff and over such other law enforcement officers as may be designated by law, in all matters pertaining to the duties of their respective offices, and may require any of said officers to make reports concerning the investigation, detection, prosecution, and punishment of crime in their respective jurisdictions as to the Attorney General may seem advisable. Whenever in the opinion of the Attorney General any law of the State is not being adequately enforced in any county, it shall be the duty of the Attorney General to prosecute any violations of law of which the superior court shall have jurisdiction, and in such cases the Attorney General shall have all the powers of a district attorney. When required by the public interest or directed by the Governor, the Attorney General shall assist any district attorney in the discharge of the duties of that office. [*As amended November 5, 1974.*]

[State Officers—Conflict of Interest—Prohibited Compensation—Earned Income]

SEC. 14.   (a) To eliminate any appearance of a conflict with the proper discharge of his or her duties and responsibilities, no state officer may knowingly receive any salary, wages, commissions, or other similar earned income from a lobbyist or lobbying firm, as defined by the Political Reform Act of 1974, or from a person who, during the previous 12 months, has been under a contract with the state agency under the jurisdiction of the state officer. The Legislature shall enact laws that define earned income. However, earned income does not include any community property interest in the income of a spouse. Any state officer who knowingly receives any salary, wages, commissions, or other similar earned income from a lobbyist employer, as defined by the Political Reform Act of 1974, may not, for a period of one year following its receipt, vote upon or make, participate in making, or in any way attempt to use his or her official position to influence an action or decision before the agency for which the state officer serves, other than an action or decision involving a bill described in subdivision (c) of Section 12 of Article IV, which he or she knows, or has reason to know, would have a direct and significant financial impact on the lobbyist employer and would not impact the public generally or a significant segment of the public in a similar manner. As used in this subdivision, "public generally" includes an industry, trade, or profession.

[*State Officers—Honoraria*]

(b) No state officer may accept any honorarium. The Legislature shall enact laws that implement this subdivision.

[*State Officers—Gifts—Conflict of Interest*]

(c) The Legislature shall enact laws that ban or strictly limit the acceptance of a gift by a state officer from any source if the acceptance of the gift might create a conflict of interest.

[*State Officers—Prohibited Compensation or Activity*]

(d) No state officer may knowingly accept any compensation for appearing, agreeing to appear, or taking any other action on behalf of another person before any state government board or agency. If a state officer knowingly accepts any compensation for appearing, agreeing to appear, or taking any other action on behalf of another person before any local government board or agency, the state officer may not, for a period of one year following the acceptance of the compensation, make, participate in making, or in any way attempt to use his or her official position to influence an action or decision before the state agency for which the state officer serves, other than an action or decision involving a bill described in subdivision (c) of Section 12 of Article IV, which he or she knows, or has reason to know, would have a direct and significant financial impact on that person and would not impact the public generally or a significant segment of the public in a similar manner. As used in this subdivision, "public generally" includes an industry, trade, or profession. However, a state officer may engage in activities involving a board or agency which are strictly on his or her own behalf, appear in the capacity of an attorney before any court or the Workers' Compensation Appeals Board, or act as an advocate without compensation or make an inquiry for information on behalf of a person before a board or agency. This subdivision does not prohibit any action of a partnership or firm of which the state officer is a member if the state officer does not share directly or indirectly in the fee, less any expenses attributable to that fee, resulting from that action.

[*State Officers—Lobbying*]

(e) The Legislature shall enact laws that prohibit a state officer, or a secretary of an agency or director of a department appointed by the Governor, who has not resigned or retired from state service prior to January 7, 1991, from lobbying, for compensation, as governed by the Political Reform Act of 1974, before the executive branch of state government for 12 months after leaving office.

[*State Officer—Definition*]

(f) "State officer," as used in this section, means the Governor, Lieutenant Governor, Attorney General, Controller, Insurance Commissioner, Secretary of State, Superintendent of Public Instruction, Treasurer, and member of the State Board of Equalization. [*New section adopted June 5, 1990. Subdivision (b) operative December 3, 1990.*]

SEC. 15. [*Repealed November 8, 1966.*]
SEC. 16. [*Repealed November 8, 1966.*]
SEC. 17. [*Repealed November 8, 1966.*]
SEC. 18. [*Repealed November 8, 1966.*]
SEC. 20. [*Repealed November 8, 1966.*]
SEC. 21. [*Repealed November 8, 1966.*]
SEC. 22. [*Repealed November 8, 1966.*]

ARTICLE VI.   [*Repealed November 8, 1966. See Article VI, below.*]

ARTICLE VI*

JUDICIAL

[*Judicial Power Vested in Courts*]

SECTION 1. The judicial power of this State is vested in the Supreme Court, courts of appeal, and superior courts, all of which are courts of record. [*As amended November 5, 2002.*]

SEC. 1a. [*Repealed November 8, 1966.*]
SEC. 1b. [*Repealed November 8, 1966.*]
SEC. 1c. [*Repealed November 8, 1966.*]

---

*New Article VI adopted November 8, 1966.

[*Supreme Court—Composition*]

SEC. 2. The Supreme Court consists of the Chief Justice of California and 6 associate justices. The Chief Justice may convene the court at any time. Concurrence of 4 judges present at the argument is necessary for a judgment.

An acting Chief Justice shall perform all functions of the Chief Justice when the Chief Justice is absent or unable to act. The Chief Justice or, if the Chief Justice fails to do so, the court shall select an associate justice as acting Chief Justice. [*As amended November 5, 1974.*]

[*Judicial Districts—Courts of Appeal*]

SEC. 3. The Legislature shall divide the State into districts each containing a court of appeal with one or more divisions. Each division consists of a presiding justice and 2 or more associate justices. It has the power of a court of appeal and shall conduct itself as a 3-judge court. Concurrence of 2 judges present at the argument is necessary for a judgment.

An acting presiding justice shall perform all functions of the presiding justice when the presiding justice is absent or unable to act. The presiding justice or, if the presiding justice fails to do so, the Chief Justice shall select an associate justice of that division as acting presiding justice. [*As amended November 5, 1974.*]

[*Superior Courts*]

SEC. 4. In each county there is a superior court of one or more judges. The Legislature shall prescribe the number of judges and provide for the officers and employees of each superior court. If the governing body of each affected county concurs, the Legislature may provide that one or more judges serve more than one superior court.

In each superior court there is an appellate division. The Chief Justice shall assign judges to the appellate division for specified terms pursuant to rules, not inconsistent with statute, adopted by the Judicial Council to promote the independence of the appellate division. [*As amended June 2, 1998.*]

SEC. 4a. [*Repealed November 8, 1966.*]

SEC. 4b. [*Repealed November 8, 1966.*]

SEC. 4c. [*Repealed November 8, 1966.*]

SEC. 4d. [*Repealed November 8, 1966.*]

SEC. 4e. [*Repealed November 8, 1966.*]

SEC. 4½. [*Repealed November 8, 1966.*]

SEC. 4¾. [*Repealed November 8, 1966.*]

SEC. 5. [*Repealed November 5, 2002.*]

SEC. 5.5. [*Repealed June 8, 1976.*]

[Judicial Council—Membership and Powers]

SEC. 6.   (a) The Judicial Council consists of the Chief Justice and one other judge of the Supreme Court, three judges of courts of appeal, 10 judges of superior courts, two nonvoting court administrators, and any other nonvoting members as determined by the voting membership of the council, each appointed by the Chief Justice for a three-year term pursuant to procedures established by the council; four members of the State Bar appointed by its governing body for three-year terms; and one member of each house of the Legislature appointed as provided by the house.

(b) Council membership terminates if a member ceases to hold the position that qualified the member for appointment. A vacancy shall be filled by the appointing power for the remainder of the term.

(c) The council may appoint an Administrative Director of the Courts, who serves at its pleasure and performs functions delegated by the council or the Chief Justice, other than adopting rules of court administration, practice and procedure.

(d) To improve the administration of justice the council shall survey judicial business and make recommendations to the courts, make recommendations annually to the Governor and Legislature, adopt rules for court administration, practice and procedure, and perform other functions prescribed by statute. The rules adopted shall not be inconsistent with statute.

(e) The Chief Justice shall seek to expedite judicial business and to equalize the work of judges. The Chief Justice may provide for the assignment of any judge to another court but only with the judge's consent if the court is of lower jurisdiction. A retired judge who consents may be assigned to any court.

(f) Judges shall report to the council as the Chief Justice directs concerning the condition of judicial business in their courts. They shall cooperate with the council and hold court as assigned. [*As amended November 5, 2002.*]

SEC. 7.   [*Repealed November 8, 1966. See Section 7, below.*]

[Commission on Judicial Appointments—Membership]

SEC. 7.   The Commission on Judicial Appointments consists of the Chief Justice, the Attorney General, and the presiding justice of the court of appeal of the affected district or, if there are 2 or more presiding justices, the one who has presided longest or, when a nomination or appointment to the Supreme Court is to be considered, the presiding justice who has presided longest on any court of appeal. [*New section adopted November 8, 1966.*]

[Commission on Judicial Performance—Membership]

SEC. 8.   (a) The Commission on Judicial Performance consists of one judge of a court of appeal and two judges of superior courts, each appointed by the Supreme Court; two members of the State Bar of California who have practiced law in this State for 10 years, each appointed by the Governor; and six citizens who are not judges, retired judges, or members of the State Bar of California, two of whom shall be appointed by the Governor, two by the Senate Committee on Rules, and two by the Speaker of the Assembly. Except as provided in subdivisions (b) and (c), all terms are for four years. No member shall serve more than two four-year terms, or for more than a total of 10 years if appointed to fill a vacancy.

(b) Commission membership terminates if a member ceases to hold the position that qualified the member for appointment. A vacancy shall be filled by the appointing power for the remainder of the term. A member whose term has expired may continue to serve until the vacancy has been filled by the appointing power. Appointing powers may appoint members who are already serving on the commission prior to March 1, 1995, to a single two-year term, but may not appoint them to an additional term thereafter.

(c) To create staggered terms among the members of the Commission on Judicial Performance, the following members shall be appointed, as follows:

(1) Two members appointed by the Supreme Court to a term commencing March 1, 1995, shall each serve a term of two years and may be reappointed to one full term.

(2) One attorney appointed by the Governor to a term commencing March 1, 1995, shall serve a term of two years and may be reappointed to one full term.

(3) One citizen member appointed by the Governor to a term commencing March 1, 1995, shall serve a term of two years and may be reappointed to one full term.

(4) One member appointed by the Senate Committee on Rules to a term commencing March 1, 1995, shall serve a term of two years and may be reappointed to one full term.

(5) One member appointed by the Speaker of the Assembly to a term commencing March 1, 1995, shall serve a term of two years and may be reappointed to one full term.

(6) All other members shall be appointed to full four-year terms commencing March 1, 1995. [*As amended November 5, 2002.*]

SEC. 9.   [*Repealed November 8, 1966. See Section 9, below.*]

[*State Bar*]

SEC. 9.   The State Bar of California is a public corporation. Every person admitted and licensed to practice law in this State is and shall be a member of the State Bar except while holding office as a judge of a court of record. [*New section adopted November 8, 1966.*]

SEC. 10.   [*Repealed November 8, 1966. See Section 10, below.*]

[Jurisdiction—Original]

SEC. 10.   The Supreme Court, courts of appeal, superior courts, and their judges have original jurisdiction in habeas corpus proceedings. Those courts also have original jurisdiction in proceedings for extraordinary relief in the nature of mandamus, certiorari, and prohibition. The appellate division of the superior court has original jurisdiction in proceedings for extraordinary relief in the nature of mandamus, certiorari, and prohibition directed to the superior court in causes subject to its appellate jurisdiction. Superior courts have original jurisdiction in all other causes.

The court may make any comment on the evidence and the testimony and credibility of any witness as in its opinion is necessary for the proper determination of the cause. [*As amended November 5, 2002.*]

SEC. 10a.   [*Repealed November 8, 1966.*]

SEC. 10b.   [*Repealed November 8, 1966.*]

[Jurisdiction—Appellate]

SEC. 11.   (a) The Supreme Court has appellate jurisdiction when judgment of death has been pronounced. With that exception courts of appeal have appellate jurisdiction when superior courts have original jurisdiction in causes of a type within the appellate jurisdiction of the courts of appeal on June 30, 1995, and in other causes prescribed by statute. When appellate jurisdiction in civil causes is determined by the amount in controversy, the Legislature may change the appellate jurisdiction of the courts of appeal by changing the jurisdictional amount in controversy.

(b) Except as provided in subdivision (a), the appellate division of the superior court has appellate jurisdiction in causes prescribed by statute.

(c) The Legislature may permit courts exercising appellate jurisdiction to take evidence and make findings of fact when jury trial is waived or not a matter of right. [*As amended June 2, 1998.*]

[Transfer of Causes—Jurisdiction—Review of Decisions]

SEC. 12.   (a) The Supreme Court may, before decision, transfer to itself a cause in a court of appeal. It may, before decision, transfer a cause from itself to a court of appeal or from one court of appeal or division to another. The court to which a cause is transferred has jurisdiction.

(b) The Supreme Court may review the decision of a court of appeal in any cause.

(c) The Judicial Council shall provide, by rules of court, for the time and procedure for transfer and for review, including, among other things, provisions for the time and procedure for transfer with instructions, for review of all or part of a decision, and for remand as improvidently granted.

(d) This section shall not apply to an appeal involving a judgment of death. [*As amended November 6, 1984. Operative May 6, 1985.*]

[Judgment—When Set Aside]

SEC. 13. No judgment shall be set aside, or new trial granted, in any cause, on the ground of misdirection of the jury, or of the improper admission or rejection of evidence, or for any error as to any matter of pleading, or for any error as to any matter of procedure, unless, after an examination of the entire cause, including the evidence, the court shall be of the opinion that the error complained of has resulted in a miscarriage of justice. [*New section adopted November 8, 1966.*]

SEC. 14. [*Repealed November 8, 1966. See Section 14, below.*]

[Supreme Court and Appellate Court—Published Opinions]

SEC. 14. The Legislature shall provide for the prompt publication of such opinions of the Supreme Court and courts of appeal as the Supreme Court deems appropriate, and those opinions shall be available for publication by any person.

Decisions of the Supreme Court and courts of appeal that determine causes shall be in writing with reasons stated. [*New section adopted November 8, 1966.*]

[Judges—Eligibility]

SEC. 15. A person is ineligible to be a judge of a court of record unless for 10 years immediately preceding selection, the person has been a member of the State Bar or served as a judge of a court of record in this State. [*As amended November 5, 2002.*]

SEC. 15.5. [*Repealed January 1, 1995.*]

[Judges—Elections—Terms—Vacancies]

SEC. 16. (a) Judges of the Supreme Court shall be elected at large and judges of courts of appeal shall be elected in their districts at general elections at the same time and places as the Governor. Their terms are 12 years beginning the Monday after January 1 following their election, except that a judge elected to an unexpired term serves the remainder of the term. In creating a new court of appeal district or division the Legislature shall provide that the first elective terms are 4, 8, and 12 years.

(b) Judges of superior courts shall be elected in their counties at general elections except as otherwise necessary to meet the requirements of federal law. In the latter case the Legislature, by two-thirds vote of the membership of each house thereof, with the advice of judges within the affected court, may provide for their election by the system prescribed in subdivision (d), or by any other arrangement. The Legislature may provide that an unopposed incumbent's name not appear on the ballot.

(c) Terms of judges of superior courts are six years beginning the Monday after January 1 following their election. A vacancy shall be filled by election to a full term at the next general election after the second January

1 following the vacancy, but the Governor shall appoint a person to fill the vacancy temporarily until the elected judge's term begins.

(d) (1) Within 30 days before August 16 preceding the expiration of the judge's term, a judge of the Supreme Court or a court of appeal may file a declaration of candidacy to succeed to the office presently held by the judge. If the declaration is not filed, the Governor before September 16 shall nominate a candidate. At the next general election, only the candidate so declared or nominated may appear on the ballot, which shall present the question whether the candidate shall be elected. The candidate shall be elected upon receiving a majority of the votes on the question. A candidate not elected may not be appointed to that court but later may be nominated and elected.

(2) The Governor shall fill vacancies in those courts by appointment. An appointee holds office until the Monday after January 1 following the first general election at which the appointee had the right to become a candidate or until an elected judge qualifies. A nomination or appointment by the Governor is effective when confirmed by the Commission on Judicial Appointments.

(3) Electors of a county, by majority of those voting and in a manner the Legislature shall provide, may make this system of selection applicable to judges of superior courts. [As amended November 5, 2002.]

[Judges—Restrictions, Other Employment, and Benefits]

SEC. 17.   A judge of a court of record may not practice law and during the term for which the judge was selected is ineligible for public employment or public office other than judicial employment or judicial office, except a judge of a court of record may accept a part-time teaching position that is outside the normal hours of his or her judicial position and that does not interfere with the regular performance of his or her judicial duties while holding office. A judge of a trial court of record may, however, become eligible for election to other public office by taking a leave of absence without pay prior to filing a declaration of candidacy. Acceptance of the public office is a resignation from the office of judge.

A judicial officer may not receive fines or fees for personal use.

A judicial officer may not earn retirement service credit from a public teaching position while holding judicial office. [As amended November 8, 1988.]

[Judges—Discipline]

SEC. 18.   (a) A judge is disqualified from acting as a judge, without loss of salary, while there is pending (1) an indictment or an information charging the judge in the United States with a crime punishable as a felony under California or federal law, or (2) a petition to the Supreme Court to review a determination by the Commission on Judicial Performance to remove or retire a judge.

(b) The Commission on Judicial Performance may disqualify a judge from acting as a judge, without loss of salary, upon notice of formal proceedings by the commission charging the judge with judicial misconduct or disability.

(c) The Commission on Judicial Performance shall suspend a judge from office without salary when in the United States the judge pleads guilty or no contest or is found guilty of a crime punishable as a felony under California or federal law or of any other crime that involves moral turpitude under that law. If the conviction is reversed, suspension terminates, and the judge shall be paid the salary for the judicial office held by the judge for the period of suspension. If the judge is suspended and the conviction becomes final, the Commission on Judicial Performance shall remove the judge from office.

(d) Except as provided in subdivision (f), the Commission on Judicial Performance may (1) retire a judge for disability that seriously interferes with the performance of the judge's duties and is or is likely to become permanent, or (2) censure a judge or former judge or remove a judge for action occurring not more than 6 years prior to the commencement of the judge's current term or of the former judge's last term that constitutes willful misconduct in office, persistent failure or inability to perform the judge's duties, habitual intemperance in the use of intoxicants or drugs, or conduct prejudicial to the administration of justice that brings the judicial office into disrepute, or (3) publicly or privately admonish a judge or former judge found to have engaged in an improper action or dereliction of duty. The commission may also bar a former judge who has been censured from receiving an assignment, appointment, or reference of work from any California state court. Upon petition by the judge or former judge, the Supreme Court may, in its discretion, grant review of a determination by the commission to retire, remove, censure, admonish, or disqualify pursuant to subdivision (b) a judge or former judge. When the Supreme Court reviews a determination of the commission, it may make an independent review of the record. If the Supreme Court has not acted within 120 days after granting the petition, the decision of the commission shall be final.

(e) A judge retired by the commission shall be considered to have retired voluntarily. A judge removed by the commission is ineligible for judicial office, including receiving an assignment, appointment, or reference of work from any California state court, and pending further order of the court is suspended from practicing law in this State. The State Bar may institute appropriate attorney disciplinary proceedings against any judge who retires or resigns from office with judicial disciplinary charges pending.

(f) A determination by the Commission on Judicial Performance to admonish or censure a judge or former judge of the Supreme Court or remove or retire a judge of the Supreme Court shall be reviewed by a tribunal of 7 court of appeal judges selected by lot.

(g) No court, except the Supreme Court, shall have jurisdiction in a civil action or other legal proceeding of any sort brought against the commission by a judge. Any request for injunctive relief or other provisional remedy shall be granted or denied within 90 days of the filing of the request for relief. A failure to comply with the time requirements of this section does not affect the validity of commission proceedings.

(h) Members of the commission, the commission staff, and the examiners and investigators employed by the commission shall be absolutely immune from suit for all conduct at any time in the course of their official duties. No civil action may be maintained against a person, or adverse employment action taken against a person, by any employer, public or private, based on statements presented by the person to the commission.

(i) The Commission on Judicial Performance shall make rules implementing this section, including, but not limited to, the following:

(1) The commission shall make rules for the investigation of judges. The commission may provide for the confidentiality of complaints to and investigations by the commission.

(2) The commission shall make rules for formal proceedings against judges when there is cause to believe there is a disability or wrongdoing within the meaning of subdivision (d).

(j) When the commission institutes formal proceedings, the notice of charges, the answer, and all subsequent papers and proceedings shall be open to the public for all formal proceedings instituted after February 28, 1995.

(k) The commission may make explanatory statements.

(*l*) The budget of the commission shall be separate from the budget of any other state agency or court.

(m) The Supreme Court shall make rules for the conduct of judges, both on and off the bench, and for judicial candidates in the conduct of their campaigns. These rules shall be referred to as the Code of Judicial Ethics. [*As amended November 8, 1994. Operative March 1, 1995.*]

[Subordinate Judicial Officers—Discipline]

SEC. 18.1.   The Commission on Judicial Performance shall exercise discretionary jurisdiction with regard to the oversight and discipline of subordinate judicial officers, according to the same standards, and subject to review upon petition to the Supreme Court, as specified in Section 18.

No person who has been found unfit to serve as a subordinate judicial officer after a hearing before the Commission on Judicial Performance shall have the requisite status to serve as a subordinate judicial officer.

This section does not diminish or eliminate the responsibility of a court to exercise initial jurisdiction to discipline or dismiss a subordinate judicial officer as its employee. [*New section adopted June 2, 1998.*]

[*Disciplined Judge Under Consideration for Judicial Appointment*]

SEC. 18.5.   (a) Upon request, the Commission on Judicial Performance shall provide to the Governor of any State of the Union the text of any private admonishment, advisory letter, or other disciplinary action together with any information that the Commission on Judicial Performance deems necessary to a full understanding of the commission's action, with respect to any applicant whom the Governor of any State of the Union indicates is under consideration for any judicial appointment.

(b) Upon request, the Commission on Judicial Performance shall provide the President of the United States the text of any private admonishment, advisory letter, or other disciplinary action together with any information that the Commission on Judicial Performance deems necessary to a full understanding of the commission's action, with respect to any applicant whom the President indicates is under consideration for any federal judicial appointment.

(c) Upon request, the Commission on Judicial Performance shall provide the Commission on Judicial Appointments the text of any private admonishment, advisory letter, or other disciplinary action together with any information that the Commission on Judicial Performance deems necessary to a full understanding of the commission action, with respect to any applicant whom the Commission on Judicial Appointments indicates is under consideration for any judicial appointment.

(d) All information released under this section shall remain confidential and privileged.

(e) Notwithstanding subdivision (d), any information released pursuant to this section shall also be provided to the applicant about whom the information was requested.

(f) "Private admonishment" refers to a disciplinary action against a judge by the Commission on Judicial Performance as authorized by subdivision (c) of Section 18 of Article VI, as amended November 8, 1988. [*New section adopted November 8, 1994. Operative March 1, 1995.*]

[*Judges—Compensation*]

SEC. 19.   The Legislature shall prescribe compensation for judges of courts of record.

A judge of a court of record may not receive the salary for the judicial office held by the judge while any cause before the judge remains pending and undetermined for 90 days after it has been submitted for decision. [*As amended November 5, 1974.*]

SEC. 20.   [*Repealed November 8, 1966. See Section 20, below.*]

[Judges—Retirement—Disability]

SEC. 20.   The Legislature shall provide for retirement, with reasonable allowance, of judges of courts of record for age or disability. [*New section adopted November 8, 1966.*]

SEC. 21.   [*Repealed November 8, 1966. See Section 21, below.*]

[Temporary Judges]

SEC. 21.   On stipulation of the parties litigant the court may order a cause to be tried by a temporary judge who is a member of the State Bar, sworn and empowered to act until final determination of the cause. [*New section adopted November 8, 1966.*]

[Appointment of Officers—Subordinate Judicial Duties]

SEC. 22.   The Legislature may provide for the appointment by trial courts of record of officers such as commissioners to perform subordinate judicial duties. [*New section adopted November 8, 1966.*]

SEC. 23.   [*Repealed November 8, 1966. See Section 23, below.*]

[Superior and Municipal Court Consolidation]

SEC. 23.   (a) The purpose of the amendments to Sections 1, 4, 5, 6, 8, 10, 11, and 16, of this article, and the amendments to Section 16 of Article I, approved at the June 2, 1998, primary election is to permit the Legislature to provide for the abolition of the municipal courts and unify their operations within the superior courts. Notwithstanding Section 8 of Article IV, the implementation of, and orderly transition under, the provisions of the measure adding this section may include urgency statutes that create or abolish offices or change the salaries, terms, or duties of offices, or grant franchises or special privileges, or create vested rights or interests, where otherwise permitted under this Constitution.

(b) When the superior and municipal courts within a county are unified, the judgeships in each municipal court in that county are abolished and the previously selected municipal court judges shall become judges of the superior court in that county. The term of office of a previously selected municipal court judge is not affected by taking office as a judge of the superior court. The 10-year membership or service requirement of Section 15 does not apply to a previously selected municipal court judge. Pursuant to Section 6, the Judicial Council may prescribe appropriate education and training for judges with regard to trial court unification.

(c) Except as provided by statute to the contrary, in any county in which the superior and municipal courts become unified, the following shall occur automatically in each preexisting superior and municipal court:

(1) Previously selected officers, employees, and other personnel who serve the court become the officers and employees of the superior court.

(2) Preexisting court locations are retained as superior court locations.

(3) Preexisting court records become records of the superior court.

(4) Pending actions, trials, proceedings, and other business of the court become pending in the superior court under the procedures previously applicable to the matters in the court in which the matters were pending.

(5) Matters of a type previously within the appellate jurisdiction of the superior court remain within the jurisdiction of the appellate division of the superior court.

(6) Matters of a type previously subject to rehearing by a superior court judge remain subject to rehearing by a superior court judge, other than the judge who originally heard the matter.

(7) Penal Code procedures that necessitate superior court review of, or action based on, a ruling or order by a municipal court judge shall be performed by a superior court judge other than the judge who originally made the ruling or order.

(d) This section shall remain in effect only until January 1, 2007, and as of that date is repealed. [*As amended and repealed November 5, 2002. Repealed on January 1, 2007.*]

SEC. 24.   [*Repealed November 8, 1966.*]

SEC. 26.   [*Repealed November 8, 1966.*]

ARTICLE VII *

PUBLIC OFFICERS AND EMPLOYEES

[Civil Service]

SECTION 1.   (a) The civil service includes every officer and employee of the State except as otherwise provided in this Constitution.

(b) In the civil service permanent appointment and promotion shall be made under a general system based on merit ascertained by competitive examination. [*New section adopted June 8, 1976.*]

[Personnel Board—Membership and Compensation]

SEC. 2.   (a) There is a Personnel Board of 5 members appointed by the Governor and approved by the Senate, a majority of the membership concurring, for 10-year terms and until their successors are appointed and qualified. Appointment to fill a vacancy is for the unexpired portion of the term. A member may be removed by concurrent resolution adopted by each house, two-thirds of the membership of each house concurring.

(b) The board annually shall elect one of its members as presiding officer.

* New Article VII adopted June 8, 1976.

(c) The board shall appoint and prescribe compensation for an executive officer who shall be a member of the civil service but not a member of the board. [*New section adopted June 8, 1976.*]

[*Personnel Board—Duties*]

SEC. 3. (a) The board shall enforce the civil service statutes and, by majority vote of all its members, shall prescribe probationary periods and classifications, adopt other rules authorized by statute, and review disciplinary actions.

(b) The executive officer shall administer the civil service statutes under rules of the board. [*New section adopted June 8, 1976.*]

[*Exempt Positions*]

SEC. 4. The following are exempt from civil service:

(a) Officers and employees appointed or employed by the Legislature, either house, or legislative committees.

(b) Officers and employees appointed or employed by councils, commissions or public corporations in the judicial branch or by a court of record or officer thereof.

(c) Officers elected by the people and a deputy and an employee selected by each elected officer.

(d) Members of boards and commissions.

(e) A deputy or employee selected by each board or commission either appointed by the Governor or authorized by statute.

(f) State officers directly appointed by the Governor with or without the consent or confirmation of the Senate and the employees of the Governor's office, and the employees of the Lieutenant Governor's office directly appointed or employed by the Lieutenant Governor.

(g) A deputy or employee selected by each officer, except members of boards and commissions, exempted under Section 4(f).

(h) Officers and employees of the University of California and the California State Colleges.

(i) The teaching staff of schools under the jurisdiction of the Department of Education or the Superintendent of Public Instruction.

(j) Member, inmate, and patient help in state homes, charitable or correctional institutions, and state facilities for mentally ill or retarded persons.

(k) Members of the militia while engaged in military service.

(*l*) Officers and employees of district agricultural associations employed less than 6 months in a calendar year.

(m) In addition to positions exempted by other provisions of this section, the Attorney General may appoint or employ six deputies or employees, the Public Utilities Commission may appoint or employ one deputy or

employee, and the Legislative Counsel may appoint or employ two deputies or employees. [*New section adopted June 8, 1976.*]

[*Temporary Appointments*]

SEC. 5. A temporary appointment may be made to a position for which
there is no employment list. No person may serve in one or more positions
under temporary appointment longer than 9 months in 12 consecutive
months. [*New section adopted June 8, 1976.*]

[*Veterans' Preferences—Special Rules*]

SEC. 6. (a) The Legislature may provide preferences for veterans and
their surviving spouses.

(b) The board by special rule may permit persons in exempt positions,
brought under civil service by constitutional provision, to qualify to continue in their positions.

(c) When the State undertakes work previously performed by a county,
city, public district of this State or by a federal department or agency, the
board by special rule shall provide for persons who previously performed
this work to qualify to continue in their positions in the state civil service
subject to such minimum standards as may be established by statute. [*New
section adopted June 8, 1976.*]

[*Dual Office Holding*]

SEC. 7. A person holding a lucrative office under the United States or
other power may not hold a civil office of profit. A local officer or postmaster whose compensation does not exceed 500 dollars per year or an
officer in the militia or a member of a reserve component of the armed
forces of the United States except where on active federal duty for more
than 30 days in any year is not a holder of a lucrative office, nor is the holding of a civil office of profit affected by this military service. [*New section
adopted June 8, 1976.*]

[*Disqualification From Holding Office or Serving on Jury—Free Suffrage*]

SEC. 8. (a) Every person shall be disqualified from holding any office
of profit in this State who shall have been convicted of having given or offered a bribe to procure personal election or appointment.

(b) Laws shall be made to exclude persons convicted of bribery, perjury,
forgery, malfeasance in office, or other high crimes from office or serving
on juries. The privilege of free suffrage shall be supported by laws regulating elections and prohibiting, under adequate penalties, all undue influence thereon from power, bribery, tumult, or other improper practice. [*New
section adopted June 8, 1976.*]

[*Persons or Organizations Advocating Overthrow of Government*]

SEC. 9. Notwithstanding any other provision of this Constitution, no
person or organization which advocates the overthrow of the Government

of the United States or the State by force or violence or other unlawful means or who advocates the support of a foreign government against the United States in the event of hostilities shall:

(a) Hold any office or employment under this State, including but not limited to the University of California, or with any county, city or county, city, district, political subdivision, authority, board, bureau, commission or other public agency of this State; or

(b) Receive any exemption from any tax imposed by this State or any county, city or county, city, district, political subdivision, authority, board, bureau, commission or other public agency of this State.

The Legislature shall enact such laws as may be necessary to enforce the provisions of this section. [*New section adopted June 8, 1976.*]

[Elected Officials—Disqualification for Libelous or Slanderous Campaign Statements]

SEC. 10.   (a) No person who is found liable in a civil action for making libelous or slanderous statements against an opposing candidate during the course of an election campaign for any federal, statewide, Board of Equalization, or legislative office or for any county, city and county, city, district, or any other local elective office shall retain the seat to which he or she is elected, where it is established that the libel or slander was a major contributing cause in the defeat of an opposing candidate.

A libelous or slanderous statement shall be deemed to have been made by a person within the meaning of this section if that person actually made the statement or if the person actually or constructively assented to, authorized, or ratified the statement.

"Federal office," as used in this section means the office of United States Senator and Member of the House of Representatives; and to the extent that the provisions of this section do not conflict with any provision of federal law, it is intended that candidates seeking the office of United States Senator or Member of the House of Representatives comply with this section.

(b) In order to determine whether libelous or slanderous statements were a major contributing cause in the defeat of an opposing candidate, the trier of fact shall make a separate, distinct finding on that issue. If the trier of fact finds that libel or slander was a major contributing cause in the defeat of an opposing candidate and that the libelous or slanderous statement was made with knowledge that it was false or with reckless disregard of whether it was false or true, the person holding office shall be disqualified from or shall forfeit that office as provided in subdivision (d). The findings required by this section shall be in writing and shall be incorporated as part of the judgment.

(c) In a case where a person is disqualified from holding office or is required to forfeit an office under subdivisions (a) and (b), that disqualification or forfeiture shall create a vacancy in office, which vacancy shall be filled in the manner provided by law for the filling of a vacancy in that particular office.

(d) Once the judgment of liability is entered by the trial court and the time for filing a notice of appeal has expired, or all possibility of direct attack in the courts of this State has been finally exhausted, the person shall be disqualified from or shall forfeit the office involved in that election and shall have no authority to exercise the powers or perform the duties of the office.

(e) This section shall apply to libelous or slanderous statements made on or after the effective date of this section. [*New section adopted June 5, 1984.*]

[Legislators' and Judges' Retirement Systems]

SEC. 11. (a) The Legislators' Retirement System shall not pay any unmodified retirement allowance or its actuarial equivalent to any person who on or after January 1, 1987, entered for the first time any state office for which membership in the Legislators' Retirement System was elective or to any beneficiary or survivor of such a person, which exceeds the higher of (1) the salary receivable by the person currently serving in the office in which the retired person served or (2) the highest salary that was received by the retired person while serving in that office.

(b) The Judges' Retirement System shall not pay any unmodified retirement allowance or its actuarial equivalent to any person who on or after January 1, 1987, entered for the first time any judicial office subject to the Judges' Retirement System or to any beneficiary or survivor of such a person, which exceeds the higher of (1) the salary receivable by the person currently serving in the judicial office in which the retired person served or (2) the highest salary that was received by the retired person while serving in that judicial office.

(c) The Legislature may define the terms used in this section.

(d) If any part of this measure or the application to any person or circumstance is held invalid, the invalidity shall not affect other provisions or applications which reasonably can be given effect without the invalid provision or application. [*As amended November 6, 1990. Initiative measure.*]

ARTICLE VIII. [*Repealed November 8, 1966.*]

ARTICLE IX

EDUCATION

[Legislative Policy]

SECTION 1. A general diffusion of knowledge and intelligence being essential to the preservation of the rights and liberties of the people, the

Legislature shall encourage by all suitable means the promotion of intellectual, scientific, moral, and agricultural improvement.

[Superintendent of Public Instruction—Election—Date of Office—Number of Terms]

SEC. 2. A Superintendent of Public Instruction shall be elected by the qualified electors of the State at each gubernatorial election. The Superintendent of Public Instruction shall enter upon the duties of the office on the first Monday after the first day of January next succeeding each gubernatorial election. No Superintendent of Public Instruction may serve more than 2 terms. [*As amended November 6, 1990. Initiative measure.*]

[Deputy and Associate Superintendents of Public Instruction]

SEC. 2.1. The State Board of Education, on nomination of the Superintendent of Public Instruction, shall appoint one Deputy Superintendent of Public Instruction and three Associate Superintendents of Public Instruction who shall be exempt from state civil service and whose terms of office shall be four years.

This section shall not be construed as prohibiting the appointment, in accordance with law, of additional Associate Superintendents of Public Instruction subject to state civil service. [*New section adopted November 5, 1946.*]

[County Superintendents of Schools]

SEC. 3. A Superintendent of Schools for each county may be elected by the qualified electors thereof at each gubernatorial election or may be appointed by the county board of education, and the manner of the selection shall be determined by a majority vote of the electors of the county voting on the question; provided, that two or more counties may, by an election conducted pursuant to Section 3.2 of this article, unite for the purpose of electing or appointing one joint superintendent for the counties so uniting. [*As amended November 2, 1976.*]

[County Superintendents of Schools—Qualifications and Salaries]

SEC. 3.1. (a) Notwithstanding any provision of this Constitution to the contrary, the Legislature shall prescribe the qualifications required of county superintendents of schools, and for these purposes shall classify the several counties in the State.

(b) Notwithstanding any provision of this Constitution to the contrary, the county board of education or joint county board of education, as the case may be, shall fix the salary of the county superintendent of schools or the joint county superintendent of schools, respectively. [*As amended November 2, 1976.*]

[Joint County Board of Education — Joint County Superintendent of Schools]

Sec. 3.2.   Notwithstanding any provision of this Constitution to the contrary, any two or more chartered counties, or nonchartered counties, or any combination thereof, may, by a majority vote of the electors of each such county voting on the proposition at an election called for that purpose in each such county, establish one joint board of education and one joint county superintendent of schools for the counties so uniting. A joint county board of education and a joint county superintendent of schools shall be governed by the general statutes and shall not be governed by the provisions of any county charter. *[New section adopted November 2, 1976.]*

[County Boards of Education — Qualifications and Terms of Office]

Sec. 3.3.   Except as provided in Section 3.2 of this article, it shall be competent to provide in any charter framed for a county under any provision of this Constitution, or by the amendment of any such charter, for the election of the members of the county board of education of such county and for their qualifications and terms of office. *[As amended November 2, 1976.]*

Sec. 4.   *[Repealed November 3, 1964.]*

[Common School System]

Sec. 5.   The Legislature shall provide for a system of common schools by which a free school shall be kept up and supported in each district at least six months in every year, after the first year in which a school has been established.

[Public Schools — Salaries]

Sec. 6.   Each person, other than a substitute employee, employed by a school district as a teacher or in any other position requiring certification qualifications shall be paid a salary which shall be at the rate of an annual salary of not less than twenty-four hundred dollars ($2,400) for a person serving full time, as defined by law.

[Public School System]

The Public School System shall include all kindergarten schools, elementary schools, secondary schools, technical schools, and state colleges, established in accordance with law and, in addition, the school districts and the other agencies authorized to maintain them. No school or college or any other part of the Public School System shall be, directly or indirectly, transferred from the Public School System or placed under the jurisdiction of any authority other than one included within the Public School System.

[*Support of Public School System — State Aid*]

The Legislature shall add to the State School Fund such other means from the revenues of the State as shall provide in said fund for apportionment in each fiscal year, an amount not less than one hundred eighty dollars ($180) per pupil in average daily attendance in the kindergarten schools, elementary schools, secondary schools, and technical schools in the Public School System during the next preceding fiscal year.

The entire State School Fund shall be apportioned in each fiscal year in such manner as the Legislature may provide, through the school districts and other agencies maintaining such schools, for the support of, and aid to, kindergarten schools, elementary schools, secondary schools, and technical schools except that there shall be apportioned to each school district in each fiscal year not less than one hundred twenty dollars ($120) per pupil in average daily attendance in the district during the next preceding fiscal year and except that the amount apportioned to each school district in each fiscal year shall be not less than twenty-four hundred dollars ($2,400).

Solely with respect to any retirement system provided for in the charter of any county or city and county pursuant to the provisions of which the contributions of, and benefits to, certificated employees of a school district who are members of such system are based upon the proportion of the salaries of such certificated employees contributed by said county or city and county, all amounts apportioned to said county or city and county, or to school districts therein, pursuant to the provisions of this section shall be considered as though derived from county or city and county school taxes for the support of county and city and county government and not money provided by the State within the meaning of this section. [*As amended November 5, 1974.*]

[*School Districts — Bonds*]

Sec. 6½.   Nothing in this Constitution contained shall forbid the formation of districts for school purposes situate in more than one county or the issuance of bonds by such districts under such general laws as have been or may hereafter be prescribed by the Legislature; and the officers mentioned in such laws shall be authorized to levy and assess such taxes and perform all such other acts as may be prescribed therein for the purpose of paying such bonds and carrying out the other powers conferred upon such districts; *provided,* that all such bonds shall be issued subject to the limitations prescribed in section eighteen † of article eleven hereof. [*New section adopted November 7, 1922.*]

[*Boards of Education*]

Sec. 7.   The Legislature shall provide for the appointment or election of the State Board of Education and a board of education in each county

---

† Former Section 18 of Article XI added to Article XIII as Section 40, June 2, 1970 and repealed November 5, 1974.

or for the election of a joint county board of education for two or more counties. [*As amended November 2, 1976.*]

[*Free Textbooks*]

SEC. 7.5. The State Board of Education shall adopt textbooks for use in grades one through eight throughout the State, to be furnished without cost as provided by statute. [*New section adopted June 2, 1970.*]

[*Sectarian Schools—Public Money—Doctrines*]

SEC. 8. No public money shall ever be appropriated for the support of any sectarian or denominational school, or any school not under the exclusive control of the officers of the public schools; nor shall any sectarian or denominational doctrine be taught, or instruction thereon be permitted, directly or indirectly, in any of the common schools of this State.

[*University of California*]

SEC. 9. (a) The University of California shall constitute a public trust, to be administered by the existing corporation known as "The Regents of the University of California," with full powers of organization and government, subject only to such legislative control as may be necessary to insure the security of its funds and compliance with the terms of the endowments of the university and such competitive bidding procedures as may be made applicable to the university by statute for the letting of construction contracts, sales of real property, and purchasing of materials, goods, and services. Said corporation shall be in form a board composed of seven ex officio members, which shall be: the Governor, the Lieutenant Governor, the Speaker of the Assembly, the Superintendent of Public Instruction, the president and the vice president of the alumni association of the university and the acting president of the university, and 18 appointive members appointed by the Governor and approved by the Senate, a majority of the membership concurring; provided, however that the present appointive members shall hold office until the expiration of their present terms.

(b) The terms of the members appointed prior to November 5, 1974, shall be 16 years; the terms of two appointive members to expire as heretofore on March 1st of every even-numbered calendar year, and two members shall be appointed for terms commencing on March 1, 1976, and on March 1 of each year thereafter; provided that no such appointments shall be made for terms to commence on March 1, 1979, or on March 1 of each fourth year thereafter, to the end that no appointment to the regents for a newly commencing term shall be made during the first year of any gubernatorial term of office. The terms of the members appointed for terms commencing on and after March 1, 1976, shall be 12 years. During the period of transition until the time when the appointive membership is comprised exclusively of persons serving for terms of 12 years, the total number of appointive members may exceed the numbers specified in the preceeding paragraph.

In case of any vacancy, the term of office of the appointee to fill such vacancy, who shall be appointed by the Governor and approved by the Senate, a majority of the membership concurring, shall be for the balance of the term for which such vacancy exists.

(c) The members of the board may, in their discretion, following procedures established by them and after consultation with representatives of faculty and students of the university, including appropriate officers of the academic senate and student governments, appoint to the board either or both of the following persons as members with all rights of participation: a member of the faculty at a campus of the university or of another institution of higher education; a person enrolled as a student at a campus of the university for each regular academic term during his service as a member of the board. Any person so appointed shall serve for not less than one year commencing on July 1.

(d) Regents shall be able persons broadly reflective of the economic, cultural, and social diversity of the State, including ethnic minorities and women. However, it is not intended that formulas or specific ratios be applied in the selection of regents.

(e) In the selection of the Regents, the Governor shall consult an advisory committee composed as follows: The Speaker of the Assembly and two public members appointed by the Speaker, the President Pro Tempore of the Senate and two public members appointed by the Rules Committee of the Senate, two public members appointed by the Governor, the chairman of the regents of the university, an alumnus of the university chosen by the alumni association of the university, a student of the university chosen by the Council of Student Body Presidents, and a member of the faculty of the university chosen by the academic senate of the university. Public members shall serve for four years, except that one each of the initially appointed members selected by the Speaker of the Assembly, the President Pro Tempore of the Senate, and the Governor shall be appointed to serve for two years; student, alumni, and faculty members shall serve for one year and may not be regents of the university at the time of their service on the advisory committee.

(f) The Regents of the University of California shall be vested with the legal title and the management and disposition of the property of the university and of property held for its benefit and shall have the power to take and hold, either by purchase or by donation, or gift, testamentary or otherwise, or in any other manner, without restriction, all real and personal property for the benefit of the university or incidentally to its conduct; provided, however, that sales of university real property shall be subject to such competitive bidding procedures as may be provided by statute. Said corporation shall also have all the powers necessary or convenient for the effective administration of its trust, including the power to sue and to be sued, to use a seal, and to delegate to its committees or to the faculty of the university, or to others, such authority or functions as it may deem wise. The Regents shall receive all funds derived from the sale of lands pursuant to the act of Congress of July 2, 1862, and any subsequent acts amendatory thereof. The university shall be entirely independent of all political or sectarian influence and kept free therefrom in the appointment of its regents and in the administration of its affairs, and no person shall be debarred admission to any department of the university on account of race, religion, ethnic heritage, or sex.

(g) Meetings of the Regents of the University of California shall be public, with exceptions and notice requirements as may be provided by statute. [*As amended November 2, 1976.*]

Sec. 10.   [*Repealed November 5, 1974.*]

Sec. 11.   [*Repealed November 5, 1974.*]

Sec. 12.   [*Repealed November 5, 1974.*]

Sec. 13.   [*Repealed November 5, 1974.*]

[*School District Incorporation and Organization—Governing Board Powers*]

Sec. 14.   The Legislature shall have power, by general law, to provide for the incorporation and organization of school districts, high school districts, and community college districts, of every kind and class, and may classify such districts.

The Legislature may authorize the governing boards of all school districts to initiate and carry on any programs, activities, or to otherwise act in any manner which is not in conflict with the laws and purposes for which school districts are established. [*As amended November 7, 1972. Operative July 1, 1973.*]

Sec. 15.   [*Repealed November 5, 1974.*]

[*Boards of Education—City Charter Provisions*]

Sec. 16.   (a) It shall be competent, in all charters framed under the authority given by Section 5 of Article XI, to provide, in addition to those provisions allowable by this Constitution, and by the laws of the State for the manner in which, the times at which, and the terms for which the members of boards of education shall be elected or appointed, for their qualifications, compensation and removal, and for the number which shall constitute any one of such boards.

[*Charter Amendments—Approval by Voters*]

(b) Notwithstanding Section 3 of Article XI, when the boundaries of a school district or community college district extend beyond the limits of a city whose charter provides for any or all of the foregoing with respect to the members of its board of education, no charter amendment effecting a change in the manner in which, the times at which, or the terms for which the members of the board of education shall be elected or appointed, for their qualifications, compensation, or removal, or for the number which shall constitute such board, shall be adopted unless it is submitted to and approved by a majority of all the qualified electors of the school district or community college district voting on the question. Any such amendment, and any portion of a proposed charter or a revised charter which would establish or change any of the foregoing provisions respecting a board of education, shall be submitted to the electors of the school district or community college district as one or more separate questions. The failure of any such separate question to be approved shall have the result of continuing in effect the applicable existing law with respect to that board of education. [*As amended June 6, 1978.*]

ARTICLE X *

WATER

[*State's Right of Eminent Domain*]

SECTION 1.   The right of eminent domain is hereby declared to exist in the State to all frontages on the navigable waters of this State. [*New section adopted June 8, 1976.*]

[*Conservation and Beneficial Use of Water—Riparian Rights*]

SEC. 2.   It is hereby declared that because of the conditions prevailing in this State the general welfare requires that the water resources of the State be put to beneficial use to the fullest extent of which they are capable, and that the waste or unreasonable use or unreasonable method of use of water be prevented, and that the conservation of such waters is to be exercised with a view to the reasonable and beneficial use thereof in the interest of the people and for the public welfare. The right to water or to the use or flow of water in or from any natural stream or water course in this State is and shall be limited to such water as shall be reasonably required for the beneficial use to be served, and such right does not and shall not extend to the waste or unreasonable use or unreasonable method of use or unreasonable method of diversion of water. Riparian rights in a stream or water course attach to, but to no more than so much of the flow thereof as may be required or used consistently with this section, for the purposes for which such lands are, or may be made adaptable, in view of such reasonable and beneficial uses; provided, however, that nothing herein contained shall be construed as depriving any riparian owner of the reasonable use of water of the stream to which the owner's land is riparian under reasonable methods of diversion and use, or as depriving any appropriator of

---

* New Article X adopted June 8, 1976.

water to which the appropriator is lawfully entitled. This section shall be self-executing, and the Legislature may also enact laws in the furtherance of the policy in this section contained. [*New section adopted June 8, 1976.*]

[*Tidelands*]

SEC. 3. All tidelands within two miles of any incorporated city, city and county, or town in this State, and fronting on the water of any harbor, estuary, bay, or inlet used for the purposes of navigation, shall be withheld from grant or sale to private persons, partnerships, or corporations; provided, however, that any such tidelands, reserved to the State solely for street purposes, which the Legislature finds and declares are not used for navigation purposes and are not necessary for such purposes may be sold to any town, city, county, city and county, municipal corporations, private persons, partnerships or corporations subject to such conditions as the Legislature determines are necessary to be imposed in connection with any such sales in order to protect the public interest. [*New section adopted June 8, 1976.*]

[*Access to Navigable Waters*]

SEC. 4. No individual, partnership, or corporation, claiming or possessing the frontage or tidal lands of a harbor, bay, inlet, estuary, or other navigable water in this State, shall be permitted to exclude the right of way to such water whenever it is required for any public purpose, nor to destroy or obstruct the free navigation of such water; and the Legislature shall enact such laws as will give the most liberal construction to this provision, so that access to the navigable waters of this State shall be always attainable for the people thereof. [*New section adopted June 8, 1976.*]

[*State Control of Water Use*]

SEC. 5. The use of all water now appropriated, or that may hereafter be appropriated, for sale, rental, or distribution, is hereby declared to be a public use, and subject to the regulation and control of the State, in the manner to be prescribed by law. [*New section adopted June 8, 1976.*]

[*Compensation for Water Use*]

SEC. 6. The right to collect rates or compensation for the use of water supplied to any county, city and county, or town, or the inhabitants thereof, is a franchise, and cannot be exercised except by authority of and in the manner prescribed by law. [*New section adopted June 8, 1976.*]

[*Acquisition of Real Property—Conformance to California Water Laws*]

SEC. 7. Whenever any agency of government, local, state, or federal, hereafter acquires any interest in real property in this State, the acceptance of the interest shall constitute an agreement by the agency to conform to the laws of California as to the acquisition, control, use, and distribution of water with respect to the land so acquired. [*New section adopted June 8, 1976.*]

ARTICLE X A *

WATER RESOURCES DEVELOPMENT

[*Article X A has no force or effect because Senate Bill No. 200 of the 1979–80 Regular Session of the Legislature was defeated by referendum vote June 8, 1982*]

[**Water Rights, Water Quality, and Fish and Wildlife Resources Guaranteed and Protected**]

SECTION 1.   The people of the State hereby provide the following guarantees and protections in this article for water rights, water quality, and fish and wildlife resources. [*New section adopted November 4, 1980. Section has no force or effect because Senate Bill No. 200 of the 1979–80 Regular Session of the Legislature was defeated by referendum vote June 8, 1982.*]

[**Statutes for Protection of Fish and Wildlife Resources, Delta, Etc.**]

SEC. 2.   No statute amending or repealing, or adding to, the provisions of the statute enacted by Senate Bill No. 200 † of the 1979–80 Regular Session of the Legislature which specify (1) the manner in which the State will protect fish and wildlife resources in the Sacramento-San Joaquin Delta, Suisun Marsh, and San Francisco Bay system westerly of the delta; (2) the manner in which the State will protect existing water rights in the Sacramento-San Joaquin Delta; and (3) the manner in which the State will operate the State Water Resources Development System to comply with water quality standards and water quality control plans, shall become effective unless approved by the electors in the same manner as statutes amending initiative statutes are approved; except that the Legislature may, by statute passed in each house by roll call vote entered in the journal, two-thirds of the membership concurring, amend or repeal, or add to, these provisions if the statute does not in any manner reduce the protection of the delta or fish and wildlife. [*New section adopted November 4, 1980. Section has no force or effect because Senate Bill No. 200 of the 1979–80 Regular Session of the Legislature was defeated by referendum vote June 8, 1982.*]

[**Appropriations of Water—Components of California Wild and Scenic Rivers System**]

SEC. 3.   No water shall be available for appropriation by storage in, or by direct diversion from, any of the components of the California Wild and

---

* New Article X A adopted November 4, 1980.

† Chapter 632, Statutes of 1980.

Scenic Rivers System, as such system exists on January 1, 1981, where such appropriation is for export of water into another major hydrologic basin of the State, as defined in the Department of Water Resources Bulletin 160-74, unless such export is expressly authorized prior to such appropriation by: (a) an initiative statute approved by the electors, or (b) the Legislature, by statute passed in each house by roll call vote entered in the journal, two-thirds of the membership concurring. [*New section adopted November 4, 1980. Section has no force or effect because Senate Bill No. 200 of the 1979–80 Regular Session of the Legislature was defeated by referendum vote June 8, 1982.*]

[*Statutes Amending, Repealing, or Adding to Delta Protection Act*]

SEC. 4.   No statute amending or repealing, or adding to, the provisions of Part 4.5 (commencing with Section 12200) of Division 6 of the Water Code (the Delta Protection Act) shall become effective unless approved by the electors in the same manner as statutes amending initiative statutes are approved; except that the Legislature may, by statute passed in each house by roll call vote entered in the journal, two-thirds of the membership concurring, amend or repeal, or add to, these provisions if the statute does not in any manner reduce the protection of the delta or fish and wildlife. [*New section adopted November 4, 1980. Section has no force or effect because Senate Bill No. 200 of the 1979–80 Regular Session of the Legislature was defeated by referendum vote June 8, 1982.*]

[*Eminent Domain Proceedings to Acquire Water Rights or Contract Rights for Water or Water Quality Maintenance in Delta Prohibited*]

SEC. 5.   No public agency may utilize eminent domain proceedings to acquire water rights, which are held for uses within the Sacramento-San Joaquin Delta as defined in Section 12220 of the Water Code, or any contract rights for water or water quality maintenance in the Delta for the purpose of exporting such water from the Delta. This provision shall not be construed to prohibit the utilization of eminent domain proceedings for the purpose of acquiring land or any other rights necessary for the construction of water facilities, including, but not limited to, facilities authorized in Chapter 8 (commencing with Section 12930) of Part 6 of Division 6 of the Water Code. [*New section adopted November 4, 1980. Section has no force or effect because Senate Bill No. 200 of the 1979–80 Regular Session of the Legislature was defeated by referendum vote June 8, 1982.*]

[*Actions and Proceedings*]

SEC. 6.   (a) The venue of any of the following actions or proceedings brought in a superior court shall be Sacramento County:

(1) An action or proceeding to attack, review, set aside, void, or annul any provision of the statute enacted by Senate Bill No. 200 † of the 1979–80 Regular Session of the Legislature.

(2) An action or proceeding to attack, review, set aside, void, or annul the determination made by the Director of Water Resources and the Director of Fish and Game pursuant to subdivision (a) of Section 11255 of the Water Code.

(3) An action or proceeding which would have the effect of attacking, reviewing, preventing, or substantially delaying the construction, operation, or maintenance of the peripheral canal unit described in subdivision (a) of Section 11255 of the Water Code.

(4) An action or proceeding to require the State Water Resources Development System to comply with subdivision (b) of Section 11460 of the Water Code.

(5) An action or proceeding to require the Department of Water Resources or its successor agency to comply with the permanent agreement specified in subdivision (a) of Section 11256 of the Water Code.

(6) An action or proceeding to require the Department of Water Resources or its successor agency to comply with the provisions of the contracts entered into pursuant to Section 11456 of the Water Code.

(b) An action or proceeding described in paragraph (1) of subdivision (a) shall be commenced within one year after the effective date of the statute enacted by Senate Bill No. 200 † of the 1979–80 Regular Session of the Legislature. Any other action or proceeding described in subdivision (a) shall be commenced within one year after the cause of action arises unless a shorter period is otherwise provided by statute.

(c) The superior court or a court of appeals shall give preference to the actions or proceedings described in this section over all civil actions or proceedings pending in the court. The superior court shall commence hearing any such action or proceeding within six months after the commencement of the action or proceeding, provided that any such hearing may be delayed by joint stipulation of the parties or at the discretion of the court for good cause shown. The provisions of this section shall supersede any provisions of law requiring courts to give preference to other civil actions or proceedings. The provisions of this subdivision may be enforced by mandamus.

(d) The Supreme Court shall, upon the request of any party, transfer to itself, before a decision in the court of appeal, any appeal or petition for extraordinary relief from an action or proceeding described in this section, unless the Supreme Court determines that the action or proceeding is unlikely to substantially affect (1) the construction, operation, or mainte-

---

† Chapter 632, Statutes of 1980.

nance of the peripheral canal unit described in subdivision (a) of Section 11255 of the Water Code, (2) compliance with subdivision (b) of Section 11460 of the Water Code, (3) compliance with the permanent agreement specified in Section 11256 of the Water Code, or (4) compliance with the provisions of the contracts entered into pursuant to Section 11456 of the Water Code. The request for transfer shall receive preference on the Supreme Court's calendar. If the action or proceeding is transferred to the Supreme Court, the Supreme Court shall commence to hear the matter within six months of the transfer unless the parties by joint stipulation request additional time or the court, for good cause shown, grants additional time.

(e) The remedy prescribed by the court for an action or proceeding described in paragraph (4), (5), or (6) of subdivision (a) shall include, but need not be limited to, compliance with subdivision (b) of Section 11460 of the Water Code, the permanent agreement specified in Section 11256 of the Water Code, or the provisions of the contracts entered into pursuant to Section 11456 of the Water Code.

(f) The Board of Supervisors of the County of Sacramento may apply to the State Board of Control for actual costs imposed by the requirements of this section upon the county, and the State Board of Control shall pay such actual costs.

(g) Notwithstanding the provisions of this section, nothing in this Article shall be construed as prohibiting the Supreme Court from exercising the transfer authority contained in Article VI, Section 12 of the Constitution. [*New section adopted November 4, 1980. Section has no force or effect because Senate Bill No. 200 of the 1979–80 Regular Session of the Legislature was defeated by referendum vote June 8, 1982.*]

[*State Agencies' Exercise of Authorized Powers*]

SEC. 7.   State agencies shall exercise their authorized powers in a manner consistent with the protections provided by this article. [*New section adopted November 4, 1980. Section has no force or effect because Senate Bill No. 200 of the 1979–80 Regular Session of the Legislature was defeated by referendum vote June 8, 1982.*]

[*Force or Effect of Article*]

SEC. 8.   This article shall have no force or effect unless Senate Bill No. 200 † of the 1979–80 Regular Session of the Legislature is enacted and takes effect. [*New section adopted November 4, 1980. Section has no force or effect because Senate Bill No. 200 of the 1979–80 Regular Session of the Legislature was defeated by referendum vote June 8, 1982.*]

---

† Chapter 632, Statutes of 1980.

ARTICLE X B *

MARINE RESOURCES PROTECTION ACT OF 1990

[*Title*]

SECTION 1.   This article shall be known and may be cited as the Marine Resources Protection Act of 1990. [*New section adopted November 6, 1990. Initiative measure.*]

[*Definitions*]

SEC. 2.   (a) "District" means a fish and game district as defined in the Fish and Game Code by statute on January 1, 1990.

(b) Except as specifically provided in this article, all references to Fish and Game Code sections, articles, chapters, parts, and divisions are defined as those statutes in effect on January 1, 1990.

(c) "Ocean waters" means the waters of the Pacific Ocean regulated by the State.

(d) "Zone" means the Marine Resources Protection zone established pursuant to this article. The zone consists of the following:

(1) In waters less than 70 fathoms or within one mile, whichever is less, around the Channel Islands consisting of the Islands of San Miguel, Santa Rosa, Santa Cruz, Anacapa, San Nicolaus, Santa Barbara, Santa Catalina, and San Clemente.

(2) The area within three nautical miles offshore of the mainland coast, and the area within three nautical miles off any manmade breakwater, between a line extending due west from Point Arguello and a line extending due west from the Mexican border.

(3) In waters less than 35 fathoms between a line running 180 degrees true from Point Fermin and a line running 270 degrees true from the south jetty of Newport Harbor. [*New section adopted November 6, 1990. Initiative measure.*]

[*Gill and Trammel Nets—Usage*]

SEC. 3.   (a) From January 1, 1991, to December 31, 1993, inclusive, gill nets or trammel nets may only be used in the zone pursuant to a nontransferable permit issued by the Department of Fish and Game pursuant to Section 5.

(b) On and after January 1, 1994, gill nets and trammel nets shall not be used in the zone. [*New section adopted November 6, 1990. Initiative measure.*]

---

* New Article X B adopted November 6, 1990. Initiative measure.

[Gill and Trammel Nets—Usage]

Sec. 4.   (a) Notwithstanding any other provision of law, gill nets and trammel nets may not be used to take any species of rockfish.

(b) In ocean waters north of Point Arguello on and after the effective date of this article, the use of gill nets and trammel nets shall be regulated by the provisions of Article 4 (commencing with Section 8660), Article 5 (commencing with Section 8680) and Article 6 (commencing with Section 8720) of Chapter 3 of Part 3 of Division 6 of the Fish and Game Code, or any regulation or order issued pursuant to these articles, in effect on January 1, 1990, except that as to Sections 8680, 8681, 8681.7, and 8682, and subdivisions (a) through (f), inclusive of Section 8681.5 of the Fish and Game Code, or any regulation or order issued pursuant to these sections, the provisions in effect on January 1, 1989, shall control where not in conflict with other provisions of this article, and shall be applicable to all ocean waters. Notwithstanding the provisions of this section, the Legislature shall not be precluded from imposing more restrictions on the use and/or possession of gill nets or trammel nets. The Director of the Department of Fish and Game shall not authorize the use of gill nets or trammel nets in any area where the use is not permitted even if the director makes specified findings. *[New section adopted November 6, 1990. Initiative measure.]*

[Gill and Trammel Nets—Usage]

Sec. 5.   The Department of Fish and Game shall issue a permit to use a gill net or trammel net in the zone for the period specified in subdivision (a) of Section 3 to any applicant who meets both of the following requirements:

(a) Has a commercial fishing license issued pursuant to Sections 7850–7852.3 of the Fish and Game Code.

(b) Has a permit issued pursuant to Section 8681 of the Fish and Game Code and is presently the owner or operator of a vessel equipped with a gill net or trammel net. *[New section adopted November 6, 1990. Initiative measure.]*

[Permit Fees]

Sec. 6.   The Department of Fish and Game shall charge the following fees for permits issued pursuant to Section 5 pursuant to the following schedule:

Calendar Year	Fee
1991	$250
1992	500
1993	1,000

[New section adopted November 6, 1990. Initiative measure.]

[Permitholder's Compensation for Discontinuing Fishing with Gill and Trammel Nets]

SEC. 7.   (a) Within 90 days after the effective date of this section, every person who intends to seek the compensation provided in subdivision (b) shall notify the Department of Fish and Game, on forms provided by the department, of that intent. Any person who does not submit the form within that 90-day period shall not be compensated pursuant to subdivision (b). The department shall publish a list of all persons submitting the form within 120 days after the effective date of this section.

(b) After July 1, 1993, and before January 1, 1994, any person who holds a permit issued pursuant to Section 5 and operates in the zone may surrender that permit to the department and agree to permanently discontinue fishing with gill or trammel nets in the zone, for which he or she shall receive, beginning on July 1, 1993, a one time compensation which shall be based upon the average annual ex vessel value of the fish other than any species of rockfish landed by a fisherman, which were taken pursuant to a valid general gill net or trammel net permit issued pursuant to Sections 8681 and 8682 of the Fish and Game Code within the zone during the years 1983 to 1987, inclusive. The department shall verify those landings by reviewing logs and landing receipts submitted to it. Any person who is denied compensation by the department as a result of the department's failure to verify landings may appeal that decision to the Fish and Game Commission.

(c) The State Board of Control shall, prior to the disbursement of any funds, verify the eligibility of each person seeking compensation and the amount of the compensation to be provided in order to ensure compliance with this section.

(d) Unless the Legislature enacts any required enabling legislation to implement this section on or before July 1, 1993, no compensation shall be paid under this article. *[New section adopted November 6, 1990. Initiative measure.]*

[Marine Resources Protection Account—Fees—Interest]

SEC. 8.   (a) There is hereby created the Marine Resources Protection Account in the Fish and Game Preservation Fund. On and after January 1, 1991, the Department of Fish and Game shall collect any and all fees required by this article. All fees received by the department pursuant to this article shall be deposited in the account and shall be expended or encumbered to compensate persons who surrender permits pursuant to Section 7 or to provide for administration of this article. All funds received by the department during any fiscal year pursuant to this article which are not expended during that fiscal year to compensate persons as set forth in Section 7 or to provide for administration of this article shall be carried over into the following fiscal year and shall be used only for those purposes. All interest accrued from the department's retention of fees received pursuant to this article shall be credited to the account. The accrued interest may only be expended for the purposes authorized by this article. The account shall continue in existence, and the requirement to pay fees under this article shall remain in effect, until the compensation provided in Section 7 has been fully funded or until January 1, 1995, whichever occurs first.

(b) An amount, not to exceed 15 percent of the total annual revenues deposited in the account excluding any interest accrued or any funds carried over from a prior fiscal year may be expended for the administration of this article.

(c) In addition to a valid California sportfishing license issued pursuant to Sections 7149, 7149.1 or 7149.2 of the Fish and Game Code and any applicable sport license stamp issued pursuant to the Fish and Game Code, a person taking fish from ocean waters south of a line extending due west from Point Arguello for sport purposes shall have permanently affixed to that person's sportfishing license a marine resources protection stamp which may be obtained from the department upon payment of a fee of three dollars ($3). This subdivision does not apply to any one-day fishing license.

(d) In addition to a valid California commercial passenger fishing boat license required by Section 7920 of the Fish and Game Code, the owner of any boat or vessel who, for profit, permits any person to fish from the boat or vessel in ocean waters south of a line extending due west from Point Arguello, shall obtain and permanently affix to the license a commercial marine resources protection stamp which may be obtained from the department upon payment of a fee of three dollars ($3).

(e) The department may accept contributions or donations from any person who wishes to donate money to be used for the compensation of commercial gill net and trammel net fishermen who surrender permits under this article.

(f) This section shall become inoperative on January 1, 1995. [*New section adopted November 6, 1990. Inoperative January 1, 1995. Initiative measure.*]

[Marine Resources Protection Account—Grants]

SEC. 9. Any funds remaining in the Marine Resources Protection Account in the Fish and Game Preservation Fund on or after January 1, 1995, shall, with the approval of the Fish and Game Commission, be used to provide grants to colleges, universities and other bonafide scientific research groups to fund marine resource related scientific research within the ecological reserves established by Section 14 of this act. [*New section adopted November 6, 1990. Initiative measure.*]

[Report to Legislature]

SEC. 10.   On or before December 31 of each year, the Director of Fish and Game shall prepare and submit a report to the Legislature regarding the implementation of this article including an accounting of all funds. *[New section adopted November 6, 1990. Initiative measure.]*

[Violations]

SEC. 11.   It is unlawful for any person to take, possess, receive, transport, purchase, sell, barter, or process any fish obtained in violation of this article. *[New section adopted November 6, 1990. Initiative measure.]*

[Commercial Fishing Daily Landings Monitoring and Evaluating Program]

SEC. 12.   To increase the State's scientific and biological information on the ocean fisheries of this State, the Department of Fish and Game shall establish a program whereby it can monitor and evaluate the daily landings of fish by commercial fishermen who are permitted under this article to take these fish. The cost of implementing this monitoring program shall be borne by the commercial fishing industry. *[New section adopted November 6, 1990. Initiative measure.]*

[Penalties for Violations—Probation—Fine]

SEC. 13.   (a) The penalty for a first violation of the provisions of Sections 3 and 4 of this article is a fine of not less than one thousand dollars ($1,000) and not more than five thousand dollars ($5,000) and a mandatory suspension of any license, permit or stamp to take, receive, transport, purchase, sell, barter or process fish for commercial purposes for six months. The penalty for a second or subsequent violation of the provisions of Sections 3 and 4 of this article is a fine of not less than two thousand five hundred dollars ($2,500) and not more than ten thousand dollars ($10,000) and a mandatory suspension of any license, permit or stamp to take, receive, transport, purchase, sell, barter, or process fish for commercial purposes for one year.

(b) Notwithstanding any other provisions of law, a violation of Section 8 of this article shall be deemed a violation of the provisions of Section 7145 of the Fish and Game Code and the penalty for such violation shall be consistent with the provisions of Section 12002.2 of said code.

(c) If a person convicted of a violation of Section 3, 4, or 8 of this article is granted probation, the court shall impose as a term or condition of probation, in addition to any other term or condition of probation, that the person pay at least the minimum fine prescribed in this section. *[New section adopted November 6, 1990. Initiative measure.]*

[New Ecological Reserves]

SEC. 14.   Prior to January 1, 1994, the Fish and Game Commission shall establish four new ecological reserves in ocean waters along the mainland coast. Each ecological reserve shall have a surface area of at least two square miles. The commission shall restrict the use of these ecological reserves to scientific research relating to the management and enhancement of marine resources. [*New section adopted November 6, 1990. Initiative measure.*]

[*Article not Preempting or Superseding Other Protective Closures*]

SEC. 15.   This article does not preempt or supersede any other closures to protect any other wildlife, including sea otters, whales, and shorebirds. [*New section adopted November 6, 1990. Initiative measure.*]

[*Severability*]

SEC. 16.   If any provision of this article or the application thereof to any person or circumstances is held invalid, that invalidity shall not affect other provisions or applications of this article which can be given effect without the invalid provision or application, and to this end the provisions of this article are severable. [*New section adopted November 6, 1990. Initiative measure.*]

ARTICLE XI.   [*Repealed June 2, 1970. See Article XI, below.*]

ARTICLE XI*

LOCAL GOVERNMENT

[*Counties—Formation, Boundaries, County Seat, Officers, and Governing Body*]

SECTION 1.   (a) The State is divided into counties which are legal subdivisions of the State. The Legislature shall prescribe uniform procedure for county formation, consolidation, and boundary change. Formation or consolidation requires approval by a majority of electors voting on the question in each affected county. A boundary change requires approval by the governing body of each affected county. No county seat shall be removed unless two-thirds of the qualified electors of the county, voting on the proposition at a general election, shall vote in favor of such removal. A proposition of removal shall not be submitted in the same county more than once in four years.

(b) The Legislature shall provide for county powers, an elected county sheriff, an elected district attorney, an elected assessor, and an elected governing body in each county. Except as provided in subdivision (b) of Section 4 of this article, each governing body shall prescribe by ordinance the compensation of its members, but the ordinance prescribing such compensation shall be subject to referendum. The Legislature or the governing body may provide for other officers whose compensation shall be prescribed by the governing body. The governing body shall provide for the

---

* New Article XI adopted June 2, 1970.

number, compensation, tenure, and appointment of employees. [*As amended June 7, 1988.*]

SEC. 2.   [*Repealed June 2, 1970. See Section 2, below.*]

[*Cities—Formation, Powers*]

SEC. 2.   (a) The Legislature shall prescribe uniform procedure for city formation and provide for city powers.

(b) Except with approval by a majority of its electors voting on the question, a city may not be annexed to or consolidated into another. [*New section adopted June 2, 1970.*]

[*County or City—Charters*]

SEC. 3.   (a) For its own government, a county or city may adopt a charter by majority vote of its electors voting on the question. The charter is effective when filed with the Secretary of State. A charter may be amended, revised, or repealed in the same manner. A charter, amendment, revision, or repeal thereof shall be published in the official state statutes. County charters adopted pursuant to this section shall supersede any existing charter and all laws inconsistent therewith. The provisions of a charter are the law of the State and have the force and effect of legislative enactments.

(b) The governing body or charter commission of a county or city may propose a charter or revision. Amendment or repeal may be proposed by initiative or by the governing body.

(c) An election to determine whether to draft or revise a charter and elect a charter commission may be required by initiative or by the governing body.

(d) If provisions of 2 or more measures approved at the same election conflict, those of the measure receiving the highest affirmative vote shall prevail. [*As amended November 5, 1974.*]

[*County Charters—Provisions*]

SEC. 4.   County charters shall provide for:

(a) A governing body of 5 or more members, elected (1) by district or, (2) at large, or (3) at large, with a requirement that they reside in a district. Charter counties are subject to statutes that relate to apportioning population of governing body districts.

(b) The compensation, terms, and removal of members of the governing body. If a county charter provides for the Legislature to prescribe the salary of the governing body, such compensation shall be prescribed by the governing body by ordinance.

(c) An elected sheriff, an elected district attorney, an elected assessor, other officers, their election or appointment, compensation, terms and removal.

(d) The performance of functions required by statute.

(e) The powers and duties of governing bodies and all other county officers, and for consolidation and segregation of county officers, and for the manner of filling all vacancies occurring therein.

(f) The fixing and regulation by governing bodies, by ordinance, of the appointment and number of assistants, deputies, clerks, attachés, and other persons to be employed, and for the prescribing and regulating by such bodies of the powers, duties, qualifications, and compensation of such persons, the times at which, and terms for which they shall be appointed, and the manner of their appointment and removal.

(g) Whenever any county has framed and adopted a charter, and the same shall have been approved by the Legislature as herein provided, the general laws adopted by the Legislature in pursuance of Section 1(b) of this article, shall, as to such county, be superseded by said charter as to matters for which, under this section it is competent to make provision in such charter, and for which provision is made therein, except as herein otherwise expressly provided.

(h) Charter counties shall have all the powers that are provided by this Constitution or by statute for counties. [*As amended June 7, 1988.*]

SEC. 5.   [*Repealed June 2, 1970. See Section 5, below.*]

[City Charters—Provisions]

SEC. 5.   (a) It shall be competent in any city charter to provide that the city governed thereunder may make and enforce all ordinances and regulations in respect to municipal affairs, subject only to restrictions and limitations provided in their several charters and in respect to other matters they shall be subject to general laws. City charters adopted pursuant to this Constitution shall supersede any existing charter, and with respect to municipal affairs shall supersede all laws inconsistent therewith.

(b) It shall be competent in all city charters to provide, in addition to those provisions allowable by this Constitution, and by the laws of the State for: (1) the constitution, regulation, and government of the city police force (2) subgovernment in all or part of a city (3) conduct of city elections and (4) plenary authority is hereby granted, subject only to the restrictions of this article, to provide therein or by amendment thereto, the manner in which, the method by which, the times at which, and the terms for which the several municipal officers and employees whose compensation is paid by the city shall be elected or appointed, and for their removal, and for their compensation, and for the number of deputies, clerks and other employees that each shall have, and for the compensation, method of appointment, qualifications, tenure of office and removal of such deputies, clerks and other employees. [*New section adopted June 2, 1970.*]

SEC. 5.1.   [*Repealed June 2, 1970.*]

SEC. 6.   [*Repealed June 2, 1970. See Section 6, below.*]

[*Charter City and County*]

SEC. 6.   (a) A county and all cities within it may consolidate as a charter city and county as provided by statute.

(b) A charter city and county is a charter city and a charter county. Its charter city powers supersede conflicting charter county powers. [*New section adopted June 2, 1970.*]

SEC. 7.   [*Repealed June 2, 1970. See Section 7, below.*]

[*Local Ordinances and Regulations*]

SEC. 7.   A county or city may make and enforce within its limits all local, police, sanitary, and other ordinances and regulations not in conflict with general laws. [*New section adopted June 2, 1970.*]

SEC. 7½.   [*Repealed June 2, 1970.*]

SEC. 7½b.   [*Repealed June 2, 1970.*]

[*Ballot Measures—Application*]

SEC. 7.5.   (a) A city or county measure proposed by the legislative body of a city, charter city, county, or charter county and submitted to the voters for approval may not do either of the following:

(1) Include or exclude any part of the city, charter city, county, or charter county from the application or effect of its provisions based upon approval or disapproval of the city or county measure, or based upon the casting of a specified percentage of votes in favor of the measure, by the electors of the city, charter city, county, charter county, or any part thereof.

(2) Contain alternative or cumulative provisions wherein one or more of those provisions would become law depending upon the casting of a specified percentage of votes for or against the measure.

(b) "City or county measure," as used in this section, means an advisory question, proposed charter or charter amendment, ordinance, proposition for the issuance of bonds, or other question or proposition submitted to the voters of a city, or to the voters of a county at an election held throughout an entire single county. [*New section adopted June 2, 1998.*]

SEC. 8.   [*Repealed June 2, 1970. See Section 8, below.*]

[*Counties—Performance of Municipal Functions*]

SEC. 8.   (a) The Legislature may provide that counties perform municipal functions at the request of cities within them.

(b) If provided by their respective charters, a county may agree with a city within it to assume and discharge specified municipal functions. [*New section adopted June 2, 1970.*]

SEC. 8½.   [*Repealed June 2, 1970.*]

[*Local Utilities*]

SEC. 9. (a) A municipal corporation may establish, purchase, and operate public works to furnish its inhabitants with light, water, power, heat, transportation, or means of communication. It may furnish those services outside its boundaries, except within another municipal corporation which furnishes the same service and does not consent.

(b) Persons or corporations may establish and operate works for supplying those services upon conditions and under regulations that the city may prescribe under its organic law. [*New section adopted June 2, 1970.*]

[*Local Government—Extra Compensation; City, County or District Employees—Residency*]

SEC. 10. (a) A local government body may not grant extra compensation or extra allowance to a public officer, public employee, or contractor after service has been rendered or a contract has been entered into and performed in whole or in part, or pay a claim under an agreement made without authority of law.

(b) A city or county, including any chartered city or chartered county, or public district, may not require that its employees be residents of such city, county, or district; except that such employees may be required to reside within a reasonable and specific distance of their place of employment or other designated location. [*As amended June 8, 1976.*]

SEC. 10.5. [*Repealed June 8, 1976.*]

[*Private Control of County or Municipal Functions—Deposit and Investment of Public Moneys*]

SEC. 11. (a) The Legislature may not delegate to a private person or body power to make, control, appropriate, supervise, or interfere with county or municipal corporation improvements, money, or property, or to levy taxes or assessments, or perform municipal functions.

(b) The Legislature may, however, provide for the deposit of public moneys in any bank in this State or in any savings and loan association in this State or any credit union in this State or in any federally insured industrial loan company in this State and for payment of interest, principal, and redemption premiums of public bonds and other evidence of public indebtedness by banks within or without this State. It may also provide for investment of public moneys in securities and the registration of bonds and other evidences of indebtedness by private persons or bodies, within or without this State, acting as trustees or fiscal agents. [*As amended November 8, 1988.*]

SEC. 12. [*As amended June 27, 1933, added to Article XIII as Section 37, June 2, 1970. See Section 12, below.*]

[Claims Against Counties or Cities, Etc.]

SEC. 12.   The Legislature may prescribe procedure for presentation, consideration, and enforcement of claims against counties, cities, their officers, agents, or employees. *[New section adopted June 2, 1970.]*

SEC. 13.   *[Repealed June 2, 1970. See Section 13, below.]*

[Distribution of Powers—Construction of Article]

SEC. 13.   The provisions of Sections 1(b) (except for the second sentence), 3(a), 4, and 5 of this Article relating to matters affecting the distribution of powers between the Legislature and cities and counties, including matters affecting supersession, shall be construed as a restatement of all related provisions of the Constitution in effect immediately prior to the effective date of this amendment, and as making no substantive change.

The terms general law, general laws, and laws, as used in this Article, shall be construed as a continuation and restatement of those terms as used in the Constitution in effect immediately prior to the effective date of this amendment, and not as effecting a change in meaning. *[New section adopted June 2, 1970.]*

SEC. 13½.   *[As amended November 3, 1914, added to Article XIII as Section 37.5, June 2, 1970.]*

[Local Government—Taxation]

SEC. 14.   A local government formed after the effective date of this section, the boundaries of which include all or part of two or more counties, shall not levy a property tax unless such tax has been approved by a majority vote of the qualified voters of that local government voting on the issue of the tax. *[New section adopted November 2, 1976.]*

[Vehicle License Fee Allocations]

SEC. 15.   (a) From the revenues derived from taxes imposed pursuant to the Vehicle License Fee Law (Part 5 (commencing with Section 10701) of Division 2 of the Revenue and Taxation Code), or its successor, other than fees on trailer coaches and mobilehomes, over and above the costs of collection and any refunds authorized by law, those revenues derived from that portion of the vehicle license fee rate that does not exceed 0.65 percent of the market value of the vehicle shall be allocated as follows:

(1) An amount shall be specified in the Vehicle License Fee Law, or the successor to that law, for deposit in the State Treasury to the credit of the Local Revenue Fund established in Chapter 6 (commencing with Section 17600) of Part 5 of Division 9 of the Welfare and Institutions Code, or its successor, if any, for allocation to cities, counties, and cities and counties as otherwise provided by law.

(2) The balance shall be allocated to cities, counties, and cities and counties as otherwise provided by law.

(b) If a statute enacted by the Legislature reduces the annual vehicle license fee below 0.65 percent of the market value of a vehicle, the Legislature shall, for each fiscal year for which the reduced fee applies, provide by statue for the allocation of an additional amount of money that is equal to the decrease, resulting from the fee reduction, in the total amount of revenues that are otherwise required to be deposited and allocated under subdivision (a) for that same fiscal year. That amount shall be allocated to cities, counties, and cities and counties in the same pro rata amounts and for the same purposes as are revenues subject to subdivision (a). [*As amended November 2, 2004.*]

SEC. 16.   [*Added to Article XIII as Section 38, June 2, 1970.*]

SEC. 16½.   [*As amended November 8, 1932, added to Article XIII as Section 39, June 2, 1970.*]

SEC. 17.   [*Repealed June 2, 1970.*]

SEC. 18.   [*As amended November 8, 1949, added to Article XIII as Section 40, June 2, 1970.*]

SEC. 18¼.   [*Repealed June 2, 1970.*]

SEC. 19.   [*Repealed June 2, 1970.*]

SEC. 20.   [*Repealed June 2, 1970.*]

ARTICLE XII.   [*Repealed November 5, 1974. See Article XII, below.*]

ARTICLE XII *

PUBLIC UTILITIES

[*Public Utilities Commission — Composition*]

SECTION 1.   The Public Utilities Commission consists of 5 members appointed by the Governor and approved by the Senate, a majority of the membership concurring, for staggered 6-year terms. A vacancy is filled for the remainder of the term. The Legislature may remove a member for in competence, neglect of duty, or corruption, two thirds of the membership of each house concurring. [*New section adopted November 5, 1974.*]

[*Public Utilities Commission — Powers and Duties*]

SEC. 2.   Subject to statute and due process, the commission may establish its own procedures. Any commissioner as designated by the commission may hold a hearing or investigation or issue an order subject to commission approval. [*New section adopted November 5, 1974.*]

---

* New Article XII adopted November 5, 1974.

[Public Utilities—Legislative Control]

SEC. 3.   Private corporations and persons that own, operate, control, or manage a line, plant, or system for the transportation of people or property, the transmission of telephone and telegraph messages, or the production, generation, transmission, or furnishing of heat, light, water, power, storage, or wharfage directly or indirectly to or for the public, and common carriers, are public utilities subject to control by the Legislature. The Legislature may prescribe that additional classes of private corporations or other persons are public utilities. *[New section adopted November 5, 1974.]*

[Rates—Discrimination in Transportation Charges, Etc.]

SEC. 4.   The commission may fix rates and establish rules for the transportation of passengers and property by transportation companies, prohibit discrimination, and award reparation for the exaction of unreasonable, excessive, or discriminatory charges. A transportation company may not raise a rate or incidental charge except after a showing to and a decision by the commission that the increase is justified, and this decision shall not be subject to judicial review except as to whether confiscation of property will result. *[New section adopted November 5, 1974.]*

[Public Utilities Commission—Compensation in Eminent Domain Proceedings]

SEC. 5.   The Legislature has plenary power, unlimited by the other provisions of this constitution but consistent with this article, to confer additional authority and jurisdiction upon the commission, to establish the manner and scope of review of commission action in a court of record, and to enable it to fix just compensation for utility property taken by eminent domain. *[New section adopted November 5, 1974.]*

[Public Utilities Commission—Powers and Duties]

SEC. 6.   The commission may fix rates, establish rules, examine records, issue subpenas, administer oaths, take testimony, punish for contempt, and prescribe a uniform system of accounts for all public utilities subject to its jurisdiction. *[New section adopted November 5, 1974.]*

[Free Passes, Public Officials—Conflict of Interest, Public Utilities Commissioner]

SEC. 7.   A transportation company may not grant free passes or discounts to anyone holding an office in this State; and the acceptance of a pass or discount by a public officer, other than a Public Utilities Commissioner, shall work a forfeiture of that office. A Public Utilities Commissioner may not hold an official relation to nor have a financial interest in a person or corporation subject to regulation by the commission. *[New section adopted November 5, 1974.]*

[*Public Utilities—Regulation*]

SEC. 8.   A city, county, or other public body may not regulate matters over which the Legislature grants regulatory power to the Commission. This section does not affect power over public utilities relating to the making and enforcement of police, sanitary, and other regulations concerning municipal affairs pursuant to a city charter existing on October 10, 1911, unless that power has been revoked by the city's electors, or the right of any city to grant franchises for public utilities or other businesses on terms, conditions, and in the manner prescribed by law. [*New section adopted November 5, 1974.*]

[*Restatement*]

SEC. 9.   The provisions of this article restate all related provisions of the Constitution in effect immediately prior to the effective date of this amendment and make no substantive change. [*New section adopted November 5, 1974.*]

SEC. 10.   [*Repealed November 5, 1974.*]

SEC. 17.   [*Repealed November 5, 1974.*]

SEC. 18.   [*Repealed November 5, 1974.*]

SEC. 19.   [*Repealed November 5, 1974.*]

SEC. 20.   [*Repealed November 5, 1974.*]

SEC. 21.   [*Repealed November 5, 1974.*]

SEC. 22.   [*Repealed November 5, 1974.*]

SEC. 23.   [*Repealed November 5, 1974.*]

SEC. 23a.   [*Repealed November 5, 1974.*]

ARTICLE XIII.   [*Repealed November 5, 1974. See Article XIII, below.*]

ARTICLE XIII *

TAXATION

SECTION 1.   [*Repealed November 5, 1974. See Section 1, below.*]

[*Uniformity Clause*]

SECTION 1.   Unless otherwise provided by this Constitution or the laws of the United States:

(a)   All property is taxable and shall be assessed at the same percentage of fair market value. When a value standard other than fair market value is prescribed by this Constitution or by statute authorized by this Constitution, the same percentage shall be applied to determine the assessed value. The value to which the percentage is applied, whether it be the fair market value or not, shall be known for property tax purposes as the full value.

---

* New Article XIII adopted November 5, 1974.

(b) All property so assessed shall be taxed in proportion to its full value. [*New section adopted November 5, 1974.*]

SEC. 1a.   [*Repealed November 5, 1974.*]

SEC. 1b.   [*Repealed November 5, 1974.*]

SEC. 1c.   [*Repealed November 5, 1974.*]

SEC. 1d.   [*Repealed November 5, 1974.*]

SEC. 1¼.   [*Repealed November 5, 1974.*]

SEC. 1¼a.   [*Repealed November 5, 1974.*]

SEC. 1¼b.   [*Repealed November 5, 1974.*]

SEC. 1½.   [*Repealed November 5, 1974.*]

SEC. 1½a.   [*Repealed November 5, 1974.*]

SEC. 1.60.   [*Repealed November 5, 1974.*]

SEC. 1.61.   [*Repealed November 5, 1974.*]

SEC. 1.62.   [*Repealed November 5, 1974.*]

SEC. 1.63.   [*Repealed November 5, 1974.*]

SEC. 1.64.   [*Repealed November 5, 1974.*]

SEC. 1.65.   [*Repealed November 5, 1974.*]

SEC. 1.66.   [*Repealed November 5, 1974.*]

SEC. 1.67.   [*Repealed November 5, 1974.*]

SEC. 1.68.   [*Repealed November 5, 1974.*]

SEC. 1.69.   [*Repealed November 5, 1974.*]

SEC. 1¾.   [*Repealed November 5, 1974.*]

SEC. 2.   [*Repealed November 5, 1974. See Section 2, below.*]

[*Personal Property Classification*]

SEC. 2.   The Legislature may provide for property taxation of all forms of tangible personal property, shares of capital stock, evidences of indebtedness, and any legal or equitable interest therein not exempt under any other provision of this article. The Legislature, two-thirds of the membership of each house concurring, may classify such personal property for differential taxation or for exemption. The tax on any interest in notes, debentures, shares of capital stock, bonds, solvent credits, deeds of trust, or mortgages shall not exceed four-tenths of one percent of full value, and the tax per dollar of full value shall not be higher on personal property than on real property in the same taxing jurisdiction. [*New section adopted November 5, 1974.*]

SEC. 2.5.   [*Repealed November 5, 1974.*]

SEC. 2.6.   [*Repealed November 5, 1974.*]

SEC. 2.8.   [*Repealed November 5, 1974.*]

[*Property Tax Exemptions*]

SEC. 3.   The following are exempt from property taxation:

[*State Owned Property*]

(a) Property owned by the State.

[*Local Government Property*]

(b) Property owned by a local government, except as otherwise provided in Section 11(a).

[*Government Bonds*]

(c) Bonds issued by the State or a local government in the State.

[*Public Property*]

(d) Property used for libraries and museums that are free and open to the public and property used exclusively for public schools, community colleges, state colleges, and state universities.

[*Educational Property*]

(e) Buildings, land, equipment, and securities used exclusively for educational purposes by a nonprofit institution of higher education.

[*Church Property*]

(f) Buildings, land on which they are situated, and equipment used exclusively for religious worship.

[*Cemetery Property*]

(g) Property used or held exclusively for the permanent deposit of human dead or for the care and maintenance of the property or the dead, except when used or held for profit. This property is also exempt from special assessment.

[*Growing Crops*]

(h) Growing crops.

[*Fruit and Nut Trees*]

(i) Fruit and nut trees until 4 years after the season in which they were planted in orchard form and grape vines until 3 years after the season in which they were planted in vineyard form.

[*Timber Exemption*]

(j) Immature forest trees planted on lands not previously bearing merchantable timber or planted or of natural growth on lands from which the merchantable original growth timber stand to the extent of 70 percent of all trees over 16 inches in diameter has been removed. Forest trees or timber shall be considered mature at such time after 40 years from the time of planting or removal of the original timber when so declared by a majority vote of a board consisting of a representative from the State Board of Forestry, a representative from the State Board of Equalization, and the assessor of the county in which the trees are located.

The Legislature may supersede the foregoing provisions with an alternative system or systems of taxing or exempting forest trees or timber, including a taxation system not based on property valuation. Any alternative system or systems shall provide for exemption of unharvested immature trees, shall encourage the continued use of timberlands for the production of trees for timber products, and shall provide for restricting the use of timberland to the production of timber products and compatible uses with provisions for taxation of timberland based on the restrictions. Nothing in this paragraph shall be construed to exclude timberland from the provisions of Section 8 of this article.

[Homeowners' Exemption]

(k) $7,000 of the full value of a dwelling, as defined by the Legislature, when occupied by an owner as his principal residence, unless the dwelling is receiving another real property exemption. The Legislature may increase this exemption and may deny it if the owner received state or local aid to pay taxes either in whole or in part, and either directly or indirectly, on the dwelling.

No increase in this exemption above the amount of $7,000 shall be effective for any fiscal year unless the Legislature increases the rate of state taxes in an amount sufficient to provide the subventions required by Section 25.

If the Legislature increases the homeowners' property tax exemption, it shall provide increases in benefits to qualified renters, as defined by law, comparable to the average increase in benefits to homeowners, as calculated by the Legislature.

[Vessels]

(*l*) Vessels of more than 50 tons burden in this State and engaged in the transportation of freight or passengers.

[Household Furnishings—Personal Effects]

(m) Household furnishings and personal effects not held or used in connection with a trade, profession, or business.

[Debt Secured by Land]

(n) Any debt secured by land.

[Veterans' Exemptions]

(o) Property in the amount of $1,000 of a claimant who—

(1) is serving in or has served in and has been discharged under honorable conditions from service in the United States Army, Navy, Air Force,

Marine Corps, Coast Guard, or Revenue Marine (Revenue Cutter) Service; and—

(2) served either

(i) in time of war, or

(ii) in time of peace in a campaign or expedition for which a medal has been issued by Congress, or

(iii) in time of peace and because of a service-connected disability was released from active duty; and—

(3) resides in the State on the current lien date.

An unmarried person who owns property valued at $5,000 or more, or a married person, who, together with the spouse, owns property valued at $10,000 or more, is ineligible for this exemption.

If the claimant is married and does not own property eligible for the full amount of the exemption, property of the spouse shall be eligible for the unused balance of the exemption.

[*Veterans' Exemptions*]

(p) Property in the amount of $1,000 of a claimant who—

(1) is the unmarried spouse of a deceased veteran who met the service requirement stated in paragraphs (1) and (2) of subsection 3(o), and

(2) does not own property in excess of $10,000, and

(3) is a resident of the State on the current lien date.

[*Veterans' Exemptions*]

(q) Property in the amount of $1,000 of a claimant who—

(1) is the parent of a deceased veteran who met the service requirement stated in paragraphs (1) and (2) of subsection 3(o), and

(2) receives a pension because of the veteran's service, and

(3) is a resident of the State on the current lien date.

Either parent of a deceased veteran may claim this exemption.

An unmarried person who owns property valued at $5,000 or more, or a married person, who, together with the spouse, owns property valued at $10,000 or more, is ineligible for this exemption.

[*Veterans' Exemptions*]

(r) No individual residing in the State on the effective date of this amendment who would have been eligible for the exemption provided by the previous section 1¼ of this article had it not been repealed shall lose eligibility for the exemption as a result of this amendment. [*As amended November 8, 1988.*]

[*Veterans' Exemptions—Change in Assessment Ratio—Adjustment*]

SEC. 3.5. In any year in which the assessment ratio is changed, the Legislature shall adjust the valuation of assessable property described in subdivisions (o), (p) and (q) of Section 3 of this article to maintain the same proportionate values of such property. [*New section adopted November 6, 1979.*]

[*Property Tax Exemption*]

SEC. 4.   The Legislature may exempt from property taxation in whole or in part:

[*Home of Veteran or Surviving Spouse*]

(a) The home of a person or a person's spouse, including an unmarried surviving spouse, if the person, because of injury incurred in military service, is blind in both eyes, has lost the use of 2 or more limbs, or is totally disabled, or if the person has, as a result of a service-connected injury or disease, died while on active duty in military service, unless the home is receiving another real property exemption.

[*Religious, Hospital and Charitable Property*]

(b) Property used exclusively for religious, hospital, or charitable purposes and owned or held in trust by corporations or other entities (1) that are organized and operating for those purposes, (2) that are nonprofit, and (3) no part of whose net earnings inures to the benefit of any private shareholder or individual.

[*Specific College Exemptions*]

(c) Property owned by the California School of Mechanical Arts, California Academy of Sciences, or Cogswell Polytechnical College, or held in trust for the Huntington Library and Art Gallery, or their successors.

[*Church Parking Lots*]

(d) Real property not used for commercial purposes that is reasonably and necessarily required for parking vehicles of persons worshipping on land exempt by Section 3(f). [*As amended November 3, 1992.*]

[*Exemption of Buildings Under Construction*]

SEC. 5.   Exemptions granted or authorized by Sections 3(e), 3(f), and 4(b) apply to buildings under construction, land required for their convenient use, and equipment in them if the intended use would qualify the property for exemption. [*New section adopted November 5, 1974.*]

SEC. 6.   [*Repealed November 5, 1974. See Section 6, below.*]

[*Exemption Waivers*]

SEC. 6.   The failure in any year to claim, in a manner required by the laws in effect at the time the claim is required to be made, an exemption or classification which reduces a property tax shall be deemed a waiver of the exemption or classification for that year. [*New section adopted November 5, 1974.*]

SEC. 7.   [*Repealed November 5, 1974. See Section 7, below.*]

[*Real Property Taxes—Exemption by County Boards of Supervisors*]

SEC. 7.   The Legislature, two-thirds of the membership of each house concurring, may authorize county boards of supervisors to exempt real property having a full value so low that, if not exempt, the total taxes and applicable subventions on the property would amount to less than the cost of assessing and collecting them. [*New section adopted November 5, 1974.*]

[*Open Space Land and Historical Property—Exemption*]

SEC. 8.   To promote the conservation, preservation and continued existence of open space lands, the Legislature may define open space land and shall provide that when this land is enforceably restricted, in a manner specified by the Legislature, to recreation, enjoyment of scenic beauty, use or conservation of natural resources, or production of food or fiber, it shall be valued for property tax purposes only on a basis that is consistent with its restrictions and uses.

To promote the preservation of property of historical significance, the Legislature may define such property and shall provide that when it is enforceably restricted, in a manner specified by the Legislature, it shall be valued for property tax purposes only on a basis that is consistent with its restrictions and uses. [*As amended June 8, 1976.*]

[*Postponement of Property Taxes*]

SEC. 8.5.   The Legislature may provide by law for the manner in which a person of low or moderate income who is 62 years of age or older may postpone ad valorem property taxes on the dwelling owned and occupied by him or her as his or her principal place of residence. The Legislature may also provide by law for the manner in which a disabled person may postpone payment of ad valorem property taxes on the dwelling owned and occupied by him or her as his or her principal place of residence. The Legislature shall have plenary power to define all terms in this section.

The Legislature shall provide by law for subventions to counties, cities and counties, cities and districts in an amount equal to the amount of revenue lost by each by reason of the postponement of taxes and for the reimbursement to the State of subventions from the payment of postponed taxes. Provision shall be made for the inclusion of reimbursement for the payment of interest on, and any costs to the State incurred in connection with, the subventions. [*As amended November 6, 1984.*]

SEC. 9.   [*Repealed November 5, 1974. See Section 9, below.*]

[Valuation of Certain Homes]

SEC. 9. The Legislature may provide for the assessment for taxation only on the basis of use of a single-family dwelling, as defined by the Legislature, and so much of the land as is required for its convenient use and occupation, when the dwelling is occupied by an owner and located on land zoned exclusively for single-family dwellings or for agricultural purposes. [*New section adopted November 5, 1974.*]

SEC. 9a.   [*Repealed November 5, 1974.*]

SEC. 9.5.   [*Repealed November 5, 1974.*]

SEC. 10.   [*Repealed November 5, 1974. See Section 10, below.*]

[Golf Course Values]

SEC. 10. Real property in a parcel of 10 or more acres which, on the lien date and for 2 or more years immediately preceding, has been used exclusively for nonprofit golf course purposes shall be assessed for taxation on the basis of such use, plus any value attributable to mines, quarries, hydrocarbon substances, or other minerals in the property or the right to extract hydrocarbons or other minerals from the property. [*New section adopted November 5, 1974.*]

SEC. 10½.   [*Repealed November 5, 1974.*]

SEC. 11.   [*Repealed November 5, 1974. See Section 11, below.*]

[Taxation of Local Government Real Property]

SEC. 11. (a) Lands owned by a local government that are outside its boundaries, including rights to use or divert water from surface or underground sources and any other interests in lands, are taxable if (1) they are located in Inyo or Mono County and (a) they were assessed for taxation to the local government in Inyo County as of the 1966 lien date, or in Mono County as of the 1967 lien date, whether or not the assessment was valid when made, or (b) they were acquired by the local government subsequent to that lien date and were assessed to a prior owner as of that lien date and each lien date thereafter, or (2) they are located outside Inyo or Mono County and were taxable when acquired by the local government. Improvements owned by a local government that are outside its boundaries are taxable if they were taxable when acquired or were constructed by the local government to replace improvements which were taxable when acquired.

(b) Taxable land belonging to a local government and located in Inyo County shall be assessed in any year subsequent to 1968 at the place where it was assessed as of the 1966 lien date and in an amount derived by multiplying its 1966 assessed value by the ratio of the statewide per capita assessed value of land as of the last lien date prior to the current lien date to $766, using civilian population only. Taxable land belonging to a local government and located in Mono County shall be assessed in any year subsequent to 1968 at the place where it was assessed as of the 1967 lien date and in an amount determined by the preceding formula except that the 1967 lien date, the 1967 assessed value, and the figure $856 shall be used in the formula. Taxable land belonging to a local government and located outside of Inyo and Mono counties shall be assessed at the place where located and in an amount that does not exceed the lower of (1) its fair market value times the prevailing percentage of fair market value at which other lands are assessed and (2) a figure derived in the manner specified in this Section for land located in Mono County.

If land acquired by a local government after the lien date of the base year specified in this Section was assessed in the base year as part of a larger parcel, the assessed value of the part in the base year shall be that fraction of the assessed value of the larger parcel that the area of the part is of the area of the larger parcel.

If a local government divests itself of ownership of land without water rights and this land was assessed in Inyo County as of the 1966 lien date or in Mono County as of the 1967 lien date, the divestment shall not diminish the quantity of water rights assessable and taxable at the place where assessed as of that lien date.

(c) In the event the Legislature changes the prevailing percentage of fair market value at which land is assessed for taxation, there shall be used in the computations required by Section 11(b) of this Article, for the first year for which the new percentage is applicable, in lieu of the statewide per capita assessed value of land as of the last lien date prior to the current lien date, the statewide per capita assessed value of land on the prior lien date times the ratio of the new prevailing percentage of fair market value to the previous prevailing percentage.

(d) If, after March 1954, a taxable improvement is replaced while owned by and in possession of a local government, the replacement improvement shall be assessed, as long as it is owned by a local government, as other improvements are except that the assessed value shall not exceed the product of (1) the percentage at which privately owned improvements are assessed times (2) the highest full value ever used for taxation of the improvement that has been replaced. For purposes of this calculation, the full value for any year prior to 1967 shall be conclusively presumed to be 4 times the assessed value in that year.

(e) No tax, charge, assessment, or levy of any character, other than those taxes authorized by Sections 11(a) to 11(d), inclusive, of this Article, shall be imposed upon one local government by another local government that is based or calculated upon the consumption or use of water outside the boundaries of the government imposing it.

(f) Any taxable interest of any character, other than a lease for agricultural purposes and an interest of a local government, in any land owned by a local government that is subject to taxation pursuant to Section 11(a) of this Article shall be taxed in the same manner as other taxable interests. The aggregate value of all the interests subject to taxation pursuant to Section 11(a), however, shall not exceed the value of all interests in the land less the taxable value of the interest of any local government ascertained as provided in Sections 11(a) to 11(e), inclusive, of this Article.

(g) Any assessment made pursuant to Sections 11(a) to 11(d), inclusive, of this Article shall be subject to review, equalization, and adjustment by the State Board of Equalization, but an adjustment shall conform to the provisions of these Sections. [*New section adopted November 5, 1974.*]

[Unsecured Property Tax Rate]

SEC. 12.   (a) Except as provided in subdivision (b), taxes on personal property, possessory interests in land, and taxable improvements located on land exempt from taxation which are not a lien upon land sufficient in value to secure their payment shall be levied at the rates for the preceding tax year upon property of the same kind where the taxes were a lien upon land sufficient in value to secure their payment.

(b) In any year in which the assessment ratio is changed, the Legislature shall adjust the rate described in subdivision (a) to maintain equality between property on the secured and unsecured rolls. [*As amended November 2, 1976.*]

SEC. 12¾.   [*Repealed November 5, 1974.*]

SEC. 13.   [*Repealed November 5, 1974. See Section 13, below.*]

[Separate Land and Improvements Assessment]

SEC. 13.   Land and improvements shall be separately assessed. [*New section adopted November 5, 1974.*]

SEC. 14.   [*Repealed November 5, 1974. See Section 14, below.*]

[Tax Situs]

SEC. 14.   All property taxed by local government shall be assessed in the county, city, and district in which it is situated. [*New section adopted November 5, 1974.*]

SEC. 14⅘.   [*Repealed November 5, 1974.*]

SEC. 15.   [*Repealed November 5, 1974. See Section 15, below.*]

[Disaster Relief]

SEC. 15.   The Legislature may authorize local government to provide for the assessment or reassessment of taxable property physically damaged or destroyed after the lien date to which the assessment or reassessment relates. [*New section adopted November 5, 1974.*]

SEC. 16.   [*Repealed November 5, 1974. See Section 16, below.*]

[*County Board of Equalization—Assessment Appeals Board*]

SEC. 16. The county board of supervisors, or one or more assessment appeals boards created by the county board of supervisors, shall constitute the county board of equalization for a county. Two or more county boards of supervisors may jointly create one or more assessment appeals boards which shall constitute the county board of equalization for each of the participating counties.

Except as provided in subdivision (g) of Section 11, the county board of equalization, under such rules of notice as the county board may prescribe, shall equalize the values of all property on the local assessment roll by adjusting individual assessments.

County boards of supervisors shall fix the compensation for members of assessment appeals boards, furnish clerical and other assistance for those boards, adopt rules of notice and procedures for those boards as may be required to facilitate their work and to insure uniformity in the processing and decision of equalization petitions, and may provide for their discontinuance.

The Legislature shall provide for: (a) the number and qualifications of members of assessment appeals boards, the manner of selecting, appointing, and removing them, and the terms for which they serve, and (b) the procedure by which two or more county boards of supervisors may jointly create one or more assessment appeals boards. [*New section adopted November 5, 1974.*]

[*Board of Equalization*]

SEC. 17. The Board of Equalization consists of 5 voting members: the Controller and 4 members elected for 4-year terms at gubernatorial elections. The State shall be divided into four Board of Equalization districts with the voters of each district electing one member. No member may serve more than 2 terms. [*As amended November 6, 1990. Initiative measure.*]

SEC. 18. [*Repealed November 5, 1974. See Section 18, below.*]

[*Intercounty Equalization*]

SEC. 18. The Board shall measure county assessment levels annually and shall bring those levels into conformity by adjusting entire secured local assessment rolls. In the event a property tax is levied by the State, however, the effects of unequalized local assessment levels, to the extent any remain after such adjustments, shall be corrected for purposes of distributing this tax by equalizing the assessment levels of locally and state-assessed properties and varying the rate of the state tax inversely with the counties' respective assessment levels. [*New section adopted November 5, 1974.*]

SEC. 19. [*Repealed November 5, 1974. See Section 19, below.*]

[*State Assessment*]

Sec. 19.   The Board shall annually assess (1) pipelines, flumes, canals, ditches, and aqueducts lying within 2 or more counties and (2) property, except franchises, owned or used by regulated railway, telegraph, or telephone companies, car companies operating on railways in the State, and companies transmitting or selling gas or electricity. This property shall be subject to taxation to the same extent and in the same manner as other property.

No other tax or license charge may be imposed on these companies which differs from that imposed on mercantile, manufacturing, and other business corporations. This restriction does not release a utility company from payments agreed on or required by law for a special privilege or franchise granted by a government body.

The Legislature may authorize Board assessment of property owned or used by other public utilities.

The Board may delegate to a local assessor the duty to assess a property used but not owned by a state assessee on which the taxes are to be paid by a local assessee. [*New section adopted November 5, 1974.*]

Sec. 20.   [*Repealed November 5, 1974. See Section 20, below.*]

[*Maximum Tax Rates—Bonding Limits*]

Sec. 20.   The Legislature may provide maximum property tax rates and bonding limits for local governments. [*New section adopted November 5, 1974.*]

Sec. 21.   [*Repealed November 5, 1974. See Section 21, below.*]

[*School District Tax*]

Sec. 21.   Within such limits as may be provided under Section 20 of this Article, the Legislature shall provide for an annual levy by county governing bodies of school district taxes sufficient to produce annual revenues for each district that the district's board determines are required for its schools and district functions. [*New section adopted November 5, 1974.*]

Sec. 21.5.   [*Repealed November 5, 1974.*]

Sec. 22.   [*Repealed November 5, 1974. See Section 22, below.*]

[*State Property Tax Limitations*]

Sec. 22.   Not more than 25 percent of the total appropriations from all funds of the State shall be raised by means of taxes on real and personal property according to the value thereof. [*New section adopted November 5, 1974.*]

Sec. 23.   [*Repealed November 5, 1974. See Section 23, below.*]

[*State Boundary Change*]

SEC. 23. If state boundaries change, the Legislature shall determine how property affected shall be taxed. [*New section adopted November 5, 1974.*]

SEC. 24. [*Repealed November 5, 1974. See Section 24, below.*]

[*State Taxes for Local Purposes*]

SEC. 24. (a) The Legislature may not impose taxes for local purposes but may authorize local governments to impose them.

(b) The Legislature may not reallocate, transfer, borrow, appropriate, restrict the use of, or otherwise use the proceeds of any tax imposed or levied by a local government solely for the local government's purposes.

[*State Funds for Local Purposes*]

(c) Money appropriated from state funds to a local government for its local purposes may be used as provided by law.

[*Subventions*]

(d) Money subvened to a local government under Section 25 may be used for state or local purposes. [*As amended November 2, 2010. Initiative measure.*]

SEC. 25. [*Repealed November 5, 1974. See Section 25, below.*]

[*Homeowners' Exemption, Reimbursement of Local Government*]

SEC. 25. The Legislature shall provide, in the same fiscal year, reimbursements to each local government for revenue lost because of Section 3(k). [*New section adopted November 5, 1974.*]

[*Ad Valorem Property Tax Revenue Allocations*]

SEC. 25.5. (a) On or after November 3, 2004, the Legislature shall not enact a statute to do any of the following:

(1) (A) Except as otherwise provided in subparagraph (B), modify the manner in which ad valorem property tax revenues are allocated in accordance with subdivision (a) of Section 1 of Article XIIIA so as to reduce for any fiscal year the percentage of the total amount of ad valorem property tax revenues in a county that is allocated among all of the local agencies in that county below the percentage of the total amount of those revenues that would be allocated among those agencies for the same fiscal year under the statutes in effect on November 3, 2004. For purposes of this subparagraph, "percentage" does not include any property tax revenues referenced in paragraph (2).

(B) In the 2009–10 fiscal year only, and except as otherwise provided in subparagraph (C), subparagraph (A) may be suspended for that fiscal year if all of the following conditions are met:

(i) The Governor issues a proclamation that declares that, due to a severe state fiscal hardship, the suspension of subparagraph (A) is necessary.

(ii) The Legislature enacts an urgency statute, pursuant to a bill passed in each house of the Legislature by rollcall vote entered in the journal, two-thirds of the membership concurring, that contains a suspension of subparagraph (A) for that fiscal year and does not contain any other provision.

(iii) No later than the effective date of the statute described in clause (ii), a statute is enacted that provides for the full repayment to local agencies of the total amount of revenue losses, including interest as provided by law, resulting from the modification of ad valorem property tax revenue allocations to local agencies. This full repayment shall be made not later than the end of the third fiscal year immediately following the fiscal year to which the modification applies.

(C) A suspension of subparagraph (A) shall not result in a total ad valorem property tax revenue loss to all local agencies within a county that exceeds 8 percent of the total amount of ad valorem property tax revenues that were allocated among all local agencies within that county for the fiscal year immediately preceding the fiscal year for which subparagraph (A) is suspended.

(2) (A) Except as otherwise provided in subparagraphs (B) and (C), restrict the authority of a city, county, or city and county to impose a tax rate under, or change the method of distributing revenues derived under, the Bradley-Burns Uniform Local Sales and Use Tax Law set forth in Part 1.5 (commencing with Section 7200) of Division 2 of the Revenue and Taxation Code, as that law read on November 3, 2004. The restriction imposed by this subparagraph also applies to the entitlement of a city, county, or city and county to the change in tax rate resulting from the end of the revenue exchange period, as defined in Section 7203.1 of the Revenue and Taxation Code as that section read on November 3, 2004.

(B) The Legislature may change by statute the method of distributing the revenues derived under a use tax imposed pursuant to the Bradley-Burns Uniform Local Sales and Use Tax Law to allow the State to participate in an interstate compact or to comply with federal law.

(C) The Legislature may authorize by statute two or more specifically identified local agencies within a county, with the approval of the governing body of each of those agencies, to enter into a contract to exchange allocations of ad valorem property tax revenues for revenues derived from a tax rate imposed under the Bradley-Burns Uniform Local Sales and Use Tax Law. The exchange under this subparagraph of revenues derived from a tax rate imposed under that law shall not require voter approval for the continued imposition of any portion of an existing tax rate from which those revenues are derived.

(3) Except as otherwise provided in subparagraph (C) of paragraph (2), change for any fiscal year the pro rata shares in which ad valorem property tax revenues are allocated among local agencies in a county other than pursuant to a bill passed in each house of the Legislature by rollcall vote entered in the journal, two-thirds of the membership concurring. The Legislature shall not change the pro rata shares of ad valorem property tax pursuant to this paragraph, nor change the allocation of the revenues described in Section 15 of Article XI, to reimburse a local government when the Legislature or any state agency mandates a new program or higher level of service on that local government.

(4) Extend beyond the revenue exchange period, as defined in Section 7203.1 of the Revenue and Taxation Code as that section read on November 3, 2004, the suspension of the authority, set forth in that section on that date, of a city, county, or city and county to impose a sales and use tax rate under the Bradley-Burns Uniform Local Sales and Use Tax Law.

(5) Reduce, during any period in which the rate authority suspension described in paragraph (4) is operative, the payments to a city, county, or city and county that are required by Section 97.68 of the Revenue and Taxation Code, as that section read on November 3, 2004.

(6) Restrict the authority of a local entity to impose a transactions and use tax rate in accordance with the Transactions and Use Tax Law (Part 1.6 (commencing with Section 7251) of Division 2 of the Revenue and Taxation Code), or change the method for distributing revenues derived under a transaction and use tax rate imposed under that law, as it read on November 3, 2004.

(7) Require a community redevelopment agency (A) to pay, remit, loan, or otherwise transfer, directly or indirectly, taxes on ad valorem real property and tangible personal property allocated to the agency pursuant to Section 16 of Article XVI to or for the benefit of the State, any agency of the State, or any jurisdiction; or (B) to use, restrict, or assign a particular purpose for such taxes for the benefit of the State, any agency of the State, or any jurisdiction, other than (i) for making payments to affected taxing agencies pursuant to Sections 33607.5 and 33607.7 of the Health and Safety Code or similar statutes requiring such payments, as those statutes read on January 1, 2008, or (ii) for the purpose of increasing, improving, and preserving the supply of low and moderate income housing available at affordable housing cost.

(b) For purposes of this section, the following definitions apply:

(1) "Ad valorem property tax revenues" means all revenues derived from the tax collected by a county under subdivision (a) of Section 1 of Article XIIIA, regardless of any of this revenue being otherwise classified by statute.

(2) "Local agency" has the same meaning as specified in Section 95 of the Revenue and Taxation Code as that section read on November 3, 2004.

(3) "Jurisdiction" has the same meaning as specified in Section 95 of the Revenue and Taxation Code as that section read on November 3, 2004. [*As amended November 2, 2010. Initiative measure.*]

[Income Tax]

Sec. 26.   (a) Taxes on or measured by income may be imposed on persons, corporations, or other entities as prescribed by law.

(b) Interest on bonds issued by the State or a local government in the State is exempt from taxes on income.

(c) Income of a nonprofit educational institution of collegiate grade within the State of California is exempt from taxes on or measured by income if both of the following conditions are met:

(1) The income is not unrelated business income as defined by the Legislature.

(2) The income is used exclusively for educational purposes.

(d) A nonprofit organization that is exempted from taxation by Chapter 4 (commencing with Section 23701) of Part 11 of Division 2 of the Revenue and Taxation Code or Subchapter F (commencing with Section 501) of Chapter 1 of Subtitle A of the Internal Revenue Code of 1986, or the successor of either, is exempt from any business license tax or fee measured by income or gross receipts that is levied by a county or city, whether charter or general law, a city and county, a school district, a special district, or any other local agency. [*As amended June 7, 1994.*]

[Bank and Corporation Taxes]

Sec. 27.   The Legislature, a majority of the membership of each house concurring, may tax corporations, including state and national banks, and their franchises by any method not prohibited by this Constitution or the Constitution or laws of the United States. Unless otherwise provided by the Legislature, the tax on state and national banks shall be according to or measured by their net income and shall be in lieu of all other taxes and license fees upon banks or their shares, except taxes upon real property and vehicle registration and license fees. [*As amended June 8, 1976.*]

[Taxation of Insurance Companies]

Sec. 28.   (a) "Insurer," as used in this section, includes insurance companies or associations and reciprocal or interinsurance exchanges together with their corporate or other attorneys in fact considered as a single unit, and the State Compensation Insurance Fund. As used in this paragraph, "companies" includes persons, partnerships, joint stock associations, companies and corporations.

(b) An annual tax is hereby imposed on each insurer doing business in this State on the base, at the rates, and subject to the deductions from the tax hereinafter specified.

(c) In the case of an insurer not transacting title insurance in this State, the "basis of the annual tax" is, in respect to each year, the amount of gross premiums, less return premiums, received in such year by such insurer upon its business done in this State, other than premiums received for reinsurance and for ocean marine insurance.

In the case of an insurer transacting title insurance in this State, the "basis of the annual tax" is, in respect to each year, all income upon business done in this State, except:

(1) Interest and dividends.

(2) Rents from real property.

(3) Profits from the sale or other disposition of investments.

(4) Income from investments.

"Investments" as used in this subdivision includes property acquired by such insurer in the settlement or adjustment of claims against it but excludes investments in title plants and title records. Income derived directly or indirectly from the use of title plants and title records is included in the basis of the annual tax.

In the case of an insurer transacting title insurance in this State which has a trust department and does a trust business under the banking laws of this State, there shall be excluded from the basis of the annual tax imposed by this section, the income of, and from the assets of, such trust department and such trust business, if such income is taxed by this State or included in the measure of any tax imposed by this State.

(d) The rate of the tax to be applied to the basis of the annual tax in respect to each year is 2.35 percent.

(f) The tax imposed on insurers by this section is in lieu of all other taxes and licenses, state, county, and municipal, upon such insurers and their property, except:

(1) Taxes upon their real estate.

(2) That an insurer transacting title insurance in this State which has a trust department or does a trust business under the banking laws of this State is subject to taxation with respect to such trust department or trust business to the same extent and in the same manner as trust companies and the trust departments of banks doing business in this State.

(3) When by or pursuant to the laws of any other state or foreign country any taxes, licenses and other fees, in the aggregate, and any fines, penalties, deposit requirements or other material obligations, prohibitions or restrictions are or would be imposed upon California insurers, or upon the agents or representatives of such insurers, which are in excess of such taxes, licenses and other fees, in the aggregate, or which are in excess of the fines, penalties, deposit requirements or other obligations, prohibitions, or restrictions directly imposed upon similar insurers, or upon the agents or representatives of such insurers, of such other state or country under the

statutes of this State; so long as such laws of such other state or country continue in force or are so applied, the same taxes, licenses and other fees, in the aggregate, or fines, penalties or deposit requirements or other material obligations, prohibitions, or restrictions, of whatever kind shall be imposed upon the insurers, or upon the agents or representatives of such insurers, of such other state or country doing business or seeking to do business in California. Any tax, license or other fee or other obligation imposed by any city, county, or other political subdivision or agency of such other state or country on California insurers or their agents or representatives shall be deemed to be imposed by such state or country within the meaning of this paragraph (3) of subdivision (f).

The provisions of this paragraph (3) of subdivision (f) shall not apply as to personal income taxes, nor as to ad valorem taxes on real or personal property nor as to special purpose obligations or assessments heretofore imposed by another state or foreign country in connection with particular kinds of insurance, other than property insurance; except that deductions, from premium taxes or other taxes otherwise payable, allowed on account of real estate or personal property taxes paid shall be taken into consideration in determining the propriety and extent of retaliatory action under this paragraph (3) of subdivision (f).

For the purposes of this paragraph (3) of subdivision (f) the domicile of an alien insurer, other than insurers formed under the laws of Canada, shall be that state in which is located its principal place of business in the United States.

In the case of an insurer formed under the laws of Canada or a province thereof, its domicile shall be deemed to be that province in which its head office is situated.

The provisions of this paragraph (3) of subdivision (f) shall also be applicable to reciprocals or interinsurance exchanges and fraternal benefit societies.

(4) The tax on ocean marine insurance.

(5) Motor vehicle and other vehicle registration license fees and any other tax or license fee imposed by the State upon vehicles, motor vehicles or the operation thereof.

(6) That each corporate or other attorney in fact of a reciprocal or interinsurance exchange shall be subject to all taxes imposed upon corporations or others doing business in the State, other than taxes on income derived from its principal business as attorney in fact.

A corporate or other attorney in fact of each exchange shall annually compute the amount of tax that would be payable by it under prevailing law except for the provisions of this section, and any management fee due from each exchange to its corporate or other attorney in fact shall be reduced pro tanto by a sum equivalent to the amount so computed.

(g) Every insurer transacting the business of ocean marine insurance in this State shall annually pay to the State a tax measured by that proportion of the underwriting profit of such insurer from such insurance written in the United States, which the gross premiums of the insurer from such insurance written in this State bear to the gross premiums of the insurer from such insurance written within the United States, at the rate of 5 per centum, which tax shall be in lieu of all other taxes and licenses, state, county and municipal, upon such insurer, except taxes upon real estate, and such other taxes as may be assessed or levied against such insurer on account of any other class of insurance written by it. The Legislature shall define the terms "ocean marine insurance" and "underwriting profit," and shall provide for the assessment, levy, collection and enforcement of the ocean marine tax.

(h) The taxes provided for by this section shall be assessed by the State Board of Equalization.

(i) The Legislature, a majority of all the members elected to each of the two houses voting in favor thereof, may by law change the rate or rates of taxes herein imposed upon insurers.

(j) This section is not intended to and does not change the law as it has previously existed with respect to the meaning of the words "gross premiums, less return premiums, received" as used in this article. [As amended June 8, 1976.]

[Local Government Tax Sharing]

SEC. 29. (a) The Legislature may authorize counties, cities and counties, and cities to enter into contracts to apportion between them the revenue derived from any sales or use tax imposed by them that is collected for them by the State. Before the contract becomes operative, it shall be authorized by a majority of those voting on the question in each jurisdiction at a general or direct primary election.

(b) Notwithstanding subdivision (a), on and after the operative date of this subdivision, counties, cities and counties, and cities may enter into contracts to apportion between them the revenue derived from any sales or use tax imposed by them pursuant to the Bradley-Burns Uniform Local Sales and Use Tax Law, or any successor provisions, that is collected for them by the State, if the ordinance or resolution proposing each contract is approved by a two-thirds vote of the governing body of each jurisdiction that is a party to the contract. [As amended November 3, 1998.]

[Tax Liens—Presumption of Payment of Taxes]

SEC. 30. Every tax shall be conclusively presumed to have been paid after 30 years from the time it became a lien unless the property subject to the lien has been sold in the manner provided by the Legislature for the payment of the tax. [New section adopted November 5, 1974.]

[*Power to Tax*]

SEC. 31.   The power to tax may not be surrendered or suspended by grant or contract. [*New section adopted November 5, 1974.*]

[*Proceedings Relating to Collection*]

SEC. 32.   No legal or equitable process shall issue in any proceeding in any court against this State or any officer thereof to prevent or enjoin the collection of any tax. After payment of a tax claimed to be illegal, an action may be maintained to recover the tax paid, with interest, in such manner as may be provided by the Legislature. [*New section adopted November 5, 1974.*]

[*Legislature to Enact Laws*]

SEC. 33.   The Legislature shall pass all laws necessary to carry out the provisions of this article. [*New section adopted November 5, 1974.*]

[*Food Products — Taxation*]

SEC. 34.   Neither the State of California nor any of its political subdivisions shall levy or collect a sales or use tax on the sale of, or the storage, use or other consumption in this State of food products for human consumption except as provided by statute as of the effective date of this section. [*New section adopted November 3, 1992. Operative January 1, 1993. Initiative measure.*]

[*Local Public Safety Services*]

SEC. 35.   (a) The people of the State of California find and declare all of the following:

(1) Public safety services are critically important to the security and well-being of the State's citizens and to the growth and revitalization of the State's economic base.

(2) The protection of the public safety is the first responsibility of local government and local officials have an obligation to give priority to the provision of adequate public safety services.

(3) In order to assist local government in maintaining a sufficient level of public safety services, the proceeds of the tax enacted pursuant to this section shall be designated exclusively for public safety.

(b) In addition to any sales and use taxes imposed by the Legislature, the following sales and use taxes are hereby imposed:

(1) For the privilege of selling tangible personal property at retail, a tax is hereby imposed upon all retailers at the rate of ½ percent of the gross receipts of any retailer from the sale of all tangible personal property sold at retail in this State on and after January 1, 1994.

(2) An excise tax is hereby imposed on the storage, use, or other consumption in this State of tangible personal property purchased from any

retailer on and after January 1, 1994, for storage, use, or other consumption in this State at the rate of ½ percent of the sales price of the property.

(c) The Sales and Use Tax Law, including any amendments made thereto on or after the effective date of this section, shall be applicable to the taxes imposed by subdivision (b).

(d) (1) All revenues, less refunds, derived from the taxes imposed pursuant to subdivision (b) shall be transferred to the Local Public Safety Fund for allocation by the Legislature, as prescribed by statute, to counties in which either of the following occurs:

(A) The board of supervisors, by a majority vote of its membership, requests an allocation from the Local Public Safety Fund in a manner prescribed by statute.

(B) A majority of the county's voters voting thereon approve the addition of this section.

(2) Moneys in the Local Public Safety Fund shall be allocated for use exclusively for public safety services of local agencies.

(e) Revenues derived from the taxes imposed pursuant to subdivision (b) shall not be considered proceeds of taxes for purposes of Article XIII B or State General Fund proceeds of taxes within the meaning of Article XVI.

(f) Except for the provisions of Section 34, this section shall supersede any other provisions of this Constitution that are in conflict with the provisions of this section, including, but not limited to, Section 9 of Article II. [*New section adopted November 2, 1993.*]

[*Protection of Schools and Local Public Safety — Temporary Income and Sales Tax Increases*]

SEC. 36.   (a) For purposes of this section:

(1) "Public Safety Services" includes the following:

(A) Employing and training public safety officials, including law enforcement personnel, attorneys assigned to criminal proceedings, and court security staff.

(B) Managing local jails and providing housing, treatment, and services for, and supervision of, juvenile and adult offenders.

(C) Preventing child abuse, neglect, or exploitation; providing services to children and youth who are abused, neglected, or exploited, or who are at risk of abuse, neglect, or exploitation, and the families of those children; providing adoption services; and providing adult protective services.

(D) Providing mental health services to children and adults to reduce failure in school, harm to self or others, homelessness, and preventable incarceration or institutionalization.

(E) Preventing, treating, and providing recovery services for substance abuse.

(2) "2011 Realignment Legislation" means legislation enacted on or before September 30, 2012, to implement the state budget plan, that is entitled 2011 Realignment and provides for the assignment of Public Safety Services responsibilities to local agencies, including related reporting responsibilities. The legislation shall provide local agencies with maximum flexibility and control over the design, administration, and delivery of Public Safety Services consistent with federal law and funding requirements, as determined by the Legislature. However, 2011 Realignment Legislation shall include no new programs assigned to local agencies after January 1, 2012, except for the early periodic screening, diagnosis, and treatment (EPSDT) program and mental health managed care.

(b) (1) Except as provided in subdivision (d), commencing in the 2011–12 fiscal year and continuing thereafter, the following amounts shall be deposited into the Local Revenue Fund 2011, as established by Section 30025 of the Government Code, as follows:

(A) All revenues, less refunds, derived from the taxes described in Sections 6051.15 and 6201.15 of the Revenue and Taxation Code, as those sections read on July 1, 2011.

(B) All revenues, less refunds, derived from the vehicle license fees described in Section 11005 of the Revenue and Taxation Code, as that section read on July 1, 2011.

(2) On and after July 1, 2011, the revenues deposited pursuant to paragraph (1) shall not be considered General Fund revenues or proceeds of taxes for purposes of Section 8 of Article XVI of the California Constitution.

(c) (1) Funds deposited in the Local Revenue Fund 2011 are continuously appropriated exclusively to fund the provision of Public Safety Services by local agencies. Pending full implementation of the 2011 Realignment Legislation, funds may also be used to reimburse the State for program costs incurred in providing Public Safety Services on behalf of local agencies. The methodology for allocating funds shall be as specified in the 2011 Realignment Legislation.

(2) The county treasurer, city and county treasurer, or other appropriate official shall create a County Local Revenue Fund 2011 within the treasury of each county or city and county. The money in each County Local Revenue Fund 2011 shall be exclusively used to fund the provision of Public Safety Services by local agencies as specified by the 2011 Realignment Legislation.

(3) Notwithstanding Section 6 of Article XIII B, or any other constitutional provision, a mandate of a new program or higher level of service on a local agency imposed by the 2011 Realignment Legislation, or by any regulation adopted or any executive order or administrative directive issued to implement that legislation, shall not constitute a mandate requiring the State to provide a subvention of funds within the meaning of that sec-

tion. Any requirement that a local agency comply with Chapter 9 (commencing with Section 54950) of Part 1 of Division 2 of Title 5 of the Government Code, with respect to performing its Public Safety Services responsibilities, or any other matter, shall not be a reimbursable mandate under Section 6 of Article XIII B.

(4) (A) Legislation enacted after September 30, 2012, that has an overall effect of increasing the costs already borne by a local agency for programs or levels of service mandated by the 2011 Realignment Legislation shall apply to local agencies only to the extent that the State provides annual funding for the cost increase. Local agencies shall not be obligated to provide programs or levels of service required by legislation, described in this subparagraph, above the level for which funding has been provided.

(B) Regulations, executive orders, or administrative directives, implemented after October 9, 2011, that are not necessary to implement the 2011 Realignment Legislation, and that have an overall effect of increasing the costs already borne by a local agency for programs or levels of service mandated by the 2011 Realignment Legislation, shall apply to local agencies only to the extent that the State provides annual funding for the cost increase. Local agencies shall not be obligated to provide programs or levels of service pursuant to new regulations, executive orders, or administrative directives, described in this subparagraph, above the level for which funding has been provided.

(C) Any new program or higher level of service provided by local agencies, as described in subparagraphs (A) and (B), above the level for which funding has been provided, shall not require a subvention of funds by the State nor otherwise be subject to Section 6 of Article XIII B. This paragraph shall not apply to legislation currently exempt from subvention under paragraph (2) of subdivision (a) of Section 6 of Article XIII B as that paragraph read on January 2, 2011.

(D) The State shall not submit to the federal government any plans or waivers, or amendments to those plans or waivers, that have an overall effect of increasing the cost borne by a local agency for programs or levels of service mandated by the 2011 Realignment Legislation, except to the extent that the plans, waivers, or amendments are required by federal law, or the State provides annual funding for the cost increase.

(E) The State shall not be required to provide a subvention of funds pursuant to this paragraph for a mandate that is imposed by the State at the request of a local agency or to comply with federal law. State funds required by this paragraph shall be from a source other than those described in subdivisions (b) and (d), ad valorem property taxes, or the Social Services Subaccount of the Sales Tax Account of the Local Revenue Fund.

(5) (A) For programs described in subparagraphs (C) to (E), inclusive, of paragraph (1) of subdivision (a) and included in the 2011 Realignment Legislation, if there are subsequent changes in federal statutes or regula-

tions that alter the conditions under which federal matching funds as described in the 2011 Realignment Legislation are obtained, and have the overall effect of increasing the costs incurred by a local agency, the State shall annually provide at least 50 percent of the nonfederal share of those costs as determined by the State.

(B) When the State is a party to any complaint brought in a federal judicial or administrative proceeding that involves one or more of the programs described in subparagraphs (C) to (E), inclusive, of paragraph (1) of subdivision (a) and included in the 2011 Realignment Legislation, and there is a settlement or judicial or administrative order that imposes a cost in the form of a monetary penalty or has the overall effect of increasing the costs already borne by a local agency for programs or levels of service mandated by the 2011 Realignment Legislation, the State shall annually provide at least 50 percent of the nonfederal share of those costs as determined by the State. Payment by the State is not required if the State determines that the settlement or order relates to one or more local agencies failing to perform a ministerial duty, failing to perform a legal obligation in good faith, or acting in a negligent or reckless manner.

(C) The state funds provided in this paragraph shall be from funding sources other than those described in subdivisions (b) and (d), ad valorem property taxes, or the Social Services Subaccount of the Sales Tax Account of the Local Revenue Fund.

(6) If the State or a local agency fails to perform a duty or obligation under this section or under the 2011 Realignment Legislation, an appropriate party may seek judicial relief. These proceedings shall have priority over all other civil matters.

(7) The funds deposited into a County Local Revenue Fund 2011 shall be spent in a manner designed to maintain the State's eligibility for federal matching funds, and to ensure compliance by the State with applicable federal standards governing the State's provision of Public Safety Services.

(8) The funds deposited into a County Local Revenue Fund 2011 shall not be used by local agencies to supplant other funding for Public Safety Services.

(d) If the taxes described in subdivision (b) are reduced or cease to be operative, the State shall annually provide moneys to the Local Revenue Fund 2011 in an amount equal to or greater than the aggregate amount that otherwise would have been provided by the taxes described in subdivision (b). The method for determining that amount shall be described in the 2011 Realignment Legislation, and the State shall be obligated to provide that amount for so long as the local agencies are required to perform the Public Safety Services responsibilities assigned by the 2011 Realignment Legislation. If the State fails to annually appropriate that amount, the Controller shall transfer that amount from the General Fund in pro rata monthly shares to the Local Revenue Fund 2011. Thereafter, the Controller shall disburse these amounts to local agencies in the manner directed by the 2011 Realignment Legislation. The state obligations under this subdivision shall have a lower priority claim to General Fund money than the first priority for money to be set apart under Section 8 of Article XVI and the second priority to pay voter-approved debts and liabilities described in Section 1 of Article XVI.

(e) (1) To ensure that public education is not harmed in the process of providing critical protection to local Public Safety Services, the Education Protection Account is hereby created in the General Fund to receive and disburse the revenues derived from the incremental increases in taxes imposed by this section, as specified in subdivision (f).

(2) (A) Before June 30, 2013, and before June 30 of each year from 2014 to 2018, inclusive, the Director of Finance shall estimate the total amount of additional revenues, less refunds, that will be derived from the incremental increases in tax rates made in subdivision (f) that will be available for transfer into the Education Protection Account during the next fiscal year. The Director of Finance shall make the same estimate by January 10, 2013, for additional revenues, less refunds, that will be received by the end of the 2012–13 fiscal year.

(B) During the last 10 days of the quarter of each of the first three quarters of each fiscal year from 2013–14 to 2018–19, inclusive, the Controller shall transfer into the Education Protection Account one-fourth of the total amount estimated pursuant to subparagraph (A) for that fiscal year, except as this amount may be adjusted pursuant to subparagraph (D).

(C) In each of the fiscal years from 2012–13 to 2020–21, inclusive, the Director of Finance shall calculate an adjustment to the Education Protection Account, as specified by subparagraph (D), by adding together the following amounts, as applicable:

(i) In the last quarter of each fiscal year from 2012–13 to 2018–19, inclusive, the Director of Finance shall recalculate the estimate made for the fiscal year pursuant to subparagraph (A), and shall subtract from this updated estimate the amounts previously transferred to the Education Protection Account for that fiscal year.

(ii) In June 2015 and in every June from 2016 to 2021, inclusive, the Director of Finance shall make a final determination of the amount of additional revenues, less refunds, derived from the incremental increases in tax rates made in subdivision (f) for the fiscal year ending two years prior. The amount of the updated estimate calculated in clause (i) for the fiscal year ending two years prior shall be subtracted from the amount of this final determination.

(D) If the sum determined pursuant to subparagraph (C) is positive, the Controller shall transfer an amount equal to that sum into the Education Protection Account within 10 days preceding the end of the fiscal year. If that amount is negative, the Controller shall suspend or reduce subsequent quarterly transfers, if any, to the Education Protection Account until the total reduction equals the negative amount herein described. For purposes of any calculation made pursuant to clause (i) of subparagraph (C), the amount of a quarterly transfer shall not be modified to reflect any suspension or reduction made pursuant to this subparagraph.

(3) All moneys in the Education Protection Account are hereby continuously appropriated for the support of school districts, county offices of education, charter schools, and community college districts as set forth in this paragraph.

(A) Eleven percent of the moneys appropriated pursuant to this paragraph shall be allocated quarterly by the Board of Governors of the California Community Colleges to community college districts to provide general purpose funding to community college districts in proportion to the amounts determined pursuant to Section 84750.5 of the Education Code, as that code section read upon voter approval of this section. The allocations calculated pursuant to this subparagraph shall be offset by the amounts specified in subdivisions (a), (c), and (d) of Section 84751 of the Education Code, as that section read upon voter approval of this section, that are in excess of the amounts calculated pursuant to Section 84750.5 of the Education Code, as that section read upon voter approval of this section, provided that no community college district shall receive less than one hundred dollars ($100) per full time equivalent student.

(B) Eighty-nine percent of the moneys appropriated pursuant to this paragraph shall be allocated quarterly by the Superintendent of Public Instruction to provide general purpose funding to school districts, county offices of education, and state general-purpose funding to charter schools in proportion to the revenue limits calculated pursuant to Sections 2558 and 42238 of the Education Code and the amounts calculated pursuant to Section 47633 of the Education Code for county offices of education, school districts, and charter schools, respectively, as those sections read upon voter approval of this section. The amounts so calculated shall be offset by the amounts specified in subdivision (c) of Section 2558 of, paragraphs (1) through (7) of subdivision (h) of Section 42238 of, and Section 47635 of, the Education Code for county offices of education, school districts, and charter schools, respectively, as those sections read upon voter approval of this section, that are in excess of the amounts calculated pursuant to Sections 2558, 42238, and 47633 of the Education Code for county offices of education, school districts, and charter schools, respectively, as those sections read upon voter approval of this section, provided that no school district, county office of education, or charter school shall receive less than two hundred dollars ($200) per unit of average daily attendance.

(4) This subdivision is self-executing and requires no legislative action to take effect. Distribution of the moneys in the Education Protection Ac-

count by the Board of Governors of the California Community Colleges and the Superintendent of Public Instruction shall not be delayed or otherwise affected by failure of the Legislature and Governor to enact an annual budget bill pursuant to Section 12 of Article IV, by invocation of paragraph (h) of Section 8 of Article XVI, or by any other action or failure to act by the Legislature or Governor.

(5) Notwithstanding any other provision of law, the moneys deposited in the Education Protection Account shall not be used to pay any costs incurred by the Legislature, the Governor, or any agency of state government.

(6) A community college district, county office of education, school district, or charter school shall have sole authority to determine how the moneys received from the Education Protection Account are spent in the school or schools within its jurisdiction, provided, however, that the appropriate governing board or body shall make these spending determinations in open session of a public meeting of the governing board or body and shall not use any of the funds from the Education Protection Account for salaries or benefits of administrators or any other administrative costs. Each community college district, county office of education, school district, and charter school shall annually publish on its Internet Web site an accounting of how much money was received from the Education Protection Account and how that money was spent.

(7) The annual independent financial and compliance audit required of community college districts, county offices of education, school districts, and charter schools shall, in addition to all other requirements of law, ascertain and verify whether the funds provided from the Education Protection Account have been properly disbursed and expended as required by this section. Expenses incurred by those entities to comply with the additional audit requirement of this section may be paid with funding from the Education Protection Account, and shall not be considered administrative costs for purposes of this section.

(8) Revenues, less refunds, derived pursuant to subdivision (f) for deposit in the Education Protection Account pursuant to this section shall be deemed "General Fund revenues," "General Fund proceeds of taxes," and "moneys to be applied by the State for the support of school districts and community college districts" for purposes of Section 8 of Article XVI.

(f) (1) (A) In addition to the taxes imposed by Part 1 (commencing with Section 6001) of Division 2 of the Revenue and Taxation Code, for the privilege of selling tangible personal property at retail, a tax is hereby imposed upon all retailers at the rate of ¼ percent of the gross receipts of any retailer from the sale of all tangible personal property sold at retail in this State on and after January 1, 2013, and before January 1, 2017.

(B) In addition to the taxes imposed by Part 1 (commencing with Section 6001) of Division 2 of the Revenue and Taxation Code, an excise tax is hereby imposed on the storage, use, or other consumption in this State of tangible personal property purchased from any retailer on and after January 1, 2013, and before January 1, 2017, for storage, use, or other consumption in this state at the rate of ¼ percent of the sales price of the property.

(C) The Sales and Use Tax Law, including any amendments enacted on or after the effective date of this section, shall apply to the taxes imposed pursuant to this paragraph.

(D) This paragraph shall become inoperative on January 1, 2017.

(2) For any taxable year beginning on or after January 1, 2012, and before January 1, 2019, with respect to the tax imposed pursuant to Section 17041 of the Revenue and Taxation Code, the income tax bracket and the rate of 9.3 percent set forth in paragraph (1) of subdivision (a) of Section 17041 of the Revenue and Taxation Code shall be modified by each of the following:

(A) (i) For that portion of taxable income that is over two hundred fifty thousand dollars ($250,000) but not over three hundred thousand dollars ($300,000), the tax rate is 10.3 percent of the excess over two hundred fifty thousand dollars ($250,000).

(ii) For that portion of taxable income that is over three hundred thousand dollars ($300,000) but not over five hundred thousand dollars ($500,000), the tax rate is 11.3 percent of the excess over three hundred thousand dollars ($300,000).

(iii) For that portion of taxable income that is over five hundred thousand dollars ($500,000), the tax rate is 12.3 percent of the excess over five hundred thousand dollars ($500,000).

(B) The income tax brackets specified in clauses (i), (ii), and (iii) of subparagraph (A) shall be recomputed, as otherwise provided in subdivision (h) of Section 17041 of the Revenue and Taxation Code, only for taxable years beginning on and after January 1, 2013.

(C) (i) For purposes of subdivision (g) of Section 19136 of the Revenue and Taxation Code, this paragraph shall be considered to be chaptered on the date it becomes effective.

(ii) For purposes of Part 10 (commencing with Section 17001) of, and Part 10.2 (commencing with Section 18401) of, Division 2 of the Revenue and Taxation Code, the modified tax brackets and tax rates established and imposed by this paragraph shall be deemed to be established and imposed under Section 17041 of the Revenue and Taxation Code.

(D) This paragraph shall become inoperative on December 1, 2019.

(3) For any taxable year beginning on or after January 1, 2012, and before January 1, 2019, with respect to the tax imposed pursuant to Section 17041 of the Revenue and Taxation Code, the income tax bracket and the rate of 9.3 percent set forth in paragraph (1) of subdivision (c) of Section

17041 of the Revenue and Taxation Code shall be modified by each of the following:

(A) (i) For that portion of taxable income that is over three hundred forty thousand dollars ($340,000) but not over four hundred eight thousand dollars ($408,000), the tax rate is 10.3 percent of the excess over three hundred forty thousand dollars ($340,000).

(ii) For that portion of taxable income that is over four hundred eight thousand dollars ($408,000) but not over six hundred eighty thousand dollars ($680,000), the tax rate is 11.3 percent of the excess over four hundred eight thousand dollars ($408,000).

(iii) For that portion of taxable income that is over six hundred eighty thousand dollars ($680,000), the tax rate is 12.3 percent of the excess over six hundred eighty thousand dollars ($680,000).

(B) The income tax brackets specified in clauses (i), (ii), and (iii) of subparagraph (A) shall be recomputed, as otherwise provided in subdivision (h) of Section 17041 of the Revenue and Taxation Code, only for taxable years beginning on and after January 1, 2013.

(C) (i) For purposes of subdivision (g) of Section 19136 of the Revenue and Taxation Code, this paragraph shall be considered to be chaptered on the date it becomes effective.

(ii) For purposes of Part 10 (commencing with Section 17001) of, and Part 10.2 (commencing with Section 18401) of, Division 2 of the Revenue and Taxation Code, the modified tax brackets and tax rates established and imposed by this paragraph shall be deemed to be established and imposed under Section 17041 of the Revenue and Taxation Code.

(D) This paragraph shall become inoperative on December 1, 2019.

(g) (1) The Controller, pursuant to his or her statutory authority, may perform audits of expenditures from the Local Revenue Fund 2011 and any County Local Revenue Fund 2011, and shall audit the Education Protection Account to ensure that those funds are used and accounted for in a manner consistent with this section.

(2) The Attorney General or local district attorney shall expeditiously investigate, and may seek civil or criminal penalties for, any misuse of moneys from the County Local Revenue Fund 2011 or the Education Protection Account. [*New section adopted November 6, 2012.*]

SEC. 37.   [*Repealed November 5, 1974.*]
SEC. 37.5.   [*Repealed November 5, 1974.*]
SEC. 38.   [*Repealed November 5, 1974.*]
SEC. 39.   [*Repealed November 5, 1974.*]
SEC. 40.   [*Repealed November 5, 1974.*]
SEC. 41.   [*Repealed November 5, 1974.*]
SEC. 42.   [*Repealed November 5, 1974.*]
SEC. 44.   [*Repealed November 5, 1974.*]

ARTICLE XIII A *

TAX LIMITATION

[*Maximum Ad Valorem Tax on Real Property—Apportionment of Tax Revenues*]

SECTION 1. (a) The maximum amount of any ad valorem tax on real property shall not exceed One percent (1%) of the full cash value of such property. The one percent (1%) tax to be collected by the counties and apportioned according to law to the districts within the counties.

[*Exceptions to Limitation*]

(b) The limitation provided for in subdivision (a) shall not apply to ad valorem taxes or special assessments to pay the interest and redemption charges on any of the following:

(1) Indebtedness approved by the voters prior to July 1, 1978.

(2) Bonded indebtedness for the acquisition or improvement of real property approved on or after July 1, 1978, by two-thirds of the votes cast by the voters voting on the proposition.

(3) Bonded indebtedness incurred by a school district, community college district, or county office of education for the construction, reconstruction, rehabilitation, or replacement of school facilities, including the furnishing and equipping of school facilities, or the acquisition or lease of real property for school facilities, approved by 55 percent of the voters of the district or county, as appropriate, voting on the proposition on or after the effective date of the measure adding this paragraph. This paragraph shall apply only if the proposition approved by the voters and resulting in the bonded indebtedness includes all of the following accountability requirements:

(A) A requirement that the proceeds from the sale of the bonds be used only for the purposes specified in Article XIII A, Section 1(b)(3), and not for any other purpose, including teacher and administrator salaries and other school operating expenses.

(B) A list of the specific school facilities projects to be funded and certification that the school district board, community college board, or county office of education has evaluated safety, class size reduction, and information technology needs in developing that list.

(C) A requirement that the school district board, community college board, or county office of education conduct an annual, independent performance audit to ensure that the funds have been expended only on the specific projects listed.

(D) A requirement that the school district board, community college board, or county office of education conduct an annual, independent finan-

---

* New Article XIII A adopted June 6, 1978. Initiative measure.

cial audit of the proceeds from the sale of the bonds until all of those proceeds have been expended for the school facilities projects.

(c) Notwithstanding any other provisions of law or of this Constitution, school districts, community college districts, and county offices of education may levy a 55 percent vote ad valorem tax pursuant to subdivision (b). [*As amended November 7, 2000. Initiative measure.*]

[*Valuation of Real Property—Appraised Value After 1975 Assessment—Replacement Dwelling*]

Sec. 2. (a) The "full cash value" means the county assessor's valuation of real property as shown on the 1975–76 tax bill under "full cash value" or, thereafter, the appraised value of real property when purchased, newly constructed, or a change in ownership has occurred after the 1975 assessment. All real property not already assessed up to the 1975–76 full cash value may be reassessed to reflect that valuation. For purposes of this section, "newly constructed" does not include real property that is reconstructed after a disaster, as declared by the Governor, where the fair market value of the real property, as reconstructed, is comparable to its fair market value prior to the disaster. For purposes of this section, the term "newly constructed" does not include that portion of an existing structure that consists of the construction or reconstruction of seismic retrofitting components, as defined by the Legislature.

However, the Legislature may provide that, under appropriate circumstances and pursuant to definitions and procedures established by the Legislature, any person over the age of 55 years who resides in property that is eligible for the homeowner's exemption under subdivision (k) of Section 3 of Article XIII and any implementing legislation may transfer the base year value of the property entitled to exemption, with the adjustments authorized by subdivision (b), to any replacement dwelling of equal or lesser value located within the same county and purchased or newly constructed by that person as his or her principal residence within two years of the sale of the original property. For purposes of this section, "any person over the age of 55 years" includes a married couple one member of which is over the age of 55 years. For purposes of this section, "replacement dwelling" means a building, structure, or other shelter constituting a place of abode, whether real property or personal property, and any land on which it may be situated. For purposes of this section, a two-dwelling unit shall be considered as two separate single-family dwellings. This paragraph shall apply to any replacement dwelling that was purchased or newly constructed on or after November 5, 1986.

In addition, the Legislature may authorize each county board of supervisors, after consultation with the local affected agencies within the county's boundaries, to adopt an ordinance making the provisions of this subdivision relating to transfer of base year value also applicable to situations in which the replacement dwellings are located in that county and the original properties are located in another county within this State. For purposes of this paragraph, "local affected agency" means any city, special district, school district, or community college district that receives an annual property tax revenue allocation. This paragraph applies to any replacement dwelling that was purchased or newly constructed on or after the date the county adopted the provisions of this subdivision relating to transfer of base year value, but does not apply to any replacement dwelling that was purchased or newly constructed before November 9, 1988.

The Legislature may extend the provisions of this subdivision relating to the transfer of base year values from original properties to replacement dwellings of homeowners over the age of 55 years to severely disabled homeowners, but only with respect to those replacement dwellings purchased or newly constructed on or after the effective date of this paragraph.

[Full Cash Value Reflecting Inflationary Rate]

(b) The full cash value base may reflect from year to year the inflationary rate not to exceed 2 percent for any given year or reduction as shown in the consumer price index or comparable data for the area under taxing jurisdiction, or may be reduced to reflect substantial damage, destruction, or other factors causing a decline in value.

["Newly Constructed"]

(c) For purposes of subdivision (a), the Legislature may provide that the term "newly constructed" does not include any of the following:

(1) The construction or addition of any active solar energy system.

(2) The construction or installation of any fire sprinkler system, other fire extinguishing system, fire detection system, or fire-related egress improvement, as defined by the Legislature, that is constructed or installed after the effective date of this paragraph.

(3) The construction, installation, or modification on or after the effective date of this paragraph of any portion or structural component of a single- or multiple-family dwelling that is eligible for the homeowner's exemption if the construction, installation, or modification is for the purpose of making the dwelling more accessible to a severely disabled person.

(4) The construction, installation, removal, or modification on or after the effective date of this paragraph of any portion or structural component of an existing building or structure if the construction, installation, removal, or modification is for the purpose of making the building more accessible to, or more usable by, a disabled person.

["Change in Ownership"]

(d) For purposes of this section, the term "change in ownership" does not include the acquisition of real property as a replacement for comparable property if the person acquiring the real property has been displaced from the property replaced by eminent domain proceedings, by acquisition by a public entity, or governmental action that has resulted in a judgment of inverse condemnation. The real property acquired shall be deemed comparable to the property replaced if it is similar in size, utility, and function, or if it conforms to state regulations defined by the Legislature governing the relocation of persons displaced by governmental actions. This subdivision applies to any property acquired after March 1, 1975, but affects only those assessments of that property that occur after the provisions of this subdivision take effect.

[*Disasters—Replacement Property*]

(e) (1) Notwithstanding any other provision of this section, the Legislature shall provide that the base year value of property that is substantially damaged or destroyed by a disaster, as declared by the Governor, may be transferred to comparable property within the same county that is acquired or newly constructed as a replacement for the substantially damaged or destroyed property.

(2) Except as provided in paragraph (3), this subdivision applies to any comparable replacement property acquired or newly constructed on or after July 1, 1985, and to the determination of base year values for the 1985–86 fiscal year and fiscal years thereafter.

(3) In addition to the transfer of base year value of property within the same county that is permitted by paragraph (1), the Legislature may authorize each county board of supervisors to adopt, after consultation with affected local agencies within the county, an ordinance allowing the transfer of the base year value of property that is located within another county in the State and is substantially damaged or destroyed by a disaster, as declared by the Governor, to comparable replacement property of equal or lesser value that is located within the adopting county and is acquired or newly constructed within three years of the substantial damage or destruction of the original property as a replacement for that property. The scope and amount of the benefit provided to a property owner by the transfer of base year value of property pursuant to this paragraph shall not exceed the scope and amount of the benefit provided to a property owner by the transfer of base year value of property pursuant to subdivision (a). For purposes of this paragraph, "affected local agency" means any city, special district, school district, or community college district that receives an annual allocation of ad valorem property tax revenues. This paragraph applies to any comparable replacement property that is acquired or newly constructed as a replacement for property substantially damaged or destroyed by a disaster, as declared by the Governor, occurring on or after October 20, 1991, and to the determination of base year values for the 1991–92 fiscal year and fiscal years thereafter.

(f) For the purposes of subdivision (e):

(1) Property is substantially damaged or destroyed if it sustains physical damage amounting to more than 50 percent of its value immediately before the disaster. Damage includes a diminution in the value of property as a result of restricted access caused by the disaster.

(2) Replacement property is comparable to the property substantially damaged or destroyed if it is similar in size, utility, and function to the property that it replaces, and if the fair market value of the acquired property is comparable to the fair market value of the replaced property prior to the disaster.

[*Real Property Transfers between Spouses*]

(g) For purposes of subdivision (a), the terms "purchased" and "change in ownership" do not include the purchase or transfer of real property between spouses since March 1, 1975, including, but not limited to, all of the following:

(1) Transfers to a trustee for the beneficial use of a spouse, or the surviving spouse of a deceased transferor, or by a trustee of such a trust to the spouse of the trustor.

(2) Transfers to a spouse that take effect upon the death of a spouse.

(3) Transfers to a spouse or former spouse in connection with a property settlement agreement or decree of dissolution of a marriage or legal separation.

(4) The creation, transfer, or termination, solely between spouses, of any coowner's interest.

(5) The distribution of a legal entity's property to a spouse or former spouse in exchange for the interest of the spouse in the legal entity in connection with a property settlement agreement or a decree of dissolution of a marriage or legal separation.

[*Real Property Transfers between Family Members*]

(h) (1) For purposes of subdivision (a), the terms "purchased" and "change in ownership" do not include the purchase or transfer of the principal residence of the transferor in the case of a purchase or transfer between parents and their children, as defined by the Legislature, and the purchase or transfer of the first one million dollars ($1,000,000) of the full cash value of all other real property between parents and their children, as defined by the Legislature. This subdivision applies to both voluntary transfers and transfers resulting from a court order or judicial decree.

(2) (A) Subject to subparagraph (B), commencing with purchases or transfers that occur on or after the date upon which the measure adding this paragraph becomes effective, the exclusion established by paragraph (1) also applies to a purchase or transfer of real property between grandparents and their grandchild or grandchildren, as defined by the Legislature, that otherwise qualifies under paragraph (1), if all of the parents of

that grandchild or those grandchildren, who qualify as the children of the grandparents, are deceased as of the date of the purchase or transfer.

(B) A purchase or transfer of a principal residence shall not be excluded pursuant to subparagraph (A) if the transferee grandchild or grandchildren also received a principal residence, or interest therein, through another purchase or transfer that was excludable pursuant to paragraph (1). The full cash value of any real property, other than a principal residence, that was transferred to the grandchild or grandchildren pursuant to a purchase or transfer that was excludable pursuant to paragraph (1), and the full cash value of a principal residence that fails to qualify for exclusion as a result of the preceding sentence, shall be included in applying, for purposes of subparagraph (A), the one-million-dollar ($1,000,000) full cash value limit specified in paragraph (1).

[*Contaminated Property*]

(i) (1) Notwithstanding any other provision of this section, the Legislature shall provide with respect to a qualified contaminated property, as defined in paragraph (2), that either, but not both, of the following apply:

(A) (i) Subject to the limitation of clause (ii), the base year value of the qualified contaminated property, as adjusted as authorized by subdivision (b), may be transferred to a replacement property that is acquired or newly constructed as a replacement for the qualified contaminated property, if the replacement real property has a fair market value that is equal to or less than the fair market value of the qualified contaminated property if that property were not contaminated and, except as otherwise provided by this clause, is located within the same county. The base year value of the qualified contaminated property may be transferred to a replacement real property located within another county if the board of supervisors of that other county has, after consultation with the affected local agencies within that county, adopted a resolution authorizing an intercounty transfer of base year value as so described.

(ii) This subparagraph applies only to replacement property that is acquired or newly constructed within five years after ownership in the qualified contaminated property is sold or otherwise transferred.

(B) In the case in which the remediation of the environmental problems on the qualified contaminated property requires the destruction of, or results in substantial damage to, a structure located on that property, the term "new construction" does not include the repair of a substantially damaged structure, or the construction of a structure replacing a destroyed structure on the qualified contaminated property, performed after the remediation of the environmental problems on that property, provided that the repaired or replacement structure is similar in size, utility, and function to the original structure.

(2) For purposes of this subdivision, "qualified contaminated property" means residential or nonresidential real property that is all of the following:

(A) In the case of residential real property, rendered uninhabitable, and in the case of nonresidential real property, rendered unusable, as the result of either environmental problems, in the nature of and including, but not limited to, the presence of toxic or hazardous materials, or the remediation of those environmental problems, except where the existence of the environmental problems was known to the owner, or to a related individual or entity as described in paragraph (3), at the time the real property was acquired or constructed. For purposes of this subparagraph, residential real property is "uninhabitable" if that property, as a result of health hazards caused by or associated with the environmental problems, is unfit for human habitation, and nonresidential real property is "unusable" if that property, as a result of health hazards caused by or associated with the environmental problems, is unhealthy and unsuitable for occupancy.

(B) Located on a site that has been designated as a toxic or environmental hazard or as an environmental cleanup site by an agency of the State of California or the federal government.

(C) Real property that contains a structure or structures thereon prior to the completion of environmental cleanup activities, and that structure or structures are substantially damaged or destroyed as a result of those environmental cleanup activities.

(D) Stipulated by the lead governmental agency, with respect to the environmental problems or environmental cleanup of the real property, not to have been rendered uninhabitable or unusable, as applicable, as described in subparagraph (A), by any act or omission in which an owner of that real property participated or acquiesced.

(3) It shall be rebuttably presumed that an owner of the real property participated or acquiesced in any act or omission that rendered the real property uninhabitable or unusable, as applicable, if that owner is related to any individual or entity that committed that act or omission in any of the following ways:

(A) Is a spouse, parent, child, grandparent, grandchild, or sibling of that individual.

(B) Is a corporate parent, subsidiary, or affiliate of that entity.

(C) Is an owner of, or has control of, that entity.

(D) Is owned or controlled by that entity.

If this presumption is not overcome, the owner shall not receive the relief provided for in subparagraph (A) or (B) of paragraph (1). The presumption may be overcome by presentation of satisfactory evidence to the assessor, who shall not be bound by the findings of the lead governmental agency in determining whether the presumption has been overcome.

(4) This subdivision applies only to replacement property that is acquired or constructed on or after January 1, 1995, and to property repairs performed on or after that date.

[*Effectiveness of Amendments*]

(j) Unless specifically provided otherwise, amendments to this section adopted prior to November 1, 1988, are effective for changes in ownership that occur, and new construction that is completed, after the effective date of the amendment. Unless specifically provided otherwise, amendments to this section adopted after November 1, 1988, are effective for changes in ownership that occur, and new construction that is completed, on or after the effective date of the amendment. [*As amended June 8, 2010.*]

[*Changes in State Taxes—Vote Requirement—Definition of "Tax"*]

SEC. 3. (a) Any change in state statute which results in any taxpayer paying a higher tax must be imposed by an act passed by not less than two-thirds of all members elected to each of the two houses of the Legislature, except that no new ad valorem taxes on real property, or sales or transaction taxes on the sales of real property may be imposed.

(b) As used in this section, "tax" means any levy, charge, or exaction of any kind imposed by the State, except the following:

(1) A charge imposed for a specific benefit conferred or privilege granted directly to the payor that is not provided to those not charged, and which does not exceed the reasonable costs to the State of conferring the benefit or granting the privilege to the payor.

(2) A charge imposed for a specific government service or product provided directly to the payor that is not provided to those not charged, and which does not exceed the reasonable costs to the State of providing the service or product to the payor.

(3) A charge imposed for the reasonable regulatory costs to the State incident to issuing licenses and permits, performing investigations, inspections, and audits, enforcing agricultural marketing orders, and the administrative enforcement and adjudication thereof.

(4) A charge imposed for entrance to or use of state property, or the purchase, rental, or lease of state property, except charges governed by Section 15 of Article XI.

(5) A fine, penalty, or other monetary charge imposed by the judicial branch of government or the State, as a result of a violation of law.

(c) Any tax adopted after January 1, 2010, but prior to the effective date of this act, that was not adopted in compliance with the requirements of this section is void 12 months after the effective date of this act unless the tax is reenacted by the Legislature and signed into law by the Governor in compliance with the requirements of this section.

(d) The State bears the burden of proving by a preponderance of the evidence that a levy, charge, or other exaction is not a tax, that the amount is no more than necessary to cover the reasonable costs of the governmental activity, and that the manner in which those costs are allocated to a payor bear a fair or reasonable relationship to the payor's burdens on, or benefits received from, the governmental activity. [*As amended November 2, 2010. Initiative measure.*]

[*Imposition of Special Taxes*]

SEC. 4.   Cities, Counties and special districts, by a two-thirds vote of the qualified electors of such district, may impose special taxes on such district, except ad valorem taxes on real property or a transaction tax or sales tax on the sale of real property within such City, County or special district. [*New section adopted June 6, 1978. Initiative measure.*]

[*Effective Date of Article*]

SEC. 5.   This article shall take effect for the tax year beginning on July 1 following the passage of this Amendment, except Section 3 which shall become effective upon the passage of this article. [*New section adopted June 6, 1978. Initiative measure.*]

[*Severability*]

SEC. 6.   If any section, part, clause, or phrase hereof is for any reason held to be invalid or unconstitutional, the remaining sections shall not be affected but will remain in full force and effect. [*New section adopted June 6, 1978. Initiative measure.*]

[*California Children and Families First Act of 1998*]

SEC. 7.   Section 3 of this article does not apply to the California Children and Families First Act of 1998. [*New section adopted November 3, 1998. Initiative measure.*]

ARTICLE XIII B *

GOVERNMENT SPENDING LIMITATION

[*Total Annual Appropriations*]

SECTION 1.   The total annual appropriations subject to limitation of the State and of each local government shall not exceed the appropriations limit of the entity of government for the prior year adjusted for the change in the cost of living and the change in population, except as otherwise provided in this article. [*As amended June 5, 1990. Operative July 1, 1990.*]

[*Appropriations Limit Annual Calculation—Review*]

SEC. 1.5.   The annual calculation of the appropriations limit under this article for each entity of local government shall be reviewed as part of an

---

* New Article XIII B adopted November 6, 1979. Operative commencing first day of fiscal year following adoption. Initiative measure.

annual financial audit. [*New section adopted June 5, 1990. Operative July 1, 1990.*]

[*Revenues in Excess of Limitation*]

SEC. 2. (a) (1) Fifty percent of all revenues received by the State in a fiscal year and in the fiscal year immediately following it in excess of the amount which may be appropriated by the State in compliance with this article during that fiscal year and the fiscal year immediately following it shall be transferred and allocated, from a fund established for that purpose, pursuant to Section 8.5 of Article XVI.

(2) Fifty percent of all revenues received by the State in a fiscal year and in the fiscal year immediately following it in excess of the amount which may be appropriated by the State in compliance with this article during that fiscal year and the fiscal year immediately following it shall be returned by a revision of tax rates or fee schedules within the next two subsequent fiscal years.

(b) All revenues received by an entity of government, other than the State, in a fiscal year and in the fiscal year immediately following it in excess of the amount which may be appropriated by the entity in compliance with this article during that fiscal year and the fiscal year immediately following it shall be returned by a revision of tax rates or fee schedules within the next two subsequent fiscal years. [*As amended June 5, 1990. Operative July 1, 1990.*]

[*Appropriations Limit—Adjustments*]

SEC. 3. The appropriations limit for any fiscal year pursuant to Sec. 1 shall be adjusted as follows:

(a) In the event that the financial responsibility of providing services is transferred, in whole or in part, whether by annexation, incorporation or otherwise, from one entity of government to another, then for the year in which such transfer becomes effective the appropriations limit of the transferee entity shall be increased by such reasonable amount as the said entities shall mutually agree and the appropriations limit of the transferor entity shall be decreased by the same amount.

(b) In the event that the financial responsibility of providing services is transferred, in whole or in part, from an entity of government to a private entity, or the financial source for the provision of services is transferred, in whole or in part, from other revenues of an entity of government, to regulatory licenses, user charges or user fees, then for the year of such transfer the appropriations limit of such entity of government shall be decreased accordingly.

(c) (1) In the event an emergency is declared by the legislative body of an entity of government, the appropriations limit of the affected entity of government may be exceeded provided that the appropriations limits in the following three years are reduced accordingly to prevent an aggregate increase in appropriations resulting from the emergency.

(2) In the event an emergency is declared by the Governor, appropriations approved by a two-thirds vote of the legislative body of an affected entity of government to an emergency account for expenditures relating to that emergency shall not constitute appropriations subject to limitation. As used in this paragraph, "emergency" means the existence, as declared by the Governor, of conditions of disaster or of extreme peril to the safety of persons and property within the State, or parts thereof, caused by such conditions as attack or probable or imminent attack by an enemy of the United States, fire, flood, drought, storm, civil disorder, earthquake, or volcanic eruption. [*As amended June 5, 1990. Operative July 1, 1990.*]

[Appropriations Limit—Establishment or Change]

Sec. 4.   The appropriations limit imposed on any new or existing entity of government by this Article may be established or changed by the electors of such entity, subject to and in conformity with constitutional and statutory voting requirements. The duration of any such change shall be as determined by said electors, but shall in no event exceed four years from the most recent vote of said electors creating or continuing such change. [*New section adopted November 6, 1979. Operative commencing first day of fiscal year following adoption. Initiative measure.*]

[Contingency, Emergency, Unemployment, Etc., Funds—Contributions—Withdrawals—Transfers]

Sec. 5.   Each entity of government may establish such contingency, emergency, unemployment, reserve, retirement, sinking fund, trust, or similar funds as it shall deem reasonable and proper. Contributions to any such fund, to the extent that such contributions are derived from the proceeds of taxes, shall for purposes of this Article constitute appropriations subject to limitation in the year of contribution. Neither withdrawals from any such fund, nor expenditures of (or authorizations to expend) such withdrawals, nor transfers between or among such funds, shall for purposes of this Article constitute appropriations subject to limitation. [*New section adopted November 6, 1979. Operative commencing first day of fiscal year following adoption. Initiative measure.*]

[Prudent State Reserve]

Sec. 5.5.   Prudent State Reserve.   The Legislature shall establish a prudent state reserve fund in such amount as it shall deem reasonable and necessary. Contributions to, and withdrawals from, the fund shall be subject to the provisions of Section 5 of this Article. [*New section adopted November 8, 1988. Initiative measure.*]

[*Mandates of New Programs or Higher Levels of Service*]

Sec. 6.   (a) Whenever the Legislature or any state agency mandates a new program or higher level of service on any local government, the State shall provide a subvention of funds to reimburse that local government for the costs of the program or increased level of service, except that the Legislature may, but need not, provide a subvention of funds for the following mandates:

(1) Legislative mandates requested by the local agency affected.

(2) Legislation defining a new crime or changing an existing definition of a crime.

(3) Legislative mandates enacted prior to January 1, 1975, or executive orders or regulations initially implementing legislation enacted prior to January 1, 1975.

(4) Legislative mandates contained in statutes within the scope of paragraph (7) of subdivision (b) of Section 3 of Article 1.

(b) (1) Except as provided in paragraph (2), for the 2005–06 fiscal year and every subsequent fiscal year, for a mandate for which the costs of a local government claimant have been determined in a preceding fiscal year to be payable by the State pursuant to law, the Legislature shall either appropriate, in the annual Budget Act, the full payable amount that has not been previously paid, or suspend the operation of the mandate for the fiscal year for which the annual Budget Act is applicable in a manner prescribed by law.

(2) Payable claims for costs incurred prior to the 2004–05 fiscal year that have not been paid prior to the 2005–06 fiscal year may be paid over a term of years, as prescribed by law.

(3) Ad valorem property tax revenues shall not be used to reimburse a local government for the costs of a new program or higher level of service.

(4) This subdivision applies to a mandate only as it affects a city, county, city and county, or special district.

(5) This subdivision shall not apply to a requirement to provide or recognize any procedural or substantive protection, right, benefit, or employment status of any local government employee or retiree, or of any local government employee organization, that arises from, affects, or directly relates to future, current, or past local government employment and that constitutes a mandate subject to this section.

(c) A mandated new program or higher level of service includes a transfer by the Legislature from the State to cities, counties, cities and counties, or special districts of complete or partial financial responsibility for a required program for which the State previously had complete or partial financial responsibility. [*As amended June 3, 2014.*]

[*Bonded Indebtedness*]

Sec. 7.   Nothing in this Article shall be construed to impair the ability of the State or of any local government to meet its obligations with respect to existing or future bonded indebtedness. [*New section adopted November 6, 1979. Operative commencing first day of fiscal year following adoption. Initiative measure.*]

[Definitions]

SEC. 8. As used in this article and except as otherwise expressly provided herein:

(a) "Appropriations subject to limitation" of the State means any authorization to expend during a fiscal year the proceeds of taxes levied by or for the State, exclusive of state subventions for the use and operation of local government (other than subventions made pursuant to Section 6) and further exclusive of refunds of taxes, benefit payments from retirement, unemployment insurance, and disability insurance funds.

(b) "Appropriations subject to limitation" of an entity of local government means any authorization to expend during a fiscal year the proceeds of taxes levied by or for that entity and the proceeds of state subventions to that entity (other than subventions made pursuant to Section 6) exclusive of refunds of taxes.

(c) "Proceeds of taxes" shall include, but not be restricted to, all tax revenues and the proceeds to an entity of government, from (1) regulatory licenses, user charges, and user fees to the extent that those proceeds exceed the costs reasonably borne by that entity in providing the regulation, product, or service, and (2) the investment of tax revenues. With respect to any local government, "proceeds of taxes" shall include subventions received from the State, other than pursuant to Section 6, and, with respect to the State, proceeds of taxes shall exclude such subventions.

(d) "Local government" means any city, county, city and county, school district, special district, authority, or other political subdivision of or within the State.

(e) (1) "Change in the cost of living" for the State, a school district, or a community college district means the percentage change in California per capita personal income from the preceding year.

(2) "Change in the cost of living" for an entity of local government, other than a school district or a community college district, shall be either (A) the percentage change in California per capita personal income from the preceding year, or (B) the percentage change in the local assessment roll from the preceding year for the jurisdiction due to the addition of local nonresidential new construction. Each entity of local government shall select its change in the cost of living pursuant to this paragraph annually by a recorded vote of the entity's governing body.

(f) "Change in population" of any entity of government, other than the State, a school district, or a community college district, shall be determined by a method prescribed by the Legislature.

"Change in population" of a school district or a community college district shall be the percentage change in the average daily attendance of the school district or community college district from the preceding fiscal year, as determined by a method prescribed by the Legislature.

"Change in population" of the State shall be determined by adding (1) the percentage change in the State's population multiplied by the percentage of the State's budget in the prior fiscal year that is expended for other than educational purposes for kindergarten and grades one to 12, inclusive, and the community colleges, and (2) the percentage change in the total statewide average daily attendance in kindergarten and grades one to 12, inclusive, and the community colleges, multiplied by the percentage of the State's budget in the prior fiscal year that is expended for educational purposes for kindergarten and grades one to 12, inclusive, and the community colleges.

Any determination of population pursuant to this subdivision, other than that measured by average daily attendance, shall be revised, as necessary, to reflect the periodic census conducted by the United States Department of Commerce, or successor department.

(g) "Debt service" means appropriations required to pay the cost of interest and redemption charges, including the funding of any reserve or sinking fund required in connection therewith, on indebtedness existing or legally authorized as of January 1, 1979, or on bonded indebtedness thereafter approved according to law by a vote of the electors of the issuing entity voting in an election for that purpose.

(h) The "appropriations limit" of each entity of government for each fiscal year is that amount which total annual appropriations subject to limitation may not exceed under Sections 1 and 3. However, the "appropriations limit" of each entity of government for fiscal year 1978–79 is the total of the appropriations subject to limitation of the entity for that fiscal year. For fiscal year 1978–79, state subventions to local governments, exclusive of federal grants, are deemed to have been derived from the proceeds of state taxes.

(i) Except as otherwise provided in Section 5, "appropriations subject to limitation" do not include local agency loan funds or indebtedness funds, investment (or authorizations to invest) funds of the State, or of an entity of local government in accounts at banks or savings and loan associations or in liquid securities. [As amended June 5, 1990. Operative July 1, 1990.]

[Exceptions to Appropriations Subject to Limitation]

SEC. 9. "Appropriations subject to limitation" for each entity of government do not include:

(a) Appropriations for debt service.

(b) Appropriations required to comply with mandates of the courts or the federal government which, without discretion, require an expenditure for additional services or which unavoidably make the provision of existing services more costly.

(c) Appropriations of any special district which existed on January 1, 1978, and which did not as of the 1977–78 fiscal year levy an ad valorem tax on property in excess of 12½ cents per $100 of assessed value; or the appropriations of any special district then existing or thereafter created by a vote of the people, which is totally funded by other than the proceeds of taxes.

(d) Appropriations for all qualified capital outlay projects, as defined by the Legislature.

(e) Appropriations of revenue which are derived from any of the following:

(1) That portion of the taxes imposed on motor vehicle fuels for use in motor vehicles upon public streets and highways at a rate of more than nine cents ($0.09) per gallon.

(2) Sales and use taxes collected on that increment of the tax specified in paragraph (1).

(3) That portion of the weight fee imposed on commercial vehicles which exceeds the weight fee imposed on those vehicles on January 1, 1990. [*As amended June 5, 1990. Operative July 1, 1990.*]

[Effective Date of Article]

Sec. 10.   This Article shall be effective commencing with the first day of the fiscal year following its adoption. [*New section adopted November 6, 1979. Operative commencing first day of fiscal year following adoption. Initiative measure.*]

[Appropriations Limit on or after July 1, 1990]

Sec. 10.5.   For fiscal years beginning on or after July 1, 1990, the appropriations limit of each entity of government shall be the appropriations limit for the 1986–87 fiscal year adjusted for the changes made from that fiscal year pursuant to this article, as amended by the measure adding this section, adjusted for the changes required by Section 3. [*New section adopted June 5, 1990. Operative July 1, 1990.*]

[Category Added or Removed from Appropriations Subject to Limitation—Severability]

Sec. 11.   If any appropriation category shall be added to or removed from appropriations subject to limitation, pursuant to final judgment of any court of competent jurisdiction and any appeal therefrom, the appropriations limit shall be adjusted accordingly. If any section, part, clause or phrase in this Article is for any reason held invalid or unconstitutional, the remaining portions of this Article shall not be affected but shall remain in full force and effect. [*New section adopted November 6, 1979. Operative commencing first day of fiscal year following adoption. Initiative measure.*]

[Exceptions to Appropriations Subject to Limitation]

SEC. 12.   "Appropriations subject to limitation" of each entity of government shall not include appropriations of revenue from the Cigarette and Tobacco Products Surtax Fund created by the Tobacco Tax and Health Protection Act of 1988. No adjustment in the appropriations limit of any entity of government shall be required pursuant to Section 3 as a result of revenue being deposited in or appropriated from the Cigarette and Tobacco Products Surtax Fund created by the Tobacco Tax and Health Protection Act of 1988. [*New section adopted November 8, 1988. Initiative measure.*]

[Exceptions to Appropriations Subject to Limitation]

SEC. 13.   "Appropriations subject to limitation" of each entity of government shall not include appropriations of revenue from the California Children and Families First Trust Fund created by the California Children and Families First Act of 1998. No adjustment in the appropriations limit of any entity of government shall be required pursuant to Section 3 as a result of revenue being deposited in or appropriated from the California Children and Families First Trust Fund. The surtax created by the California Children and Families First Act of 1998 shall not be considered General Fund revenues for the purposes of Section 8 of Article XVI. [*New section adopted November 3, 1998. Initiative measure.*]

ARTICLE XIII C *

VOTER APPROVAL FOR LOCAL TAX LEVIES

SECTION 1.   Definitions.   As used in this article:

(a) "General tax" means any tax imposed for general governmental purposes.

(b) "Local government" means any county, city, city and county, including a charter city or county, any special district, or any other local or regional governmental entity.

(c) "Special district" means an agency of the State, formed pursuant to general law or a special act, for the local performance of governmental or proprietary functions with limited geographic boundaries including, but not limited to, school districts and redevelopment agencies.

(d) "Special tax" means any tax imposed for specific purposes, including a tax imposed for specific purposes, which is placed into a general fund.

(e) As used in this article, "tax" means any levy, charge, or exaction of any kind imposed by a local government, except the following:

(1) A charge imposed for a specific benefit conferred or privilege granted directly to the payor that is not provided to those not charged, and

---

* New Article XIII C adopted November 5, 1996. Initiative measure.

which does not exceed the reasonable costs to the local government of conferring the benefit or granting the privilege.

(2) A charge imposed for a specific government service or product provided directly to the payor that is not provided to those not charged, and which does not exceed the reasonable costs to the local government of providing the service or product.

(3) A charge imposed for the reasonable regulatory costs to a local government for issuing licenses and permits, performing investigations, inspections, and audits, enforcing agricultural marketing orders, and the administrative enforcement and adjudication thereof.

(4) A charge imposed for entrance to or use of local government property, or the purchase, rental, or lease of local government property.

(5) A fine, penalty, or other monetary charge imposed by the judicial branch of government or a local government, as a result of a violation of law.

(6) A charge imposed as a condition of property development.

(7) Assessments and property-related fees imposed in accordance with the provisions of Article XIIID.

The local government bears the burden of proving by a preponderance of the evidence that a levy, charge, or other exaction is not a tax, that the amount is no more than necessary to cover the reasonable costs of the governmental activity, and that the manner in which those costs are allocated to a payor bear a fair or reasonable relationship to the payor's burdens on, or benefits received from, the governmental activity. [*As amended November 2, 2010. Initiative measure.*]

SEC. 2.   Local Government Tax Limitation.   Notwithstanding any other provision of this Constitution:

(a) All taxes imposed by any local government shall be deemed to be either general taxes or special taxes. Special purpose districts or agencies, including school districts, shall have no power to levy general taxes.

(b) No local government may impose, extend, or increase any general tax unless and until that tax is submitted to the electorate and approved by a majority vote. A general tax shall not be deemed to have been increased if it is imposed at a rate not higher than the maximum rate so approved. The election required by this subdivision shall be consolidated with a regularly scheduled general election for members of the governing body of the local government, except in cases of emergency declared by a unanimous vote of the governing body.

(c) Any general tax imposed, extended, or increased, without voter approval, by any local government on or after January 1, 1995, and prior to the effective date of this article, shall continue to be imposed only if approved by a majority vote of the voters voting in an election on the issue of the imposition, which election shall be held within two years of the effective date of this article and in compliance with subdivision (b).

(d) No local government may impose, extend, or increase any special tax unless and until that tax is submitted to the electorate and approved by a two-thirds vote. A special tax shall not be deemed to have been increased if it is imposed at a rate not higher than the maximum rate so approved. [*New section adopted November 5, 1996. Initiative measure.*]

SEC. 3.   Initiative Power for Local Taxes, Assessments, Fees and Charges.   Notwithstanding any other provision of this Constitution, including, but not limited to, Sections 8 and 9 of Article II, the initiative power shall not be prohibited or otherwise limited in matters of reducing or repealing any local tax, assessment, fee or charge. The power of initiative to affect local taxes, assessments, fees and charges shall be applicable to all local governments and neither the Legislature nor any local government charter shall impose a signature requirement higher than that applicable to statewide statutory initiatives. [*New section adopted November 5, 1996. Initiative measure.*]

ARTICLE XIII D *

ASSESSMENT AND PROPERTY-RELATED FEE REFORM

SECTION 1.   Application.   Notwithstanding any other provision of law, the provisions of this article shall apply to all assessments, fees and charges, whether imposed pursuant to state statute or local government charter authority. Nothing in this article or Article XIII C shall be construed to:

(a) Provide any new authority to any agency to impose a tax, assessment, fee, or charge.

(b) Affect existing laws relating to the imposition of fees or charges as a condition of property development.

(c) Affect existing laws relating to the imposition of timber yield taxes. [*New section adopted November 5, 1996. Initiative measure.*]

SEC. 2.   Definitions.   As used in this article:

(a) "Agency" means any local government as defined in subdivision (b) of Section 1 of Article XIII C.

(b) "Assessment" means any levy or charge upon real property by an agency for a special benefit conferred upon the real property. "Assessment" includes, but is not limited to, "special assessment," "benefit assessment," "maintenance assessment" and "special assessment tax."

(c) "Capital cost" means the cost of acquisition, installation, construction, reconstruction, or replacement of a permanent public improvement by an agency.

---

*New Article XIII D adopted November 5, 1996. Initiative measure.

(d) "District" means an area determined by an agency to contain all parcels which will receive a special benefit from a proposed public improvement or property-related service.

(e) "Fee" or "charge" means any levy other than an ad valorem tax, a special tax, or an assessment, imposed by an agency upon a parcel or upon a person as an incident of property ownership, including a user fee or charge for a property-related service.

(f) "Maintenance and operation expenses" means the cost of rent, repair, replacement, rehabilitation, fuel, power, electrical current, care, and supervision necessary to properly operate and maintain a permanent public improvement.

(g) "Property ownership" shall be deemed to include tenancies of real property where tenants are directly liable to pay the assessment, fee, or charge in question.

(h) "Property-related service" means a public service having a direct relationship to property ownership.

(i) "Special benefit" means a particular and distinct benefit over and above general benefits conferred on real property located in the district or to the public at large. General enhancement of property value does not constitute "special benefit." [*New section adopted November 5, 1996. Initiative measure.*]

SEC. 3. Property Taxes, Assessments, Fees and Charges Limited.   (a) No tax, assessment, fee, or charge shall be assessed by any agency upon any parcel of property or upon any person as an incident of property ownership except:

(1) The ad valorem property tax imposed pursuant to Article XIII and Article XIII A.

(2) Any special tax receiving a two-thirds vote pursuant to Section 4 of Article XIII A.

(3) Assessments as provided by this article.

(4) Fees or charges for property-related services as provided by this article.

(b) For purposes of this article, fees for the provision of electrical or gas service shall not be deemed charges or fees imposed as an incident of property ownership. [*New section adopted November 5, 1996. Initiative measure.*]

SEC. 4. Procedures and Requirements for All Assessments. (a) An agency which proposes to levy an assessment shall identify all parcels which will have a special benefit conferred upon them and upon which an assessment will be imposed. The proportionate special benefit derived by each identified parcel shall be determined in relationship to the entirety of the capital cost of a public improvement, the maintenance and operation expenses of a public improvement, or the cost of the property-related service being provided. No assessment shall be imposed on any parcel which exceeds the reasonable cost of the proportional special benefit conferred on that parcel. Only special benefits are assessable, and an agency shall separate the general benefits from the special benefits conferred on a parcel. Parcels within a district that are owned or used by any agency, the State of California or the United States shall not be exempt from assessment unless the agency can demonstrate by clear and convincing evidence that those publicly owned parcels in fact receive no special benefit.

(b) All assessments shall be supported by a detailed engineer's report prepared by a registered professional engineer certified by the State of California.

(c) The amount of the proposed assessment for each identified parcel shall be calculated and the record owner of each parcel shall be given written notice by mail of the proposed assessment, the total amount thereof chargeable to the entire district, the amount chargeable to the owner's particular parcel, the duration of the payments, the reason for the assessment and the basis upon which the amount of the proposed assessment was calculated, together with the date, time, and location of a public hearing on the proposed assessment. Each notice shall also include, in a conspicuous place thereon, a summary of the procedures applicable to the completion, return, and tabulation of the ballots required pursuant to subdivision (d), including a disclosure statement that the existence of a majority protest, as defined in subdivision (e), will result in the assessment not being imposed.

(d) Each notice mailed to owners of identified parcels within the district pursuant to subdivision (c) shall contain a ballot which includes the agency's address for receipt of the ballot once completed by any owner receiving the notice whereby the owner may indicate his or her name, reasonable identification of the parcel, and his or her support or opposition to the proposed assessment.

(e) The agency shall conduct a public hearing upon the proposed assessment not less than 45 days after mailing the notice of the proposed assessment to record owners of each identified parcel. At the public hearing, the agency shall consider all protests against the proposed assessment and tabulate the ballots. The agency shall not impose an assessment if there is a majority protest. A majority protest exists if, upon the conclusion of the hearing, ballots submitted in opposition to the assessment exceed the ballots submitted in favor of the assessment. In tabulating the ballots, the ballots shall be weighted according to the proportional financial obligation of the affected property.

(f) In any legal action contesting the validity of any assessment, the burden shall be on the agency to demonstrate that the property or properties in question receive a special benefit over and above the benefits conferred on the public at large and that the amount of any contested assessment is proportional to, and no greater than, the benefits conferred on the property or properties in question.

(g) Because only special benefits are assessable, electors residing within the district who do not own property within the district shall not be deemed under this Constitution to have been deprived of the right to vote for any assessment. If a court determines that the Constitution of the United States or other federal law requires otherwise, the assessment shall not be imposed unless approved by a two-thirds vote of the electorate in the district in addition to being approved by the property owners as required by subdivision (e). [*New section adopted November 5, 1996. Initiative measure.*]

SEC. 5.   Effective Date.   Pursuant to subdivision (a) of Section 10 of Article II, the provisions of this article shall become effective the day after the election unless otherwise provided. Beginning July 1, 1997, all existing, new, or increased assessments shall comply with this article. Notwithstanding the foregoing, the following assessments existing on the effective date of this article shall be exempt from the procedures and approval process set forth in Section 4:

(a) Any assessment imposed exclusively to finance the capital costs or maintenance and operation expenses for sidewalks, streets, sewers, water, flood control, drainage systems or vector control. Subsequent increases in such assessments shall be subject to the procedures and approval process set forth in Section 4.

(b) Any assessment imposed pursuant to a petition signed by the persons owning all of the parcels subject to the assessment at the time the assessment is initially imposed. Subsequent increases in such assessments shall be subject to the procedures and approval process set forth in Section 4.

(c) Any assessment the proceeds of which are exclusively used to repay bonded indebtedness of which the failure to pay would violate the Contract Impairment Clause of the Constitution of the United States.

(d) Any assessment which previously received majority voter approval from the voters voting in an election on the issue of the assessment. Subsequent increases in those assessments shall be subject to the procedures and approval process set forth in Section 4. [*New section adopted November 5, 1996. Initiative measure.*]

SEC. 6.   Property-Related Fees and Charges.   (a) Procedures for New or Increased Fees and Charges.   An agency shall follow the procedures pursuant to this section in imposing or increasing any fee or charge as defined pursuant to this article, including, but not limited to, the following:

(1) The parcels upon which a fee or charge is proposed for imposition shall be identified. The amount of the fee or charge proposed to be imposed upon each parcel shall be calculated. The agency shall provide written notice by mail of the proposed fee or charge to the record owner of

each identified parcel upon which the fee or charge is proposed for imposition, the amount of the fee or charge proposed to be imposed upon each, the basis upon which the amount of the proposed fee or charge was calculated, the reason for the fee or charge, together with the date, time, and location of a public hearing on the proposed fee or charge.

(2) The agency shall conduct a public hearing upon the proposed fee or charge not less than 45 days after mailing the notice of the proposed fee or charge to the record owners of each identified parcel upon which the fee or charge is proposed for imposition. At the public hearing, the agency shall consider all protests against the proposed fee or charge. If written protests against the proposed fee or charge are presented by a majority of owners of the identified parcels, the agency shall not impose the fee or charge.

(b) Requirements for Existing, New or Increased Fees and Charges. A fee or charge shall not be extended, imposed, or increased by any agency unless it meets all of the following requirements:

(1) Revenues derived from the fee or charge shall not exceed the funds required to provide the property-related service.

(2) Revenues derived from the fee or charge shall not be used for any purpose other than that for which the fee or charge was imposed.

(3) The amount of a fee or charge imposed upon any parcel or person as an incident of property ownership shall not exceed the proportional cost of the service attributable to the parcel.

(4) No fee or charge may be imposed for a service unless that service is actually used by, or immediately available to, the owner of the property in question. Fees or charges based on potential or future use of a service are not permitted. Standby charges, whether characterized as charges or assessments, shall be classified as assessments and shall not be imposed without compliance with Section 4.

(5) No fee or charge may be imposed for general governmental services including, but not limited to, police, fire, ambulance or library services, where the service is available to the public at large in substantially the same manner as it is to property owners.

Reliance by an agency on any parcel map, including, but not limited to, an assessor's parcel map, may be considered a significant factor in determining whether a fee or charge is imposed as an incident of property ownership for purposes of this article. In any legal action contesting the validity of a fee or charge, the burden shall be on the agency to demonstrate compliance with this article.

(c) Voter Approval for New or Increased Fees and Charges. Except for fees or charges for sewer, water, and refuse collection services, no property-related fee or charge shall be imposed or increased unless and until that fee or charge is submitted and approved by a majority vote of the property owners of the property subject to the fee or charge or, at the option of the agency, by a two-thirds vote of the electorate residing in the affected area. The election shall be conducted not less than 45 days after the public hearing. An agency may adopt procedures similar to those for increases in assessments in the conduct of elections under this subdivision.

(d) Beginning July 1, 1997, all fees or charges shall comply with this section. [*New section adopted November 5, 1996. Initiative measure.*]

ARTICLE XIV.   [*Repealed June 8, 1976. See Article XIV, below.*]

ARTICLE XIV *

LABOR RELATIONS

SECTION 1.   [*Repealed June 8, 1976. See Section 1, below.*]

[Minimum Wages and General Welfare of Employees]

SECTION 1.   The Legislature may provide for minimum wages and for the general welfare of employees and for those purposes may confer on a commission legislative, executive, and judicial powers. [*New section adopted June 8, 1976.*]

SEC. 2.   [*Repealed June 8, 1976. See Section 2, below.*]

[Eight-hour Workday]

SEC. 2.   Worktime of mechanics or workers on public works may not exceed eight hours a day except in wartime or extraordinary emergencies that endanger life or property. The Legislature shall provide for enforcement of this section. [*New section adopted June 8, 1976.*]

SEC. 3.   [*Repealed June 8, 1976. See Section 3, below.*]

[Mechanics' Liens]

SEC. 3.   Mechanics, persons furnishing materials, artisans, and laborers of every class, shall have a lien upon the property upon which they have bestowed labor or furnished material for the value of such labor done and material furnished; and the Legislature shall provide, by law, for the speedy and efficient enforcement of such liens. [*New section adopted June 8, 1976.*]

SEC. 4.   [*Repealed June 8, 1976. See Section 4, below.*]

[Workers' Compensation]

SEC. 4.   The Legislature is hereby expressly vested with plenary power, unlimited by any provision of this Constitution, to create, and enforce a complete system of workers' compensation, by appropriate legislation, and in that behalf to create and enforce a liability on the part of any or all persons to compensate any or all of their workers for injury or disability,

---

* New Article XIV adopted June 8, 1976.

and their dependents for death incurred or sustained by the said workers in the course of their employment, irrespective of the fault of any party. A complete system of workers' compensation includes adequate provisions for the comfort, health and safety and general welfare of any and all workers and those dependent upon them for support to the extent of relieving from the consequences of any injury or death incurred or sustained by workers in the course of their employment, irrespective of the fault of any party; also full provision for securing safety in places of employment; full provision for such medical, surgical, hospital and other remedial treatment as is requisite to cure and relieve from the effects of such injury; full provision for adequate insurance coverage against liability to pay or furnish compensation; full provision for regulating such insurance coverage in all its aspects, including the establishment and management of a state compensation insurance fund; full provision for otherwise securing the payment of compensation; and full provision for vesting power, authority and jurisdiction in an administrative body with all the requisite governmental functions to determine any dispute or matter arising under such legislation, to the end that the administration of such legislation shall accomplish substantial justice in all cases expeditiously, inexpensively, and without incumbrance of any character; all of which matters are expressly declared to be the social public policy of this State, binding upon all departments of the state government.

The Legislature is vested with plenary powers, to provide for the settlement of any disputes arising under such legislation by arbitration, or by an industrial accident commission, by the courts, or by either, any, or all of these agencies, either separately or in combination, and may fix and control the method and manner of trial of any such dispute, the rules of evidence and the manner of review of decisions rendered by the tribunal or tribunals designated by it; provided, that all decisions of any such tribunal shall be subject to review by the appellate courts of this State. The Legislature may combine in one statute all the provisions for a complete system of workers' compensation, as herein defined.

The Legislature shall have power to provide for the payment of an award to the State in the case of the death, arising out of and in the course of the employment, of an employee without dependents, and such awards may be used for the payment of extra compensation for subsequent injuries beyond the liability of a single employer for awards to employees of the employer.

Nothing contained herein shall be taken or construed to impair or render ineffectual in any measure the creation and existence of the industrial accident commission of this State or the state compensation insurance fund, the creation and existence of which, with all the functions vested in them, are hereby ratified and confirmed. [*New section adopted June 8, 1976.*]

SEC. 5.   [*Repealed November 6, 1990. See Section 5, below.*]

[Inmate Labor]

SECTION 5. (a) The Director of Corrections or any county Sheriff or other local government official charged with jail operations, may enter into contracts with public entities, nonprofit or for profit organizations, entities, or businesses for the purpose of conducting programs which use inmate labor. Such programs shall be operated and implemented pursuant to statutes enacted by or in accordance with the provisions of the Prison Inmate Labor Initiative of 1990, and by rules and regulations prescribed by the Director of Corrections and, for county jail programs, by local ordinances.

(b) No contract shall be executed with an employer that will initiate employment by inmates in the same job classification as non-inmate employees of the same employer who are on strike, as defined in Section 1132.6 of the Labor Code, as it reads on January 1, 1990, or who are subject to lockout, as defined in Section 1132.8 of the Labor Code, as it reads on January 1, 1990. Total daily hours worked by inmates employed in the same job classification as non-inmate employees of the same employer who are on strike, as defined in Section 1132.6 of the Labor Code, as it reads on January 1, 1990, or who are subject to lockout, as defined in Section 1132.8 of the Labor Code, as it reads on January 1, 1990, shall not exceed, for the duration of the strike, the average daily hours worked for the preceding six months, or if the program has been in operation for less than six months, the average for the period of operation.

(c) Nothing in this section shall be interpreted as creating a right of inmates to work. [*New section adopted November 6, 1990. Initiative measure.*]

ARTICLE XV.   [*Repealed June 8, 1976. See Article XV, below.*]

ARTICLE XV *

USURY

[Rate of Interest]

SECTION 1. The rate of interest upon the loan or forbearance of any money, goods, or things in action, or on accounts after demand, shall be 7 percent per annum but it shall be competent for the parties to any loan or forbearance of any money, goods or things in action to contract in writing for a rate of interest:

(1) For any loan or forbearance of any money, goods, or things in action, if the money, goods, or things in action are for use primarily for personal, family, or household purposes, at a rate not exceeding 10 percent per an-

---

* New Article XV adopted June 8, 1976.

num; provided, however, that any loan or forbearance of any money, goods or things in action the proceeds of which are used primarily for the purchase, construction or improvement of real property shall not be deemed to be a use primarily for personal, family or household purposes; or

(2) For any loan or forbearance of any money, goods, or things in action for any use other than specified in paragraph (1), at a rate not exceeding the higher of (a) 10 percent per annum or (b) 5 percent per annum plus the rate prevailing on the 25th day of the month preceding the earlier of (i) the date of execution of the contract to make the loan or forbearance, or (ii) the date of making the loan or forbearance established by the Federal Reserve Bank of San Francisco on advances to member banks under Sections 13 and 13a of the Federal Reserve Act as now in effect or hereafter from time to time amended (or if there is no such single determinable rate of advances, the closest counterpart of such rate as shall be designated by the Superintendent of Banks of the State of California unless some other person or agency is delegated such authority by the Legislature).

[Charges]

No person, association, copartnership or corporation shall by charging any fee, bonus, commission, discount or other compensation receive from a borrower more than the interest authorized by this section upon any loan or forbearance of any money, goods or things in action.

[Exemptions]

However, none of the above restrictions shall apply to any obligations of, loans made by, or forbearances of, any building and loan association as defined in and which is operated under that certain act known as the "Building and Loan Association Act," approved May 5, 1931, as amended, or to any corporation incorporated in the manner prescribed in and operating under that certain act entitled "An act defining industrial loan companies, providing for their incorporation, powers and supervision," approved May 18, 1917, as amended, or any corporation incorporated in the manner prescribed in and operating under that certain act entitled "An act defining credit unions, providing for their incorporation, powers, management and supervision," approved March 31, 1927, as amended or any duly licensed pawnbroker or personal property broker, or any loans made or arranged by any person licensed as a real estate broker by the State of California and secured in whole or in part by liens on real property, or any bank as defined in and operating under that certain act known as the "Bank Act," approved March 1, 1909, as amended, or any bank created and operating under and pursuant to any laws of this State or of the United States of America or any nonprofit cooperative association organized under Chapter 1 (commencing with Section 54001) of Division 20 of the Food and Agricultural Code in loaning or advancing money in connection with any activity mentioned in said title or any corporation, association, syndicate, joint stock company, or partnership engaged exclusively in the business of marketing agricultural, horticultural, viticultural, dairy, live stock, poultry and bee products on a cooperative nonprofit basis in loaning or advancing money to the members thereof or in connection with any such business or any corporation securing money or credit from any federal intermediate credit bank, organized and existing pursuant to the provisions of an act of Congress entitled "Agricultural Credits Act of 1923," as amended in loaning or advancing credit so secured, or any other class of persons authorized by statute, or to any successor in interest to any loan or forbearance exempted under this article, nor shall any such charge of any said exempted classes of persons be considered in any action or for any purpose as increasing or affecting or as connected with the rate of interest hereinbefore fixed. The Legislature may from time to time prescribe the maximum rate per annum of, or provide for the supervision, or the filing of a schedule of, or in any manner fix, regulate or limit, the fees, bonuses, commissions, discounts or other compensation which all or any of the said exempted classes of persons may charge or receive from a borrower in connection with any loan or forbearance of any money, goods or things in action.

[*Judgments Rendered in Court—Rate of Interest*]

The rate of interest upon a judgment rendered in any court of this State shall be set by the Legislature at not more than 10 percent per annum. Such rate may be variable and based upon interest rates charged by federal agencies or economic indicators, or both.

In the absence of the setting of such rate by the Legislature, the rate of interest on any judgment rendered in any court of the State shall be 7 percent per annum.

[*Scope of Section*]

The provisions of this section shall supersede all provisions of this Constitution and laws enacted thereunder in conflict therewith. [*As amended November 6, 1979.*]

SEC. 2.   [*Repealed June 8, 1976.*]

SEC. 3.   [*Repealed June 8, 1976.*]

ARTICLE XVI

PUBLIC FINANCE

[*Heading as amended November 5, 1974.*]

[*State Indebtedness—Limitation—Two-thirds Vote to Submit Bond Law— Submission of Law to Electors*]

SECTION 1.   The Legislature shall not, in any manner create any debt or debts, liability or liabilities, which shall, singly or in the aggregate with any previous debts or liabilities, exceed the sum of three hundred thousand dollars ($300,000), except in case of war to repel invasion or suppress insurrection, unless the same shall be authorized by law for some single object or work to be distinctly specified therein which law shall provide ways and means, exclusive of loans, for the payment of the interest of such debt or liability as it falls due, and also to pay and discharge the principal of such debt or liability within 50 years of the time of the contracting thereof, and shall be irrepealable until the principal and interest thereon shall be paid and discharged, and such law may make provision for a sinking fund to pay the principal of such debt or liability to commence at a time after the incurring of such debt or liability of not more than a period of one-fourth of the time of maturity of such debt or liability; but no such law shall take effect unless it has been passed by a two-thirds vote of all the members elected to each house of the Legislature and until, at a general election or at a direct primary, it shall have been submitted to the people and shall have received a majority of all the votes cast for and against it at such election; and all moneys raised by authority of such law shall be applied only to the specific object therein stated or to the payment of the debt thereby created. Full publicity as to matters to be voted upon by the people is afforded by the setting out of the complete text of the proposed laws, together with the arguments for and against them, in the ballot pamphlet mailed to each elector preceding the election at which they are submitted, and the only requirement for publication of such law shall be that it be set out at length in ballot pamphlets which the Secretary of State shall cause to be printed. The Legislature may, at any time after the approval of such law by the people, reduce the amount of the indebtedness authorized by the law to an amount not less than the amount contracted at the time of the reduction, or it may repeal the law if no debt shall have been contracted in pursuance thereof.

Notwithstanding any other provision of this Constitution, Members of the Legislature who are required to meet with the State Allocation Board shall have equal rights and duties with the nonlegislative members to vote and act upon matters pending or coming before such board for the allocation and apportionment of funds to school districts for school construction purposes or purposes related thereto.

Notwithstanding any other provision of this constitution, or of any bond act to the contrary, if any general obligation bonds of the State heretofore or hereafter authorized by vote of the people have been offered for sale and not sold, the Legislature may raise the maximum rate of interest payable on all general obligation bonds authorized but not sold, whether or not such bonds have been offered for sale, by a statute passed by a two-thirds vote of all members elected to each house thereof.

The provisions of Senate Bill No. 763 † of the 1969 Regular Session, which authorize an increase of the state general obligation bond maximum interest rate from 5 percent to an amount not in excess of 7 percent and eliminate the maximum rate of interest payable on notes given in anticipation of the sale of such bonds, are hereby ratified. [*As amended June 2, 1970.*]

[*Budget Deficits*]

SEC. 1.3.   (a) For the purposes of Section 1, a "single object or work," for which the Legislature may create a debt or liability in excess of three hundred thousand dollars ($300,000) subject to the requirements set forth in Section 1, includes the funding of an accumulated state budget deficit to the extent, and in the amount, that funding is authorized in a measure submitted to the voters at the March 2, 2004, statewide primary election.

(b) As used in subdivision (a), "accumulated state budget deficit" means the aggregate of both of the following, as certified by the Director of Finance:

(1) The estimated negative balance of the Special Fund for Economic Uncertainties arising on or before June 30, 2004, not including the effect of the estimated amount of net proceeds of any bonds issued or to be issued pursuant to the California Fiscal Recovery Financing Act (Title 17 (commencing with Section 99000) of the Government Code) and any bonds issued or to be issued pursuant to the measure submitted to the voters at the March 2, 2004, statewide primary election as described in subdivision (a).

(2) Other General Fund obligations incurred by the State prior to June 30, 2004, to the extent not included in that negative balance.

(c) Subsequent to the issuance of any state bonds described in subdivision (a), the State may not obtain moneys to fund a year-end state budget deficit, as may be defined by statute, pursuant to any of the following: (1) indebtedness incurred pursuant to Section 1 of this article, (2) a debt obligation under which funds to repay that obligation are derived solely from a designated source of revenue, or (3) a bond or similar instrument for the borrowing of moneys for which there is no legal obligation of repayment. This subdivision does not apply to funding obtained through a short-term obligation incurred in anticipation of the receipt of tax proceeds or other revenues that may be applied to the payment of that obligation, for the purposes and not exceeding the amounts of existing appropriations to which the resulting proceeds are to be applied. For purposes of this subdivision, "year-end state budget deficit" does not include an obligation within the accumulated state budget deficit as defined by subdivision (b). [*New section adopted March 2, 2004.*]

† Chapter 740.

[General Obligation Bond Proceeds Fund]

SEC. 1.5. The Legislature may create and establish a "General Obligation Bond Proceeds Fund" in the State Treasury, and may provide for the proceeds of the sale of general obligation bonds of the State heretofore or hereafter issued, including any sums paid as accrued interest thereon, under any or all acts authorizing the issuance of such bonds, to be paid into or transferred to, as the case may be, the "General Obligation Bond Proceeds Fund." Accounts shall be maintained in the "General Obligation Bond Proceeds Fund" of all moneys deposited in the State Treasury to the credit of that fund and the proceeds of each bond issue shall be maintained as a separate and distinct account and shall be paid out only in accordance with the law authorizing the issuance of the particular bonds from which the proceeds were derived. The Legislature may abolish, subject to the conditions of this section, any fund in the State Treasury heretofore or hereafter created by any act for the purpose of having deposited therein the proceeds from the issuance of bonds if such proceeds are transferred to or paid into the "General Obligation Bond Proceeds Fund" pursuant to the authority granted in this section; provided, however, that nothing in this section shall prevent the Legislature from re-establishing any bond proceeds fund so abolished and transferring back to its credit all proceeds in the "General Obligation Bond Proceeds Fund" which constitute the proceeds of the particular bond fund being re-established. [*New section adopted November 6, 1962.*]

SEC. 2. [*Repealed November 6, 1962. See Section 2, below.*]

[Bond Issues—Submission by Constitutional Amendment Prohibited—Repeal of Certain Constitutional Provisions]

SEC. 2. (a) No amendment to this Constitution which provides for the preparation, issuance and sale of bonds of the State of California shall hereafter be submitted to the electors, nor shall any such amendment to the Constitution hereafter submitted to or approved by the electors become effective for any purpose.

Each measure providing for the preparation, issuance and sale of bonds of the State of California shall hereafter be submitted to the electors in the form of a bond act or statute.

(b) The provisions of this Constitution enumerated in subdivision (c) of this section are repealed and such provisions are continued as statutes which have been approved, adopted, legalized, ratified, validated, and made fully and completely effective, by means of the adoption by the electorate of a ratifying constitutional amendment, except that the Legislature, in addition to whatever powers it possessed under such provisions, may amend or repeal such provisions when the bonds issued thereunder have been fully retired and when no rights thereunder will be damaged.

(c) The enumerated provisions of this Constitution are: Article XVI, Sections 2, 3, 4, 4½, 5, 6, 8, 8½, 15, 16, 16.5, 17, 18, 19, 19.5, 20 and 21. [*New section adopted November 6, 1962.*]

[*Appropriations*]

Sec. 3.   No money shall ever be appropriated or drawn from the State Treasury for the purpose or benefit of any corporation, association, asylum, hospital, or any other institution not under the exclusive management and control of the State as a state institution, nor shall any grant or donation of property ever be made thereto by the State, except that notwithstanding anything contained in this or any other section of the Constitution:

[*Federal Funds*]

(1) Whenever federal funds are made available for the construction of hospital facilities by public agencies and nonprofit corporations organized to construct and maintain such facilities, nothing in this Constitution shall prevent the Legislature from making state money available for that purpose, or from authorizing the use of such money for the construction of hospital facilities by nonprofit corporations organized to construct and maintain such facilities.

[*Institution for Support of Orphans or Aged Indigents*]

(2) The Legislature shall have the power to grant aid to the institutions conducted for the support and maintenance of minor orphans, or half-orphans, or abandoned children, or children of a father who is incapacitated for gainful work by permanent physical disability or is suffering from tuberculosis in such a stage that he cannot pursue a gainful occupation, or aged persons in indigent circumstances—such aid to be granted by a uniform rule, and proportioned to the number of inmates of such respective institutions.

[*Needy Blind*]

(3) The Legislature shall have the power to grant aid to needy blind persons not inmates of any institution supported in whole or in part by the State or by any of its political subdivisions, and no person concerned with the administration of aid to needy blind persons shall dictate how any applicant or recipient shall expend such aid granted him, and all money paid to a recipient of such aid shall be intended to help him meet his individual needs and is not for the benefit of any other person, and such aid when granted shall not be construed as income to any person other than the blind recipient of such aid, and the State Department of Social Welfare shall take all necessary action to enforce the provisions relating to aid to needy blind persons as heretofore stated.

[*Physically Handicapped Persons*]

(4) The Legislature shall have power to grant aid to needy physically handicapped persons not inmates of any institution under the supervision of the Department of Mental Hygiene and supported in whole or in part by the State or by any institution supported in whole or part by any political subdivision of the State.

[*Management of Institutions*]

(5) The State shall have at any time the right to inquire into the management of such institutions.

[*Orphans, Aged Indigents, Needy Blind—County Support*]

(6) Whenever any county, or city and county, or city, or town, shall provide for the support of minor orphans, or half-orphans, or abandoned children, or children of a father who is incapacitated for gainful work by permanent physical disability or is suffering from tuberculosis in such a stage that he cannot pursue a gainful occupation, or aged persons in indigent circumstances, or needy blind persons not inmates of any institution supported in whole or in part by the State or by any of its political subdivisions, or needy physically handicapped persons not inmates of any institution under the supervision of the Department of Mental Hygiene and supported in whole or in part by the State or by any institution supported in whole or part by any political subdivision of the State; such county, city and county, city, or town shall be entitled to receive the same pro rata appropriations as may be granted to such institutions under church, or other control.

[*Receipts and Expenditures of Public Moneys*]

An accurate statement of the receipts and expenditures of public moneys shall be attached to and published with the laws at every regular session of the Legislature. [*New section adopted November 5, 1974.*]

[*Loan Guarantees re Nonprofit Corporations and Public Agencies*]

SEC. 4.   The Legislature shall have the power to insure or guarantee loans made by private or public lenders to nonprofit corporations and public agencies, the proceeds of which are to be used for the construction, expansion, enlargement, improvement, renovation or repair of any public or nonprofit hospital, hospital facility, or extended care facility, facility for the treatment of mental illness, or all of them, including any outpatient facility and any other facility useful and convenient in the operation of the hospital and any original equipment for any such hospital or facility, or both.

No provision of this Constitution, including but not limited to, Section 1 of Article XVI and Section 14 of Article XI, shall be construed as a limitation upon the authority granted to the Legislature by this section. [*New section adopted November 5, 1974.*]

SEC. 4½.   [*Repealed November 6, 1962.*]

[*Religious Institutions—Grants Prohibited*]

SEC. 5.   Neither the Legislature, nor any county, city and county, township, school district, or other municipal corporation, shall ever make an appropriation, or pay from any public fund whatever, or grant anything to or in aid of any religious sect, church, creed, or sectarian purpose, or help to support or sustain any school, college, university, hospital, or other institution controlled by any religious creed, church, or sectarian denomination whatever; nor shall any grant or donation of personal property or real estate ever be made by the State, or any city, city and county, town, or other municipal corporation for any religious creed, church, or sectarian purpose whatever; provided, that nothing in this section shall prevent the Legislature granting aid pursuant to Section 3 of Article XVI. [*New section adopted November 5, 1974.*]

[*Gifts or Loans of Public Moneys or Pledging of Credit Prohibited—Stock of Corporations*]

SEC. 6.   The Legislature shall have no power to give or to lend, or to authorize the giving or lending, of the credit of the State, or of any county, city and county, city, township or other political corporation or subdivision of the State now existing, or that may be hereafter established, in aid of or to any person, association, or corporation, whether municipal or otherwise, or to pledge the credit thereof, in any manner whatever, for the payment of the liabilities of any individual, association, municipal or other corporation whatever; nor shall it have power to make any gift or authorize the making of any gift, of any public money or thing of value to any individual, municipal or other corporation whatever; provided, that nothing in this section shall prevent the Legislature granting aid pursuant to Section 3 of Article XVI; and it shall not have power to authorize the State, or any political subdivision thereof, to subscribe for stock, or to become a stockholder in any corporation whatever; provided, further, that irrigation districts for the purpose of acquiring the control of any entire international water system necessary for its use and purposes, a part of which is situated in the United States, and a part thereof in a foreign country, may in the manner authorized by law, acquire the stock of any foreign corporation which is the owner of, or which holds the title to the part of such system situated in a foreign country; provided, further, that irrigation districts for the purpose of acquiring water and water rights and other property necessary for their uses and purposes, may acquire and hold the stock of corporations, domestic or foreign, owning waters, water rights, canals, waterworks, franchises or concessions subject to the same obligations and liabilities as are imposed by law upon all other stockholders in such corporation; and

[*Insurance Pooling Arrangements*]

Provided, further, that this section shall not prohibit any county, city and county, city, township, or other political corporation or subdivision of the State from joining with other such agencies in providing for the payment of workers' compensation, unemployment compensation, tort liability, or public liability losses incurred by such agencies, by entry into an insurance pooling arrangement under a joint exercise of powers agreement, or by membership in such publicly-owned nonprofit corporation or other public agency as may be authorized by the Legislature; and

[*Aid to Veterans*]

Provided, further, that nothing contained in this Constitution shall prohibit the use of state money or credit, in aiding veterans who served in the military or naval service of the United States during the time of war, in the acquisition of, or payments for, (1) farms or homes, or in projects of land settlement or in the development of such farms or homes or land settlement projects for the benefit of such veterans, or (2) any business, land or any interest therein, buildings, supplies, equipment, machinery, or tools, to be used by the veteran in pursuing a gainful occupation; and

[*Disaster Assistance*]

Provided, further, that nothing contained in this Constitution shall prohibit the State, or any county, city and county, city, township, or other political corporation or subdivision of the State from providing aid or assistance to persons, if found to be in the public interest, for the purpose of clearing debris, natural materials, and wreckage from privately owned lands and waters deposited thereon or therein during a period of a major disaster or emergency, in either case declared by the President. In such case, the public entity shall be indemnified by the recipient from the award of any claim against the public entity arising from the rendering of such aid or assistance. Such aid or assistance must be eligible for federal reimbursement for the cost thereof.

[*Temporary Transfers of Funds to Political Subdivisions*]

And provided, still further, that notwithstanding the restrictions contained in this Constitution, the treasurer of any city, county, or city and county shall have power and the duty to make such temporary transfers from the funds in custody as may be necessary to provide funds for meeting the obligations incurred for maintenance purposes by any city, county, city and county, district, or other political subdivision whose funds are in custody and are paid out solely through the treasurer's office. Such temporary transfer of funds to any political subdivision shall be made only upon resolution adopted by the governing body of the city, county, or city and county directing the treasurer of such city, county, or city and county to make such temporary transfer. Such temporary transfer of funds to any political subdivision shall not exceed 85 percent of the anticipated revenues accruing to such political subdivision, shall not be made prior to the first day of the fiscal year nor after the last Monday in April of the current fiscal year, and shall be replaced from the revenues accruing to such political subdivision before any other obligation of such political subdivision is met from such revenue. [*As amended November 2, 1982.*]

[*Controller's Warrants*]

SEC. 7.   Money may be drawn from the Treasury only through an appropriation made by law and upon a Controller's duly drawn warrant. [*New section adopted November 5, 1974.*]

[*School Funding Priority*]

SEC. 8.   (a) From all state revenues there shall first be set apart the moneys to be applied by the State for support of the public school system and public institutions of higher education.

(b) Commencing with the 1990–91 fiscal year, the moneys to be applied by the State for the support of school districts and community college districts shall be not less than the greater of the following amounts:

(1) The amount which, as a percentage of General Fund revenues which may be appropriated pursuant to Article XIII B, equals the percentage of General Fund revenues appropriated for school districts and community college districts, respectively, in fiscal year 1986–87.

(2) The amount required to ensure that the total allocations to school districts and community college districts from General Fund proceeds of taxes appropriated pursuant to Article XIII B and allocated local proceeds of taxes shall not be less than the total amount from these sources in the prior fiscal year, excluding any revenues allocated pursuant to subdivision (a) of Section 8.5, adjusted for changes in enrollment and adjusted for the change in the cost of living pursuant to paragraph (1) of subdivision (e) of Section 8 of Article XIII B. This paragraph shall be operative only in a fiscal year in which the percentage growth in California per capita personal income is less than or equal to the percentage growth in per capita General Fund revenues plus one half of one percent.

(3) (A) The amount required to ensure that the total allocations to school districts and community college districts from General Fund proceeds of taxes appropriated pursuant to Article XIII B and allocated local proceeds of taxes shall equal the total amount from these sources in the prior fiscal year, excluding any revenues allocated pursuant to subdivision (a) of Section 8.5, adjusted for changes in enrollment and adjusted for the change in per capita General Fund revenues.

(B) In addition, an amount equal to one-half of one percent times the prior year total allocations to school districts and community colleges from General Fund proceeds of taxes appropriated pursuant to Article XIII B and allocated local proceeds of taxes, excluding any revenues allocated pursuant to subdivision (a) of Section 8.5, adjusted for changes in enrollment.

(C) This paragraph (3) shall be operative only in a fiscal year in which the percentage growth in California per capita personal income in a fiscal year is greater than the percentage growth in per capita General Fund revenues plus one half of one percent.

(c) In any fiscal year, if the amount computed pursuant to paragraph (1) of subdivision (b) exceeds the amount computed pursuant to paragraph (2) of subdivision (b) by a difference that exceeds one and one-half percent of General Fund revenues, the amount in excess of one and one-half percent of General Fund revenues shall not be considered allocations to school districts and community colleges for purposes of computing the amount of state aid pursuant to paragraph (2) or 3 of subdivision (b) in the subsequent fiscal year.

(d) In any fiscal year in which school districts and community college districts are allocated funding pursuant to paragraph (3) of subdivision (b) or pursuant to subdivision (h), they shall be entitled to a maintenance factor, equal to the difference between (1) the amount of General Fund moneys which would have been appropriated pursuant to paragraph (2) of subdivision (b) if that paragraph had been operative or the amount of General Fund moneys which would have been appropriated pursuant to subdivision (b) had subdivision (b) not been suspended, and (2) the amount of General Fund moneys actually appropriated to school districts and community college districts in that fiscal year.

(e) The maintenance factor for school districts and community college districts determined pursuant to subdivision (d) shall be adjusted annually for changes in enrollment, and adjusted for the change in the cost of living pursuant to paragraph (1) of subdivision (e) of Section 8 of Article XIII B, until it has been allocated in full. The maintenance factor shall be allocated in a manner determined by the Legislature in each fiscal year in which the percentage growth in per capita General Fund revenues exceeds the percentage growth in California per capita personal income. The maintenance factor shall be reduced each year by the amount allocated by the Legislature in that fiscal year. The minimum maintenance factor amount to be allocated in a fiscal year shall be equal to the product of General Fund revenues from proceeds of taxes and one-half of the difference between the percentage growth in per capita General Fund revenues from proceeds of taxes and in California per capita personal income, not to exceed the total dollar amount of the maintenance factor.

(f) For purposes of this section, "changes in enrollment" shall be measured by the percentage change in average daily attendance. However, in any fiscal year, there shall be no adjustment for decreases in enrollment between the prior fiscal year and the current fiscal year unless there have been decreases in enrollment between the second prior fiscal year and the prior fiscal year and between the third prior fiscal year and the second prior fiscal year.

(h) Subparagraph (B) of paragraph (3) of subdivision (b) may be suspended for one year only when made part of or included within any bill enacted pursuant to Section 12 of Article IV. All other provisions of subdivision (b) may be suspended for one year by the enactment of an urgency statute pursuant to Section 8 of Article IV, provided that the urgency statute may not be made part of or included within any bill enacted pursuant to Section 12 of Article IV. [*As amended June 5, 1990. Operative July 1, 1990.*]

Sec. 8½.   [*Repealed November 6, 1962.*]

[Allocations to State School Fund]

Sec. 8.5.   (a) In addition to the amount required to be applied for the support of school districts and community college districts pursuant to Section 8, the Controller shall during each fiscal year transfer and allocate all revenues available pursuant to paragraph 1 of subdivision (a) of Section 2 of Article XIII B to that portion of the State School Fund restricted for elementary and high school purposes, and to that portion of the State School Fund restricted for community college purposes, respectively, in proportion to the enrollment in school districts and community college districts respectively.

(1) With respect to funds allocated to that portion of the State School Fund restricted for elementary and high school purposes, no transfer or allocation of funds pursuant to this section shall be required at any time that the Director of Finance and the Superintendent of Public Instruction mutually determine that current annual expenditures per student equal or exceed the average annual expenditure per student of the 10 states with the highest annual expenditures per student for elementary and high schools, and that average class size equals or is less than the average class size of the 10 states with the lowest class size for elementary and high schools.

(2) With respect to funds allocated to that portion of the State School Fund restricted for community college purposes, no transfer or allocation of funds pursuant to this section shall be required at any time that the Director of Finance and the Chancellor of the California Community Colleges mutually determine that current annual expenditures per student for community colleges in this State equal or exceed the average annual expenditure per student of the 10 states with the highest annual expenditures per student for community colleges.

(b) Notwithstanding the provisions of Article XIII B, funds allocated pursuant to this section shall not constitute appropriations subject to limitation.

(c) From any funds transferred to the State School Fund pursuant to subdivision (a), the Controller shall each year allocate to each school district and community college district an equal amount per enrollment in school districts from the amount in that portion of the State School Fund restricted for elementary and high school purposes and an equal amount per enrollment in community college districts from that portion of the State School Fund restricted for community college purposes.

(d) All revenues allocated pursuant to subdivision (a) shall be expended solely for the purposes of instructional improvement and accountability as required by law.

(e) Any school district maintaining an elementary or secondary school shall develop and cause to be prepared an annual audit accounting for such funds and shall adopt a School Accountability Report Card for each school. [*As amended June 5, 1990. Operative July 1, 1990.*]

[*Fish and Game*]

SEC. 9. Money collected under any state law relating to the protection or propagation of fish and game shall be used for activities relating thereto. [*New section adopted November 5, 1974.*]

[*Aged Aid—Federal-State Co-operation*]

SEC. 10. Whenever the United States government or any officer or agency thereof shall provide pensions or other aid for the aged, co-operation by the State therewith and therein is hereby authorized in such manner and to such extent as may be provided by law.

The money expended by any county, city and county, municipality, district or other political subdivision of this State made available under the provisions of this section shall not be considered as a part of the base for determining the maximum expenditure for any given year permissible under Section 20 † of Article XI of this Constitution independent of the vote of the electors or authorization by the State Board of Equalization. [*As amended November 6, 1962.*]

[*Relief Administration*]

SEC. 11. The Legislature has plenary power to provide for the administration of any constitutional provisions or laws heretofore or hereafter enacted concerning the administration of relief, and to that end may modify, transfer, or enlarge the powers vested in any state agency or officer concerned with the administration of relief or laws appertaining thereto. The Legislature, or the people by initiative, shall have power to amend,

---

† Section 20, Article XI, repealed June 2, 1970.

alter, or repeal any law relating to the relief of hardship and destitution, whether such hardship and destitution results from unemployment or from other causes, or to provide for the administration of the relief of hardship and destitution, whether resulting from unemployment or from other causes, either directly by the State or through the counties of the State, and to grant such aid to the counties therefor, or make such provision for reimbursement of the counties by the State, as the Legislature deems proper. [*As amended November 6, 1962.*]

SEC. 12.   [*Repealed November 6, 1962.*]

[*Legislative Power to Release Encumbrances Taken as Security for Aid to Aged*]

SEC. 13.   Notwithstanding any other provision of this Constitution, the Legislature shall have power to release, rescind, cancel, or otherwise nullify in whole or in part any encumbrance on property, personal obligation, or other form of security heretofore or hereafter exacted or imposed by the Legislature to secure the repayment to, or reimbursement of, the State, and the counties or other agencies of the state government, of aid lawfully granted to and received by aged persons. [*As amended November 6, 1962.*]

[*Bonds—Environmental Pollution Control Facilities*]

SEC. 14.   The Legislature may provide for the issuance of revenue bonds to finance the acquisition, construction, and installation of environmental pollution control facilities, including the acquisition of all technological facilities necessary or convenient for pollution control, and for the lease or sale of such facilities to persons, associations, or corporations, other than municipal corporations; provided, that such revenue bonds shall not be secured by the taxing power of the State; and provided, further, that the Legislature may, by resolution adopted by either house, prohibit or limit any proposed issuance of such revenue bonds. No provision of this Constitution, including, but not limited to, Section 25 of Article XIII and Sections 1 and 2 of Article XVI, shall be construed as a limitation upon the authority granted to the Legislature pursuant to this section. Nothing herein contained shall authorize any public agency to operate any industrial or commercial enterprise. [*New section adopted November 7, 1972.*]

[*Energy Alternative Sources Facilities—Acquisition, Construction, Etc.—Revenue Bond Issuance*]

SEC. 14.5.   The Legislature may provide for the issuance of revenue bonds to finance the acquisition, construction, and installation of facilities utilizing cogeneration technology, solar power, biomass, or any other alternative source the Legislature may deem appropriate, including the acquisition of all technological facilities necessary or convenient for the use of alternative sources, and for the lease or sale of such facilities to persons, associations, or corporations, other than municipal corporations; provided, that such revenue bonds shall not be secured by the taxing power of the

State; and provided, further, that the Legislature may, by resolution adopted by both houses, prohibit or limit any proposed issuance of such revenue bonds. No provision of this Constitution, including, but not limited to, Sections 1, 2, and 6, of this article, shall be construed as a limitation upon the authority granted to the Legislature pursuant to this section. Nothing contained herein shall authorize any public agency to operate any industrial or commercial enterprise. [*New section adopted June 3, 1980.*]

[*Parking Meter Revenues*]

SEC. 15.   A public body authorized to issue securities to provide public parking facilities and any other public body whose territorial area includes such facilities are authorized to make revenues from street parking meters available as additional security. [*New section adopted November 5, 1974.*]

[*Taxation of Redevelopment Projects*]

SEC. 16.   All property in a redevelopment project established under the Community Redevelopment Law as now existing or hereafter amended, except publicly owned property not subject to taxation by reason of that ownership, shall be taxed in proportion to its value as provided in Section 1 of this article, and those taxes (the word "taxes" as used herein includes, but is not limited to, all levies on an ad valorem basis upon land or real property) shall be levied and collected as other taxes are levied and collected by the respective taxing agencies.

The Legislature may provide that any redevelopment plan may contain a provision that the taxes, if any, so levied upon the taxable property in a redevelopment project each year by or for the benefit of the State of California, any city, county, city and county, district, or other public corporation (hereinafter sometimes called "taxing agencies") after the effective date of the ordinance approving the redevelopment plan, shall be divided as follows:

(a) That portion of the taxes which would be produced by the rate upon which the tax is levied each year by or for each of those taxing agencies upon the total sum of the assessed value of the taxable property in the redevelopment project as shown upon the assessment roll used in connection with the taxation of that property by the taxing agency, last equalized prior to the effective date of the ordinance, shall be allocated to, and when collected shall be paid into, the funds of the respective taxing agencies as taxes by or for those taxing agencies on all other property are paid (for the purpose of allocating taxes levied by or for any taxing agency or agencies which did not include the territory in a redevelopment project on the effective date of the ordinance but to which that territory has been annexed or otherwise included after the ordinance's effective date, the assessment roll of the county last equalized on the effective date of that ordinance shall be used in determining the assessed valuation of the taxable property in the project on that effective date); and

(b) Except as provided in subdivision (c), that portion of the levied taxes each year in excess of that amount shall be allocated to and when collected shall be paid into a special fund of the redevelopment agency to pay the principal of and interest on loans, moneys advanced to, or indebtedness (whether funded, refunded, assumed or otherwise) incurred by the redevelopment agency to finance or refinance, in whole or in part, the redevelopment project. Unless and until the total assessed valuation of the taxable property in a redevelopment project exceeds the total assessed value of the taxable property in the project as shown by the last equalized assessment roll referred to in subdivision (a), all of the taxes levied and collected upon the taxable property in the redevelopment project shall be paid into the funds of the respective taxing agencies. When the loans, advances, and indebtedness, if any, and interest thereon, have been paid, then all moneys thereafter received from taxes upon the taxable property in the redevelopment project shall be paid into the funds of the respective taxing agencies as taxes on all other property are paid.

(c) That portion of the taxes identified in subdivision (b) which are attributable to a tax rate levied by a taxing agency for the purpose of producing revenues in an amount sufficient to make annual repayments of the principal of, and the interest on, any bonded indebtedness for the acquisition or improvement of real property shall be allocated to, and when collected shall be paid into, the fund of that taxing agency. This paragraph shall only apply to taxes levied to repay bonded indebtedness approved by the voters of the taxing agency on or after January 1, 1989.

The Legislature may also provide that in any redevelopment plan or in the proceedings for the advance of moneys, or making of loans, or the incurring of any indebtedness (whether funded, refunded, assumed, or otherwise) by the redevelopment agency to finance or refinance, in whole or in part, the redevelopment project, the portion of taxes identified in subdivision (b), exclusive of that portion identified in subdivision (c), may be irrevocably pledged for the payment of the principal of and interest on those loans, advances, or indebtedness.

It is intended by this section to empower any redevelopment agency, city, county, or city and county under any law authorized by this section to exercise the provisions hereof separately or in combination with powers granted by the same or any other law relative to redevelopment agencies. This section shall not affect any other law or laws relating to the same or a similar subject but is intended to authorize an alternative method of procedure governing the subject to which it refers.

The Legislature shall enact those laws as may be necessary to enforce the provisions of this section. [*As amended November 8, 1988.*]

SEC. 16.5.   [*Repealed November 6, 1962.*]

[*State's Credit—Investment of Public Pension or Retirement Funds*]

SEC. 17. The State shall not in any manner loan its credit, nor shall it subscribe to, or be interested in the stock of any company, association, or corporation, except that the State and each political subdivision, district, municipality, and public agency thereof is hereby authorized to acquire and hold shares of the capital stock of any mutual water company or corporation when the stock is so acquired or held for the purpose of furnishing a supply of water for public, municipal or governmental purposes; and the holding of the stock shall entitle the holder thereof to all of the rights, powers and privileges, and shall subject the holder to the obligations and liabilities conferred or imposed by law upon other holders of stock in the mutual water company or corporation in which the stock is so held.

Notwithstanding any other provisions of law or this Constitution to the contrary, the retirement board of a public pension or retirement system shall have plenary authority and fiduciary responsibility for investment of moneys and administration of the system, subject to all of the following:

(a) The retirement board of a public pension or retirement system shall have the sole and exclusive fiduciary responsibility over the assets of the public pension or retirement system. The retirement board shall also have sole and exclusive responsibility to administer the system in a manner that will assure prompt delivery of benefits and related services to the participants and their beneficiaries. The assets of a public pension or retirement system are trust funds and shall be held for the exclusive purposes of providing benefits to participants in the pension or retirement system and their beneficiaries and defraying reasonable expenses of administering the system.

(b) The members of the retirement board of a public pension or retirement system shall discharge their duties with respect to the system solely in the interest of, and for the exclusive purposes of providing benefits to, participants and their beneficiaries, minimizing employer contributions thereto, and defraying reasonable expenses of administering the system. A retirement board's duty to its participants and their beneficiaries shall take precedence over any other duty.

(c) The members of the retirement board of a public pension or retirement system shall discharge their duties with respect to the system with the care, skill, prudence, and diligence under the circumstances then prevailing that a prudent person acting in a like capacity and familiar with these matters would use in the conduct of an enterprise of a like character and with like aims.

(d) The members of the retirement board of a public pension or retirement system shall diversify the investments of the system so as to minimize the risk of loss and to maximize the rate of return, unless under the circumstances it is clearly not prudent to do so.

(e) The retirement board of a public pension or retirement system, consistent with the exclusive fiduciary responsibilities vested in it, shall have the sole and exclusive power to provide for actuarial services in order to assure the competency of the assets of the public pension or retirement system.

(f) With regard to the retirement board of a public pension or retirement system which includes in its composition elected employee members, the number, terms, and method of selection or removal of members of the retirement board which were required by law or otherwise in effect on July 1, 1991, shall not be changed, amended, or modified by the Legislature unless the change, amendment, or modification enacted by the Legislature is ratified by a majority vote of the electors of the jurisdiction in which the participants of the system are or were, prior to retirement, employed.

(g) The Legislature may by statute continue to prohibit certain investments by a retirement board where it is in the public interest to do so, and provided that the prohibition satisfies the standards of fiduciary care and loyalty required of a retirement board pursuant to this section.

(h) As used in this section, the term "retirement board" shall mean the board of administration, board of trustees, board of directors, or other governing body or board of a public employees' pension or retirement system; provided, however, that the term "retirement board" shall not be interpreted to mean or include a governing body or board created after July 1, 1991 which does not administer pension or retirement benefits, or the elected legislative body of a jurisdiction which employs participants in a public employees' pension or retirement system. [*As amended November 3, 1992. Initiative measure.*]

[*Municipal Debt Exceeding Income*]

SEC. 18.   (a) No county, city, town, township, board of education, or school district, shall incur any indebtedness or liability in any manner or for any purpose exceeding in any year the income and revenue provided for such year, without the assent of two-thirds of the voters of the public entity voting at an election to be held for that purpose, except that with respect to any such public entity which is authorized to incur indebtedness for public school purposes, any proposition for the incurrence of indebtedness in the form of general obligation bonds for the purpose of repairing, reconstructing or replacing public school buildings determined, in the manner prescribed by law, to be structurally unsafe for school use, shall be adopted upon the approval of a majority of the voters of the public entity voting on the proposition at such election; nor unless before or at the time of incurring such indebtedness provision shall be made for the collection of an annual tax sufficient to pay the interest on such indebtedness as it falls due, and to provide for a sinking fund for the payment of the principal thereof, on or before maturity, which shall not exceed forty years from the time of contracting the indebtedness.

(b) Notwithstanding subdivision (a), on or after the effective date of the measure adding this subdivision, in the case of any school district, community college district, or county office of education, any proposition for the incurrence of indebtedness in the form of general obligation bonds for the construction, reconstruction, rehabilitation, or replacement of school facilities, including the furnishing and equipping of school facilities, or the acquisition or lease of real property for school facilities, shall be adopted upon the approval of 55 percent of the voters of the district or county, as appropriate, voting on the proposition at an election. This subdivision shall apply only to a proposition for the incurrence of indebtedness in the form of general obligation bonds for the purposes specified in this subdivision if the proposition meets all of the accountability requirements of paragraph (3) of subdivision (b) of Section 1 of Article XIII A.

(c) When two or more propositions for incurring any indebtedness or liability are submitted at the same election, the votes cast for and against each proposition shall be counted separately, and when two-thirds or a majority or 55 percent of the voters, as the case may be, voting on any one of those propositions, vote in favor thereof, the proposition shall be deemed adopted. [*As amended November 7, 2000. Initiative measure.*]

[*Public Improvement Proceedings by Chartered City or County*]

SEC. 19.   All proceedings undertaken by any chartered city, or by any chartered county or by any chartered city and county for the construction of any public improvement, or the acquisition of any property for public use, or both, where the cost thereof is to be paid in whole or in part by special assessment or other special assessment taxes upon property, whether the special assessment will be specific or a special assessment tax upon property wholly or partially according to the assessed value of such property, shall be undertaken only in accordance with the provisions of law governing: (a) limitations of costs of such proceedings or assessments for such proceedings, or both, in relation to the value of any property assessed therefor; (b) determination of a basis for the valuation of any such property; (c) payment of the cost in excess of such limitations; (d) avoidance of such limitations; (e) postponement or abandonment, or both, of such proceedings in whole or in part upon majority protest, and particularly in accordance with such provisions as contained in Sections 10, 11 and 13a of the Special Assessment Investigation, Limitation and Majority Protest Act of 1931 or any amendments, codification, reenactment or restatement thereof.

Notwithstanding any provisions for debt limitation or majority protest as in this section provided, if, after the giving of such reasonable notice by publication and posting and the holding of such public hearing as the legislative body of any such chartered county, chartered city or chartered city and county shall have prescribed, such legislative body by no less than a four-fifths vote of all members thereof, finds and determines that the public convenience and necessity require such improvements or acquisitions, such debt limitation and majority protest provisions shall not apply.

Nothing contained in this section shall require the legislative body of any such city, county, or city and county to prepare or to cause to be prepared, hear, notice for hearing or report the hearing of any report as to any such proposed construction or acquisition or both. [*New section adopted November 5, 1974.*]

SEC. 19.5.   [*Repealed November 6, 1962.*]

SEC. 20.   [*Repealed November 4, 2014. See Section 20, below.*]

[Budget Stabilization Account]

SEC. 20.   (a) (1) The Budget Stabilization Account is hereby created in the General Fund.

(2) For the 2015–16 fiscal year and each fiscal year thereafter, based on the Budget Act for the fiscal year, the Controller shall transfer from the General Fund to the Budget Stabilization Account, no later than October 1, a sum equal to 1.5 percent of the estimated amount of General Fund revenues for that fiscal year.

(b) (1) For the 2015–16 fiscal year and each fiscal year thereafter, based on the Budget Act for the fiscal year, the Department of Finance shall provide to the Legislature all of the following information:

(A) An estimate of the amount of General Fund proceeds of taxes that may be appropriated pursuant to Article XIII B for that fiscal year.

(B) (i) An estimate of that portion of the General Fund proceeds of taxes identified in subparagraph (A) that is derived from personal income taxes paid on net capital gains.

(ii) The portion of the estimate in clause (i) that exceeds 8 percent of the estimate made under subparagraph (A).

(C) That portion of the state's funding obligation under Section 8 that results from including the amount calculated under clause (ii) of subparagraph (B), if any, as General Fund proceeds of taxes.

(D) The amount of any appropriations described in clause (ii) of subparagraph (B) of paragraph (1) of, or subparagraph (C) of paragraph (2) of, subdivision (c), that are made from the revenues described in clause (ii) of subparagraph (B) of this paragraph.

(E) The amount resulting from subtracting the combined values calculated under subparagraphs (C) and (D) from the value calculated under clause (ii) of subparagraph (B). If less than zero, the amount shall be considered zero for this purpose.

(F) The lesser of the amount calculated under subparagraph (E) or the amount of transfer resulting in the balance in the Budget Stabilization Account reaching the limit specified in subdivision (e).

(2) In the 2016–17 fiscal year, with respect to the 2015–16 fiscal year only, and in the 2017–18 fiscal year and each fiscal year thereafter, separately with respect to each of the two next preceding fiscal years, the Department of Finance shall calculate all of the following, using the same methodology used for the relevant fiscal year, and provide those calculations to the Legislature:

(A) An updated estimate of the amount of General Fund proceeds of taxes that may be appropriated pursuant to Article XIII B.

(B) (i) An updated estimate of that portion of the General Fund proceeds of taxes identified in subparagraph (A) that is derived from personal income taxes paid on net capital gains.

(ii) That portion of the updated estimate in clause (i) that exceeds 8 percent of the updated estimate made under subparagraph (A).

(C) The updated calculation of that portion of the state's funding obligation under Section 8 that results from including the updated amount calculated under clause (ii) of subparagraph (B), if any, as General Fund proceeds of taxes.

(D) The amount of any appropriations described in clause (ii) of subparagraph (B) of paragraph (1) of, or subparagraph (C) of paragraph (2) of, subdivision (c), that are made from the revenues described in clause (ii) of subparagraph (B) of paragraph (1).

(E) The amount resulting from subtracting the combined values calculated under subparagraphs (C) and (D) from the value calculated under clause (ii) of subparagraph (B). If less than zero, the amount shall be considered zero for this purpose.

(F) The amount previously transferred for the fiscal year by the Controller from the General Fund to the Budget Stabilization Account pursuant to subdivisions (c) and (d).

(G) The lesser of (i) the amount, not less than zero, resulting from subtracting, from the amount calculated under subparagraph (E), the value of any suspension or reduction of transfer pursuant to paragraph (1) of subdivision (a) of Section 22 previously approved by the Legislature for the relevant fiscal year, and the amount previously transferred for that fiscal year by the Controller as described in subparagraph (F), or (ii) the amount of transfer resulting in the balance in the Budget Stabilization Account reaching the limit as specified in subdivision (e).

(c) (1) (A) By October 1 of the 2015–16 fiscal year and each fiscal year thereafter to the 2029–30 fiscal year, inclusive, based on the estimates set forth in the annual Budget Act pursuant to paragraphs (2) and (3) of subdivision (h), and the sum identified in paragraph (2) of subdivision (a), the Controller shall transfer amounts from the General Fund and the Budget Stabilization Account, pursuant to a schedule provided by the Director of Finance, as provided in subparagraph (B).

(B) Notwithstanding any other provision of this section, in the fiscal year to which the Budget Act identified in subparagraph (A) applies:

(i) Fifty percent of both the amount identified in paragraph (2) of subdivision (a), and the amount resulting from subtracting the value calculated under subparagraph (C) of paragraph (1) of subdivision (b) from the value calculated under clause (ii) of subparagraph (B) of paragraph (1) of subdivision (b), shall be transferred from the General Fund to the Budget Stabilization Account.

(ii) The remaining 50 percent shall be appropriated by the Legislature for one or more of the following obligations and purposes:

(I) Unfunded prior fiscal year General Fund obligations pursuant to Section 8 that existed on July 1, 2014.

(II) Budgetary loans to the General Fund, from funds outside the General Fund, that had outstanding balances on January 1, 2014.

(III) Payable claims for mandated costs incurred prior to the 2004–05 fiscal year that have not yet been paid, and that pursuant to paragraph (2) of subdivision (b) of Section 6 of Article XIII B are permitted to be paid over a term of years, as prescribed by law.

(IV) Unfunded liabilities for state-level pension plans and prefunding other postemployment benefits, in excess of current base amounts as established for the fiscal year in which the funds would otherwise be transferred to the Budget Stabilization Account. For the purpose of this subclause, current base amounts are those required to be paid pursuant to law, an approved memorandum of understanding, benefit schedules established by the employer or entity authorized to establish those contributions for employees excluded or exempted from collective bargaining, or any combination of these. To qualify under this subclause, the appropriation shall supplement and not supplant funding that would otherwise be made available to pay for the obligations described in this subclause for the fiscal year or the subsequent fiscal year.

(2) (A) By October 1 of the 2030–31 fiscal year and each fiscal year thereafter, based on the estimates set forth in the annual Budget Act pursuant to paragraphs (2) and (3) of subdivision (h), the Controller shall transfer amounts from the General Fund to the Budget Stabilization Account, pursuant to a schedule provided by the Director of Finance, as provided in subparagraph (B).

(B) In the fiscal year to which the Budget Act identified in subparagraph (A) applies, both the amount identified in paragraph (2) of subdivision (a), and the amount resulting from subtracting the value calculated under subparagraph (C) of paragraph (1) of subdivision (b) from the value calculated under clause (ii) of subparagraph (B) of paragraph (1) of subdivision (b), shall be transferred from the General Fund to the Budget Stabilization Account.

(C) Notwithstanding any other provision of this section, the Legislature may appropriate up to 50 percent of both the amount identified in paragraph (2) of subdivision (a), and of the amount resulting from subtracting the value calculated under subparagraph (C) of paragraph (1) of subdivision (b) from the value calculated under clause (ii) of subparagraph (B) of paragraph (1) of subdivision (b), for one or more of the obligations and purposes described in clause (ii) of subparagraph (B) of paragraph (1).

(3) The transfers described in this subdivision are subject to suspension or reduction pursuant to paragraph (1) of subdivision (a) of Section 22.

(d) By October 1 of the 2016–17 fiscal year and each fiscal year thereafter, based on the estimates set forth in the annual Budget Act pursuant to paragraphs (4) and (5) of subdivision (h), the Controller shall transfer amounts between the General Fund and the Budget Stabilization Account pursuant to a schedule provided by the Director of Finance, as follows:

(1) If the amount in subparagraph (G) of paragraph (2) of subdivision (b) is greater than zero, transfer that amount from the General Fund to the Budget Stabilization Account, subject to any suspension or reduction of this transfer pursuant to paragraph (1) of subdivision (a) of Section 22.

(2) If the amount described in subparagraph (F) of paragraph (2) of subdivision (b) is greater than the amount calculated under subparagraph (E) of paragraph (2) of subdivision (b), transfer that excess amount from the Budget Stabilization Account back to the General Fund.

(e) Notwithstanding any other provision of this section, the amount of a transfer to the Budget Stabilization Account pursuant to paragraph (2) of subdivision (a) and subdivisions (c) and (d) for any fiscal year shall not exceed an amount that would result in a balance in the account that, when the transfer is made, exceeds 10 percent of the amount of General Fund proceeds of taxes for the fiscal year estimated pursuant to subdivision (b). For any fiscal year, General Fund proceeds of taxes that, but for this paragraph, would have been transferred to the Budget Stabilization Account may be expended only for infrastructure, as defined by Section 13101 of the Government Code, as that section read on January 1, 2014, including deferred maintenance thereon.

(f) The funds described in subdivision (b) as General Fund proceeds of taxes are General Fund proceeds of taxes for purposes of Section 8 for the fiscal year to which those proceeds are attributed, but are not deemed to be additional General Fund proceeds of taxes on the basis that the funds are thereafter transferred from the Budget Stabilization Account to the General Fund.

(g) The Controller may utilize funds in the Budget Stabilization Account, that he or she determines to currently be unnecessary for the purposes of this section, to help manage General Fund daily cashflow needs.

Any use pursuant to this subdivision shall not interfere with the purposes of the Budget Stabilization Account.

(h) The annual Budget Act shall include the estimates described in all of the following:

(1) Paragraph (2) of subdivision (a).

(2) Clause (ii) of subparagraph (B) of paragraph (1) of subdivision (b).

(3) Subparagraph (F) of paragraph (1) of subdivision (b).

(4) Clause (ii) of subparagraph (B) of paragraph (2) of subdivision (b).

(5) Subparagraph (G) of paragraph (2) of subdivision (b). [*New section adopted November 4, 2014.*]

[*Public School System Stabilization Account*]

SEC. 21.   (a) The Public School System Stabilization Account is hereby created in the General Fund.

(b) On or before October 1 of each fiscal year, commencing with the 2015–16 fiscal year, based on the amounts identified in the annual Budget Act pursuant to subdivision (b) of Section 20, the Controller shall transfer, pursuant to a schedule provided by the Director of Finance, amounts from the General Fund to the Public School System Stabilization Account as follows:

(1) (A) For the 2015–16 fiscal year, and for each fiscal year thereafter, any positive amount identified in subparagraph (C) of paragraph (1) of subdivision (b) of Section 20 shall be transferred from the General Fund to the Public School System Stabilization Account in the amount calculated under subparagraph (B), subject to any reduction or suspension of this transfer pursuant to any other provision of this section or paragraph (3) of subdivision (a) of Section 22.

(B) The Director of Finance shall calculate the amount by which the positive amount identified in subparagraph (C) of paragraph (1) of subdivision (b) of Section 20, in combination with all other moneys required to be applied by the State for the support of school districts and community college districts for that fiscal year pursuant to Section 8, exceeds the sum of the total allocations to school districts and community college districts from General Fund proceeds of taxes appropriated pursuant to Article XIII B and allocated local proceeds of taxes in the prior fiscal year, plus any allocations from the Public School System Stabilization Account in the prior fiscal year, less any transfers to the Public School System Stabilization Account pursuant to this section in the prior fiscal year and any revenues allocated pursuant to subdivision (a) of Section 8.5, adjusted for the percentage change in average daily attendance and adjusted for the higher of the change in the cost of living pursuant to paragraph (1) of subdivision (e) of Section 8 of Article XIII B or the cost of living adjustment applied to school district and community college district general purpose apportionments.

(2) (A) Commencing with the 2016–17 fiscal year, and for each fiscal year thereafter, to the extent the amount calculated under this paragraph exceeds the amounts previously transferred by the Controller from the General Fund to the Public School System Stabilization Account for a preceding fiscal year, any positive amount calculated pursuant to subparagraph (C) of paragraph (2) of subdivision (b) of Section 20 for that fiscal year shall be transferred from the General Fund to the Public School System Stabilization Account in the amount calculated under subparagraph (B), subject to any reduction or suspension of this transfer pursuant to any other provision of this section or paragraph (3) of subdivision (a) of Section 22.

(B) The Director of Finance shall calculate the amount by which the positive amount identified in subparagraph (C) of paragraph (2) of subdivision (b) of Section 20, in combination with all other moneys required to be applied by the State for the support of school districts and community college districts for that fiscal year pursuant to Section 8, exceeds the sum of the total allocations to school districts and community college districts from General Fund proceeds of taxes appropriated pursuant to Article XIII B and allocated local proceeds of taxes in the prior fiscal year, plus any allocations from the Public School System Stabilization Account in the prior fiscal year, less any transfers to the Public School System Stabilization Account pursuant to this section in the prior fiscal year and any revenues allocated pursuant to subdivision (a) of Section 8.5, adjusted for the percentage change in average daily attendance and adjusted for the higher of the change in the cost of living pursuant to the paragraph (1) of subdivision (e) of Section 8 of Article XIII B or the cost of living adjustment applied to school district and community college district general purpose apportionments.

(c) Commencing with the 2016–17 fiscal year, and for each fiscal year thereafter, if the amount calculated pursuant to subparagraph (C) of paragraph (2) of subdivision (b) of Section 20 for a fiscal year is less than the amounts previously transferred by the Controller from the General Fund to the Public School System Stabilization Account for that fiscal year, the amount of this difference shall be appropriated and allocated by the State from the Public School System Stabilization Account for the support of school districts and community college districts.

(d) Notwithstanding any other provision of this section, the amount transferred to the Public School System Stabilization Account pursuant to subdivision (b) for a fiscal year shall not exceed the amount by which the amount of state support calculated pursuant to paragraph (1) of subdivision (b) of Section 8 exceeds the amount of state support calculated pursuant to paragraph (2) of subdivision (b) of Section 8 for that fiscal year. If the amount of state support calculated pursuant to paragraph (1) of subdivision (b) of Section 8 does not exceed the amount of state support calculated pursuant to paragraph (2) of subdivision (b) of Section 8 for a fiscal year, no amount shall be transferred to the Public School System Stabilization Account pursuant to subdivision (b) for that fiscal year.

(e) Notwithstanding any other provision of this section, no amount shall be transferred to the Public School System Stabilization Account pursuant to subdivision (b) for a fiscal year for which a maintenance factor is determined pursuant to subdivision (d) of Section 8.

(f) Notwithstanding any other provision of this section, no amount shall be transferred to the Public School System Stabilization Account pursuant to subdivision (b) until the maintenance factor determined pursuant to subdivisions (d) and (e) of Section 8 for fiscal years prior to the 2014–15 fiscal year has been fully allocated. Transfers may be made beginning in the fiscal year following the fiscal year in which it is determined, based on the Budget Act for that fiscal year, that this condition will be met. If a transfer is made for a fiscal year for which it is later determined that this condition has not been met, the amount of the transfer shall be appropriated and allocated from the Public School System Stabilization Account for the support of school districts and community college districts. No transfer shall be made for a year for which it was determined, based on the Budget Act for that fiscal year, that this condition would not be met but was subsequently determined to have been met in that year or a prior fiscal year.

(g) Notwithstanding any other provision of this section, no amount shall be transferred to the Public School System Stabilization Account for any fiscal year for which any of the provisions of subdivision (b) of Section 8 are suspended pursuant to subdivision (h) of Section 8.

(h) Notwithstanding any other provision of this section, for any fiscal year, the amount of a transfer to the Public School System Stabilization Account pursuant to subdivision (b) shall not exceed an amount that would result in a balance in the account that is in excess of 10 percent of the total allocations to school districts and community college districts from General Fund proceeds of taxes appropriated pursuant to Article XIII B and allocated local proceeds of taxes for that fiscal year pursuant to Section 8. For any fiscal year, General Fund proceeds of taxes that, but for this subdivision, would have been transferred to the Public School System Stabilization Account shall be applied by the State for the support of school districts and community colleges.

(i) In any fiscal year in which the amount required to be applied by the State for the support of school districts and community college districts for that fiscal year pursuant to Section 8 is less than the total allocations to school districts and community college districts from General Fund proceeds of taxes appropriated pursuant to Article XIII B and allocated local proceeds of taxes in the prior fiscal year, plus any allocations from the Public School System Stabilization Account in the prior fiscal year, less any transfers to the Public School System Stabilization Account in the prior fiscal year and any revenues allocated pursuant to subdivision (a) of Section 8.5, adjusted for the percentage change in average daily attendance and adjusted for the higher of the change in the cost of living pursuant to paragraph (1) of subdivision (e) of Section 8 of Article XIII B or the cost of living adjustment applied to school district and community college district general purpose apportionments, the amount of the deficiency shall be appropriated and allocated by the State from the Public School System Stabilization Account for the support of school districts and community college districts.

(j) Funds transferred to the Public School System Stabilization Account shall be deemed, for purposes of Section 8, to be moneys applied by the State for the support of school districts and community college districts in the fiscal year for which the transfer is made, and not in the fiscal year in which moneys are appropriated from the account.

(k) Nothing in this section shall be construed to reduce the amount of the moneys required to be applied by the State for the support of school districts and community college districts pursuant to Sections 8 and 8.5.

(l) The Controller may utilize funds in the Public School System Stabilization Account, that he or she determines to currently be unnecessary for the purposes of this section, to help manage General Fund daily cashflow needs. Any use of funds by the Controller pursuant to this subdivision shall not interfere with the purposes of the Public School System Stabilization Account. [New section adopted November 4, 2014.]

[Budget Emergency]

SEC. 22.   (a) Upon the Governor's proclamation declaring a budget emergency and identifying the conditions constituting the emergency, the Legislature may pass a bill that does any of the following:

(1) Suspends or reduces by a specified dollar amount for one fiscal year the transfer of moneys from the General Fund to the Budget Stabilization Account required by Section 20.

(2) (A) Returns funds that have been transferred to the Budget Stabilization Account pursuant to Section 20 to the General Fund for appropriation to address the budget emergency.

(B) Not more than 50 percent of the balance in the Budget Stabilization Account may be returned to the General Fund for appropriation pursuant to subparagraph (A) in any fiscal year, unless funds in the Budget Stabilization Account have been returned to the General Fund for appropriation in the immediately preceding fiscal year.

(3) Suspends or reduces by a specified dollar amount for one fiscal year the transfer of moneys from the General Fund to the Public School System Stabilization Account required by Section 21.

(4) Appropriates funds transferred to the Public School System Stabilization Account pursuant to Section 21 and allocates those funds for the support of school districts and community college districts.

(b) For purposes of this section, "budget emergency" means any of the following:

(1) An emergency declared by the Governor, within the meaning of paragraph (2) of subdivision (c) of Section 3 of Article XIII B.

(2) (A) A determination by the Governor that estimated resources are inadequate to fund General Fund expenditures for the current or ensuing fiscal year, after setting aside funds for the reserve for liquidation of encumbrances, at a level equal to the highest amount of total General Fund expenditures estimated at the time of enactment of any of the three most recent Budget Acts, adjusted for both of the following:

(i) The annual percentage change in the cost of living for the State, as measured by the California Consumer Price Index.

(ii) The annual percentage growth in the civilian population of the State pursuant to subdivision (b) of Section 7901 of the Government Code.

(B) The maximum amount that may be withdrawn for a budget emergency determined under this paragraph shall not exceed either an amount that would result in a total General Fund expenditure level for a fiscal year that is greater than the highest amount of total General Fund expenditures estimated at the time of enactment of any of the three most recent Budget Acts, as calculated pursuant to subparagraph (A), or any limit imposed by subparagraph (B) of paragraph (2) of subdivision (a). [*New section adopted November 4, 2014.*]

ARTICLE XVII.   [*Repealed June 8, 1976.*]

ARTICLE XVIII.   [*Repealed November 3, 1970. See Article XVIII, below.*]

ARTICLE XVIII *

AMENDING AND REVISING THE CONSTITUTION

SECTION 1.   [*Repealed November 3, 1970. See Section 1, below.*]

[*By Legislature*]

SECTION 1.   The Legislature by rollcall vote entered in the journal, two-thirds of the membership of each house concurring, may propose an amendment or revision of the Constitution and in the same manner may amend or withdraw its proposal. Each amendment shall be so prepared and submitted that it can be voted on separately. [*New section adopted November 3, 1970.*]

SEC. 2.   [*Repealed November 3, 1970. See Section 2, below.*]

---

* New Article XVIII adopted November 3, 1970.

[*Constitutional Convention*]

SEC. 2.   The Legislature by rollcall vote entered in the journal, two-thirds of the membership of each house concurring, may submit at a general election the question whether to call a convention to revise the Constitution. If the majority vote yes on that question, within 6 months the Legislature shall provide for the convention. Delegates to a constitutional convention shall be voters elected from districts as nearly equal in population as may be practicable. [*New section adopted November 3, 1970.*]

[*Initiatives*]

SEC. 3.   The electors may amend the Constitution by initiative. [*New section adopted November 3, 1970.*]

[*Effective Date—Conflict*]

SEC. 4.   A proposed amendment or revision shall be submitted to the electors and if approved by a majority of votes thereon takes effect the day after the election unless the measure provides otherwise. If provisions of 2 or more measures approved at the same election conflict, those of the measure receiving the highest affirmative vote shall prevail. [*New section adopted November 3, 1970.*]

ARTICLE XIX *

MOTOR VEHICLE REVENUES

[*Highway Users Tax Account Revenues*]

SECTION 1.   The Legislature shall not borrow revenue from the Highway Users Tax Account, or its successor, and shall not use these revenues for purposes, or in ways, other than those specifically permitted by this article. [*New section adopted November 2, 2010. Initiative measure.*]

[*Use of Fuel Taxes*]

SEC 2.   Revenues from taxes imposed by the State on motor vehicle fuels for use in motor vehicles upon public streets and highways, over and above the costs of collection and any refunds authorized by law, shall be deposited into the Highway Users Tax Account (Section 2100 of the Streets and Highways Code) or its successor, which is hereby declared to be a trust fund, and shall be allocated monthly in accordance with Section 4, and shall be used solely for the following purposes:

(a) The research, planning, construction, improvement, maintenance, and operation of public streets and highways (and their related public facilities for nonmotorized traffic), including the mitigation of their environmental effects, the payment for property taken or damaged for such pur-

---

* Former Article XXVI, as renumbered June 8, 1976.

poses, and the administrative costs necessarily incurred in the foregoing purposes.

(b) The research, planning, construction, and improvement of exclusive public mass transit guideways (and their related fixed facilities), including the mitigation of their environmental effects, the payment for property taken or damaged for such purposes, the administrative costs necessarily incurred in the foregoing purposes, and the maintenance of the structures and the immediate right-of-way for the public mass transit guideways, but excluding the maintenance and operating costs for mass transit power systems and mass transit passenger facilities, vehicles, equipment, and services. [*Former Section 1, as renumbered November 2, 2010. Initiative measure.*]

[Use of Motor Vehicle Fees and Taxes]

SEC. 3.   Revenues from fees and taxes imposed by the State upon vehicles or their use or operation, over and above the costs of collection and any refunds authorized by law, shall be used for the following purposes:

(a) The state administration and enforcement of laws regulating the use, operation, or registration of vehicles used upon the public streets and highways of this State, including the enforcement of traffic and vehicle laws by state agencies and the mitigation of the environmental effects of motor vehicle operation due to air and sound emissions.

(b) The purposes specified in Section 2 of this article. [*Former Section 2, as renumbered November 2, 2010. Initiative measure.*]

[Appropriations by the Legislature—Regulation of Expenditures, Etc.]

SEC. 4.   (a) Except as provided in subdivision (b), the statutory formulas in effect on June 30, 2009, which allocate the revenues described in Section 2 to cities, counties, and areas of the State shall remain in effect.

(b) The Legislature shall not modify the statutory allocations in effect on June 30, 2009, unless and until both of the following have occurred:

(1) The Legislature determines in accordance with this subdivision that another basis for an equitable, geographical, and jurisdictional distribution exists. Any future statutory revisions shall (A) provide for the allocation of these revenues, together with other similar revenues, in a manner which gives equal consideration to the transportation needs of all areas of the State and all segments of the population; and (B) be consistent with the orderly achievement of the adopted local, regional, and statewide goals for ground transportation in local general plans, regional transportation plans, and the California Transportation Plan;

(2) The process described in subdivision (c) has been completed.

(c) The Legislature shall not modify the statutory allocation pursuant to subdivision (b) until all of the following have occurred:

(1) The California Transportation Commission has held no less than four public hearings in different parts of the State to receive public input about the local and regional goals for ground transportation in that part of the State;

(2) The California Transportation Commission has published a report describing the input received at the public hearings and how the modification to the statutory allocation is consistent with the orderly achievement of local, regional, and statewide goals for ground transportation in local general plans, regional transportation plans, and the California Transportation Plan; and

(3) Ninety days have passed since the publication of the report by the California Transportation Commission.

(d) A statute enacted by the Legislature modifying the statutory allocations must be by a bill passed in each house of the Legislature by rollcall vote entered in the journal, two-thirds of the membership concurring, provided that the bill does not contain any other unrelated provision.

(e) The revenues allocated by statute to cities, counties, and areas of the State pursuant to this article may be used solely by the entity to which they are allocated, and solely for the purposes described in Sections 2, 5, or 6 of this article.

(f) The Legislature may not take any action which permanently or temporarily does any of the following: (1) changes the status of the Highway Users Tax Account as a trust fund; (2) borrows, diverts, or appropriates these revenues for purposes other than those described in subdivision (e); or (3) delays, defers, suspends, or otherwise interrupts the payment, allocation, distribution, disbursal, or transfer of revenues from taxes described in Section 2 to cities, counties, and areas of the State pursuant to the procedures in effect on June 30, 2009. [*Former Section 3, as renumbered November 2, 2010. Initiative measure.*]

[Authorization and Approval for Expenditures]

Sec. 5. Revenues allocated pursuant to Section 4 may not be expended for the purposes specified in subdivision (b) of Section 2, except for research and planning, until such use is approved by a majority of the votes cast on the proposition authorizing such use of such revenues in an election held throughout the county or counties, or a specified area of a county or counties, within which the revenues are to be expended. The Legislature may authorize the revenues approved for allocation or expenditure under this section to be pledged or used for the payment of principal and interest on voter-approved bonds issued for the purposes specified in subdivision (b) of Section 2. [*Former Section 4, as renumbered November 2, 2010. Initiative measure.*]

[*Expenditures for Payment of Bonds*]

SEC. 6.   (a) Up to 25 percent of the revenues allocated to the State pursuant to Section 4 for the purposes specified in subdivision (a) of Section 2 of this article may be pledged or used by the State, upon approval by the voters and appropriation by the Legislature, for the payment of principal and interest on voter-approved bonds for such purposes issued by the State on and after November 2, 2010.

(b) Up to 25 percent of the revenues allocated to any city or county pursuant to Section 4 for the purposes specified in subdivision (a) of Section 2 of this article may be pledged or used only by any city or county for the payment of principal and interest on voter-approved bonds issued by that city or county for such purposes. [*Former Section 5, as renumbered November 2, 2010. Initiative measure.*]

SEC. 6.   [*Repealed November 2, 2010. Initiative measure.*]

[*Replacement Revenue*]

SEC. 7.   If the Legislature reduces or repeals the taxes described in Section 2 and adopts an alternative source of revenue to replace the moneys derived from those taxes, the replacement revenue shall be deposited into the Highway Users Tax Account, dedicated to the purposes listed in Section 2, and allocated to cities, counties, and areas of the State pursuant to Section 4. All other provisions of this article shall apply to any revenues adopted by the Legislature to replace the moneys derived from the taxes described in Section 2. [*New section adopted November 2, 2010. Initiative measure.*]

[*Scope of Article*]

SEC. 8.   This article shall not affect or apply to fees or taxes imposed pursuant to the Sales and Use Tax Law or the Vehicle License Fee Law, and all amendments and additions now or hereafter made to such statutes. [*Former Section 7, as renumbered November 2, 2010. Initiative measure.*]

[*Use of Excess Lands for Parks and Recreation*]

SEC. 9.   Notwithstanding Sections 2 and 3 of this article, any real property acquired by the expenditure of the designated tax revenues by an entity other than the State for the purposes authorized in those sections, but no longer required for such purposes, may be used for local public park and recreational purposes. [*Former Section 8, as renumbered November 2, 2010. Initiative measure.*]

[*Transfer of Surplus State Property Located in Coastal Zone*]

SEC. 10.   Notwithstanding any other provision of this Constitution, the Legislature, by statute, with respect to surplus state property acquired by the expenditure of tax revenues designated in Sections 2 and 3 and located in the coastal zone, may authorize the transfer of such property, for a consideration at least equal to the acquisition cost paid by the State to acquire the property, to the Department of Parks and Recreation for state park purposes, or to the Department of Fish and Game for the protection and preservation of fish and wildlife habitat, or to the Wildlife Conservation Board for purposes of the Wildlife Conservation Law of 1947, or to the State Coastal Conservancy for the preservation of agricultural lands.

As used in this section, "coastal zone" means "coastal zone" as defined by Section 30103 of the Public Resources Code as such zone is described on January 1, 1977. [*Former Section 9, as renumbered November 2, 2010. Initiative measure.*]

ARTICLE XIX A*

LOANS FROM THE PUBLIC TRANSPORTATION ACCOUNT OR LOCAL TRANSPORTATION FUNDS

[Loans to State General Fund—Use of Funds]

SECTION 1. (a) The Legislature shall not borrow revenues from the Public Transportation Account, or any successor account, and shall not use these revenues for purposes, or in ways, other than those specifically permitted by this article.

(b) The Public Transportation Account in the State Transportation Fund, or any successor account, is a trust fund. The Legislature may not change the status of the Public Transportation Account as a trust fund. Funds in the Public Transportation Account may not be loaned or otherwise transferred to the General Fund or any other fund or account in the State Treasury.

(c) All revenues specified in paragraphs (1) through (3), inclusive, of subdivision (a) of Section 7102 of the Revenue and Taxation Code, as that section read on June 1, 2001, shall be deposited no less than quarterly into the Public Transportation Account (Section 99310 of the Public Utilities Code), or its successor. The Legislature may not take any action which temporarily or permanently diverts or appropriates these revenues for purposes other than those described in subdivision (d), or delays, defers, suspends, or otherwise interrupts the quarterly deposit of these funds into the Public Transportation Account.

(d) Funds in the Public Transportation Account may only be used for transportation planning and mass transportation purposes. The revenues described in subdivision (c) are hereby continuously appropriated to the Controller without regard to fiscal years for allocation as follows:

(1) Fifty percent pursuant to subdivisions (a) through (f), inclusive, of Section 99315 of the Public Utilities Code, as that section read on July 30, 2009.

_____

* New Article XIX A adopted November 3, 1998.

(2) Twenty-five percent pursuant to subdivision (b) of Section 99312 of the Public Utilities Code, as that section read on July 30, 2009.

(3) Twenty-five percent pursuant to subdivision (c) of Section 99312 of the Public Utilities Code, as that section read on July 30, 2009.

(e) For purposes of paragraph (I) of subdivision (d), "transportation planning" means only the purposes described in subdivisions (c) through (f), inclusive, of Section 99315 of the Public Utilities Code, as that section read on July 30, 2009.

(f) For purposes of this article, "mass transportation," "public transit," and "mass transit" have the same meaning as "public transportation." "Public transportation" means:

(1) (A) Surface transportation service provided to the general public, complementary paratransit service provided to persons with disabilities as required by 42 U.S.C. 12143, or similar transportation provided to people with disabilities or the elderly; (B) operated by bus, rail, ferry, or other conveyance on a fixed route, demand response, or otherwise regularly available basis; (C) generally for which a fare is charged; and (D) provided by any transit district, included transit district, municipal operator, included municipal operator, eligible municipal operator, or transit development board, as those terms were defined in Article 1 of Chapter 4 of Part 11 of Division 10 of the Public Utilities Code on January 1, 2009, a joint powers authority formed to provide mass transportation services, an agency described in subdivision (f) of Section 15975 of the Government Code, as that section read on January 1, 2009, any recipient of funds under Sections 99260, 99260.7, 99275, or subdivision (c) of Section 99400 of the Public Utilities Code, as those sections read on January 1, 2009, or a consolidated agency as defined in Section 132353.1 of the Public Utilities Code, as that section read on January 1, 2009.

(2) Surface transportation service provided by the Department of Transportation pursuant to subdivision (a) of Section 99315 of the Public Utilities Code, as that section read on July 30, 2009.

(3) Public transit capital improvement projects, including those identified in subdivision (b) of Section 99315 of the Public Utilities Code, as that section read on July 30, 2009. [*As amended November 2, 2010. Initiative Measure.*]

[*"Local Transportation Fund"*]

SEC. 2. (a) As used in this section, a "local transportation fund" is a fund created under Section 29530 of the Government Code, or any successor to that statute.

(b) All local transportation funds are hereby designated trust funds. The Legislature may not change the status of local transportation funds as trust funds.

(c) A local transportation fund that has been created pursuant to law may not be abolished.

(d) Money in a local transportation fund shall be allocated only by the local government that created the fund, and only for the purposes authorized under Article 11 (commencing with Section 29530) of Chapter 2 of Division 3 of Title 3 of the Government Code and Chapter 4 (commencing with Section 99200) of Part 11 of Division 10 of the Public Utilities Code, as those provisions existed on October 1, 1997. Neither the county nor the Legislature may authorize the expenditure of money in a local transportation fund for purposes other than those specified in this subdivision.

(e) This section constitutes the sole method of allocating, distributing, and using the revenues in a local transportation fund. The purposes described in subdivision (d) are the sole purposes for which the revenues in a local transportation fund may be used. The Legislature may not enact a statute or take any other action which, permanently or temporarily, does any of the following:

(1) Transfers, diverts, or appropriates the revenues in a local transportation fund for any other purpose than those described in subdivision (d);

(2) Authorizes the expenditures of the revenue in a local transportation fund for any other purpose than those described in subdivision (d);

(3) Borrows or loans the revenues in a local transportation fund, regardless of whether these revenues remain in the Retail Sales Tax Fund in the State Treasury or are transferred to another fund or account.

(f) The percentage of the tax imposed pursuant to Section 7202 of the Revenue and Taxation Code allocated to local transportation funds shall not be reduced below the percentage that was transmitted to such funds during the 2008 calendar year. Revenues allocated to local transportation funds shall be transmitted in accordance with Section 7204 of the Revenue and Taxation Code and deposited into local transportation funds in accordance with Section 29530 of the Government Code, as those sections read on June 30, 2009. [*As amended November 2, 2010. Initiative measure.*]

ARTICLE XIX B *

MOTOR VEHICLE FUEL SALES TAX REVENUES AND TRANSPORTATION IMPROVEMENT FUNDING

[*Use of Funds*]

SECTION 1.   The Legislature shall not borrow revenues from the Transportation Investment Fund, or its successor, and shall not use these revenues for purposes, or in ways, other than those specifically permitted by this article. [*New section added November 2, 2010. Initiative measure.*]

---

* New Article XIX B adopted November 5, 2002.

[*Allocation of Funds*]

SEC. 2. For the 2003–04 fiscal year and each fiscal year thereafter, all revenues that are collected during the fiscal year from taxes under the Sales and Use Tax Law (Part 1 (commencing with Section 6001) of Division 2 of the Revenue and Taxation Code), or any successor to that law, upon the sale, storage, use, or other consumption in this State of motor vehicle fuel, as defined for purposes of the Motor Vehicle Fuel License Tax Law (Part 2 (commencing with Section 7301) of Division 2 of the Revenue and Taxation Code), shall be deposited into the Transportation Investment Fund or its successor, which is hereby created in the State Treasury and which is hereby declared to be a trust fund. The Legislature may not change the status of the Transportation Investment Fund as a trust fund.

(b) (1) For the 2003–04 to 2007–08 fiscal years, inclusive, moneys in the Transportation Investment Fund shall be allocated, upon appropriation by the Legislature, in accordance with Section 7104 of the Revenue and Taxation Code as that section read on March 6, 2002.

(2) For the 2008–09 fiscal year and each fiscal year thereafter, moneys in the Transportation Investment Fund shall be allocated solely for the following purposes:

(A) Public transit and mass transportation. Moneys appropriated for public transit and mass transportation shall be allocated as follows: (i) Twenty-five percent pursuant to subdivision (b) of Section 99312 of the Public Utilities Code, as that section read on July 30, 2009; (ii) Twenty-five percent pursuant to subdivision (c) of Section 99312 of the Public Utilities Code, as that section read on July 30, 2009; and (iii) Fifty percent for the purposes of subdivisions (a) and (b) of Section 99315 of the Public Utilities Code, as that section read on July 30, 2009.

(B) Transportation capital improvement projects, subject to the laws governing the State Transportation Improvement Program, or any successor to that program.

(C) Street and highway maintenance, rehabilitation, reconstruction, or storm damage repair conducted by cities, including a city and county.

(D) Street and highway maintenance, rehabilitation, reconstruction, or storm damage repair conducted by counties, including a city and county.

(c) For the 2008–09 fiscal year and each fiscal year thereafter, moneys in the Transportation Investment Fund are hereby continuously appropriated to the Controller without regard to fiscal years, which shall be allocated as follows:

(A) Twenty percent of the moneys for the purposes set forth in subparagraph (A) of paragraph (2) of subdivision (b).

(B) Forty percent of the moneys for the purposes set forth in subparagraph (B) of paragraph (2) of subdivision (b).

(C) Twenty percent of the moneys for the purposes set forth in subparagraph (C) of paragraph (2) of subdivision (b).

(D) Twenty percent of the moneys for the purposes set forth in subparagraph (D) of paragraph (2) of subdivision (b).

(d) The Legislature may not enact a statute that modifies the percentage shares set forth in subdivision (c) until all of the following have occurred:

(1) The California Transportation Commission has held no less than four public hearings in different parts of the State to receive public input about the need for public transit, mass transportation, transportation capital improvement projects, and street and highway maintenance;

(2) The California Transportation Commission has published a report describing the input received at the public hearings and how the modification to the statutory allocation is consistent with the orderly achievement of local, regional and statewide goals for public transit, mass transportation, transportation capital improvements, and street and highway maintenance in a manner that is consistent with local general plans, regional transportation plans, and the California Transportation Plan;

(3) Ninety days have passed since the publication of the report by the California Transportation Commission.

(4) The statute enacted by the Legislature pursuant to this subdivision must be by a bill passed in each house of the Legislature by rollcall vote entered in the journal, two-thirds of the membership concurring, provided that the bill does not contain any other unrelated provision and that the revenues described in subdivision (a) are expended solely for the purposes set forth in paragraph (2) of subdivision (b).

(e) (1) An amount equivalent to the total amount of revenues that were not transferred from the General Fund of the State to the Transportation Investment Fund, as of July 1, 2007, because of a suspension of transfer of revenues pursuant to this section as it read on January 1, 2006, but excluding the amount to be paid to the Transportation Deferred Investment Fund pursuant to Section 63048.65 of the Government Code, shall be transferred from the General Fund to the Transportation Investment Fund no later than June 30, 2016. Until this total amount has been transferred, the amount of transfer payments to be made in each fiscal year shall not be less than one-tenth of the total amount required to be transferred by June 30, 2016. The transferred revenues shall be allocated solely for the purposes set forth in this section as if they had been received in the absence of a suspension of transfer of revenues.

(2) The Legislature may provide by statute for the issuance of bonds by the state or local agencies, as applicable, that are secured by the minimum transfer payments required by paragraph (1). Proceeds from the sale of those bonds shall be allocated solely for the purposes set forth in this section as if they were revenues subject to allocation pursuant to paragraph (2) of subdivision (b).

(f) This section constitutes the sole method of allocating, distributing, and using the revenues described in subdivision (a). The purposes described in paragraph (2) of subdivision (b) are the sole purposes for which the revenues described in subdivision (a) may be used. The Legislature may not enact a statute or take any other action which, permanently or temporarily, does any of the following:

(1) Transfers, diverts, or appropriates the revenues described in subdivision (a) for any other purposes than those described in paragraph (2) of subdivision (b);

(2) Authorizes the expenditures of the revenues described in subdivision (a) for any other purposes than those described in paragraph (2) of subdivision (b) or;

(3) Borrows or loans the revenues described in subdivision (a), regardless of whether these revenues remain in the Transportation Investment Fund or are transferred to another fund or account such as the Public Transportation Account, a trust fund in the State Transportation Fund.

(g) For purposes of this article, "mass transportation," "public transit" and "mass transit" have the same meanings as "public transportation." "Public transportation" means:

(1) (A) Surface transportation service provided to the general public, complementary paratransit service provided to persons with disabilities as required by 42 U.S.C. 12143, or similar transportation provided to people with disabilities or the elderly; (B) operated by bus, rail, ferry, or other conveyance on a fixed route, demand response, or otherwise regularly available basis; (C) generally for which a fare is charged; and (D) provided by any transit district, included transit district, municipal operator, included municipal operator, eligible municipal operator, or transit development board, as those terms were defined in Article 1 of Chapter 4 of Part 11 of Division 10 of the Public Utilities Code on January 1, 2009, a joint powers authority formed to provide mass transportation services, an agency described in subdivision (f) of Section 15975 of the Government Code, as that section read on January 1, 2009, any recipient of funds under Sections 99260, 99260.7, 99275, or subdivision (c) of Section 99400 of the Public Utilities Code, as those sections read on January 1, 2009, or a consolidated agency as defined in Section 132353.1 of the Public Utilities Code, as that section read on January 1, 2009.

(2) Surface transportation service provided by the Department of Transportation pursuant to subdivision (a) of Section 99315 of the Public Utilities Code, as that section read on July 30, 2009.

(3) Public transit capital improvement projects, including those identified in subdivision (b) of Section 99315 of the Public Utilities Code, as that section read on July 30, 2009.

(h) If the Legislature reduces or repeals the taxes described in subdivision (a) and adopts an alternative source of revenue to replace the moneys derived from those taxes, the replacement revenue shall be deposited into the Transportation Investment Fund, dedicated to the purposes listed in paragraph (2) of subdivision (b), and allocated pursuant to subdivision (c). All other provisions of this article shall apply to any revenues adopted by the Legislature to replace the moneys derived from the taxes described in subdivision (a). [*Former Section 1, as renumbered November 2, 2010. Initiative measure.*]

ARTICLE XIX C *

ENFORCEMENT OF CERTAIN PROVISIONS

[*Challenge to Invalidate an Action*]

SECTION 1.   If any challenge to invalidate an action that violates Article XIX, XIXA, or XIXB is successful either by way of a final judgment, settlement, or resolution by administrative or legislative action, there is hereby continuously appropriated from the General Fund to the Controller, without regard to fiscal years, that amount of revenue necessary to restore the fund or account from which the revenues were unlawfully taken or diverted to its financial status had the unlawful action not been taken. [*New section adopted November 2, 2010. Initiative measure.*]

[*Challenge to Invalidate an Action*]

SEC. 2.   If any challenge to invalidate an action that violates Section 24 or Section 25.5 of Article XIII is successful either by way of a final judgment, settlement, or resolution by administrative or legislative action, there is hereby continuously appropriated from the General Fund to the local government an amount of revenue equal to the amount of revenue unlawfully taken or diverted. [*New section adopted November 2, 2010. Initiative measure.*]

[*Interest*]

SEC. 3.   Interest calculated at the Pooled Money Investment Fund rate from the date or dates the revenues were unlawfully taken or diverted shall accrue to the amounts required to be restored pursuant to this section. Within 30 days from the date a challenge is successful, the Controller shall make the transfer required by the continuous appropriation and issue a notice to the parties that the transfer has been completed. [*New section adopted November 2, 2010. Initiative measure.*]

[*Restraining Order or Preliminary Injunction*]

SEC. 4.   If in any challenge brought pursuant to this section a restraining order or preliminary injunction is issued, the plaintiffs or petitioners shall not be required to post a bond obligating the plaintiffs or petitioners to indemnify the government defendants or the State of California for any

---

* New Article XIX C adopted November 2, 2010. Initiative measure.

damage the restraining order or preliminary injunction may cause. [*New section adopted November 2, 2010. Initiative measure.*]

ARTICLE XX

MISCELLANEOUS SUBJECTS

[*Sacramento County Consolidation With City or Cities*]

SECTION 1. Notwithstanding the provisions of Section 6 of Article XI, the County of Sacramento and all or any of the cities within the County of Sacramento may be consolidated as a charter city and county as provided by statute, with the approval of a majority of the electors of the county voting on the question of such consolidation and upon such other vote as the Legislature may prescribe in such statute. The charter City and County of Sacramento shall be a charter city and a charter county. Its charter city powers supersede conflicting charter county powers. [*New section adopted June 4, 1974.*]

[*Protection of Homesteads*]

SEC. 1.5. The Legislature shall protect, by law, from forced sale a certain portion of the homestead and other property of all heads of families. [*New section adopted June 8, 1976.*]

[*Leland Stanford Junior University—Henry E. Huntington Library and Art Gallery*]

SEC. 2. Except for tax exemptions provided in Article XIII, the rights, powers, privileges, and confirmations conferred by Sections 10 † and 15 † of Article IX in effect on January 1, 1973, relating to Stanford University and the Huntington Library and Art Gallery, are continued in effect. [*Former Section 6, as renumbered June 8, 1976.*]

[*Oath of Office*]

SEC. 3. Members of the Legislature, and all public officers and employees, executive, legislative, and judicial, except such inferior officers and employees as may be by law exempted, shall, before they enter upon the duties of their respective offices, take and subscribe the following oath or affirmation:

"I, _____, do solemnly swear (or affirm) that I will support and defend the Constitution of the United States and the Constitution of the State of California against all enemies, foreign and domestic; that I will bear true faith and allegiance to the Constitution of the United States and the Constitution of the State of California; that I take this obligation freely, without any mental reservation or purpose of evasion; and that I will well and faithfully discharge the duties upon which I am about to enter.

---

† Sections 10 and 15 of Article IX repealed November 5, 1974.

"And I do further swear (or affirm) that I do not advocate, nor am I a member of any party or organization, political or otherwise, that now advocates the overthrow of the Government of the United States or of the State of California by force or violence or other unlawful means; that within the five years immediately preceding the taking of this oath (or affirmation) I have not been a member of any party or organization, political or otherwise, that advocated the overthrow of the Government of the United States or of the State of California by force or violence or other unlawful means except as follows:

_____

(If no affiliations, write in the words "No Exceptions")
and that during such time as I hold the office of _____
(name of office)
I will not advocate nor become a member of any party or organization, political or otherwise, that advocates the overthrow of the Government of the United States or of the State of California by force or violence or other unlawful means."

And no other oath, declaration, or test, shall be required as a qualification for any public office or employment.

"Public officer and employee" includes every officer and employee of the State, including the University of California, every county, city, city and county, district, and authority, including any department, division, bureau, board, commission, agency, or instrumentality of any of the foregoing. [*As amended November 4, 1952.*]

SEC. 3.5.   [*Repealed November 3, 1970.*]

[*Franchises*]

SEC. 4.   The Legislature shall not pass any laws permitting the leasing or alienation of any franchise, so as to relieve the franchise or property held thereunder from the liabilities of the lessor or grantor, lessee, or grantee, contracted or incurred in the operation, use, or enjoyment of such franchise, or any of its privileges. [*Former Section 7, as renumbered June 8, 1976.*]

SEC. 5.   [*Repealed June 8, 1976. See Section 5, below.*]

[*Laws Concerning Corporations*]

SEC. 5.   All laws now in force in this State concerning corporations and all laws that may be hereafter passed pursuant to this section may be altered from time to time or repealed. [*Former Section 24, as renumbered June 8, 1976.*]

SEC. 6.   [*Renumbered Section 2 June 8, 1976. See Section 6, below.*]

[Reduction in Legislator's Term of Office—Retirement Benefits, Etc.]

SEC. 6. Any legislator whose term of office is reduced by operation of the amendment to subdivision (a) of Section 2 of Article IV adopted by the people in 1972 shall, notwithstanding any other provision of this Constitution, be entitled to retirement benefits and compensation as if the term of office had not been so reduced. *[Former Section 25, as renumbered June 8, 1976.]*

[Constitutional Officers—Number of Terms]

SEC. 7. The limitations on the number of terms prescribed by Section 2 of Article IV, Sections 2 and 11 of Article V, Section 2 of Article IX, and Section 17 of Article XIII apply only to terms to which persons are elected or appointed on or after November 6, 1990, except that an incumbent Senator whose office is not on the ballot for the general election on that date may serve only one additional term. Those limitations shall not apply to any unexpired term to which a person is elected or appointed if the remainder of the term is less than half of the full term. *[New section adopted November 6, 1990. Initiative measure.]*

SEC. 8.   *[Renumbered Section 21 of Article I and amended November 5, 1974.]*

SEC. 9.   *[Repealed November 3, 1970.]*

SEC. 10.   *[Repealed June 8, 1976.]*

SEC. 11.   *[Repealed June 8, 1976.]*

SEC. 12.   *[Repealed November 3, 1970.]*

SEC. 13.   *[Repealed November 3, 1970.]*

SEC. 14.   *[Repealed November 3, 1970.]*

SEC. 15.   *[Repealed June 8, 1976.]*

SEC. 16.   *[Repealed November 7, 1972.]*

SEC. 17.   *[Repealed June 8, 1976.]*

SEC. 17½.   *[Repealed June 8, 1976.]*

SEC. 18.   *[Renumbered Section 8 of Article I and amended November 5, 1974.]*

SEC. 19.   *[Repealed June 8, 1976.]*

SEC. 20.   *[Repealed June 8, 1976.]*

SEC. 21.   *[Repealed June 8, 1976.]*

[Liquor Control]

SEC. 22. The State of California, subject to the internal revenue laws of the United States, shall have the exclusive right and power to license and regulate the manufacture, sale, purchase, possession and transportation of alcoholic beverages within the State, and subject to the laws of the United States regulating commerce between foreign nations and among the states shall have the exclusive right and power to regulate the importation into and exportation from the State, of alcoholic beverages. In the exercise of these rights and powers, the Legislature shall not constitute the State or any agency thereof a manufacturer or seller of alcoholic beverages.

[Licensed Premises — Types of Licenses]

All alcoholic beverages may be bought, sold, served, consumed and otherwise disposed of in premises which shall be licensed as provided by the Legislature. In providing for the licensing of premises, the Legislature may provide for the issuance of, among other licenses, licenses for the following types of premises where the alcoholic beverages specified in the licenses may be sold and served for consumption upon the premises:

(a) For bona fide public eating places, as defined by the Legislature.

(b) For public premises in which food shall not be sold or served as in a bona fide public eating place, but upon which premises the Legislature may permit the sale or service of food products incidental to the sale and service of alcoholic beverages. No person under the age of 21 years shall be permitted to enter and remain in any such premises without lawful business therein.

(c) For public premises for the sale and service of beers alone.

(d) Under such conditions as the Legislature may impose, for railroad dining or club cars, passenger ships, common carriers by air, and bona fide clubs after such clubs have been lawfully operated for not less than one year.

[Service or Sale to Minors]

The sale, furnishing, giving, or causing to be sold, furnished, or giving away of any alcoholic beverage to any person under the age of 21 years is hereby prohibited, and no person shall sell, furnish, give, or cause to be sold, furnished, or given away any alcoholic beverage to any person under the age of 21 years, and no person under the age of 21 years shall purchase any alcoholic beverage.

[Director of Alcoholic Beverage Control]

The Director of Alcoholic Beverage Control shall be the head of the Department of Alcoholic Beverage Control, shall be appointed by the Governor subject to confirmation by a majority vote of all of the members elected to the Senate, and shall serve at the pleasure of the Governor. The director may be removed from office by the Governor, and the Legislature shall have the power, by a majority vote of all members elected to each house, to remove the director from office for dereliction of duty or corruption or incompetency. The director may appoint three persons who shall be exempt from civil service, in addition to the person he is authorized to appoint by Section 4 of Article XXIV.

[*Department of Alcoholic Beverage Control—Powers—Duties*]

The Department of Alcoholic Beverage Control shall have the exclusive power, except as herein provided and in accordance with laws enacted by the Legislature, to license the manufacture, importation and sale of alcoholic beverages in this State, and to collect license fees or occupation taxes on account thereof. The department shall have the power, in its discretion, to deny, suspend or revoke any specific alcoholic beverages license if it shall determine for good cause that the granting or continuance of such license would be contrary to public welfare or morals, or that a person seeking or holding a license has violated any law prohibiting conduct involving moral turpitude. It shall be unlawful for any person other than a licensee of said department to manufacture, import or sell alcoholic beverages in this State.

[*Alcoholic Beverage Control Appeals Board*]

The Alcoholic Beverage Control Appeals Board shall consist of three members appointed by the Governor, subject to confirmation by a majority vote of all of the members elected to the Senate. Each member, at the time of his initial appointment, shall be a resident of a different county from the one in which either of the other members resides. The members of the board may be removed from office by the Governor, and the Legislature shall have the power, by a majority vote of all members elected to each house, to remove any member from office for dereliction of duty or corruption or incompetency.

[*Appeals—Reviews—Reversals*]

When any person aggrieved thereby appeals from a decision of the department ordering any penalty assessment, issuing, denying, transferring, suspending or revoking any license for the manufacture, importation, or sale of alcoholic beverages, the board shall review the decision subject to such limitations as may be imposed by the Legislature. In such cases, the board shall not receive evidence in addition to that considered by the department. Review by the board of a decision of the department shall be limited to the questions whether the department has proceeded without or in excess of its jurisdiction, whether the department has proceeded in the manner required by law, whether the decision is supported by the findings, and whether the findings are supported by substantial evidence in the light of the whole record. In appeals where the board finds that there is relevant evidence which, in the exercise of reasonable diligence, could not have been produced or which was improperly excluded at the hearing before the department it may enter an order remanding the matter to the department for reconsideration in the light of such evidence. In all other appeals the board shall enter an order either affirming or reversing the decision of the department. When the order reverses the decision of the department, the board may direct the reconsideration of the matter in the light of its order and may direct the department to take such further action as is specially enjoined upon it by law, but the order shall not limit or control in any way the discretion vested by law in the department. Orders of the board shall be subject to judicial review upon petition of the director or any party aggrieved by such order.

[*Removal of Director or Board Members*]

A concurrent resolution for the removal of either the director or any member of the board may be introduced in the Legislature only if five Members of the Senate, or 10 Members of the Assembly, join as authors.

[*Licenses—Regulation—Fees*]

Until the Legislature shall otherwise provide, the privilege of keeping, buying, selling, serving, and otherwise disposing of alcoholic beverages in bona fide hotels, restaurants, cafes, cafeterias, railroad dining or club cars, passenger ships, and other public eating places, and in bona fide clubs after such clubs have been lawfully operated for not less than one year, and the privilege of keeping, buying, selling, serving, and otherwise disposing of beers on any premises open to the general public shall be licensed and regulated under the applicable provisions of the Alcoholic Beverage Control Act, insofar as the same are not inconsistent with the provisions hereof, and excepting that the license fee to be charged bona fide hotels, restaurants, cafes, cafeterias, railroad dining or club cars, passenger ships, and other public eating places, and any bona fide clubs after such clubs have been lawfully operated for not less than one year, for the privilege of keeping, buying, selling, or otherwise disposing of alcoholic beverages, shall be the amounts prescribed as of the operative date hereof, subject to the power of the Legislature to change such fees.

The State Board of Equalization shall assess and collect such excise taxes as are or may be imposed by the Legislature on account of the manufacture, importation and sale of alcoholic beverages in this State.

The Legislature may authorize, subject to reasonable restrictions, the sale in retail stores of alcoholic beverages contained in the original packages, where such alcoholic beverages are not to be consumed on the premises where sold; and may provide for the issuance of all types of licenses necessary to carry on the activities referred to in the first paragraph of this section, including, but not limited to, licenses necessary for the manufacture, production, processing, importation, exportation, transportation, wholesaling, distribution, and sale of any and all kinds of alcoholic beverages.

The Legislature shall provide for apportioning the amounts collected for license fees or occupation taxes under the provisions hereof between the State and the cities, counties and cities and counties of the State, in such manner as the Legislature may deem proper.

All constitutional provisions and laws inconsistent with the provisions hereof are hereby repealed.

The provisions of this section shall be self-executing, but nothing herein shall prohibit the Legislature from enacting laws implementing and not inconsistent with such provisions.

This amendment shall become operative on January 1, 1957. [*As amended November 6, 1956. Operative January 1, 1957.*]

[*State Colleges—Speaker, Member of Governing Body*]

SEC. 23.   Notwithstanding any other provision of this Constitution, the Speaker of the Assembly shall be an ex officio member, having equal rights and duties with the nonlegislative members, of any state agency created by the Legislature in the field of public higher education which is charged with the management, administration, and control of the State College System of California. [*New section adopted November 3, 1970.*]

SEC. 24.   [*Renumbered Section 5 June 8, 1976.*]

SEC. 25.   [*Renumbered Section 6 June 8, 1976.*]

ARTICLE XXI*

REDISTRICTING OF SENATE, ASSEMBLY, CONGRESSIONAL AND
BOARD OF EQUALIZATION DISTRICTS

[*Heading as amended November 4, 2008. Initiative measure.*]

[*Redistricting Following National Census*]

SECTION 1.   In the year following the year in which the national census is taken under the direction of Congress at the beginning of each decade, the Citizens Redistricting Commission described in Section 2 shall adjust the boundary lines of the congressional, State Senatorial, Assembly, and Board of Equalization districts (also known as "redistricting") in conformance with the standards and process set forth in Section 2. [*As amended November 2, 2010. Initiative measure.*]

[*The Citizens Redistricting Commission*]

SEC. 2.   (a) The Citizens Redistricting Commission shall be created no later than December 31 in 2010, and in each year ending in the number zero thereafter.

(b) The commission shall: (1) conduct an open and transparent process enabling full public consideration of and comment on the drawing of district lines; (2) draw district lines according to the redistricting criteria specified in this article; and (3) conduct themselves with integrity and fairness.

---

* New Article XXI adopted June 3, 1980.

(c) (1) The selection process is designed to produce a commission that is independent from legislative influence and reasonably representative of this State's diversity.

(2) The commission shall consist of 14 members, as follows: five who are registered with the largest political party in California based on registration, five who are registered with the second largest political party in California based on registration, and four who are not registered with either of the two largest political parties in California based on registration.

(3) Each commission member shall be a voter who has been continuously registered in California with the same political party or unaffiliated with a political party and who has not changed political party affiliation for five or more years immediately preceding the date of his or her appointment. Each commission member shall have voted in two of the last three statewide general elections immediately preceding his or her application.

(4) The term of office of each member of the commission expires upon the appointment of the first member of the succeeding commission.

(5) Nine members of the commission shall constitute a quorum. Nine or more affirmative votes shall be required for any official action. The four final redistricting maps must be approved by at least nine affirmative votes which must include at least three votes of members registered from each of the two largest political parties in California based on registration and three votes from members who are not registered with either of these two political parties.

(6) Each commission member shall apply this article in a manner that is impartial and that reinforces public confidence in the integrity of the redistricting process. A commission member shall be ineligible for a period of 10 years beginning from the date of appointment to hold elective public office at the federal, state, county, or city level in this State. A member of the commission shall be ineligible for a period of five years beginning from the date of appointment to hold appointive federal, state, or local public office, to serve as paid staff for, or as a paid consultant to, the Board of Equalization, the Congress, the Legislature, or any individual legislator, or to register as a federal, state or local lobbyist in this State.

(d) The commission shall establish single-member districts for the Senate, Assembly, Congress, and State Board of Equalization pursuant to a mapping process using the following criteria as set forth in the following order of priority:

(1) Districts shall comply with the United States Constitution. Congressional districts shall achieve population equality as nearly as is practicable, and Senatorial, Assembly, and State Board of Equalization districts shall have reasonably equal population with other districts for the same office, except where deviation is required to comply with the federal Voting Rights Act or allowable by law.

(2) Districts shall comply with the federal Voting Rights Act (42 U.S.C. Sec. 1971 and following).

(3) Districts shall be geographically contiguous.

(4) The geographic integrity of any city, county, city and county, local neighborhood, or local community of interest shall be respected in a manner that minimizes their division to the extent possible without violating the requirements of any of the preceding subdivisions. A community of interest is a contiguous population which shares common social and economic interests that should be included within a single district for purposes of its effective and fair representation. Examples of such shared interests are those common to an urban area, a rural area, an industrial area, or an agricultural area, and those common to areas in which the people share similar living standards, use the same transportation facilities, have similar work opportunities, or have access to the same media of communication relevant to the election process. Communities of interest shall not include relationships with political parties, incumbents, or political candidates.

(5) To the extent practicable, and where this does not conflict with the criteria above, districts shall be drawn to encourage geographical compactness such that nearby areas of population are not bypassed for more distant population.

(6) To the extent practicable, and where this does not conflict with the criteria above, each Senate district shall be comprised of two whole, complete, and adjacent Assembly districts, and each Board of Equalization district shall be comprised of 10 whole, complete, and adjacent Senate districts.

(e) The place of residence of any incumbent or political candidate shall not be considered in the creation of a map. Districts shall not be drawn for the purpose of favoring or discriminating against an incumbent, political candidate, or political party.

(f) Districts for the Congress, Senate, Assembly, and State Board of Equalization shall be numbered consecutively commencing at the northern boundary of the State and ending at the southern boundary.

(g) By August 15 in 2011, and in each year ending in the number one thereafter, the commission shall approve four final maps that separately set forth the district boundary lines for the congressional, Senatorial, Assembly, and State Board of Equalization districts. Upon approval, the commission shall certify the four final maps to the Secretary of State.

(h) The commission shall issue, with each of the four final maps, a report that explains the basis on which the commission made its decisions in achieving compliance with the criteria listed in subdivision (d) and shall include definitions of the terms and standards used in drawing each final map.

(i) Each certified final map shall be subject to referendum in the same manner that a statute is subject to referendum pursuant to Section 9 of Article II. The date of certification of a final map to the Secretary of State shall be deemed the enactment date for purposes of Section 9 of Article II.

(j) If the commission does not approve a final map by at least the requisite votes or if voters disapprove a certified final map in a referendum, the Secretary of State shall immediately petition the California Supreme Court for an order directing the appointment of special masters to adjust the boundary lines of that map in accordance with the redistricting criteria and requirements set forth in subdivisions (d), (e), and (f). Upon its approval of the masters' map, the court shall certify the resulting map to the Secretary of State, which map shall constitute the certified final map for the subject type of district. [*As amended November 2, 2010. Initiative measure.*]

[*Defense of Certified Final Map*]

SEC. 3.   (a) The commission has the sole legal standing to defend any action regarding a certified final map, and shall inform the Legislature if it determines that funds or other resources provided for the operation of the commission are not adequate. The Legislature shall provide adequate funding to defend any action regarding a certified map. The commission has sole authority to determine whether the Attorney General or other legal counsel retained by the commission shall assist in the defense of a certified final map.

(b) (1) The California Supreme Court has original and exclusive jurisdiction in all proceedings in which a certified final map is challenged or is claimed not to have taken timely effect.

(2) Any registered voter in this state may file a petition for a writ of mandate or writ of prohibition, within 45 days after the commission has certified a final map to the Secretary of State, to bar the Secretary of State from implementing the plan on the grounds that the filed plan violates this Constitution, the United States Constitution, or any federal or state statute. Any registered voter in this state may also file a petition for a writ of mandate or writ of prohibition to seek relief where a certified final map is subject to a referendum measure that is likely to qualify and stay the timely implementation of the map.

(3) The California Supreme Court shall give priority to ruling on a petition for a writ of mandate or a writ of prohibition filed pursuant to paragraph (2). If the court determines that a final certified map violates this Constitution, the United States Constitution, or any federal or state statute, the court shall fashion the relief that it deems appropriate, including, but not limited to, the relief set forth in subdivision (j) of Section 2. [*As amended November 2, 2010. Initiative measure.*]

ARTICLE XXII*

ARCHITECTURAL AND ENGINEERING SERVICES

[Authority of Government to Contract for Architectural and Engineering Services]

SECTION 1. The State of California and all other governmental entities, including, but not limited to, cities, counties, cities and counties, school districts and other special districts, local and regional agencies and joint power agencies, shall be allowed to contract with qualified private entities for architectural and engineering services for all public works of improvement. The choice and authority to contract shall extend to all phases of project development including permitting and environmental studies, rights-of-way services, design phase services and construction phase services. The choice and authority shall exist without regard to funding sources whether federal, state, regional, local or private, whether or not the project is programmed by a state, regional or local governmental entity, and whether or not the completed project is a part of any state owned or state operated system or facility. *[New section adopted November 7, 2000. Initiative measure.]*

[Construction of Article VII]

SEC. 2. Nothing contained in Article VII of this Constitution shall be construed to limit, restrict or prohibit the State or any other governmental entities, including, but not limited to, cities, counties, cities and counties, school districts and other special districts, local and regional agencies and joint power agencies, from contracting with private entities for the performance of architectural and engineering services. *[New section adopted November 7, 2000. Initiative measure.]*

ARTICLE XXIII. *[Repealed June 8, 1976.]*

ARTICLE XXIV. *[Repealed June 8, 1976.]*

ARTICLE XXV. *[Repealed November 8, 1949. Initiative measure.]*

ARTICLE XXVI. *[Renumbered Article XIX June 8, 1976.]*

ARTICLE XXVII. *[Repealed November 3, 1970.]*

ARTICLE XXVIII. *[Repealed November 5, 1974.]*

ARTICLE XXIX to XXXIII. *[No articles have been adopted.]*

---

* New Article XXII adopted November 7, 2000. Initiative measure.

ARTICLE XXXIV *

PUBLIC HOUSING PROJECT LAW

[*Approval of Low Rent Housing Projects by Electors*]

SECTION 1.   No low rent housing project shall hereafter be developed, constructed, or acquired in any manner by any state public body until, a majority of the qualified electors of the city, town or county, as the case may be, in which it is proposed to develop, construct, or acquire the same, voting upon such issue, approve such project by voting in favor thereof at an election to be held for that purpose, or at any general or special election.

[*"Low Rent Housing Project"*]

For the purposes of this article the term "low rent housing project" shall mean any development composed of urban or rural dwellings, apartments or other living accommodations for persons of low income, financed in whole or in part by the Federal Government or a state public body or to which the Federal Government or a state public body extends assistance by supplying all or part of the labor, by guaranteeing the payment of liens, or otherwise. For the purposes of this Article only there shall be excluded from the term "low rent housing project" any such project where there shall be in existence on the effective date hereof, a contract for financial assistance between any state public body and the Federal Government in respect to such project.

[*"Persons of Low Income"*]

For the purposes of this Article only "persons of low income" shall mean persons or families who lack the amount of income which is necessary (as determined by the state public body developing, constructing, or acquiring the housing project) to enable them, without financial assistance, to live in decent, safe and sanitary dwellings, without overcrowding.

[*"State Public Body"*]

For the purposes of this Article the term "state public body" shall mean this State, or any city, city and county, county, district, authority, agency, or any other subdivision or public body of this State.

[*"Federal Government"*]

For the purposes of this Article the term "Federal Government" shall mean the United States of America, or any agency or instrumentality, corporate or otherwise, of the United States of America. [*New section adopted November 7, 1950. Initiative measure.*]

---

* New Article XXXIV adopted November 7, 1950. Initiative measure.

[*Self-executing Provisions*]

SEC. 2.   The provisions of this Article shall be self-executing but legislation not in conflict herewith may be enacted to facilitate its operation. [*New section adopted November 7, 1950. Initiative measure.*]

[*Constitutionality of Article*]

SEC. 3.   If any portion, section or clause of this Article, or the application thereof to any person or circumstance, shall for any reason be declared unconstitutional or held invalid, the remainder of this Article, or the application of such portion, section or clause to other persons or circumstances, shall not be affected thereby. [*New section adopted November 7, 1950. Initiative measure.*]

[*Scope of Article*]

SEC. 4.   The provisions of this Article shall supersede all provisions of this Constitution and laws enacted thereunder in conflict therewith. [*New section adopted November 7, 1950. Initiative measure.*]

ARTICLE XXXV *

MEDICAL RESEARCH

[*California Institute for Regenerative Medicine*]

SECTION 1.   There is hereby established the California Institute for Regenerative Medicine. [*New section adopted November 2, 2004. Initiative measure.*]

[*California Institute for Regenerative Medicine — Purposes*]

SEC. 2.   The institute shall have the following purposes:

(a) To make grants and loans for stem cell research, for research facilities, and for other vital research opportunities to realize therapies, protocols, and/or medical procedures that will result in, as speedily as possible, the cure for, and/or substantial mitigation of, major diseases, injuries, and orphan diseases.

(b) To support all stages of the process of developing cures, from laboratory research through successful clinical trials.

(c) To establish the appropriate regulatory standards and oversight bodies for research and facilities development. [*New section adopted November 2, 2004. Initiative measure.*]

[*California Institute for Regenerative Medicine — Use of Funds for Cloning Research*]

SEC. 3.   No funds authorized for, or made available to, the institute shall be used for research involving human reproductive cloning. [*New section adopted November 2, 2004. Initiative measure.*]

---

* New Article XXXV adopted November 2, 2004. Initiative measure.

[*California Institute for Regenerative Medicine — Funds*]

SEC. 4.   Funds authorized for, or made available to, the institute shall be continuously appropriated without regard to fiscal year, be available and used only for the purposes provided in this article, and shall not be subject to appropriation or transfer by the Legislature or the Governor for any other purpose. [*New section adopted November 2, 2004. Initiative measure.*]

[*Right to Conduct Stem Cell Research*]

SEC. 5.   There is hereby established a right to conduct stem cell research which includes research involving adult stem cells, cord blood stem cells, pluripotent stem cells, and/or progenitor cells. Pluripotent stem cells are cells that are capable of self-renewal, and have broad potential to differentiate into multiple adult cell types. Pluripotent stem cells may be derived from somatic cell nuclear transfer or from surplus products of in vitro fertilization treatments when such products are donated under appropriate informed consent procedures. Progenitor cells are multipotent or precursor cells that are partially differentiated, but retain the ability to divide and give rise to differentiated cells. [*New section adopted November 2, 2004. Initiative measure.*]

[*California Institute for Regenerative Medicine — Utilization of Bonds*]

SEC. 6.   Notwithstanding any other provision of this Constitution or any law, the institute, which is established in state government, may utilize state issued tax-exempt and taxable bonds to fund its operations, medical and scientific research, including therapy development through clinical trials, and facilities. [*New section adopted November 2, 2004. Initiative measure.*]

[*California Institute for Regenerative Medicine — Civil Service Exemption*]

SEC. 7.   Notwithstanding any other provision of this Constitution, including Article VII, or any law, the institute and its employees are exempt from civil service. [*New section adopted November 2, 2004. Initiative measure.*]

Index
Constitution of California

INDEX TO CALIFORNIA CONSTITUTION

A

C

D

E

F   *Article   Section*

H

J

M

N

Q

R

U

V

Z

Appendix
Governors, Lieutenant Governors,
Officers of the Senate,
Officers of the Assembly, Chief Justices,
Legislative Counsels, and
Legislative Analysts

1849–2015

APPENDIX

GOVERNORS OF CALIFORNIA—1849–2015

Name	Party	Date of Inauguration	Notes
Peter H. Burnett	Ind. D.	Dec. 20, 1849	Resigned January 8, 1851.
John McDougal	Ind. D.	Jan. 9, 1851	Lieutenant Governor, succeeded Burnett.
John Bigler	D.	Jan. 8, 1852	Former Assembly Speaker, 1849–1851.
John Bigler	D.	Jan. 7, 1854	Re-elected, September 7, 1853.
J. Neeley Johnson	Amer.	Jan. 9, 1856	Assemblyman, 1853.
John B. Weller	D.	Jan. 8, 1858	U.S. Senator, 1851–1857.
Milton S. Latham	Lecomp. D.	Jan. 9, 1860	Resigned Jan. 14, 1860. U.S. Senator, 1860–1863.
John G. Downey	Lecomp. D.	Jan. 14, 1860	Lieutenant Governor, succeeded Latham.
Leland Stanford	R.	Jan. 10, 1862	U.S. Senator, 1885–1897.
Frederick F. Low	Union	Dec. 10, 1863	Representative in Congress, 1861–1863.
Henry H. Haight	D.	Dec. 5, 1867	Member of Second Constitutional Convention.
Newton Booth	R.	Dec. 8, 1871	Resigned Feb. 27, 1875. U.S. Senator, 1875–1881.
Romualdo Pacheco	R.	Feb. 27, 1875	Lieutenant Governor, succeeded Booth.
William Irwin	D.	Dec. 9, 1875	Harbor Commission, 1883–1886.
George C. Perkins	R.	Jan. 8, 1880	U.S. Senator, 1893–1903.
George Stoneman	D.	Jan. 10, 1883	Transportation Commissioner.
Washington Bartlett	D.	Jan. 8, 1887	Railroad Commissioner.
Robert W. Waterman	R.	Sept. 13, 1887	Lieutenant Governor, succeeded Bartlett.
Henry H. Markham	R.	Jan. 8, 1891	Representative in Congress, 1885–1887.
James H. Budd	D.	Jan. 11, 1895	Representative in Congress, 1883–1885.
Henry T. Gage	R.	Jan. 4, 1899	Minister to Portugal, Dec. 21, 1909.
George C. Pardee	R.	Jan. 6, 1903	Regent of University of California, 1899.
James N. Gillett	R.	Jan. 8, 1907	Representative in Congress, 1903–1906.
Hiram W. Johnson	R.	Jan. 3, 1911	Re-elected Nov. 3, 1914.
Hiram W. Johnson	Prog.	Jan. 5, 1915	Elected U.S. Senator, Nov. 7, 1916. Resigned as Governor, March 15, 1917.
William D. Stephens	R.	Mar. 15, 1917	Member of Congress, 10th Dist., 1910–1916. Appointed Lieutenant Governor, July 19, 1916.
William D. Stephens	R.	Jan. 7, 1919	Elected 1918.
Friend Wm. Richardson	R.	Jan. 9, 1923	State Treasurer, 1915–1922.
C. C. Young†	R.	Jan. 4, 1927	Former Assembly Speaker, Lieutenant Governor, 1919–1927.
James Rolph, Jr.	R.	Jan. 6, 1931	Mayor of San Francisco, 1911–1930. Deceased, June 2, 1934.
Frank F. Merriam†	R.	June 7, 1934	Former Assembly Speaker, Lieutenant Governor, succeeded Rolph.
Frank F. Merriam	R.	Jan. 8, 1935	Lieutenant Governor, 1931–1934.
Culbert L. Olson	D.	Jan. 2, 1939	State Senator, 1935–1938.
Earl Warren	R.	Jan. 4, 1943	Attorney General, 1939–1943.
Earl Warren	R.	Jan. 6, 1947	Re-elected Nov. 5, 1946.
Earl Warren	R., D.	Jan. 8, 1951	Re-elected Nov. 7, 1950. Resigned as Governor, Oct. 4, 1953. Appointed Chief Justice, U.S. Supreme Court, Oct. 5, 1953.
Goodwin J. Knight	R.	Oct. 5, 1953	Lieutenant Governor succeeded Warren.
Goodwin J. Knight	R.	Jan. 3, 1955	Elected Governor Nov. 2, 1954.
Edmund G. Brown	D.	Jan. 5, 1959	Attorney General, 1951–1958.
Edmund G. Brown	D.	Jan. 7, 1963	Re-elected Nov. 6, 1962.
Ronald Reagan	R.	Jan. 2, 1967	
Ronald Reagan	R.	Jan. 4, 1971	Re-elected Nov. 3, 1970.
Edmund G. Brown Jr.	D.	Jan. 6, 1975	Secretary of State, 1971–1974.
Edmund G. Brown Jr.	D.	Jan. 8, 1979	Re-elected Nov. 7, 1978.
George Deukmejian	R.	Jan. 3, 1983	Attorney General, 1979–1982.
George Deukmejian	R.	Jan. 5, 1987	Re-elected Nov. 4, 1986.
Pete Wilson	R.	Jan. 7, 1991	Assemblyman, 1967–1972. U.S. Senator 1983–91; Resigned as U.S. Senator Jan. 7, 1991.
Pete Wilson	R.	Jan. 2, 1995	Re-elected Nov. 1, 1994.
Gray Davis	D.	Jan. 4, 1999	Former Assembly Member, State Controller, and Lieutenant Governor.

GOVERNORS OF CALIFORNIA—1849–2015—Continued

Name	Party	Date of Inauguration	Notes
Gray Davis	D.	Jan. 6, 2003	Recalled Oct. 7, 2003. First Governor to be recalled.
Arnold Schwarzenegger	R.	Nov. 17, 2003	Elected in recall election, Oct. 7, 2003.
Arnold Schwarzenegger	R.	Jan. 5, 2007	Re-elected Nov. 7, 2006.
Edmund G. Brown Jr.	D.	Jan. 3, 2011	Previous service as Governor, 1975–1983. Former Secretary of State and Attorney General.
Edmund G. Brown Jr.	D.	Jan. 5, 2015	Re-elected Nov. 4, 2014.

† The only persons in California history to serve as Governor, Lt. Governor, and Speaker were C. C. Young and Frank Merriam.

LIEUTENANT GOVERNORS OF CALIFORNIA—1849-2015

Name	Party	Date of Inauguration		Notes
John McDougall	Ind. D.	Dec.	20, 1849	Became Governor January 9, 1851, succeeding Governor Burnett, resigned.
David C. Broderick (Acting) ..	D.	Jan.	9, 1851	Elected President of Senate January 9, 1851, thereby becoming Acting Lieutenant Governor, vice John McDougall, resigned.
Samuel Purdy.........................	D.	Jan.	8, 1852	
Samuel Purdy.........................	D.	Jan.	7, 1854	
Robert M. Anderson	Amer.	Jan.	9, 1856	
John Walkup	D.	Jan.	8, 1858	
John G. Downey	Lecomp. D.	Jan.	9, 1860	Became Governor January 14, 1860, succeeding Governor Latham, resigned.
Isaac N. Quinn (Acting).........	D.	Jan.	20, 1860	Elected President of Senate January 20, 1860, thereby becoming Acting Lieutenant Governor, vice John G. Downey, resigned.
Pablo de la Guerra (Acting)	D.	Jan.	7, 1861	Elected President of Senate January 7, 1861, thereby becoming Acting Lieutenant Governor, vice Isaac N. Quinn, resigned.
John F. Chellis	R.	Jan.	10, 1862	
T. N. Machin	Union	Dec.	10, 1863	
William Holden	D.	Dec.	5, 1867	
Romualdo Pacheco	R.	Dec.	8, 1871	Became Governor February 27, 1875, succeeding Governor Booth, resigned.
William Irwin (Acting)	D.	Feb.	27, 1875	Elected President of Senate February 27, 1875, thereby becoming Acting Lieutenant Governor, vice Romualdo Pacheco, resigned.
James A. Johnson...................	D.	Dec.	9, 1875	
John Mansfield.......................	R.	Jan.	8, 1880	
John Daggett	D.	Jan.	10, 1883	
Robert W. Waterman	R.	Jan.	8, 1887	Became Governor September 13, 1887, succeeding Governor Bartlett, who died in office.
Stephen M. White (Acting).....	D.	Sept.	13, 1887	Elected President pro Tempore of Senate January 5, 1887, thereby becoming Acting Lieutenant Governor, vice Robert W. Waterman, resigned.
John B. Reddick.....................	R.	Jan.	8, 1891	
Spencer G. Millard	R.	Jan.	11, 1895	Died in office October 24, 1895.
William T. Jeter	D.	Oct.	25, 1896	Appointed October 25, 1895, by Governor Budd, vice Spencer G. Millard, deceased.
Jacob H. Neff	R.	Jan.	3, 1899	
Alden Anderson	R.	Jan.	6, 1903	Former Assembly Speaker.
Warren R. Porter	R.	Jan.	8, 1907	
A. J. Wallace	R.	Jan.	3, 1911	
John M. Eshleman	Prog.	Jan.	5, 1915	Died in office February 28, 1916.
William D. Stephens	R.	July	22, 1916	Appointed July 22, 1916, by Governor Johnson, vice John M. Eshleman, deceased. Became Governor March 15, 1917, vice Hiram W. Johnson, resigned.
Vacancy from March 15, 1917, to Jan. 7, 1919				
C. C. Young	R.	Jan.	7, 1919	Former Assembly Speaker.
C. C. Young	R.	Jan.	9, 1923	Elected Governor November 2, 1926.
Buron Fitts	R.	Jan.	4, 1927	Resigned November 30, 1928.
H. L. Carnahan	R.	....		Appointed December 4, 1928, by Governor Young, vice Buron Fitts, resigned.
Frank F. Merriam	R.	Jan.	6, 1931	Former Assembly Speaker. Became Governor June 7, 1934, succeeding Governor Rolph who died in office.
Vacancy from June 7, 1934, to Jan. 8, 1935				
George J. Hatfield	R.	Jan.	8, 1935	
Ellis E. Patterson	D.	Jan.	2, 1939	
Frederick F. Houser	R.	Jan.	4, 1943	
Goodwin J. Knight.................	R.	Jan.	6, 1947	
Goodwin J. Knight.................	R.	Jan.	8, 1951	Became Governor October 5, 1953, succeeding Governor Warren, resigned.
Harold J. Powers	R.	Oct.	5, 1953	Served as President pro Tempore of Senate from 1947 until October 5, 1953, when he became Lieutenant Governor, vice Goodwin J. Knight, resigned.

LIEUTENANT GOVERNORS OF CALIFORNIA—1849–2015—Continued

Name	Party	Date of Inauguration	Notes
Harold J. Powers	R.	Jan. 3, 1955	
Glenn M. Anderson	D.	Jan. 5, 1959	
Glenn M. Anderson	D.	Jan. 7, 1963	
Robert H. Finch	R.	Jan. 2, 1967	Resigned January 20, 1969, to become Secretary, U.S. Department of Health, Education, and Welfare.
Ed Reinecke	R.	Jan. 21, 1969	Appointed January 21, 1969, by Governor Reagan, vice Robert H. Finch, resigned.
Ed Reinecke	R.	Jan. 4, 1971	Resigned October 2, 1974.
John L. Harmer	R.	Oct. 4, 1974	Appointed October 4, 1974, by Governor Reagan, vice Ed Reinecke, resigned.
Mervyn M. Dymally	D.	Jan. 6, 1975	Former Assembly Member and State Senator. Later served in Congress.
Mike Curb	R.	Jan. 8, 1979	
Leo T. McCarthy	D.	Jan. 3, 1983	Speaker of the Assembly, June 28, 1974–1980.
Leo T. McCarthy	D.	Jan. 5, 1987	
Leo T. McCarthy	D.	Jan. 7, 1991	
Gray Davis	D.	Jan. 2, 1995	Former State Assembly Member and State Controller.
Cruz M. Bustamante	D.	Jan. 4, 1999	Former Assembly Speaker.
Cruz M. Bustamante	D.	Jan. 6, 2003	
John Garamendi	D.	Jan. 7, 2007	Former Insurance Commissioner, Assembly Member, and State Senator. Deputy Secretary of the Interior under President Clinton. Elected to Congress on Nov. 3, 2009, resigned as Lt. Gov. on Nov. 5, 2009.
Mona Pasquil (Acting)	D.	Nov. 5, 2009	Assumed statutory duties as Acting Lt. Governor pursuant to Gov. Code 1775. Served from Nov. 5, 2009 to April 27, 2010.
Abel Maldonado	R.	April 27, 2010	Nominated to fill vacancy, Nov. 24, 2009. Senate confirmed Feb. 11, 2010. Assembly refused to confirm, February 11, 2010. Governor re-submitted nomination, Feb. 16, 2010. Assembly confirmed, April 22, 2010. Senate confirmed, April 26, 2010. Former Assembly Member and Senator.
Gavin Newsom	D.	Jan. 10, 2011	Former Mayor of San Francisco.
Gavin Newsom	D.	Jan. 5, 2015	

OFFICERS OF THE SENATE—1849-2015

Session	President pro Tempore	Secretary	Sergeant at Arms
1849	E. Kirby Chamberlain	James F. Howe	Thomas J. Austin
1851	Elcan Heydenfeldt (W)[1]	James F. Howe	Clark Burnham
1852	Benj. F. Keene (D)	A. C. Bradford	Clark Burnham
1853	Benj. F. Keene (D)	A. C. Bradford	G. W. Tenbrook
1854	Benj. F. Keene (D)[2]	John Y. Lind	W. H. Harvey
1855	Royal T. Sprague (D)	Wm. A. Cornwall[3]	John T. Knox
1856	Delos R. Ashley (Am.)	William Bausman	J. W. Ross
1857	Samuel H. Dosh (D)	George S. Evans	Alex Hunter
1858	Samuel A. Merritt (D)	Thomas N. Cazneau	James W. Hawkins
1859	W. B. Dickinson (D)	Edwin C. Palmer	James W. Hawkins
1860	Isaac N. Quinn (D)[4]	Joseph R. Beard	W. H. Bell
	Charles J. Lansing (D)		
1861	Richard Irwin (Doug. D)[5]	Charles W. Tozer	William F. Williamson
1862	James McM. Shafter (Rep.)	Thomas Hill	Archibald G. Turner
1863	A. M. Crane (Union)	John White	George I. Lytl
1864	R. Burnell (Union)	Charles Westmoreland	John Hemsley
1866	S. P. Wright (Union)	John White	John H. Morgan
1868	Lansing B. Mizner (Union)	John White	F. S. Lardner
1870	Edward J. Lewis (D)	Joseph Roberts, Jr.	Nat Boyce
1872	James T. Farley (D)	Robert Ferral	James W. Hawkins
1874	William Irwin (D)	T. J. Shackelford	James W. Hawkins
1876	Benj. F. Tuttle (D)	T. J. Shackelford	James W. Hawkins
1878	Edward J. Lewis (D)	Rufus Shoemaker	William H. Bell
1880	George F. Baker (R)	Marcus D. Boruck	Andrew Wasson
1881	William Johnston (R)	Marcus D. Boruck	Andrew Wasson
1883	R. F. Del Valle (D)	Edwin F. Smith[6]	I. G. Messec
1885	Benj. Knight, Jr. (D)	Edwin F. Smith	I. G. Messec
1887	Stephen M. White (D)	Edward H. Hamilton	John W. Wilcox
1889	Stephen M. White (D)	George W. Peckham	George W. Taylor
1891	Thomas Fraser (R)	Frank J. Brandon	Thomas Rogers
1893	R. B. Carpenter (R)	Frank J. Brandon	Thomas Rogers
1895	Thomas Flint, Jr. (R)	Frank J. Brandon	L. B. Blackburn
1897	Thomas Flint, Jr. (R)	Frank J. Brandon	L. B. Blackburn
1899	Thomas Flint, Jr. (R)	Frank J. Brandon	J. Louis Martin
1901	Thomas Flint, Jr. (R)	Frank J. Brandon	J. Louis Martin
1903	Thomas Flint, Jr. (R)	Frank J. Brandon	J. Louis Martin
1905	Edward I. Wolfe (R)	Lewis A. Hilborn	J. Louis Martin
1907	Edward I. Wolfe (R)	Lewis A. Hilborn	J. Louis Martin
1909	Edward I. Wolfe (R)	Lewis A. Hilborn	J. Louis Martin
1911	A. E. Boynton (R)	Walter N. Parrish	Joseph L. Coughlin
1913	A. E. Boynton (R)	Walter N. Parrish	Joseph L. Coughlin
1915	N. W. Thompson (R)	Edwin F. Smith	Thomas A. Brown
1917	Arthur H. Breed (R)	Clifton E. Brooks	Thomas A. Brown
1919	Arthur H. Breed (R)	Joseph A. Beek	Thomas A. Brown
1921	Arthur H. Breed (R)	Grace S. Stoermer	Thomas A. Brown
1923	Arthur H. Breed (R)	Joseph A. Beek	Joseph F. Nolan
1925	Arthur H. Breed (R)	Joseph A. Beek	Joseph F. Nolan
1927	Arthur H. Breed (R)	Joseph A. Beek	Joseph F. Nolan
1929	Arthur H. Breed (R)	Joseph A. Beek	Joseph F. Nolan
1931	Arthur H. Breed (R)	Joseph A. Beek	Joseph F. Nolan
1933	Arthur H. Breed (R)	Joseph A. Beek	Joseph F. Nolan
1935	William P. Rich (R)	Joseph A. Beek	Joseph F. Nolan
1937	William P. Rich (R)	Joseph A. Beek	Joseph F. Nolan
1939	Jerrold L. Seawell (R)	Joseph A. Beek	Joseph F. Nolan
1941	William P. Rich (R)	Joseph A. Beek	Joseph F. Nolan
1943	Jerrold L. Seawell (R)	Joseph A. Beek	Joseph F. Nolan
1945	Jerrold L. Seawell (R)	Joseph A. Beek	Joseph F. Nolan
1947	Harold J. Powers (R)	Joseph A. Beek	Joseph F. Nolan
1948	Harold J. Powers (R)	Joseph A. Beek	Joseph F. Nolan
1949	Harold J. Powers (R)	Joseph A. Beek	Joseph F. Nolan
1950	Harold J. Powers (R)	Joseph A. Beek	Joseph F. Nolan
1951	Harold J. Powers (R)	Joseph A. Beek	Joseph F. Nolan
1952	Harold J. Powers (R)	Joseph A. Beek	Joseph F. Nolan
1953	Harold J. Powers (R)[7]	Joseph A. Beek	Joseph F. Nolan
1954	Clarence C. Ward (R)	Joseph A. Beek	Joseph F. Nolan
1955	Clarence C. Ward (R)[8]	Joseph A. Beek	Joseph F. Nolan
	Ben Hulse (R)		
1956	Ben Hulse (R)	Joseph A. Beek	Joseph F. Nolan
1957	Hugh M. Burns (D)	Joseph A. Beek	Joseph F. Nolan
1958	Hugh M. Burns (D)	Joseph A. Beek	Joseph F. Nolan
1959	Hugh M. Burns (D)	Joseph A. Beek	Joseph F. Nolan

OFFICERS OF THE SENATE—1849–2015—Continued

Session	President pro Tempore	Secretary	Sergeant at Arms
1960	Hugh M. Burns (D)	Joseph A. Beek	Joseph F. Nolan
1961	Hugh M. Burns (D)	Joseph A. Beek	Joseph F. Nolan
1962	Hugh M. Burns (D)	Joseph A. Beek	Joseph F. Nolan
1963	Hugh M. Burns (D)	Joseph A. Beek	P. H. Kenealy
1964	Hugh M. Burns (D)	Joseph A. Beek	P. H. Kenealy
1965	Hugh M. Burns (D)	Joseph A. Beek	P. H. Kenealy
1966	Hugh M. Burns (D)	Joseph A. Beek	P. H. Kenealy
1967	Hugh M. Burns (D)	Joseph A. Beek	P. H. Kenealy
1968	Hugh M. Burns (D)	Joseph A. Beek[9]	P. H. Kenealy
1969	Hugh M. Burns (D)	C.D. Alexander	P. H. Kenealy
	Howard Way (R)[10]		
1970	Howard Way (R)	Darryl R. White	P. H. Kenealy
	Jack Schrade (R)[11]		
1971	James R. Mills (D)	Darryl R. White	P. H. Kenealy
1972	James R. Mills (D)	Darryl R. White	P. H. Kenealy
1973–74	James R. Mills (D)	Darryl R. White	P. H. Kenealy
1975–76	James R. Mills (D)	Darryl R. White	Frank Thomas
1977–78	James R. Mills (D)	Darryl R. White	Frank Thomas
1979–80	James R. Mills (D)	Darryl R. White	Frank Thomas[12]
			Tony Beard, Jr.[13]
1981–82	David A. Roberti (D)	Darryl R. White	Tony Beard, Jr.[14]
1983–84	David A. Roberti (D)	Darryl R. White	Tony Beard, Jr.
1985–86	David A. Roberti (D)	Darryl R. White	Tony Beard, Jr.
1987–88	David A. Roberti (D)	Darryl R. White	Tony Beard, Jr.
1989–90	David A. Roberti (D)	Darryl R. White	Tony Beard, Jr.
1991–92	David A. Roberti (D)	Darryl R. White[15]	Tony Beard, Jr.
		John W. Rovane[16]	
		Rick Rollens[17]	
1993–94	David A. Roberti (D)	Rick Rollens	Tony Beard, Jr.
	Bill Lockyer (D)[18]		
1995–96	Bill Lockyer (D)	Rick Rollens[19]	Tony Beard, Jr.
		John W. Rovane[20]	
		Gregory Schmidt[21]	
1997–98	Bill Lockyer (D)	Gregory Schmidt	Tony Beard, Jr.
	John Burton (D)[22]		
1999–2000	John Burton (D)	Gregory Schmidt	Tony Beard, Jr.
2001–02	John Burton (D)	Gregory Schmidt	Tony Beard, Jr.
2003–04	John Burton (D)	Gregory Schmidt	Tony Beard, Jr.
2005–06	Don Perata (D)[23]	Gregory Schmidt	Tony Beard, Jr.
2007–08	Don Perata (D)	Gregory Schmidt	Tony Beard, Jr.
2009–10	Darrell Steinberg (D)[24]	Gregory Schmidt	Tony Beard, Jr.
2011–12	Darrell Steinberg (D)	Gregory Schmidt	Tony Beard, Jr.
2013–14	Darrell Steinberg (D)	Gregory Schmidt	Tony Beard, Jr.[25]
			Katrina Rodriguez[26]
			Debbie Manning[27]
	Kevin de León (D)[28]	Daniel Alvarez[29]	
2015–16	Kevin de León (D)	Daniel Alvarez	Debbie Manning[30]

[1] David C. Broderick was elected President of the Senate January 9, 1851, when McDougall was inaugurated Governor; and on the 24th, Heydenfeldt was elected President pro Tempore.

[2] Elected January 10, 1853.

[3] Removed March 22, 1855, and Charles Dickinson elected Secretary.

[4] Became Acting Lieutenant Governor on the resignation of Governor Latham, having been elected President of the Senate January 20, 1860, and Charles J. Lansing was elected President pro Tempore.

[5] Pablo de la Guerra was elected President of the Senate and Acting Lieutenant Governor, and Richard Irwin was elected President pro Tempore.

[6] Edwin F. Smith served as Secretary of the Constitutional Convention of 1879.

[7] Harold J. Powers became Lieutenant Governor on October 5, 1953, when Goodwin J. Knight resigned to become Governor.

[8] Clarence C. Ward died in office on May 9, 1955, and Ben Hulse was elected President pro Tempore on June 6, 1955.

[9] Joseph A. Beek died in office October 20, 1968.

[10] Howard Way elected President pro Tempore May 14, 1969.

[11] Jack Schrade elected President pro Tempore February 10, 1970.

[12] Resigned October 31, 1980.

[13] Tony Beard, Jr. appointed Sergeant at Arms November 1, 1980.

[14] Continued as Sergeant at Arms without election until January 14, 1982. Government Code, Section 9150. Elected January 14, 1982.

[15] Resigned January 31, 1991.

[16] Assumed duties as Acting Secretary, February 1, 1991.

[17] Elected February 15, 1991.

[18] Bill Lockyer elected President pro Tempore January 31, 1994.

[19] Resigned December 31, 1995.

[20] Assumed duties as Acting Secretary, January 1, 1996.

[21] Elected August 31, 1996. Also served as Executive Officer of Senate Rules Committee.

APPENDIX

OFFICERS OF THE SENATE—1849–2015—Continued

[22] John Burton was elected President pro Tempore February 5, 1998, and sworn in on February 5, 1998.

[23] Don Perata was elected President pro Tempore August 26, 2004, and sworn in on November 30, 2004.

[24] Darrell Steinberg was elected President pro Tempore August 21, 2008, and sworn in on November 30, 2008.

[25] Tony Beard Jr. resigned May 6, 2014.

[26] Katrina Rodriguez assumed duties as Acting Chief Sergeant at Arms May 7, 2014.

[27] Debbie Manning was appointed Acting Chief Sergeant at Arms August 1, 2014.

[28] Kevin de León was elected President pro Tempore June 16, 2014, and sworn in October 15, 2014.

[29] Daniel Alvarez was elected Secretary of the Senate August 29, 2014, and sworn in October 15, 2014.

[30] Debbie Manning was elected Chief Sergeant at Arms December 1, 2014.

OFFICERS OF THE ASSEMBLY—1849-2015

Session	Speaker	Speaker pro Tem.	Chief Clerk	Sergeant at Arms
1849	Thomas J. White[1]	George B. Tingley[2]	E. H. Tharp[3]	Samuel N. Houston
	John Bigler[4]		John Nugent[5]	
1851	John Bigler (D)		George O. McMullin	William W. Gift
1852	Richard P. Hammond (D)		Blanton McAlpin	C. C. Hornsby
1853	Isaac B. Wall (D)	Patrick Canney (D)[6]	Blanton McAlpin[7]	G. W. Coffey
			J. G. Stebbins[8]	
1854	Charles S. Fairfax (D)	Jas. W. Mandeville (D)[9]	Blanton McAlpin	George H. Blake
1855	William W. Stow (Whig)		J. M. Anderson	Blanton McAlpin
1856	James T. Farley (Am.)[†]		J. M. Anderson	E. Gates
1857	Elwood T. Beatty (D)	James O'Neil (D)[10]	William Campbell	Silas Brown
1858	N. E. Whiteside (D)		Joseph W. Scoby	James F. Quinn
1859	William C. Stratton (D)		Caleb Gilman	James H. Moore
1860	Philip Moore (D)	E. A. Stevenson (D)[11]	J. M. Anderson	Charles W. Tozer
1861	R. Burnell (Doug. D)[†]	D. Showalter (Breck. D)[12]	J. M. Anderson	M. Gray
1862	George Barstow (R)		John Sedgwick	H. J. Clayton
1863	Tim N. Machin (Union)	James Collins (D)	H. G. Worthington	Thomas Eager
1864	William H. Sears (Union)	J. J. Owen (Union)	Osgood C. Wheeler	W. M. Rider
1866	John Yule (Union)	John W. Wilcox (Union)	Marcus D. Boruck	Benjamin Dore
1868	Caius T. Ryland (D)	J. J. O'Malley (D)	John A. Eagon	John K. Luttrell
1870	George H. Rogers (D)	Charles Gildea (D)	Robert Ferral	W. Dana Perkins
1872	Thomas B. Shannon (R)	Peter J. Hopper (R)	Marcus D. Boruck	A. J. Rhodes
1874	Morris M. Estee (Ind.)	Robert Howe (D)	D. T. Loofbourrow	Wm. M. Crutcher
1876	G. J. Carpenter (D)	James E. Murphy (D)	Robert Ferral	W. Dana Perkins
1878	Campbell P. Berry (D)	James E. Murphy (D)	Robert C. Page	J. M. Farrelly
1880	Jabez F. Cowdery (D)	Thomas Fraser (R)	C. E. Gunn	Robert W. Parker
1881	William H. Parks (R)	Thomas Fraser (R)	George E. McStay	E. Walters
1883	Hugh M. LaRue (D)	John T. Campbell (D)	M. C. Haley	J. M. Farrelly
1885	William H. Parks (R)	J. H. G. Weaver (R)	Frank D. Ryan	Jerome Porter
1887	William H. Jordan (R)	John R. Brierly (R)	Frank D. Ryan	P. R. Klein
1889	Robert Howe (D)	T. W. H. Shanahan (D)	Edward E. Leake	J. J. Driscoll
1891	Frank L. Coombs (R)	Nestor A. Young (R)	H. A. Mason	H. J. McKusick
1893	F. H. Gould (D)	William P. Mathews (D)	George W. Peckham	Thomas E. Healy
1895	John C. Lynch (R)	E. V. Spencer (R)	S. J. Duckworth	George C. Parkinson
1897	Frank L. Coombs (R)	Brewster C. Kenyon (R)	S. J. Duckworth	William O. Banks
1899	Howard E. Wright (R)[13]	Alden Anderson (R)	C. W. Kyle	William O. Banks
	Alden Anderson (R)[14]	F. E. Dunlap (R)[15]		
1901	Cornelius W. Pendleton (R)	William C. Ralston (R)	Clio Lloyd	William O. Banks
1903	Arthur G. Fisk (R)	Henry E. Carter (R)	Clio Lloyd	John T. Stafford
1905	Frank C. Prescott (R)	T. E. Atkinson (R)[16]	Clio Lloyd	John T. Stafford
1907	R. L. Beardslee (R)	J. P. Transue (R)	Clio Lloyd	John T. Stafford
1909	P. A. Stanton (R)	George M. Perine (R)	Clio Lloyd[17]	John T. Stafford
			Thomas G. Walker[18]	
1911	A. H. Hewitt (R)	H. G. Cattell (R)	L. B. Mallory	E. H. Whyte
1913	C. C. Young (R)	W. A. Johnstone (R)	L. B. Mallory	Ed E. Reese
1915	C. C. Young (Prog)	Howard J. Fish (R)	L. B. Mallory	H. B. Miller
1917	C. C. Young (R)	James J. Ryan (R)	B. O. Boothby	W. J. Leflar
1919	Henry W. Wright (R)	Clarence W. Morris (R)	B. O. Boothby[19]	W. J. Leflar
1921	Henry W. Wright (R)	Albert A. Rosenshine (R)	J. B. Kavanaugh	W. J. Leflar
1923	Frank F. Merriam (R)	Frank W. Anderson (R)	Arthur A. Ohnimus	W. J. Leflar
1925	Frank F. Merriam (R)	Homer R. Spence (R)	Arthur A. Ohnimus	Charles H. Wilkinson
1927	Edgar C. Levey (R)	William M. Byrne (R)	Arthur A. Ohnimus	William J. McQuillan
1929	Edgar C. Levey (R)	William M. Byrne (R)	Arthur A. Ohnimus	Arthur Ferguson
1931	Edgar C. Levey (R)	Chester M. Kline (R)	Arthur A. Ohnimus	Arthur Ferguson
1933	Walter J. Little (R)	F. C. Clowdsley (D)	Arthur A. Ohnimus	Michael Connolly
1934 (Ex.)	F. C. Clowdsley (D)	Harry B. Riley (R)	Arthur A. Ohnimus	Michael Connolly
1935	Edward Craig (R)	John H. O'Donnell (D)	Arthur A. Ohnimus	Joseph Moloney
1937	Wm. Moseley Jones (D)	Henry P. Meehan (D)	James G. Smyth	Delwin W. Smith
1939	Paul Peek (D)	Hugh P. Donnelly (D)	Jack Carl Greenburg	David V. Gill
1940 (Ex.)	Gordon H. Garland (D)[20]	Gardiner Johnson (R)[21]		Wilkie Ogg[22]
1941	Gordon H. Garland (D)	Earl D. Desmond (D)	Arthur A. Ohnimus	Wilkie Ogg
1943	Charles W. Lyon (R)	Thomas A. Maloney (R)	Arthur A. Ohnimus	Wilkie Ogg
1945	Charles W. Lyon (R)	Thomas A. Maloney (R)	Arthur A. Ohnimus	Wilkie Ogg
1947	Sam L. Collins (R)	Thomas A. Maloney (R)	Arthur A. Ohnimus	Wilkie Ogg
1948	Sam L. Collins (R)	Thomas A. Maloney (R)	Arthur A. Ohnimus	Wilkie Ogg
1949	Sam L. Collins (R)	Thomas A. Maloney (R)	Arthur A. Ohnimus	Wilkie Ogg

[†] The only persons in California history to serve as Assembly Speaker and Senate President pro Tempore were Ransom Burnell and James T. Farley.

OFFICERS OF THE ASSEMBLY—1849-2015—Continued

Session	Speaker	Speaker pro Tem.	Chief Clerk	Sergeant at Arms
1950	Sam L. Collins (R)	Thomas A. Maloney (R)	Arthur A. Ohnimus	Wilkie Ogg
1951	Sam L. Collins (R)	Thomas A. Maloney (R)	Arthur A. Ohnimus	Wilkie Ogg
1952	Sam L. Collins (R)	Thomas A. Maloney (R)	Arthur A. Ohnimus	Wilkie Ogg
1953	James W. Silliman (R)	Thomas A. Maloney (R)	Arthur A. Ohnimus	Wilkie Ogg
1954	James W. Silliman (R)	Thomas A. Maloney (R)	Arthur A. Ohnimus	Wilkie Ogg
1955	L. H. Lincoln (R)	Thomas A. Maloney (R)	Arthur A. Ohnimus	Wilkie Ogg[23]
1956	L. H. Lincoln (R)	Thomas A. Maloney (R)	Arthur A. Ohnimus	Tony Beard
1957	L. H. Lincoln (R)	Charles J. Conrad (R)	Arthur A. Ohnimus	Tony Beard
1958	L. H. Lincoln (R)	Charles J. Conrad (R)	Arthur A. Ohnimus	Tony Beard
1959	Ralph M. Brown (D)	Carlos Bee (D)	Arthur A. Ohnimus	Tony Beard
1960	Ralph M. Brown (D)	Carlos Bee (D)	Arthur A. Ohnimus	Tony Beard
1961	Ralph M. Brown (D)[24]	Carlos Bee (D)	Arthur A. Ohnimus	Tony Beard
	Jesse M. Unruh (D)[25]			
1962	Jesse M. Unruh (D)	Carlos Bee (D)	Arthur A. Ohnimus	Tony Beard
1963	Jesse M. Unruh (D)	Carlos Bee (D)	Arthur A. Ohnimus[26]	Tony Beard
			James D. Driscoll[27]	
1964	Jesse M. Unruh (D)	Carlos Bee (D)	James D. Driscoll	Tony Beard
1965	Jesse M. Unruh (D)	Carlos Bee (D)	James D. Driscoll	Tony Beard
1966	Jesse M. Unruh (D)	Carlos Bee (D)	James D. Driscoll	Tony Beard
1967	Jesse M. Unruh (D)	Carlos Bee (D)	James D. Driscoll	Tony Beard
1968	Jesse M. Unruh (D)	Carlos Bee (D)	James D. Driscoll	Tony Beard
1969	Bob Monagan (R)	Charles J. Conrad (R)	James D. Driscoll	Tony Beard
1970	Bob Monagan (R)	Charles J. Conrad (R)	James D. Driscoll	Tony Beard
1971	Bob Moretti (D)	Carlos Bee (D)	James D. Driscoll	Tony Beard
1972	Bob Moretti (D)	Carlos Bee (D)	James D. Driscoll	Tony Beard
1973–74	Bob Moretti (D)[28]	Carlos Bee (D)[29]	James D. Driscoll	Tony Beard
	Leo T. McCarthy (D)[30]			
1975–76	Leo T. McCarthy (D)	Louis J. Papan (D)[31]	James D. Driscoll	Tony Beard
		John T. Knox (D)[32]		
1977–78	Leo T. McCarthy (D)	John T. Knox (D)	James D. Driscoll	Tony Beard[33]
				Charles E. Greene[34]
1979–80	Leo T. McCarthy (D)	John T. Knox (D)	James D. Driscoll	Charles E. Greene
1981–82	Willie L. Brown, Jr. (D)	Leo T. McCarthy (D)	James D. Driscoll[35]	Charles E. Greene[36]
1983–84	Willie L. Brown, Jr. (D)	Frank Vicencia (D)	James D. Driscoll[37]	Charles E. Greene[38]
				Charles E. Bell[39]
1985–86	Willie L. Brown, Jr. (D)	Frank Vicencia (D)	James D. Driscoll	Charles E. Bell
1987–88	Willie L. Brown, Jr. (D)	Mike Roos (D)	James D. Driscoll[40]	Charles E. Bell
			R. Brian Kidney[41]	
1989–90	Willie L. Brown, Jr. (D)	Mike Roos (D)	R. Brian Kidney	Charles E. Bell
1991–92	Willie L. Brown, Jr. (D)	Mike Roos (D)[42]	R. Brian Kidney[43]	Charles E. Bell
		Jack O'Connell (D)[44]	Lawrence A. Murman[45]	
			E. Dotson Wilson[46]	
1993–94	Willie L. Brown, Jr. (D)	Jack O'Connell (D)	E. Dotson Wilson	Charles E. Bell
1995–96	Willie L. Brown, Jr. (D)[47]	Joe Baca (D)[48]	E. Dotson Wilson	Charles E. Bell[49]
	Doris Allen (R)[50]	Brian Setencich (R)		
	(Majority)[51]	(Minority)[52]		
		Joe Baca (D)		
	Brian Setencich (R)[53]	Doris Allen (R)		
		(Majority)[54]		
		Joe Baca (D)		
		(Minority)		
		Fred Aguiar (R)		
		(Majority)[55]		
	Curt Pringle (R)[56]	Fred Aguiar (R)[57]		Ronald E. Pane[58]
1997–98	Cruz M. Bustamante (D)	Sheila James Kuehl (D)	E. Dotson Wilson	Ronald E. Pane
	Antonio R. Villaraigosa (D)[59]			
1999–2000	Antonio R. Villaraigosa (D)	Fred Keeley (D)	E. Dotson Wilson	Ronald E. Pane[60]
	Robert M. Hertzberg (D)[61]			
2001–02	Robert M. Hertzberg (D)	Fred Keeley (D)	E. Dotson Wilson	Ronald E. Pane
	Herb J. Wesson, Jr. (D)[62]			
2003–04	Herb J. Wesson, Jr. (D)	Christine Kehoe (D)[63]	E. Dotson Wilson	Ronald E. Pane
	Fabian Núñez (D)[64]	Leland Yee (D)[65]		
2005–06	Fabian Núñez (D)	Leland Yee (D)	E. Dotson Wilson	Ronald E. Pane
2007–08	Fabian Núñez (D)	Sally Lieber (D)	E. Dotson Wilson	Ronald E. Pane
	Karen Bass (D)[66]			
2009–10	Karen Bass (D)	Lori Saldaña (D)	E. Dotson Wilson	Ronald E. Pane
	John A. Pérez (D)[67]			
		Fiona Ma (D)[68]		
2011–12	John A. Pérez (D)	Fiona Ma (D)	E. Dotson Wilson	Ronald E. Pane
		Nora Campos (D)[69]		

438 APPENDIX

OFFICERS OF THE ASSEMBLY—1849–2015—Continued

Session	Speaker	Speaker pro Tem.	Chief Clerk	Sergeant at Arms
2013–14	John A. Pérez (D) .... Toni G. Atkins (D)[70]	Nora Campos (D)	E. Dotson Wilson	Ronald E. Pane
2015–16	Toni G. Atkins (D)	Kevin Mullin (D)	E. Dotson Wilson	Ronald E. Pane

[1] Resigned February 6, 1850.

[2] Elected March 25, 1850.

[3] Resigned February 21, 1850. E. H. Tharp was elected Clerk of the Supreme Court. (*See Assembly Journal*, February 20, 1850, p. 888–889.) Initial references to the title "Principal Clerk" were abandoned for the title "Chief Clerk."

[4] Elected February 6, 1850.

[5] Elected February 21, 1850. Nugent won election over A.D. Ohr (Asst. Clerk) and E. Dickey. (*See Assembly Journal*, February 21, 1850, p. 895.)

[6] Elected April 2, 1853.

[7] Resigned February 15, 1853.

[8] Elected February 15, 1853.

[9] Elected January 11, 1854.

[10] Elected January 9, 1857.

[11] Elected February 13, 1860.

[12] Elected April 12, 1861.

[13] Resigned January 30, 1899.

[14] Elected January 30, 1899.

[15] Elected January 30, 1899.

[16] Assumed duties of the Speakership for the 1906 1st Extraordinary Session when Frank C. Prescott resigned January 1, 1906.

[17] Clio Lloyd served as Chief Clerk in the 1910 First Extraordinary Session on September 6, 1910 but did not run for re-election for the Second Extraordinary Session, convened the following month.

[18] Thomas G. Walker was elected Chief Clerk in the 1910 Second Extraordinary Session on October 3, 1910. (*See Assembly Journal*, Second Extraordinary Session, page 46.) Additionally, Walker presided over the January 2, 1911 organizational session, where L.B. Mallory was elected Chief Clerk.

[19] John H. Martin served as Minute Clerk and was elected Acting Chief Clerk. (*See Assembly Journal*, April 22, 1919, p. 2100–2101.)

[20] Elected January 29, 1940.

[21] Elected January 29, 1940.

[22] Elected January 29, 1940.

[23] Died in office November 23, 1955.

[24] Resigned September 19, 1961.

[25] Elected by Assembly Caucus September 30, 1961.

[26] Resigned October 4, 1963.

[27] Appointed by the Rules Committee October 5, 1963.

[28] Resigned June 27, 1974.

[29] Died in office November 29, 1974.

[30] Elected June 28, 1974.

[31] Elected December 2, 1974 (convening of 1975–76 Regular Session). Resigned January 19, 1976.

[32] Elected January 19, 1976.

[33] Resigned January 15, 1977.

[34] Elected January 3, 1978.

[35] Continued as Chief Clerk without election until February 1, 1982, *Government Code*, Section 9150. Elected February 1, 1982.

[36] Continued as Sergeant at Arms without election until February 1, 1982, *Government Code*, Section 9150. Elected February 1, 1982.

[37] Continued as Chief Clerk without election until July 19, 1983, *Government Code*, Section 9150. Elected July 19, 1983.

[38] Resigned March 31, 1983.

[39] Elected July 19, 1983.

[40] Resigned December 30, 1986.

[41] Assumed duties of Chief Clerk for the 1987–88 Regular Session on January 1, 1987. Elected Chief Clerk January 4, 1988.

[42] Resigned March 20, 1991.

[43] Resigned January 31, 1991.

[44] Elected March 18, 1991.

[45] Assumed duties as Acting Chief Clerk, February 1, 1991 to January 6, 1992. Former Assembly Member John T. Knox served as "Parliamentarian" in 1991, during time when the Chief Clerk position was vacant.

[46] Elected January 6, 1992. Continued as Chief Clerk without election until January 4, 1996 pursuant to *Government Code*, Section 9150. Re-elected January 4, 1996 and every subsequent session. As of March 2015, E. Dotson Wilson is the longest serving Chief Clerk of the Assembly in California history (continuous service).

[47] Served January 23, 1995–June 5, 1995.

[48] Elected Speaker pro Tempore February 23, 1995. *See also*, footnote 52.

[49] Replaced January 4, 1996.

[50] Served June 5, 1995–September 14, 1995.

[51] Appointed Majority Speaker pro Tempore June 21, 1995. Served until September 14, 1995. (*Pursuant to the Isenberg Substitute Rules, Assembly Rule 6, 1995–96 Regular Session, adopted June 5, 1995, there were two Speakers pro Tempore appointed, a Majority and a Minority. See Assembly Journal, page 2000.*)

[52] Appointed Minority Speaker pro Tempore June 26, 1995. Served until January 4, 1996.

[53] Served September 14, 1995–January 4, 1996.

[54] Appointed Majority Speaker pro Tempore September 14, 1995 but did not take oath of office.

[55] Appointed Majority Speaker pro Tempore December 7, 1995, succeeding Doris Allen, recalled.

[56] Served January 4, 1996–November 30, 1996.

[57] Appointed Speaker pro Tempore January 4, 1996. Served until November 30, 1996. *(Pursuant to the Motion by Assembly Member Richter, relative to Legislative Powers and Duties, adopted January 3, 1996, there was one Speaker pro Tempore appointed. See Assembly Journal, pages 4252 and 4264.)*

[58] Appointed Acting Chief Sergeant at Arms January 4, 1996. Elected Chief Sergeant at Arms April 22, 1996 and re-elected December 2, 1996.

[59] Elected Speaker on January 26, 1998; took oath of office on February 26, 1998.

[60] Continued as Sergeant at Arms without election until April 24, 2000, *Government Code*, Section 9150. Elected April 24, 2000. Re-elected December 4, 2000 and every subsequent session.

[61] Elected Speaker on January 24, 2000; took oath of office on April 13, 2000.

[62] Elected Speaker on January 10, 2002; took oath of office on February 6, 2002.

[63] Served until February 9, 2004.

[64] Elected Speaker on January 8, 2004; took oath of office on February 9, 2004.

[65] Appointed Speaker pro Tempore on February 9, 2004.

[66] Elected Speaker on February 28, 2008; took oath of office on May 13, 2008.

[67] Elected Speaker on January 7, 2010; took oath of office on March 1, 2010.

[68] Appointed Speaker pro Tempore on March 18, 2010.

[69] Appointed Speaker pro Tempore September 1, 2012.

[70] Elected Speaker on March 17, 2014; took oath of office on May 12, 2014.

APPENDIX
CALIFORNIA'S SUPREME COURT
Chief Justices of California
1849–2015

Name	Tenure
Serranus Clinton Hastings	January 1850–January 1852
Henry A. Lyons	January 1852–March 1852
Hugh C. Murray	March 1852–September 1857
David S. Terry	October 1857–September 1859
Steven J. Field	September 1859–May 1863
W. W. Cope	May 1863–January 1864
Silas W. Sanderson	January 1864–January 1866
John Currey	January 1866–January 1868
Lorenzo Sawyer	January 1868–January 1870
Augustus L. Rhodes	January 1870–January 1872
Royal T. Sprague	January 1872–February 1872
William T. Wallace	February 1872–November 1879
Robert F. Morrison	November 1879–March 1887
Niles Searls	April 1887–January 1889
William H. Beatty	January 1889–August 1914
Matt I. Sullivan	August 1914–January 1915
Frank M. Angellotti	January 1915–November 1921
Lucien Shaw	November 1921–January 1923
Curtis D. Wilbur	January 1923–March 1924
Louis W. Myers	March 1924–January 1926
William H. Waste	January 1926–June 1940
Phil S. Gibson	June 1940–August 1964
Roger J. Traynor	September 1964–February 1970
Donald R. Wright	April 1970–February 1977
Rose Elizabeth Bird *	March 1977–January 1987
Malcolm M. Lucas	February 1987–April 1996
Ronald M. George	May 1996–January 2011
Tani G. Cantil-Sakauye	January 2011–

*Not elected to a new term, Nov. 4, 1986 general election.

LEGISLATIVE COUNSELS OF CALIFORNIA
1914–2015

Legislative Counsel	Tenure	Notes
Arthur Will[1]	1914–1920	Selected by a board consisting of Governor Hiram W. Johnson and two Members of each house of the Legislature.
George Bush[2]	1921	Appointed by Governor William D. Stephens.
John McGilvray	1923	Appointed by Governor Friend William Richardson.
Thomas Gannon	1925	Appointed by Governor Friend William Richardson.
Fred B. Wood[3]	1927–1950	Selected by adoption of a concurrent resolution. Justice, First District Court of Appeals, 1950–1959.
Ralph N. Kleps	1950–1961	.
Angus C. Morrisson	1961–1964	
George H. Murphy	1964–1976	
Bion M. Gregory	1976–2002	Longest serving Legislative Counsel in California history.
Diane Boyer-Vine	2002–	

[1] The first Legislative Counsel was selected by a board consisting of the Governor and two Members of each house of the Legislature.

[2] In 1917, the Legislative Counsel position was made appointive at the pleasure of the Governor.

[3] The law was changed in 1927 to the present procedure for the selection of the Legislative Counsel by the Legislature—the adoption of a concurrent resolution at the beginning of each session.

APPENDIX

LEGISLATIVE ANALYSTS OF CALIFORNIA
1941–2015

Legislative Analyst*	Tenure
Rolland A. Vandegrift	1941–1949
A. Alan Post	1949–1977
William G. Hamm	1977–1986
Elizabeth G. Hill	1986–2008
Mac Taylor	2008–

*From 1941 to 1957, the title was "Legislative Auditor." Chapter 176, *Statutes of 1957*, changed the title to Legislative Analyst.

OSP 15 2139—100

Photoelectronic composition by
CALIFORNIA OFFICE OF STATE PUBLISHING